Uncle John's Bathroom Reader
Nature Calls

The Bathroom Readers' Institute
Ashland, Oregon, and San Diego, California

OUR "REGULAR" READERS RAVE

"I have learned so much from you guys. Thank you for being amazing!"

—Reece T.

"Your books have been part of my life since the very first one was published. Every Christmas, the newest edition is my gift to myself. I've also gotten several of the specialist titles, dealing with music, Hollywood, etc. I love them."

—Matt C.

"My dad got the calendar when I was 11. I sat and read the whole thing in one afternoon."

—Kelli W.

"Before the BRI came along, I had a small library of just books. After BRI, I now have a great library filled with incredible books."

—Green S.

"I remember reading the first *Bathroom Reader* as a kid, and learning that Barbie had a last name. (Roberts!)"

—Katie F.

"*Uncle John's Bathroom Readers* are the entire reason I started collecting rubber ducks. I have over seventy."

—Sara C.

"I inadvertently stole one from my teacher in 1991. (Sorry, Mr. Mont!) I got hooked, my family got hooked, and now I have my nieces and nephews hooked!"

—Michael C.

"Long live Uncle John!"

—Denis S.

UNCLE JOHN'S BATHROOM READER®
NATURE CALLS

For information, write…
The Bathroom Readers' Institute
P.O. Box 1117, Ashland, OR 97520
www.bathroomreader.com
e-mail: mail@bathroomreader.com

ISBN 13: 978-1-60710-428-5 / ISBN 10: 1-60710-428-8

Library of Congress Cataloging-in-Publication Data

Uncle John's bathroom reader nature calls.
p. cm.
ISBN 978-1-60710-428-5 (pbk.)
1. Natural history--Miscellanea. 2. Nature--Miscellanea. 3. Nature--Humor.
QH45.5.U63 2012
081--dc23
2011053135

Printed in the United States of America
First printing: June 2012
17 16 15 14 13 12 6 5 4 3 2 1

THANK YOU!

Gordon Javna
JoAnn Padgett
Melinda Allman
Thom Little
Sue Steiner
Stephanie Spadaccini
Jay Newman
Michael Brunsfeld
Laura Egendorf
Jeff Altemus
Angie Kern
Jef Fretwell
J. Carroll
Derek Fairbridge
Jenness Crawford
Terri Schlichenmeyer
Joe O'Connell
Michele Miller
Dan Mansfield
True Sims
Trina Hedgpeth
Brian Boone

Lilian Nordland
Monica Maestas
Annie Lam
Ginger Winters
Mana Monzavi
Jennifer Frederick
Bonnie Vandewater
Kim T. Griswell
Sydney Stanley
David Cully
Margaret Faherty
Cynthia Francisco
Amy L. and Amy M.
Christine Little
R. R. Donnelley
Jane Goodall
John Muir
Euell Gibbons
Steve Irwin
Mr. Natural
Sophie and JJ
Thomas Crapper

Hiya Morgan! Hiya Malia! Hiya Max!

CONTENTS

Because the BRI understands your reading needs, we've divided the contents by length as well as subject.

Short—a quick read

Medium—2 to 3 pages

Long—for those extended visits, when something a little more involved is required.

IN FROM THE WILD

We've poured the stinky sludge from our cracked and cudgeled walking boots, ripped the burrs from our fried and frazzled hair, picked the ticks and leeches from our bums and backs, taken the gophers from our pockets, the vipers from our armpits, and the elephants from our trunks—and we've tucked them all inside this fat little book you are holding in your hands right this very instant. (Careful: Some of those critters are venomous!) Welcome to *Uncle John's Bathroom Reader Nature Calls*, the latest—and wildest—publication from all of us at the BRI...right down to Proudfoot and Fangorn, Ol' Jay's pet turtles. That's Proudfoot roaring his great turtle roar on the cover!

We had so much fun making this book! Well, we always have fun making our books, but we're all such animal and all-around nature freaks that this one pretty much put us over the moon. We learned so many cool, bizarre, hilarious, eye-widening—and just plain freaky and creepy—things in the course of making this book that, at times, we thought we'd go a little mad with happiness. Here are just a few examples of what we mean:

• There's a family of whales called beaked whales. The males have only two teeth, which grow from their lower jaws, up around their upper jaws—sort of like the tusks of wild boars. (We did not know this!)

• Cane toads have been known to try to mate with dead cane toads. And dead pythons. And dead bunny rabbits. (We did not want to know this! Okay, we lie—we did want to know this.)

• There's a species of moth that spends its *entire* adult life in the fur of sloths. Only pregnant females ever leave those furry confines...when the host sloths climb down from their trees to poop, at which time the females fly out of the fur to lay eggs in the poop.

• In the late 1670s, Dutch scholar Nicolas Hartsoeker, using that still-new invention—the microscope—announced that he'd seen tiny, complete humans inside sperm cells. This, he said, explained how babies were made. Hartsoeker's "discovery" launched the "spermist" movement, one of the foremost schools on human reproduction for the next hundred years.

You're hooked already, aren't you?! We understand. These are fairly mind-blowing things. And we have tons more! Along with *Bathroom Reader* usuals such as name origins, hilarious police logs, and weird news stories (of the wild variety), there are a couple of quizzes—and much, much more. Some sample articles we think you'll like:

• "A Very Dirty Story" (page 56): what everyone should know about the soil beneath their feet

• "Hornywinks, Shags, and Stinkpots" (page 144): actual animal names you should not giggle at in front of the kids

• "The Critters Are Coming" (page 152): every 48 years a plague of rats visits a forest in India...and other plague-ridden stories

• "Nature Films: Before Cousteau" (page 209): the evolution of the nature documentary, all the way back to the silent film era

• "Mud-Luscious and Puddle-Wonderful" (page 270): wonderful quotes about our wonderful natural world

One more thing. As usual, thanks to the entire BRI staff and our far-flung team of freelancers—especially Thom and Sue—for their endless inspirations, triple hard work, adventurous spirits…and all the bad animal puns. (We worked so hard that we were nearly catatonic! That's even worse than dog-tired! We're not lyin'!)

We hope this book gives you many hours of wonder and giggling and learning and good old-fashioned bathroom-reading fun. And as always...

Go with the Flow!

—Uncle John, Felix the Dog,
and the BRI Staff

BIZARRE BEASTIES

Come for the spider that fibs. Stay for the ape that cooks.

BEAUTIES ON THE QUACK WALK

The Duck Fashion Show is exactly what it sounds like: Ducks wear fancy outfits, including little hats, and waddle up and down a catwalk to the delight of onlookers. Duck handler Brian Harrington has been dressing up his "Pied Piper Ducks" since the 1980s. He takes them to agricultural fairs throughout Australia, where the not-so-ugly ducklings show off the latest quack fashions—including "evening wear," "bridal wear," and "off to the races." They're always a big hit.

FISH OUT OF WATER

Ginger the goldfish lives in a bowl on top of a cabinet in the home of Barbara and Alan Woodward. In late 2008, Barbara awoke to discover that Ginger had jumped out of his bowl and was lying on the floor behind the cabinet. The cabinet was too heavy for Barbara to move, she was late for work, and Alan wasn't there. So she left. When Barbara returned 13 hours later, she expected to find a dead fish, but there was Ginger, flopping around in the middle of the floor. "It's a Christmas miracle!" Barbara told reporters. (Biologists have been unable to explain how the fish survived for so long without water.) Ginger doesn't swim as well as he used to, but there is now a cover over his bowl just to be safe.

SHORT-ORDER COOK

Kanzi is a 31-year-old bonobo (a pygmy chimpanzee) who lives at the Great Ape Trust in Des Moines, Iowa. Under the tutelage of Dr. Sue Savage-Rumbaugh, the primate can understand 3,000 words and "say" 500 words by pointing at symbols. But Kanzi's most amazing ability is that he cooks his own food. It started when he was young. Said Savage-Rumbaugh, "Kanzi used to watch the film *Quest for Fire*...about early man struggling to control fire. He watched it spellbound over and over." Then she taught the bonobo how to light a match. Now (with human supervision) Kanzi can pan-fry his own hamburgers and roast marshmallows on a stick.

The Indian emperor Ashoka created the first known nature preserve in 242 BC.

MY, WHAT A PRETTY EYE YOU HAVE

When the "Cyclops Shark" showed up on the Internet in 2011, most people dismissed it as a Photoshopped hoax. But it turns out that the picture is real. The dead fetal shark was removed from the belly of a pregnant female caught by an angler in the Gulf of California. Like an actual cyclops, it has one large eye located in the center of its face. The strange shark was sent to Mexican biologist Felipe Galván-Magaña, who confirmed that the lone eye had all its optic nerves, so had the animal been born, it most likely would have been able to see. However, it was too malformed to survive for long. Calling the find "extremely rare," Galván-Magaña said such genetic mutations are not unheard of—there have been a few other documented cases of cyclops animals.

MALE CHAUVINIST SPIDER

In 2011 scientists at Denmark's Aarhus University observed a previously unknown behavior in nursery web spiders. The researchers already knew that males attract females by giving them a present of an insect carefully wrapped in silk. If the female accepts the gift, it's mating time. But there's a newly observed behavior that's a bit more shocking: If the male can't find a good bug to gift, it will instead use a small part of a plant and disguise it as a bug. To delay her from discovering his secret, the male spider winds the silk in such a complicated way that is very difficult for the female to unwrap it. Then, as she fruitlessly tries to open her gift, he takes the opportunity to mount her while she is distracted.

WHERE THE SUN DON'T SHINE

"The key thing for fish living on coral reefs is to find somewhere to hide and not get eaten," said Martin Attrill, a marine biologist from England's Plymouth University. He's talking about pearlfish, found along Australia's Great Barrier Reef. They will take up residence in any "hole" they find suitable, even an oyster (hence the name). But the pearlfish's preferred home is actually inside the butt of a sea cucumber (known as the "ocean's slug"). "The pearlfish are essentially living in a burrow," said Attrill. "They come out at night to feed from the sea cucumber's colonic cavity. It is moist and safe in there, and quite often, the pearlfish live in there in pairs."

The odd way gazelles jump is called "pronking."

BRANCHING OUT

Do trees contemplate us as much as we contemplate them?

"It is not so much for its beauty that the forest makes a claim upon men's hearts, as for that subtle something, that quality of air, that emanation from old trees, that so wonderfully changes and renews a weary spirit."

—**Robert Louis Stevenson**

"Coconut trees, lithe and graceful, crowd the beach in their ordered rows like a minuet of slender elderly virgins adopting flippant poses."

—**William Manchester**

"Break open a cherry tree and there are no flowers, but the spring breeze brings forth myriad blossoms."

—**Ikkyu Sojun**

"A woodland in full color is awesome as a forest fire, but a single tree is like a dancing tongue of flame to warm the heart."

—**Hal Borland**

"Nothing is more beautiful than the loveliness of the woods before sunrise."

—**George Washington Carver**

"A tree is an incomprehensible mystery."

—**Jim Woodring**

"The clearest way into the universe is through a forest wilderness."

—**John Muir**

"Wilderness is not a luxury but a necessity of the human spirit."

—**Edward Abbey**

"In an orchard there should be enough to eat, enough to lay up, enough to be stolen, and enough to rot on the ground."

—**James Boswell**

"A society grows great when old men plant trees whose shade they know they shall never sit in."

—**Greek proverb**

"Sometimes our fate resembles a fruit tree in winter. Who would think that those branches would turn green again and blossom, but we hope it, we know it."

—**Johann Wolfgang von Goethe**

BUFFALO BLOTTERS

Actual police reports involving actual animals—and several trees—all from the area around Buffalo, New York. (Maybe it's the name?)

• A possum was destroyed by patrol in a backyard. The homeowner reported the possum acting "aggressively," doing things like standing on its back feet—and smiling.

• A woman on Grover Cleveland Highway reported that a large animal was behind her dryer making a lot of noise. A large rat refused to come out of the hole.

• A Harlem Road resident reported that the house had been hit with paint balls for the second time in a week. Police said it actually appeared to be bird droppings.

• A Midway resident reported a "suspicious-looking" fox in a field behind his home. The resident worried that it might be chasing rabbits.

• A man reported that he went to get his car from a Genesee Street parking lot when he lost his 13-year-old son. Reportedly the youth saw a spider, panicked, and was hiding somewhere in the lot. He was located.

• A motorist traveling on Ellicott Road complained of an irrational deer. Looks like it was dancing.

• An elderly resident reported a bird in the house on Kensington Avenue. The resident was advised to open windows and doors, but it was determined that there was really a dead battery in a smoke detector. There was no bird.

• A bird was reported in a house on South Avenue. Patrols 4, 7, & 9 responding.

• Officers received a complaint of suspicious activity on Fourth Avenue. A man was reported hugging several trees.

• Troopers investigated an accident on Clarence Center Road. Car #1 stopped to avoid a turtle. The driver of car #1 said car #2 drove into the back end of car #1. The driver of car #2 said the driver of car #1 stopped to avoid the turtle in the road and then backed up, hitting car #2. Troopers said the turtle was unable to offer any information.

Difference between human and chimpanzee DNA: Less than 1%.

A FISHY STORY

In late 1994 a particularly fishy news story swept the globe. A short time later, it got even fishier...

BACKGROUND

In early September 1994, Cor Stoop, of Amsterdam lost his dentures in the North Sea while on a chartered fishing trip. (He'd been seasick, and lost them vomiting over the side of the boat.) In late November, Hugo Slamat, an Amsterdam-based North Sea charter boat captain, caught a 19-pound cod. When he gutted the fish...he found a set of dentures in its belly. He showed them to another boat captain, who happened to be the one Stoop had been fishing with. A couple of days later, Slamat, the other captain, and Stoop got together, and Stoop tried the dentures on. They fit. Slamat had actually found Stoop's dentures. By December 1994 that story had become an international news sensation. National Public Radio in the United States even did a segment on it, interviewing both Slamat and Stoop.

DEEPER BACKGROUND...

Two weeks later, however, two Dutch taxi drivers, Roel Pool and Klaas Reinders, contacted the media. The dentures didn't belong to Cor Stoop, they said. How did they know? Because they were friends of Hugo Slamat, and had been with him on the fateful fishing trip, and they'd put the dentures in the cod's belly as a joke. They were coming forward, they explained, because the whole thing had gotten out of hand...and because Pool's wife Janet wanted her spare set of dentures back. News organizations around the world, including NPR, had to retract their stories. Stoop, for his part, confirmed with his dentist that the dentures were indeed not his. (He didn't feel too bad about the whole thing: he'd been paid a large amount of money for his story, and because he himself had been duped—he didn't have to pay it back!) Stoop gave the dentures to Slamat to return to Janet Pool—but Slamat, furious with Pool and Reinders for making him the butt of an internationally famous joke, refused. He admitted months later that he threw the dentures into the North Sea. So maybe some other fisherman will have another toothy fish story to tell us someday?

Tulips continue to grow after being cut.

SNOW BIG DEAL

Think you know about snow? Well, there's a winter storm watch...starting on this page.

• Snowflakes get their start when water vapor in the atmosphere condenses and becomes ice. In the middle of the flake is usually a teensy bit of dust that collected the vapor, which in turn collected more moisture and froze into a water crystal.

• The shape of snow crystals is determined by atmospheric moisture and temperature—the warmer the air, the bigger the crystals. The shapes of the flakes also depend on air temperature. Most snowflakes are six-sided, but if you took a microscope outside during a snowstorm, you might see rod-shaped flakes, cup-shaped flakes, and eight- or twelve-pointed stars.

• The best snowmen are made when the air temperature is closer to the freezing point. That's because snow that's slightly melted will stick together better than the dry, fluffy stuff.

• According to one report, the largest snowflakes ever fell near Fort Keogh, Montana, in January 1887. People claimed the monster flakes were "larger than milk pans." Some scientists say that might have been possible, noting that snowflakes measuring 6 inches across are real (though rare) occurrences.

• Although it can vary greatly depending on the wetness or dryness of the snow, the general rule of thumb is that 10 inches of snow equals an inch of rain. If the snow is dry and fluffy, the amount of snow is higher. If the snow is wet and heavy, the ratio can be as low as 3 inches of snow to an inch of rain.

• In 1941 New Hampshire became the first state to create an official policy for using salt on snowy and icy roads. Salt lowers the melting point of snow, making roads more wet than icy.

• The U.S. record for the most snow came in the 1998–99 season in Washington State when the Mt. Baker Ski Area received 1,140 inches...which made a snowbank about the height of a nine-story building.

In proportion to their body size, hummingbirds have the largest brains of all bird species.

THE TWO ELEPHANTS

When we think of elephants we tend to think of, well, elephants. But the two elephant types—the Asian and the African—are pretty different animals. Let's take a look.

SIZE: African elephants are larger, reaching 13½ feet in height and weighing up to 15,000 pounds. Asian elephants reach about 12 feet and 14,000 pounds.

HEAD: Asian elephants have an indent in their foreheads and two pronounced domes on top of their heads. African elephants lack these features.

EARS: African elephants have large ears that extend above the top of the neck. Asian elephants' much smaller ears don't extend above the neck. (This is the easiest way to tell the two types apart.)

LOWER LIP: Asians have long, pointed lower lips; Africans' are short and round.

TUSKS: All African elephants can grow tusks, with males having larger tusks than females. But only some male Asian elephants have tusks. Also, many female and some male Asians have small tusk-like teeth known as *tushes*.

TRUNK: African elephants have two "fingers" at the tip of the trunk, one on top, one on bottom, with which they can grip objects; Asian elephants have just one finger on top of the tip, and grips by pressing objects against the underside of the trunk's tip.

BACK: Africans have convex, dipped backs; Asians have concave, rounded backs.

RIBS: Numbers vary for both, but Africans can have up to 21 pairs; Asians, up to 19.

TOES: Africans have four or five toes on their front feet and three on the rear; Asians have five on the front feet and four on the rear.

DIET: Varies for both, but Asians eat mostly grass; Africans eat mostly leaves.

EXTRA: Asian elephants consist of just one species; Africans, two: *savanna* and *forest* elephants. (Forest elephants have rounder ears, for starters.) Scientists made that species split in 2010, so the forest elephant is the "newest "elephant in the world.

A mosquito's wings beat 300 to 600 times per second.

A SEGANKU BY ANY OTHER NAME...

Was Shakespeare right when he wrote that a rose by any other name wouldn't smell as sweet? And if so, would a skunk smell the same if we still called it a seganku?

• The Algonquian natives used the word *seganku*, which means "one who squirts." Colonial settlers spelled it "squunck," which eventually became "skunk."

• Another Algonquian name comes from the Narragansetts of Rhode Island, who called the big beast a *moosu*, which means "he strips off," referring to the moose's ability to remove bark from a tree while foraging for food.

• The Masai people of Africa call the elephant an *olenkaina*, which roughly means "he with hand," referring to the elephant's trunk, which it uses to prepare food, feed itself, pick up objects—and as a portable shower head.

• A long-standing legend said that when explorer James Cook asked the aboriginals of Australia for the name of "that jumping animal," they answered, "*kanguru*," which meant "I don't understand you." Cute, but not true. The tale was debunked in the 1970s. *Kanguru* was, in fact, the aboriginal name for the gray kangaroo, which eventually became the general English name for all kangaroos.

• The Arabic people—who probably got the name from an African language—called giraffes *zarafa*, which means "one who walks swiftly," because the animals can really move when they need to. Afrikaaners called it a *kameelperd* ("cameleopard" in English) from "camel" and "leopard," referring to the giraffe's camel-like body and leopardlike spots.

• It's easy to see how the rhinoceros got its name: *Rhino* is Latin for "nose," and *ceros* is Latin for "horn." Though it's commonly thought that the white rhino is called "white" based on the

You're 16 times more likely to be hit by lightning under an oak tree than under a beech tree.

corruption of a Dutch word for "wide" (referring to the animal's mouth, which is wider than the hooked lip of the black rhino), that is a fallacy. The truth is that etymologists aren't sure exactly why the white rhinoceros is so named. One theory suggests the animal's name comes from its appearance during a favorite pastime: wallowing in wet, chalky soil.

• The term *hippopotamus*, meaning "river horse," comes from the ancient Greek. However, the semiaquatic hippo's closest relatives aren't horses—or even pigs, which some say they resemble—but cetaceans, like whales and porpoises.

• Ancient aboriginals called koalas *gula*, which loosely means "no drink." The reason: The koala gets most of its liquids from the eucalyptus plants it eats.

* * *

STAND-UP FOLKS

"A new study shows that licking the sweat off a frog can cure depression. The downside is, the minute you stop licking, the frog gets depressed again."

—Jay Leno

"Cigarettes are like weasels. Perfectly harmless unless you put one in your mouth and try to set fire to it."

—Boothby Graffoe

"An Australian relief effort is knitting sweaters to protect the feathers of penguins being affected by an oil spill. The sweaters are being refused by many penguins who'd rather die then dress casual."

—Conan O'Brien

"A friend of mine rang and asked me to help him with the crossword. The clue was 'A flightless bird found in Iceland,' and the answer was two words, six and seven letters long. 'I've got it!' I said. 'Frozen chicken!'"

—Tommy Cooper

Q: What do you get if you cross a giraffe and a hedgehog? A: An extra-long toilet brush.

"THE ART OF PAINTING ANIMALS ON ROCKS"

And other real-life, actually authentic, totally not-made-up book titles that will make you laugh so hard your kidneys might explode. (Hey—that would be a good title for a book!)

Pets Who Want to Kill Themselves
Duncan Birmingham (2009)

Be Bold with Bananas
The Australian Banana Growers Council (1975)

Beyond Leaf Raking
Peter L. Benson (1993)

Grandma's Dead: Breaking Bad News with Baby Animals
Amanda McCall; and Ben Schwartz (2008)

A Compendium of the Biographical Literature on Deceased Entomologists
Pamela Gilbert (1977)

The Art of Faking Exhibition Poultry
George Ryley Scott (1934)

The Joy of Chickens
Dennis Nolan (1981)

Prehistoric Humans in Film and Television
Michael Klossner (2006)

A Popular History of British Seaweeds, Comprising Their Structure, Fructification, Specific Characters, Arrangement, and General Distribution, with Notices of Some of the Fresh-Water Algae
Rev. D. Landsborough (1857)

How Green Were the Nazis?
by Franz-Josef Bruggemeier, Mark Cioc, and Thomas Zeller (2005)

Proceedings of the Second International Workshop on Nude Mice
Various authors (1977)

Stick Making: A Complete Course
Andrew Jones and Clive George (2007)

Explosive Spiders and How to Make Them
John Scoffern (1881)

A Letter to the Man Who Killed My Dog
Richard Joseph (1956)

Antlers are shed every year; horns are permanent.

Oral Sadism and the Vegetarian Personality
Glenn C. Ellenbogen (1987)

The Art of Painting Animals on Rocks
Lin Wellford (1994)

Cold Meat and How to Disguise It
Ms. M. E. Rattray (1904)

Microscopic Objects: How to Mount Them
Jean C. Johnson (1948)

The Coming Disaster, Worse Than the H-bomb: Astronomically, Geologically and Scientifically Proven. The Coal Beds, Ice Ages, Tides, and Coming Soon, a Great Wave and Flood Caused by a Shift of the Axis of the Earth from the Gyroscopic Action of Our Solar System
Adam D. Barber (1954)

Shag the Pony
Peter Crabbe (1952)

* * *

IN MY BARNACLE BALLOON

For several years, researchers had found species of barnacles native to the Mediterranean Sea in waters off Scandinavia. That's not so surprising: barnacles attach themselves to ships, and in this way, they have been transported around the world's oceans for as long as ships have been around. But in 2010 researchers found that the creatures may have discovered another mode of travel: flight. Clumps of live barnacles were observed attached to the leg-tags of seagulls that had been tagged for migration studies—and the migration route of these particular gulls happened to include a path between the Mediterranean Sea and waters off Scandinavia. The theory, experts said, is plausible. Barnacles are able to close themselves up and endure long periods without water to accommodate the coming and going of tides. So they could feasibly survive the gulls' long flights by closing themselves up, only to reopen when the gulls got to water once again. The research- ers said further study was needed before the "invasion of the flying barnacles" theory could be fully confirmed. (We'll let you know what they find out…so stick around.)

12 ODD WHALE FACTS

There was a lot we didn't know about whales. How about you?

• Whale poop comes out as a slurrylike liquid. It floats. (We thought you'd like to know that.) It's very nutrient-rich, too, and an important part of ocean ecosystems.

• The only mammals whose females regularly live for decades after they've lost the ability to bear young: humans, apes, and whales.

• In 1991 an all-white humpback whale calf was spotted off Australia. It was named Migaloo—an Aboriginal word meaning "whitefella."

• *Toothed* whales (e.g., dolphins) have one blowhole. *Baleen* whales (e.g., humpback whales) have two—side by side—which gives them their characteristic V-shaped spouts.

• Whales (and seals) can suffer decompression sickness—or "the bends"—if they ascend from deep dives too quickly.

• There are 21 beaked whale species. They have long beaks, like dolphins, and are the least known of all the whales.

• For most beaked whale species, only the teeth of males erupt from the gums, and the animals have just one pair of teeth. The teeth grow from the lower jaw, up around the upper jaw—like tusks.

• Beaked whale researchers say females choose mates by the size and shape of their tusks, meaning beaked whale tusks, are, in a way, whale antlers.

• Whales can hiccup.

• Four whales you may not have heard of: Bryde's whale, sei whale, Gervais' beaked whale, melon-headed whale.

• *Sounding*, in regards to whales, means diving, and usually refers to the deep *sounding dives* whales regularly make for food.

• *Atavism* is a genetic phenomenon whereby an organism shows ancestral traits that it normally doesn't. An example is when humans are born with tails. Whales show this occasionally...by growing partly developed hind limbs.

MOCHA DICK?

Here's the story of a sperm whale that helped inspire one of history's greatest novels. The drawing is by Captain Charles M. Scammon, from his book The Marine Mammals of the North-Western Coast of North America, Described and Illustrated *(1874).*

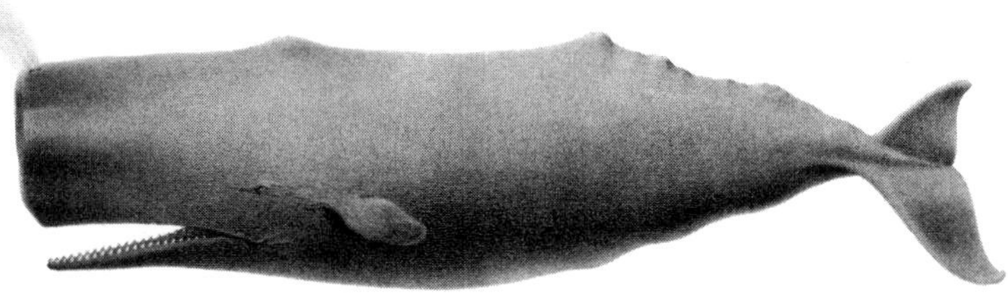

LORD OF THE WHALES

Sometime around 1810, a whaling ship in the South Pacific Ocean encountered a sperm whale. It was huge, bizarrely aggressive—and white. The whalers went after it, but were not only unable to kill it...they were attacked by it. This was the first of several reports of a very large and very aggressive albino sperm whale that whaling ships in the region encountered over the next almost 50 years. Some accounts say the whale was harpooned by a hundred different whaling crews—and escaped them all after ramming and battering many of their boats, killing dozens of men in the process. More reasonable accounts lowered those numbers drastically, but there is no doubt that for at least five decades, a large albino whale did wreak havoc on whaling crews in the region. It was finally killed sometime in the late 1850s.

That whale's nickname? Mocha Dick. Why? Whalers most often encountered the animal near Mocha, an island off Chile's south coast. "Dick" was just a common nickname (like "Tom" and "Harry"). In 1839 American author Jeremiah N. Reynolds wrote about the legendary whale in an article for the *Knickerbocker*, a monthly magazine headquartered in New York City. Mocha Dick was also at least part of the inspiration for another, much more famous, and fictional, white sperm whale: Captain Ahab's nemesis in Herman Melville's 1851 novel *Moby-Dick*.

The jack-o'-lantern mushroom emits an eerie green glow at night.

BEYOND WEIRD

We've always got lots of weird news stories—but some need their own special category.

In April 2011, scientists in China announced that they had successfully introduced human genes into cows...and they now had 200 cows that produced human breast milk. The scientists said they hoped there would one day be herds of cows all over the world producing human breast milk for hungry human babies.

• **Winged beetles started** flying out of a hole in a 13-year-old Indian boy's groin one day in June 2003. Doctors said the boy was suffering from *myiasis*, wherein an insect's eggs somehow hatch inside a human body. The beetles continued to fly out of the hole for at least 18 days.

• **The cane toad** is native to Central America, and is a devastating invasive species in Australia. But the toads are also known for something else: Male cane toads will try to mate with just about anything. They have been observed mounting and trying—sometimes for hours—to mate with *dead* cane toads, male or female, as well as dead frogs, lizards, pythons, and even small dead mammals such as rabbits.

• **A pack of** vicious squirrels attacked and killed a dog in the village of Lazo in far eastern Russia in December 2005. The dog had been barking at the squirrels when they attacked en masse. The squirrels ran off when people intervened, witnesses told the BBC, "some carrying pieces of flesh" in their mouths.

• **Japanese scientists announced** in January 2012 that they had created a mouse that tweets like a bird. They had long been cross-breeding mice and monitoring them for abnormalities. "We checked the newly born mice one by one," lead researcher Arikuni Uchimura said. "One day, we found a mouse that was singing like a bird." He added that he hoped his research would lead to the creation of a talking mouse. "I know it's a long shot," he said, "but I'm doing this with hopes of making a Mickey Mouse someday."

Sea horses can move their eyes in opposite directions.

THE WONDERFUL WORLD OF WEEDS, PART I

Step away from that weed killer and listen up! Those plants you're aiming at don't all deserve to die. In fact, some of the little green heads sticking up through the cracks in your driveway might even come in handy.

CHICKWEED

Humans have used chickweed for centuries in folk medicine, but it's also a favorite food of chickens, hence the name.

How to find it: This plant is native to Europe, but now grows throughout North America. It looks like a ground cover and has a tough, shallow root system. The light green leaves grow to be about 1¼ inches long, and its star-shaped flowers are white. It thrives in the shade and is usually found growing at the foot of trees—especially oak trees. It likes moisture, too, so you might even find it flourishing at the base of a leaky faucet.

What it's good for: Not only is chickweed an old folk remedy for weight loss, it can also be used to treat a variety of illnesses (including ailments of the liver and kidneys), as a blood purifier, and as a cleansing tonic in the spring after a sedentary winter spent indulging in rich foods and drinks.

Internal medicine: The uses of chickweed are many. It tastes a little like spinach, so it can be eaten raw in a salad or wilted as a side dish or as part of a cooked dish. You might use it in an omelet: just add a handful or two of chickweed and some cheese and/or other ingredients. As the omelet finishes cooking, the chickweed will wilt and make for a filling, nutritious meal.

Taking chickweed in tea or juice form (with a little carrot juice to offset the bitterness) helps the body rid itself of toxins and waste, thereby smoothing the skin, boosting energy levels, and easing the aches and pains of arthritis.

External medicine: Herbalists add chickweed to oils and salves that treat skin disorders like rashes, eczema, abscesses, boils, and skin ulcers. Adding the leaves directly to bathwater can soothe itchy or inflamed skin (hives or chicken pox, for example). If you prefer homemade remedies, you can treat cuts and relieve itching from eczema and psoriasis by making a poultice out of chickweed (by grinding it, adding heated water, and placing the resulting paste in a piece of cloth) and applying it to your skin.

Nutrients: Chickweed is rich in vitamin C, beta-carotene, B vitamins, magnesium, potassium, calcium, and lots of other stuff that's good for you.

DANDELION

The word dandelion is from the Old French *dent-de-lion*, meaning "lion's tooth," because the leaves look like sharp teeth. It's been used as food and an herbal remedy throughout recorded history.

How to find it: Dandelion is a low-growing plant with leaves up to 2½ inches wide and 3 to 12 inches long spread out in a circle. Its flowers are bright yellow, one flower to a stem. The flower blooms are replaced by "puff-ball" seed heads, which all of us (admit it) enjoyed blowing across the yard when we were kids.

What it's good for: Dandelion acts as a diuretic at the same time it's adding potassium back into the body. Dandelion root is most potent and cleansing when harvested in the fall. In the old days, dandelion was used as a tonic, and was best known for purifying the liver, gallbladder, and kidneys.

Internal medicine: The leaves can be eaten in a salad or turned into a tea. Dandelion leaves are at their tastiest when they've just come up. With a drizzle of honey and a fresh squeeze of lemon, the leaves make for a nutritious cup of tea. And let's not forget the flowers: They can be eaten fresh, dipped in batter and fried, or pickled with vinegar and spices.

Nutrients: Bursting with vitamins A through E and loaded with antioxidants, the leaves contain more beta-carotene than carrots do. Even spinach doesn't have as much calcium and iron. There's also zinc, magnesium, potassium, phosphorus, and more.

For more wonderful weeds, turn to page 141.

SANDIER SARDINE?!

And a few other amazing (or just plain annoying) animal anagrams...

Q: What ate your **parrot**?
A: A **raptor**.

Q: She writes deer **odes**?
A: She **does**. To **does**.

Q: That's a nice **loin** cloth. What's it made from?
A: Lion.

Q: Is that a new **gun**?
A: No, it's a **gnu** gun. Just got it today!

Q: Do **trout** school?
A: If they get a **tutor** they do.

Q: Uh, Brian, why did you kiss that **lamb**?
A: Lanolin—cheap, sheep-based lip **balm**.

Q: Why is that **grizzly bear** wearing a three-piece suit?
A: You wouldn't want him to be a **grizzly bare**, would you?

Q: What's that thing floating in your **Tang**?
A: A **gnat**.

Bloke #1: Mate, your **echidna** is vicious!
Bloke #2: That's why I keep him **chained** up!

Q: Hey, Bill the Bull, what happened to your **horns**?
A: Shorn.

Q: Why is that **orangutan** throwing his feces around?
A: Aw, he's just on some kind of **guano rant**.

Cat: I'm sick of having **paws**! I want hooves!
Cow: Swap?

Q: Are you telling me the **leopard** was set free?
A: Yeah. He was **paroled**.

Q: Why won't the **giraffe** eat these Newtons?
A: Fig fear.

Deckhand: Skipper, we've got too many **mackerel**!
Skipper: That's all right, open the **keel, cram** them in!

Q: What goes with **pickerel**?
A: Kelp, rice...

Q: What's that **hippopotamus** doing in an outhouse in Pennsylvania?
A: He likes to **put Amish poop** on his dry skin.

Q: What's that **dingo** up to?
A: Seems to be **doing** something with the baby.

Q: What did that **wolf** with the *Bathroom Reader* say?
A: Go with the **flow**!

WILD MOVIES

Need an idea for a great nature film to watch? (And no, 1966's The Wild World of Batwoman *does not count.) Here are a few suggestions from Uncle John's own collection.*

PLANET EARTH (2006)

"Seven continents. Five years. A $25 million budget. A total run time of 530 minutes. *Planet Earth* is an undertaking so epic in scope that it earns comparisons to the grandest Hollywood blockbusters. It's the *Titanic* of television nature documentaries. The production employed over a dozen of the world's most renowned nature photographers, sent them out to traverse the globe for over 60 months, capturing the planet's most amazing landscapes and creatures in stunning high-definition. Even the title of the series is ballsy—you don't name your documentary 'Planet Earth' if you're not aspiring to something monumental." (Peter M. Bracke, *High-Def Digest*)

SERENGETI SHALL NOT DIE **(1959)**

"Described by legendary wildlife filmmaker Alan Root as 'perhaps the best-known and most influential wildlife film ever made,' *Serengeti Shall Not Die* is an intimate and evocative account of the wildebeests' yearly migration. Hoping one day the boundaries of Serengeti National Park would encompass the entire movement of these massive herds, German conservationist Professor Bernhard Grzimek researched the route of the herds. *Serengeti Shall Not Die* is widely credited with alerting the world to the plight of Africa's wildlife, the Grzimek's aerial census bringing to life the dwindling numbers of numerous species." (*WildFilmHistory.org*)

NEVER CRY WOLF **(1983)**

"This is the haunting story of a scientist who is sent to the Arctic to study wolves. Unfamiliar with the wilderness, Tyler (Charles Martin Smith) finds himself unprepared for his stay in the frozen desolation. Based on Farley Mowat's study of wolves for the Ottawa Wildlife Service, this beautifully photographed wilderness film is as fine as director Carroll Ballard's previous film, *Black Stal-*

lion. Capturing the changes a man goes through as he learns about life in the wilds, *Never Cry Wolf* is very informative, but it is Smith's performance that makes the film a resounding success. (*TV Guide*)

WALKABOUT (1971)

"In its simplest terms it's the story of an attractive fourteen-year-old girl (Jenny Agutter) and her six-year-old little brother (Lucien John, the real-life son of [director Nicholas] Roeg) residing in a luxury apartment in Sydney, Australia, with their depressed upper-class English geologist father (John Meillon), who takes the children to the outback and tries to shoot them, and when that fails blows up the car and shoots himself. The children are left in the harsh Australian outback. They are saved by a sixteen-year-old aborigine on walkabout (a tribal initiation into manhood), who helps the kids by getting them to tune in to nature." (Dennis Schwartz, *Ozus' World Movie Reviews*)

GRIZZLY MAN (2005)

"We know this about Timothy Treadwell: He lived with bears in Alaska for thirteen summers and died by being eaten by one. The movie, built mostly from Treadwell's sometimes extraordinary and always self-dramatizing video footage, expects our morbid curiosity; it is a check on a culture that elevates the Crocodile Hunter to pop hero and probably an indulgence of that culture's darkest fantasy. Its power is in the way Herzog authenticates and complicates the suggestion that Treadwell 'got what he deserved.'" (Jonathan Kiefer, *Sacramento News & Review*)

THE COVE (2009)

"The narrator is Richard O'Barry who, in the 1960s, trained the dolphins used in the *Flipper* TV show. But when one of these intelligent mammals apparently committed suicide in his arms by closing her blowhole, he realized something was terribly wrong. Now a passionate animal-rights activist, he attempts here to film a secretive dolphin hunt at a remote cove in Taiji, Japan, where thousands are caught each year, some to be killed for meat, the rest to be sold to theme parks. Richard and his team set up camouflaged cameras and underwater recorders in a bid to capture the

A frog's tongue is attached at the front of its mouth.

slaughter. The result is shocking, electrifying and enough to put you off a trip to SeaWorld for good." (David Edwards, *The Daily Mirror*)

THE SILENT WORLD (1956)

"Fans of underwater diving and sea life will be both shocked and disturbed to visit this Oscar-winning documentary by famed diver and explorer Jacques Cousteau. Although he's known as a pioneering marine conservationist, this film demonstrates a horrifying level of disrespect towards marine animal life, with various sequences showing the crew 'riding' on the backs of sea turtles; attacking a school of sharks because they 'dare' to circle around a dead whale and eat its flesh; and dynamiting a coral reef. With that said, those who can stomach these scenes should at least appreciate Cousteau's groundbreaking work in the field of underwater cinematography. Assisted by a young Louis Malle, Cousteau captured haunting footage of life underwater—the type of imagery we take for granted now, but which was remarkably innovative at the time." (*FilmFanatic.org*)

THE BEAR (1988)

"Storytelling doesn't get much purer than this—a film with virtually no dialogue and not a minute that isn't fascinating, either for the plot it pursues or the way director Jean-Jacques Annaud gets his ursine stars to do what he wants. The story deals with a young cub who, after his mother is killed in a landslide, bonds to a lumbering male Kodiak. The two of them then must cope with an invasion of hunters into their territory—and Annaud makes it clear whose side he's on. Aside from stunning scenery, the film offers startlingly close-up looks at bear behavior. They say the best actors are the ones that let you see what they're thinking, a trick Annaud manages with his big, furry stars." (Marshall Fine, Gannett Newspapers)

* * *

The world's largest dog was an English mastiff that measured more than 8 feet from nose to tail. The world's smallest dog: a Jack Russell terrier that measured less than 4 inches high.

BUGGY PROVERBS

Humans can learn some important lessons from segmented invertebrates with exoskeletons.

"When spiders' webs unite, they can tie up a lion."

—Ethiopia

"Do not kill a single wasp; for then a hundred will come to its funeral."

—Russia

"The hand of compassion gets stung when it pets a scorpion."

—Persia

"One bee is better than a thousand flies."

—Spain

"When the moth flies around the flame, it burns itself."

—China

"We keep an eye on the scorpion, but do not watch out for the millipede."

—Italy

"The camel carries the load, it is the tick that complains."

—Morocco

"The butterfly often forgets it once was a caterpillar."

—Sweden

"In a battle between the elephants, it is the ants that get squashed."

—Thailand

"The beetle is a beauty in the eyes of its mother."

—Egypt

"The way to kill the bedbug is to set fire to the bed."

—Mexico

"The termite can do nothing to a stone but lick it."

—Sudan

"One dead fly spoils much good ointment."

—New England

"A centipede though dead will not fall."

—Japan

"The death throes of an elephant are not so annoying as a living flea."

—Zanzibar

"Fly like a butterfly, sting like a bee."

—Muhammad Ali

VERY WEIRD DISEASES

Sometimes diseases aren't just scary—they're weird too. Here are a few memorable examples.

STONE MAN SYNDROME

Technically known as *fibrodysplasia ossificans progressiva*, this is a particularly perverse disease because it's the result of a malfunction of the body's own repair system. When nonaffected people injure fibrous tissue—things like muscles and tendons—their bodies jump into gear to fix the problem. But in the case of people with this disease, their bodies go too far and cause the injured tissue to *ossify*...or turn into bone. Real, actual bone. That means if you injure your wrist, your body responds by turning all the tendons, ligaments, and muscles in your wrist to bone, with the obvious result that you can't move your wrist anymore. In the most extreme cases, the victim can be rendered completely immobile, hence the "stone man" name. There is no cure, and there's not even any effective treatment: Surgery to fix the ossified tissue just results in the body rushing to add more bone to the area.

AQUAGENIC URTICARIA

This is hands down one of—if not *the*—weirdest afflictions ever. Why? Because it causes its victims to have an allergic reaction... to water. People with aquagenic urticaria react to having water on their skin as if it were acid: It causes intense pain, itching, and a severe red rash with weltlike bumps. (The *urticaria*, or hives, in the name refers to this rash.) Added to this weirdness is the fact that victims have the same reaction to their own sweat. And their own tears. And if they drink water, their throats can swell up. The cause of aquegenic urticaria is unknown. Fortunately, it's very rare, with only a few known cases in history, and it's not permanent, occurring only in episodes with symptoms lasting for a few hours.

Extra: Another type of urticaria is known as "cold urticaria." What does that mean? Instead of being allergic to water, victims of this condition are allergic to cold, and they suffer itching and burning hives when they're exposed to cold temperatures.

PROGERIA

This is an especially depressing disease that causes small children to physically age far more rapidly than normal. A young child afflicted with progeria can look 80 or 90 years old, and can already show symptoms regularly associated with old age, including wrinkled skin, hair loss, arthritis, loss of vision, and debilitated organ function. Progeria is caused by a mutation to a specific section of a specific gene, the full function of which scientists have yet to determine, although part of its function is obviously related to aging. (For that reason, the gene has been the subject of intense study by geneticists all over the world since its discovery in 2003.) Progeria is very rare, occurring in only about one in 8 million births. There is no known cure, and victims seldom live past their early teens.

TRIMETHYLAMINURIA

People with this metabolic disorder are unable to produce an enzyme used to break down *trimethylamine*, a compound found in many foods. That means trimethylamine builds up in the body, until there is so much that it is finally emitted through urine, sweat, and breathing. And that's bad...because trimethylamine smells like stinky fish. In fact, it's the very chemical compound that makes stinky fish smell like stinky fish in the first place. People with this disorder can smell so strongly that—as you can imagine—it can make work and social situations difficult. Trimethylaminuria is a genetic disease, and there is no cure, though the strength of the fishy odor can be made less powerful through diet.

Extra: The gene mutation that causes trimethylaminuria was discovered in 1997, but the disease has been around for a long time. The earliest known mention of it may come from the ancient Sanskrit epic the *Mahabharata*, a collection of Indian folk tales more than 2,000 years old. One of those tales includes a maiden who "grew to be comely and fair, but a fishy odor ever clung to her."

* * *

DID YOU KNOW?

A "zedonk" is a cross between a zebra and another equine species, such as a donkey.

THE PETRIFYING WELL

And other fascinating phenomena brought to you free of charge by Mother Earth.

ROLL CLOUDS

Also known as "morning glory clouds," roll clouds are long, tube-shaped clouds that look like they're rolling across the sky. They're usually low to the ground—just a few hundred feet up—and enormous: The tubes can be several hundred feet across and more than a mile long. They've been known to move at speeds of up to 35 miles per hour, so it's like looking up at a giant rolling pin moving across the sky. And sometimes they travel in crowds of clouds: you might see more than one, moving along in succession. Meteorologists still aren't sure what causes them. They're rare—the only place where they appear regularly is in the sky above the Gulf of Carpentaria in Australia's far north, where they're seen every year in the early morning from September to mid-November.

PENITENTES

If you were high in South America's Andes Mountains on a summer day, you might come across a shocking sight: what looks like forest of hard, icy spikes—hundreds of them—all standing close to one another, many up to 15 feet high. They're a rare snow formation known as *penitentes*, Spanish for "penitent ones," and are so named because a field of them resembles a procession of monks in white robes. Scientists say the phenomenon is caused by a combination of the very cold, dry, and windy conditions along with bright summer sunlight, which causes snow to melt in the strange, penitente-forming way.

THE PETRIFYING WELL

Do you have a teddy bear that you'd like to turn to stone? (Who doesn't?!) Just stuff it in a suitcase and take it to the town of Knaresborough in North Yorkshire, England. There, on the banks of the river Nidd, you'll find a huge, barrel-shaped, smooth, and oddly sculpted rock, from the top of which spring water flows

Besides blue, sapphires can also be clear, brown, black, or gray.

continuously. Hanging from ropes across the rock's face, in the path of the falling water, are a bunch of items, including hats, shoes, and teddy bears, and they've all been turned to, or are in the process of turning into, stone. That's because the water has an especially high mineral content—so high, in fact, that the giant rock itself was created by the dripping water over thousands of years. Anything that's hung on the rock and exposed to the rush of the water gets slowly covered in the minerals and becomes petrified. (Small, soft toys like teddy bears take three to five months to petrify, the site's owners say, while larger, nonporous items can take up to 18 months.) The Knaresborough Petrifying Well has been a tourist attraction in England since 1630, when the grounds were sold by the English crown to a local lord. Petrified items that once belonged to famous people are on display at the site's museum. They include a purse left there by author Agatha Christie and a cowboy hat brought by John Wayne. (Similar wells can be found in other locations around the world, but Knaresborough's is by far the most famous.)

* * *

COCK-A-DOODLE-DOO...

"Swedish scientists have scooped an Ig Nobel Prize [an American parody of the Nobel Prize] for demonstrating that chickens prefer beautiful humans. The trophies, which offer an antidote to next week's more serious Nobels, honor research that makes people laugh, then think. 'There are many people who have done work that will never win a Nobel Prize, but that deserve recognition,' says organizer Marc Abrahams. The winning team trained birds to peck portraits of preference. The fowl favored hunky guys and longhaired ladies with bee-stung lips—as did Swedish college students. This suggests that man and chicken share similar wiring, explains coauthor Magnus Enquist of Stockholm University. It could be one in the eye, he suggests, for the evolutionary theory that we chose 'fit' mates to share their genes with our offspring."

—*Nature*, October 2003

THE RACCOON REPORT

Wherever there are humans in North America, there are also raccoons. These are just a few of their stories.

Memphis, Tennessee: Police found a man barbecuing a raccoon in the parking lot of an apartment complex in October 2011. A subsequent search discovered a meth lab in the apartment where the man was staying.

Miami, Florida: A 77-year-old man in was bitten by a raccoon in July 2008. The man told police he was feeding his pet monkeys in his backyard when the raccoon suddenly appeared and bit him.

Bristol, Tennessee: Police were called to a NASCAR race in August 2011 after reports of a drunk man "waving and spinning in circles" in the crowd. The man was naked. Police found a raccoon in his car.

Pasadena, Texas: In October 2011 a man struck a metal pole in his front yard with an ax several times, saw a raccoon run by, then chased the raccoon with the ax. This behavior was reported to police by a neighbor. The man told police he hadn't done anything wrong. Police took his ax away.

Toronto, Ontario: A man found a baby albino raccoon in his garage in May 2011. "Some neighbors thought it was a bear or a fox," the man said, "but then we found a black one and knew it was a raccoon." A wildlife control officer soon found three more albino babies. The four young raccoons were put in a box and left at the home—their mother came and took them away that night. The wildlife officer said the chances of finding four albino raccoons in one litter was "one in ten million."

St. Augustine, Florida: A raccoon got its head stuck in a peanut butter jar in February 2012. Sheriff's deputies caught it and removed the jar, but then the raccoon lost consciousness. A deputy performed chest compressions on the raccoon; it woke up and ran away. "Its whereabouts," a sheriff's department spokesman told reporters, "are unknown at this point."

TAKE TWO WORMS AND CALL ME IN THE MORNING

We've all heard that plants and herbs have healing properties, but what about maggots, leeches, and other gross things?

MAGGOT THERAPY

Eww, That's Gross: It sounds like a horror film—fat, cream-colored maggots eating their way through infected sores and wounds. But it's actually just a scene from modern medicine. Since ancient times, physicians have used maggots to prevent wounds from getting infected. Western docs started using them to clean wounds during the American Civil War—they stopped after World War II when antibiotics made the creepy crawlies seem obsolete.

But as bacteria have developed resistance to antibiotics, maggot therapy has made a comeback. Today, thousands of patients with abscesses, ulcers, gangrene, and burn wounds that haven't responded to traditional medical care are being treated with maggots.

How It Works: Surgeons use scalpels and lasers to remove dead tissue and expose healthy tissue, a procedure called *debridement*. But maggots do it by secreting digestive enzymes that feed on the dead tissue; the enzymes also kill bacteria in the wound and speed up healing. The maggots are kept in place with a mesh covering that's affixed to the borders of the wound. Inside are usually 200 to 300 maggots—30 per square inch—that are left in place for 48 to 72 hours. When the maggots are done feeding, doctors remove them.

Maggots to the Rescue: Wounds that haven't healed for months, or even years, often respond relatively quickly to maggot medicine. Many patients require only two or three treatments.

HIRUDOTHERAPY

Eww, That's Gross: If you've seen the movie *The African Queen*, you know that leeches are worms that live in fresh water and latch onto their victims to suck up their blood. When these creatures bite, they secrete an anticoagulant called *hirudin* that prevents the victim's blood from clotting, thus making it easier for the leeches to feed. After being bitten by a leech, a person can bleed for hours. For thousands of years, doctors used leeches on patients in a treatment called bloodletting, thinking that it would cure everything from headaches to hemorrhoids. By the mid-1800s, it became clear that bloodletting was pretty useless, and leeches went down in history as a medical mistake.

But then in the 1980s, leeches made a comeback. Plastic surgeon Joseph Upton had reattached the severed ear of a five-year-old boy—an amazing medical feat at the time—but the tissues in the ear were dying. Upton rounded up some leeches, attached them to the boy's ear...and it healed. The operation was a well-publicized success, and hirudotherapy again became an important part of medicine. Medicinal leeches are now raised for use in reconstructive and plastic surgery, and in cases where blood coagulation and blood pooling impede the healing process.

How It Works: When a body part is reattached, the blood often doesn't drain properly inside the small sutured veins. Instead, the blood pools and clots, blocking circulation. Leeches suck up the extra blood to prevent swelling. Plus, their saliva not only releases the hirudin that keeps blood from clotting, it also releases other chemicals that numb pain, fight infection, calm inflammation, and even act as anesthetics. Leeches cause fresh blood to flow to damaged tissue, allowing it to heal and produce new growth.

Leeches to the Rescue: Leeches are mainly used to help patients heal after surgery, but the ability of their saliva to fight inflammation, pain, infection, and blood clots has led to their being used in the treatment of glaucoma, varicose veins, heart disease, strokes, painful joints, and arthritis.

FECAL TRANSPLANTS

Eww, That's Gross: Who knew you could fight a difficult and potentially fatal disease with plain old poop? The disease is caused by a bacterium—*Clostridium difficile* (C. *diff*)—that infects about 250,000 people the United States annually. C. *diff* causes constant diarrhea and can be fatal in severe cases. Antibiotics are the first line of defense, but they don't always work, and thousands of people die of C. *diff* every year. These days, some doctors and hospitals are using a remarkable substance to save lives and kill antibiotic-resistant C. *diff*: a blend of saline water and…poop.

How It Works: The cure is relatively simple (or simply weird, depending on your point of view). Using healthy feces from a relative of the patient, a doctor mixes it with a saline solution, and then transplants the mixture into the patient's colon via an enema, a colonoscopy, or a nasogastric (nose-to-tummy) tube. After the treatment, beneficial bacteria from the stool colonize the intestines, killing off the C. *diff*.

Poop to the Rescue: In more than 90 percent of cases, patients are cured with one fecal transplant, and there are no relapses. All the same, in the 50-odd years since fecal transplants were first reported to cure C. *diff* patients—some of them near death—there have been no large-scale studies done on the procedure. One problem is that extensive tests cost millions of dollars, and of course, no pharmaceutical company can make a profit on feces. But that's not the only hurdle: One gastroenterologist who has cured C. *diff* with fecal transplants remarked that, even for doctors, there can be a problem with the "ick" factor.

HELMINTHIC THERAPY

Eww, That's Gross: Whipworms are a type of *helminth*—a worm that's classified as parasitic. Long, thin, and pale, whipworms thrive in places that lack proper bathroom sanitation. They're ingested as microscopic eggs that hatch inside the body. Then the newly hatched worms migrate to the intestines, where they attach to and feed off the intestinal walls. Whipworms have largely been eradicated in developed countries, but are common in places like Africa, where they can cause everything from intense stomach distress to retardation in children.

But now some Westerners are swallowing whipworm eggs on purpose. In 2011 an episode of *The Dr. Oz Show* featured whipworms as a "weird cure" for irritable bowel disease (IBD), a painful and incurable ailment that can get so serious the entire colon has to be removed. (Much better to swallow some worm eggs, we say.)

How It Works: IBD is an autoimmune disease, which means that

Brazil nuts contain small amounts of the radioactive element radium.

a patient's immune systems attack his or her own body. On the other hand, people who are infected with parasites like whipworm rarely suffer from autoimmune diseases. This caused some doctors to wonder if our very hygienic society, with its lack of germs and parasites, sometimes makes our immune systems misfire. Maybe that's why we're susceptible to autoimmune diseases in which the immune systems overreact and attack our bodies instead of only attacking bad bacteria. The doctors decided to try using whipworms to calm and reeducate patients' immune systems, so that they attack only bad bacteria and the worms, and leave the body alone.

All it takes to start treatment with whipworms is to swallow the eggs. Patients slurp down a dose of several hundred whipworm eggs in small amounts of salty liquid and then let them grow. For now, this treatment is still being used in clinical trials, but according to Dr. Oz and other medical experts, the little wrigglers are proving themselves valuable and may soon be available by prescription.

Whipworms to the Rescue: In the clinical trials, whipworms have put IBD patients into remission. In one study, a patient's symptoms returned when the whipworms died off; the symptoms disappeared again when he was reinfected with more worms.

Whipworms are also being used in clinical trials as a treatment for multiple sclerosis (MS), another autoimmune disease with no known cure. So far, whipworm therapy has been shown to reduce the harmful brain lesions caused by MS. Although more study is needed, researchers are optimistic because, in some cases, the worms do a better job of treating these debilitating diseases than traditional medicines do.

* * *

GREEN LIVING TIP

Want an air freshener that isn't loaded with nasty chemicals like propellants and fake fragrances? Mix even parts vodka and distilled water in a small spray bottle, and add 30 to 40 drops of the essential oil of your choice. (Lime and lavender is nice.) And then spray away.

Even the eggs of the harlequin poison dart frog are poisonous.

THERE'S A _____ IN MY BATHROOM!

No, we don't mean an Uncle John's Bathroom Reader*—we knew that was in there! We mean creepy, animal-y, living things.*

ALLIGATOR. Alexis Dunbar returned to her Palmetto, Florida, home after a night away in April 2011 and went to the bathroom—where she was greeted with a hiss from a seven-foot-long alligator. She screamed, closed the door, and called wildlife officials, who came and took it away. Dunbar told reporters the alligator came in through her catdoor. (Her two cats were fine.) "My furniture was all moved around," she said. "My blinds were all discombobulated."

DEER. Colleen Slattery and Beau Williams were sitting in their apartment in Eagan, Minnesota, one morning in February 2011 when they were startled by a huge crash: a deer had smashed through their bathroom window. The couple found the deer with both of its front legs stuck in the toilet bowl. Police officers got the deer out of the toilet. "It was a pretty bloody mess," Sergeant Dan Mason said. Officers guided the deer outside, and it ran off.

SPIDER! EXPLOSION! One night in September 2010, Christopher Robinson of Clacton-on-Sea, England, was called to the bathroom by his wife, Janine. She told Christopher there was a spider in the bathroom. Christopher, wanting to play the good husband, it seems, chased the spider around the bathroom, cornered it behind the toilet and—having no bug spray handy—sprayed deodorant. Not sure he'd killed it, he leaned in for a closer look...lit his lighter to help him see...and was blown out of the bathroom and into the hallway by a sizable explosion. "There was just this big puff of flame," he said later. The explosion left the bathroom scorched, and Christopher with burns on his legs and arms. "Luckily, I was wearing my boxer shorts," he told reporters later, "so I did not get burned in a more sensitive area." A fireman said there was no sign of the spider.

Good news! Of 35,000 known species of spiders, only about 500 can bite humans.

FEATHER FACTS

Clothes may make the man (or woman), but feathers make the bird.

DRESSED FOR SUCCESS

Birds are found on every continent, and there are more than 10,000 bird species. From penguins in the Antarctic to desert eagles in the Sahara, birds live in all sorts of habitats and come in all sizes, shapes, and colors. What they have in common—and what makes them different from other animals—isn't the fact that they can fly (penguins and ostriches don't fly, whereas bats, which aren't birds, do). It's feathers that make birds unique—all birds have them, and no other animal does.

And feathers are the reason why so many varieties of birds can thrive in so many different habitats. They protect a bird from heat and cold, attract a mate, provide material for a nest, and of course, they help a lot in that flying thing.

FEATHERY FUN

Feathers grow out of follicles in a bird's skin, overlapping so that no skin shows. They're made of keratin, the same material that lizards' scales and human hair and fingernails are made of. Keratin is strong and flexible, so feathers can bend without breaking. It's also a very light material, so gravity has less pull on the birds when they fly—a large swan feather that's about 18 inches long, for instance, weighs only about half an ounce.

Feathers are surprisingly complex. They have a nearly hollow shaft made up of two parts, a quill area that attaches to the bird's skin and a central area called a *rachis*. Spreading out of the two sides of the rachis are the "vanes," the soft, flat parts of the feather that give it shape, texture, and color. But on close examination, you can see just how complicated a single feather is. The vanes are made up of more than a million parts, including...

• **Barbs:** The thousands of slender parallel branches that grow out of both sides of the feather shaft.

• **Barbules:** The extremely skinny and tiny parallel branches that grow out of each side of those thousands of barbs.

• **Barbicels:** The microscopic hooks on the barbules that work like Velcro to hold the barbs together and make a flat, interlocked surface. It's this surface that makes a bird's outer feathers so smooth and shiny.

THE LAYERED LOOK

By changing one or more of all those intricate parts, nature creates several different types of feathers on most birds.

• **Contour feathers** cover a bird's body, wings, and tail. These are the feathers that you see when you look at a bird. They're sleek, flat, and sometimes bright and colorful. Contour feathers protect a bird's delicate skin from the sun, rain, wind, and injury.

• **Semiplumes** are hidden beneath the contour feathers; their purpose is to give the outer feathers shape while providing extra warmth. In keeping with their function, semiplumes have a very flexible shaft. In fact, they're the feathers that are used in ostrich feather dusters.

• **Down feathers** have a very short shaft and have no barbicules to make the feather stiff. Instead, down feathers are fluffy with a loose structure that traps insulating air.

• **Filoplumes** are delicate, hairlike feathers with only a few barbs on their tips. They grow near contour feathers, and their nerve cells tell a bird when to adjust its contour feathers.

For more feathery facts, fly over to page 363.

* * *

PLUCKING FEATHERS

In the late 1800s and early 1900s, feathers were fashionable on hats, and birds were hunted for them. Egrets and other birds with beautiful and delicate feathers were hunted almost to extinction. So in 1905, the National Audubon Society was founded in the United States to protect birds from being killed for fashion. It's now illegal in the U.S. to possess any native wild bird feathers.

FIVE FISH A-MIGRATING

Next time someone asks you to name a type of catadromous fish—you'll be ready. (No "thank you" necessary!)

Many species of fish migrate at some stage of their lives, either for breeding or for feeding purposes. They're broken down into five different categories:

• **Anadromous** (Greek for "running up") fish are born in freshwater, migrate to the ocean where they spend most of their lives, and return to freshwater to spawn (that's where the "running up" comes in, as in running up a river). Half of all migrating fish are anadromous. They include salmon, steelheads, many species of sturgeons, some species of bass, and lampreys.

• **Catadromous** ("running down") fish are born in salt water, migrate to freshwater where they spend most of their lives, and migrate back to the ocean to spawn. They include many species of true eels, including the only one found in North America: the American eel. In this eel's case, the journey may be as long as 4,000 miles from its ocean breeding grounds to its freshwater home, and it may stay in that home for as long as 40 years before returning to the deep sea to mate.

• **Amphidromous** (*amphi* means "both") fish move between freshwater and the ocean for feeding reasons and can spawn in either. Examples include gobies, jollytails, and bull sharks. (Yes, bull sharks—which can grow to more than 11 feet in length and are very aggressive—can be found far up rivers.)

• **Potamodromous** ("river running") fish migrate significant distances, but only in freshwater. They include carp, catfish, northern pike, and walleyes, the latter of which regularly migrate hundreds of miles from lake to lake via rivers and streams throughout the Great Lakes region. And they do it all over the course of a year.

• **Oceanodromous** fish migrate in salt water only, normally between feeding and spawning grounds. They include herring, sea perch, cod, tuna, swordfish, and several shark species, all of which migrate thousands of miles throughout the year.

IT'S FERAL CAT DAY!

Here are the stories behind some fun animal-themed holidays.

SQUIRREL APPRECIATION DAY

Date: January 21

Origin: This holiday was created in 2001 by Christy Hargrove, a wildlife rehabilitator from Asheville, North Carolina. At first, the holiday was just a fun way to get local kids interested in the region's many squirrel species, some of which are endangered. But over the last few years, Squirrel Appreciation Day has grown more and more popular at schools throughout the United States. Why is it in January? That's when food for squirrels is the most scarce, so celebrants are encouraged to put out some seeds, nuts, or suet for the furry little creatures. The holiday is also a great way to pass on some cool squirrel facts, like this one: The word goes back to the Greek *skiouros*, a combination of "shade" and "tail," which meant "creature who sits in the shadow of his tail."

NATIONAL PIG DAY

Date: March 1

Origin: Ellen Stanley didn't think that people gave pigs enough credit as intelligent animals that make great pets. So in 1972 the art teacher from Lubbock, Texas, cofounded National Pig Day with her sister Mary. Today it's celebrated by pig owners (and plain old pig lovers) all over the country. A recommended present for your favorite pig: apples—pigs just love apples!

INTERNATIONAL MIGRATORY BIRD DAY

Date: The second Saturday of May

Origin: This holiday was started in 1993 by ornithologists at the Smithsonian Migratory Bird Center and the Cornell Laboratory of Ornithology. Their goal: to increase awareness of the many migratory bird species in the Western Hemisphere. Government-sponsored events take place on the big day from Canada down to Latin America. Want to take part? Go to birdday.org and download a bird-count form. Then print it out, go for a birdwatching walk, and submit your data back to the Web site.

In Japan, May 4 is Greenery Day, a holiday that celebrates nature.

NATIONAL COBRA DAY

Date: The fifth day of the moonlit fortnight in the Hindu month of Shravan (translation: sometime in July or August)

Origin: This Hindu holy day, known locally as Nag Panchami, has been celebrated all over India for centuries. Different regions have their own ways of revering the sacred serpent. In the state of Punjab in the northwest, huge "dough snakes" are made from flour and butter and carried in noisy, colorful processions through the streets, after which the "snake" is blessed and buried. In the state of Maharashtra on India's west coast, snake charmers carry baskets with live cobras inside them through crowds of celebrants. The charmers play their flutes and cry out, "Nagoba-la dudh, de Mayi!" ("Give milk to the Cobra, oh mother!") Women come running out from their houses dressed in their finest saris. The deadly snakes are released and the women sprinkle spices and flowers on their heads and feed them sweetened milk.

NATIONAL FERAL CAT DAY

Date: October 16

Origin: This holiday is celebrated all over the world by feral cats who get together for mice-and-beer parties. Okay, not really. It was actually started in 2001 by humans at Alley Cat Allies, a national cat-protection organization in Bethesda, Maryland. Their goal is a serious one: ending the mistreatment and killing of feral cats in the United States. (An estimated 70 percent of the cats that go to U.S. shelters are killed.)

LEARN ABOUT BUTTERFLIES DAY

Date: March 14

Origin: This holiday is so unofficial that we couldn't even find out who created it. But we're guessing it was a teacher, because every March 14, schoolkids all over North America learn about butterflies. They watch butterfly videos, read butterfly books, and draw pictures of not just butterflies but caterpillars and cocoons, too! (We're not sure why a holiday about a summertime insect takes place in the winter, but it does give the kids something to look forward to.)

DUTCH NATIONAL OWL DAY

Date: November 3

Origin: Created in 1986 by one of the world's premier owl experts, Johan de Jong, founder of the Dutch Barn Owl Working Group, the holiday helps raise money and awareness for the endangered European barn owl. The group's efforts have paid off, and the barn owl's numbers are steadily rising. This success has prompted de Jong to get the day recognized around the world, as there are many more endangered owl species. You can do your own part by holding a National Owl Day celebration in your community this November. They're a real hoot!

PENGUIN AWARENESS DAY

Date: January 20

Origin: This began in the 1980s as a lark by biologists studying penguins in the Antarctic. Few people (in the Northern Hemisphere, anyway) gave the holiday much thought until 2006, after two penguin-themed movies had taken the world by storm—the French documentary *March of the Penguins* and the animated musical *Happy Feet*. Thrilled with the sudden interest, penguin advocates publicized the holiday as a means to educate people about the world's endangered penguin species. Suggested activities for Penguin Awareness Day:

- Organize a field trip to the nearest zoo that has penguins.
- Rent a tux (or just wear black and white) and waddle around handing out literature about penguins.
- Rent one or all of these lesser-known penguin films: *The Adventures of Scamper the Penguin* (a 1988 cartoon about a young Adélie penguin), *Little Kings* (a 1999 documentary about penguin expert Mike Bingham), or our all-time favorite, a 1950 animated short called *8 Ball Bunny* in which Bugs Bunny must help a lost "pen-gu-in" find his way home to the South Pole. (Every time the little guy cries an ice cube, it just breaks Uncle John's heart.)

CRYPTIDS

We asked our friend Andy the Talking Humpback Whale to settle this once and for all: Do these creatures exist or not? We'd tell you what Andy's answer was... but then we'd have to krill you.

BACKGROUND

You've possibly heard of *cryptozoology*. It's the study of animals that some people think exist, but whose existence has yet to be proven. Of course, the field includes a lot of wackadoodle creatures (Uh-oh—here comes the angry letters from Bigfoot and Chupacabra!), but there's some serious science involved, too. That includes the study of animals that are *believed* to be extinct...but not by everybody. Meanwhile, take these possibly imaginary creatures...please.

RHINOCEROS DOLPHIN. This odd cetacean (a marine mammal such as a porpoise, dolphin, or whale) was first sighted in the Mediterranean Sea in the 1800s. The reports, which claimed the animal was a dolphin with two dorsal fins—hence the name "rhinoceros dolphin"—were not taken seriously, because no other known cetacean has two dorsal fins. (They all have either none or one.) That would have been that, but in 1819 two respected French naturalists, Joseph Paul Gaimard and Jean René Constant Quoy, backed up the story when they reported seeing very similar creatures while sailing the South Pacific: "Every one on board was surprised to perceive that they had a fin on their head bent backwards, the same as that on their backs," they wrote. The naturalist duo even gave the creature the scientific name *Delphinus rhinoceros*. Sightings of similar two-finned dolphins have been recorded over the years since, but none have been confirmed. (If you see one—take a picture and send it to us!)

GIGLIOLI'S WHALE. On September 4, 1867, Italian zoologist Enrico Hillyer Giglioli was on the Italian warship *Magenta* in the Pacific Ocean, about 1,200 miles off the coast of Chile, when a whale surfaced very close to the ship and stayed alongside for several minutes. Giglioli wrote that it looked like a member of the baleen whale family, which includes blue whales and humpbacks, was about 60 feet long—and had two dorsal fins. Again: No known cetaceans have two dorsal fins, and no such creature has ever been captured. But (also again) there have been other sightings since, one of the most recent in 1983, when sailors on a boat between Corsica and France reported that a large whale with two dorsal fins followed their ship for several hours. Whale experts still think it very unlikely such creatures exist, mostly because large whales were so heavily hunted during the whaling era that surely at least one whale with two dorsal fins would have been seen.

AGOGWE. The earliest credible sighting of this small, human-like biped was reported by British explorer Captain William Hichens. Writing in the British magazine *Discovery*, Hichens claimed he saw two of the creatures in what is now Tanzania in the 1920s. He described them as standing about four feet tall, covered in russet-colored hair, and walking upright like humans. His local guide called them *agogwe*, explaining they were legendary creatures that would, for example, work in people's gardens in exchange for food and beer. Similar creatures with a variety of names are said to exist all across the region. There have been many reported sightings of small, bipedal "humans" over the years, but no solid confirmation. Some say agogwes could be ancient hominids long thought to be extinct, many of which were small in stature, like the agogwe. If they exist, that is.

BERGMAN'S BEAR. In the 1920s Swedish zoologist Sten Bergman identified what he claimed was a subspecies of the brown bear on the Kamchatka Peninsula in northeast Russia. He described it as significantly larger than common brown bears, and much darker, almost black in color. But here's the thing: Bergman never actually *saw* one of the bears: He saw a hide, and saw what he said were very large tracks of the animals. There have been no further sightings of what is still known as Bergman's bear.

IRKUIEM. The story of Bergman's bear was understandably mostly forgotten—until the 1980s, when Russian biologist N. K. Vereshchagin heard that native peoples in Kamchatka were talking about having seen a strange bear there. They called it *irkuiem*, meaning "trousers pulled down" because it had bunches of fat that hung down between its rear legs, which made it look like it was wearing falling-down trousers. The reports revived the stories of Bergman's bear, but Vereshchagin suggested the animal might be something much more remarkable: a surviving strain of *Arctodus simus*, one of the largest bears that ever lived. Before it went extinct, the bear inhabited North America for millions of years, from Mississippi to Alaska—right across the land bridge from Russia, where the locals were telling their irkuiem stories.

DINGONEK. This fanciful creature is supposed to resemble an anteater, except that it lives in rivers and lakes, can grow to 18 feet in length, has a horn on its head, a poison-secreting tail like a scorpion, and tusks like a walrus (hence its other name: the "jungle walrus.") According to legend, dingoneks inhabit the jungles of western Africa, where they prey on crocodiles, hippos, and people. They're best known from a description by British explorer John Alfred Jordan, who claimed to have seen and shot at one in the river Maggori in Kenya in 1907. Alas, it got away. (The origin of the name "dingonek" is unknown.)

NANDI BEAR. The forested mountains of eastern Africa are the supposed home of this supposed creature, whose name is taken from the Nandi people of Kenya. It's been described as about four feet tall at the shoulders, with reddish-brown fur, and much longer forelegs than hind legs, which makes it look more like a hyena than an actual bear. According to legend, it's a ferocious carnivore that eats only the brains of its victims, which include humans (a kind of zombie bear!). Sightings have been reported for centuries, but no Nandi bear has ever been captured or photographed. Some cryptozoologists say it may be a surviving *Pachycrocuta brevirostris*, or "giant hyena," which most paleontologists say went extinct 500,000 years ago. Others say it could be a relative of the Atlas bear, Africa's only known native bear, which roamed the Atlas Mountains of northwest Africa before being driven to extinction by overhunting in the late 1800s. Even famed paleoanthropologist Louis Leakey added his two cents to the debate, wondering if the Nandi bear could be related to the *Chalicotherium*, which according to fossil evidence has been extinct for more than 7 million years, and rather than being a brain-eating carnivore (zombie bear!) was an herbivore.

A watermelon is 92% water, the highest water content of any fruit.

CITIZEN CANINE

Store owners like to come up with clever names for their stores. Sometimes the names make you crack up—sometimes they make you wish those people were severely pun-ished. (Sorry.) Some examples.

Steve's Dog and Cat Repair
(Edwards, Colorado)

Furberry
(online designer pet store, Australia)

Bon A-Pet-Treat Pet Bakery
(Calgary, Alberta)

Fi-Dough Pet Bakery
(Boston, Massachusetts)

Owlcatraz: Native Bird and Wildlife Park
(Palmerston North, New Zealand)

Canis Minor: Dog & Cat Boutique
(New York City)

Get Stuffed Taxidermy
(Derby Line, Vermont)

Paws for Thought
(Erdington, West Midlands, England)

The Dirty Hoe
(gardening and landscaping, Seattle, Washington)

Citizen Canine
(dog kennel, Oakland, California)

Indiana Bones and Temple of Groom
(Thousand Oaks, California)

Shady Business Nursery
(Bangor, Pennsylvania)

Pride and Pedigree
(Oakland, California)

Doggie Style Bowtique
(Kansas City, Missouri)

Murphy's Paw
(Pleasanton, California)

Reigning Cats and Dogs
(Glenmont, New York)

Dirty Dogs Done Dirt Cheap
(dog grooming service, Melbourne, Australia)

Master Baiter's Sportfishing
(Puerto Vallarta, Mexico)

Wetspot Aquatics: High Quality Tropical Fish
(South Bend, Indiana)

The Crate Escape
(doggie daycare, South Burlington Vermont)

Nuts Landing: Dog Neutering Clinic
(*The Simpsons*)

THE LURE OF THE ORCHID

They're not just for prom night anymore.

SEX AND THE SINGLE ORCHID

The difference between orchids and ordinary flowers has a lot to do with reproduction. Unlike the reproductive parts on most flowers, an orchid's male and female parts are fused together. Plus, orchid pollen is thicker than the dusty stuff you find on most flowers—it clumps into a waxy goo called *pollinium*. This system works out just fine for the genus *Orchidaceae*. They're the most diverse flowering plants in the world, growing in the wild on six of the seven continents and coming in somewhere between 20,000 and 35,000 species. There are also hybrids, which number another 60,000 or so, bringing the total number of species close to 100,000.

THAT "COME HITHER" LOOK

All flowers have to pollinate to survive; it's a simple process of luring bees and other insects with nectar to get pollen on the insect's body; the pollen can then be transferred to another flower. Some orchid varieties have taken the process to a higher level: Take *Ophrys apifera* (the "bee orchid"), for example. It doesn't need nectar as its lure. This orchid tantalizes the bee with a tricky game. The plant's *labellum*, or lip, looks a whole lot like the backside of a female bee and even gives off the same sexual odor. So the male bee jumps on board, tries to mate, and in the ensuing hubbub, the orchid releases pollen that sticks to the bee's back like glue. The bee eventually gets frustrated and moves on to the next fake female bee (er, orchid), where he drops off the pollen.

DEPARTMENT OF MYTHINFORMATION

Even the name *orchid* has a sexual origin; it comes from the Greek word for "testicle." Its source is the myth of Orchis, the son of a nymph and satyr who in Greek mythology tried to have his way with a priestess during a feast of Dionysius, which is a big-time no-

no, even at bacchanalian festivals where pretty much anything goes. Or went. Anyway, the kid drank too much and got carried away. His punishment? He was torn to pieces. His father prayed for him to live again, but the gods instead transformed him into a flower...the orchid.

MAKES SCENTS TO ME

• Most people have been eating orchids for most of their lives. There's one species of orchid, *Vanilla planifolia*, that produces vanilla beans (which aren't really "beans"—they're seedpods). These can then be ground into a powder or produced as an extract and added to most of the desserts we love. European explorers discovered *Vanilla planifolia* in Mexico in the 1500s and brought it back home. Even though, over the centuries, vanilla became synonymous with plain and ordinary, it's still an expensive spice because it's so hard to raise and prepare the orchids.

• Then there's the *Satyrium pumilum* orchid of South Africa, which reeks of roadkill, and which you wouldn't think would be all that attractive—until you remember that putrefying roadkill is to flies what nectar is to bees. The flies buzz around a bit, then dart off to pollinate other flowers. Some female flies are so fooled by the odor that they attempt to lay their eggs in the orchid as if it were a dead creature.

• Not to be outdone, orchids of the genus *Dracula* (so named because they look like little bats flying through the forest) simulate the smell of small mushrooms to attract a particular variety of fruit flies.

PETAL PUSHER

Some rare orchids can sell for close to $1,000 each, so even though international laws have been put in place to save the species from extinction, smugglers still comb the rain forests of Madagascar, Thailand, and Brazil looking for the plants. In the mid-1990s, 1,500 rare lady slipper orchids were intercepted in Redondo Beach, California, with an estimated value of $150,000. The culprit—Harto Kolopaking—belongs to an Indonesian family so closely tied to the orchid trade that one species (*Paphiopedilum kolopakingii*) is named for them.

...Prospective dads ate large orchid roots if they wanted a boy; moms ate small ones for a girl.

CROSSWORD CRITTERS

These animals might be spotted in a crossword puzzle as often as in the wild.

Pity the poor crossword puzzle writer; he or she tries to include only words that solvers would readily recognize (really!), but sometimes only an obscure animal name will do. Here are some of the most popular, accompanied by their typical clues. How many have you seen skulking around your crossword puzzles?

Clue: Dwarf buffalo of Indonesia
Answer: ANOA

Clue: Anaconda's cousin
Answer: BOA

Clue: Raccoon relative
Answer: COATI

Clue: Wild Asian dog
Answer: DHOLE

Clue: "Snowy" wading bird
Answer: EGRET

Clue: Sea eagle
Answer: ERN (also spelled ERNE)

Clue: African antelope
Answer: ELAND

Clue: Sacred Egyptian bird
Answer: IBIS

Clue: Alpine goat
Answer: IBEX

Clue: Twisty-horned antelope
Answer: KUDU

Clue: Giraffe relative
Answer: OKAPI

Clue: Arctic seabird
Answer: SKUA

Clue: South American monkey
Answer: TITI

Clue: Indian beast of burden
Answer: ZEBU

Fun fact: Of the critters on our list, the ERN (without the second E) is by far the most popular, having made more than 100 appearances in *New York Times* crossword puzzles since 1998.

VIRGIN BIRTHS: ANIMAL EDITION

Some insects and other invertebrates don't need to mate to reproduce, but for vertebrates, reproducing that way is rare—less than 0.1 percent. So what about the ones that have done it? Read on.

WHO? A boa constrictor snake
WHERE? At a pet store in Tennessee
WHAT? Although she had given birth naturally years before, this female boa delivered twice more in 2009 and 2010 under different circumstances. DNA testing determined that none of the male snakes she lived with were the father of her 22 (only female) babies. It turned out that all of them were "half-clones" (two eggs fused together) of their mama and had no dad. This marked the first time a boa had ever reproduced asexually.
WHY? No one seems to know. Interestingly, the boa mom did apparently need to be around males before she could become pregnant, though, even if she didn't breed with them. Geneticist Warren Booth points out, "Only in years that she was housed with males has she produced offspring. It appears that some interaction with a male is required. However, why she does not utilize his sperm is at present unknown."

WHO? A zebra shark named Zebedee
WHERE? Burj Al Arab Hotel aquarium, Dubai
WHAT? In 2007 Zebedee shocked the aquarium's staff (and the world) by laying eggs that contained live embryos, even though she wasn't housed with any other sharks. The assistant manager of the aquarium explains: "We were actually moving the eggs, and one of our guys felt something move inside the egg, and we checked the eggs with light, and there were babies inside." The pups that hatched were genetically similar to Zebedee but not identical clones, suggesting that her body recombined her DNA to reproduce without a male's contribution. Some of the babies survived, and Zebedee got pregnant again...and again...for four years in a row. That's the most

virgin pregnancies ever recorded. By early 2012, she had produced a total of 21 living pups.

WHY? Recently, researchers have discovered that other species of sharks, including hammerheads, have this ability too. This evolutionary adaptation seems to help the creatures thrive in tough or new habitats without having to find a mate. It isn't ideal, though, because the pups are less likely to survive without the genetic diversity that comes from having two parents.

WHO? Sungai, a Komodo dragon

WHERE? The London Zoo, England

WHAT? Born and raised in captivity, Sungai had not interacted with a male Komodo dragon in more than two years. Even so, she laid a clutch of 22 fertilized eggs in 2005. Four of the eggs hatched, all male, and did not contain DNA that would have come from a daddy dragon. The birth stunned scientists, who had not known Komodo dragons could reproduce asexually. It is unclear whether this occurred through cloning—which, researchers note, should have produced all females, not males—or perhaps a process called *selfing*, in which an animal's body stores some cells that act like sperm and others that behave like eggs.

WHY? Here's what the scientists think: Komodo dragons are the biggest lizards on earth, but in the wild, they are confined to one small part of the world—a few volcanic islands in Indonesia. They are also an endangered species. All this makes keeping the species going a tricky business. But with this unique reproduction ability, females could produce offspring all on their own—even colonize a new island if necessary—all without the help of a partner and perhaps saving the species from total extinction.

* * *

NATURE IN CHIEF

Three species named after U.S. presidents:

- *Caloplaca obamae* (a lichen): Barack Obama
- *Agathidium bushi* (a slime mold beetle): George W. Bush
- *Stenomorpha roosevelti* (a darkling beetle): Teddy Roosevelt

A panda has to eat about 45 pounds of bamboo per day to survive.

NATURE'S PIRATES

Some animals are nasty, deceitful, thieving little cads, with behavior more reminiscent of Bluebeard than Bambi. Here are a few of our favorites.

ANIMAL: Cuckoo

BACKGROUND: Cuckoos make up a large family of birds found all over the world. Of the roughly 140 species, about 60 are really bad parents.

NASTY: When it's time for a female cuckoo to lay eggs, she hangs around the egg-heavy nest of a different bird species (always a *smaller* species), and when Mom and Dad are busy, she swoops down, kicks one egg out of the nest, lays one of her own in its place...and flies off. She can be done in 10 seconds. When the cuckoo chick hatches, it's much larger than the other hatchlings, and it kicks them all out of the nest, too—killing them. Thereafter, it is raised by the tricked parents as their own. Different cuckoos target different species for this behavior (which biologists call "brood-parasitism"), and each cuckoo has even evolved in such a way that its eggs actually resemble those of the unwitting hosts, the better to fool them into taking care of the baby.

ANIMAL: Cuckoo bee

BACKGROUND: Another type of brood-parasitism is used by many bee species. These are cuckoo bees (named after the birds).

NASTY: Almost everywhere on earth where there are pollen-gathering, nest-building bees, there are also cuckoo bees, which *don't* collect pollen or build nests, but have evolved to physically resemble their busy neighbors. When the time comes for a female cuckoo bee to lay eggs, she takes advantage of that resemblance, and enters her neighbor's nest. There she lays her eggs in cells in the nest's walls—cells already inhabited by the host's eggs. The resident bees unwittingly fill the cells with pollen, and seal up the cells. The cuckoo bee's eggs hatch early—the newborns eat the host eggs and then grow fat on the pollen supply. In some species, the larvae leave after emerging from the cells as adults; in others they stay, kill the queen, and take over the nest as their own.

Male smallmouth bass guard their eggs, scooping them into their mouths if they sense danger.

ANIMAL: Slavemaker ant

BACKGROUND: This is a name given to several different species of ants found in the United States and Canada that have a "special" relationship with other ant species.

NASTY: When a scout slavemaker ant comes across a nest of a foreign ant species (each slavemaker species has specific target species), it hurries back to its own nest and mobilizes a whole troop of slavemaker ants, which rush to storm the foreigner's nest. Once there, they release chemical compounds that induce the foreign ants to flee, after which the slavemakers grab the enemy's eggs and carry them back to their own nest. There they care for the eggs until they hatch—at which point the just-born ants are enslaved: They spend the rest of their lives taking care of the slavemaker's nests, eggs, and young. Some slavemaker ant species have done this for so long that they don't even know how to take care of their own nests anymore. They actually need the "slaves" to survive.

ANIMAL: Slavemaker ant (again)

BACKGROUND: This concerns a particular species of slave-maker ant—*Rossomyrmex minuchae*—native to Spain's Sierra Nevada Mountains. They do things a little differently.

NASTY: After a female *R. minuchae* ant mates, she leaves her nest and goes on a solo journey in search of a nest of another ant species, *Proformica longiseta*. When she finds one, she enters it. Normally this would result in a lethal attack by the nest's workers, but the invading female releases a concoction of pheromones that induces the workers to be calm and meek. The invader waltzes right into the nest, locates the resident queen, bites her...and licks the ooze that comes out of the wound. Why? To steal her scent, basically. This goes until the queen finally dies. Then her once-loyal subjects accept the invader as their new queen—because she smells like the old queen. The ants proceed to take care of their pirate queen and the eggs she soon begins to lay.

ANIMAL: Antbird

BACKGROUND: These are several bird species in Central and South America that have learned to live on the spoils of war.

NASTY: Army ants in Central and South America don't build permanent nests like other ants do. Instead, they make above-ground bivouac camps in between their notorious foraging swarms. These swarms are a force of nature: Hundreds of thousands of ants form frighteningly fast-moving columns that can be 65 feet wide—killing, eating, and generally terrorizing everything in their paths. That includes other ants, spiders, scorpions, snakes, lizards , and much more. And what about the lucky creatures that manage to escape the swarm? There's a good chance an antbird will get them. These birds spend their days following army ant swarms, capturing the terrified animals that flee them.

ANIMAL: Vampire finch

BACKGROUND: This small, creepy finch species is found on the Galápagos Islands. They feed primarily on seeds and insects, and occasionally flower nectar. But every year, a long dry season makes those foods scarce, and the vampire finch has evolved some creative feeding habits to deal with this problem.

NASTY: When a female boobie (a large seabird found on the islands) is laying an egg (right on the rocky ground with no nest), it's common for a vampire finch to sneak up behind her and drink the lubricating fluids that accompany the egg—as the fluid is leaving the boobie's body. This is a good source of protein.

NASTIER: Almost as soon as a vampire finch is finished eating the fluid, it steals the egg. The finches have learned to roll boobie eggs—which are nearly as large as they are—over little rocky drops to break them, thereby gaining access to the nourishing insides.

NASTIEST: Vampire finches regularly peck the wings and bodies of boobies and other seabirds until they bleed, and then they drink the blood. Stranger still, the seabirds let them do this. Biologists believe that the reason for this bizarre behavior—the only of its kind in all the bird world—is that it began eons ago with the finches eating parasites off the bigger birds' skin. Over time, it evolved to the pecking, then the bleeding—and then the vampire bird got its very deserved name.

The Cowardly Lion's costume in *The Wizard of Oz* was made from two real lion skins.

THIS BITES

This article, we mean. Or, more precisely, the things in it.

CHOMP. In 2002 Mac Bosco Chawinga was swimming in a lake in the African nation of Malawi when he was attacked by a crocodile. The giant reptile had both of the 43-year-old businessman's arms in its mouth—so Chawinga bit the croc on the nose. Local policeman Bob Mtekama told the BBC that the bite was so deep, the snake had to let go. Chawinga made it to shore and was rushed to a hospital. Nicknamed the "Crocodile Biter," he was treated and released some weeks later.

CHOMP. In September 2011 David Elmer Senk was arrested on animal torture charges after he bit a 3½-foot-long python in a Sacramento, California, convenience store. The snake's owner had brought the python in to show it off, police said later, when Senk showed up and bit it. Twice. The snake had to have two ribs removed, and needed several stitches—but it made a full recovery. Senk said he had been drinking, and didn't remember the incident. "I'm not too fond of snakes," he said, "but I try not to bite them."

CHOMP. In 2003 the American submarine *Connecticut* surfaced in ice-choked waters between Alaska and the North Pole—right next to a polar bear. Over the next 30 minutes, the polar brear bit the 350-foot-long attack submarine's exposed rudder several times, and swatted it with its huge paws for good measure. Eventually, the sub left—with minor polar bear–battle damages—and the bear ambled off.

CHOMP. In February 2012 British tourist Jackson Scott was squatting and urinating in a yard after a night at the pub in Tasmania, Australia, when he was bitten on the testicles by a venomous tiger snake. Scott's friend Roddy Andrews rushed him to the hospital in Hobart, 40 minutes away, where Scott was given a dose of antivenin in time to save his life (and his testicles). "Needless to say," Scott told reporters the next day, "Rod was not of a mind to suck out the poison."

YOU SHOULD'VE ASKED YOUR MOTHER, PART I

Got a problem? Mom usually has the answer, especially if she's Mother Nature.

MIMIC THIS

Technologists and engineers are turning to a surprising place for inspiration—the zoo. The San Diego Zoo, for instance, provides a study center where innovators use the resident animals as an inspiration for their own designs, a process called *biomimicry*. It's based on the idea that, since nature has been coming up with successful approaches to living on earth for about 3.8 billion years, it pays to turn to nature when solving modern problems.

Biomimicry has a long history. In the 15th century, Leonardo Da Vinci studied birds in flight as an inspiration for designing "flying machines." His machines never got off the ground, but other inventors were more successful, including Orville and Wilbur Wright, whose study of pigeon flight helped them build the first successful airplane in 1903. Biomimicry has continued to progress, and today, it's found in every part of the world. Here are a few examples.

TERMITES ARE COOL

Termites in Zimbabwe live in huge clay mounds. While outside temperatures can soar above 100°F, the termites stay comfortable in their mounds and underground nests, which are insulated by the earth and are also self-cooling. The mounds have vents, tunnels, and chimneys. The vents bring cool ground air in, and the chimneys allow the warm air to rise and flow out of the mound.

The self-cooling termite mounds were an inspiration for architect Mick Pearce, who designed the Eastgate Centre, a large store and office complex in Harare, Zimbabwe. The structure doesn't use air conditioners at all. Instead, air currents and heat-absorbing materials control the temperature. At night, cold, dense air enters through vents under the floors, leaving Eastgate's interior cool in the morning. During the day, heat is absorbed by the massive concrete building, and fans push the rising warm air out through the

Monkeys peel their bananas.

building's chimneys. In the evening, the process begins again. Eastgate Centre's termite-based system works so well that it uses only 10 percent of the energy of a conventional building its size.

HOOKED ON VELCRO

In 1941 Swiss engineer George de Mestral took a walk in the woods with his Irish pointer. When he got home, he found that annoying burdock thistles were stuck to his clothing. Instead of getting angry about it, de Mestral wondered why the burrs clung so well and reattached so easily. Examining them under a microscope, he found hundreds of hooks along their edges that were speared into the looped fibers of his clothing.

For years, de Mestral experimented with similar hook-and-loop systems created from man-made materials. Eventually he created a way to bind materials together, allow them to be pulled apart, and then reattach. He called it Velcro, a combination of the French words *velours* (velvet) and *crochet* (hook). At first, de Mestral had trouble convincing people to try Velcro, but that changed after NASA used it to make fasteners for their space suits. Suddenly Velcro hit the mainstream.

BOXFISH GO BIONIC

Forget those powerful jaguars and mustangs. In 2007, when Mercedes-Benz built the Bionic, the company was inspired by a tropical fish that's only 18 inches long. *Ostracion cubicus* (yellow boxfish) swims in the Indian and Pacific Oceans. It has a unique, boxy shape with a face that's small in proportion to its overall length, giving it a slick, aerodynamic design.

The Bionic is a concept car (rather than one produced for consumers) that demonstrates high efficiency, and its fishy design helps it speed along without a lot of the air turbulence, or "drag," that can reduce fuel efficiency. The year it was built, the four-seater Bionic had the least amount of drag of any car ever produced. Its aerodynamic design helped the Bionic get a fuel economy of 70 miles per gallon in city driving, and an amazing 84 mpg when driven consistently at 56 mph.

For more on biomimicry, turn to page 202.

Tsunami waves can travel at speeds of 600 mph, as fast as a jet plane.

HOLLYWILD

Uncle John told us to find really wacky quotes about animals, so naturally we looked to the entertainment industry.

"Every woman should have four pets in her life. A mink in her closet, a jaguar in her garage, a tiger in her bed, and a jackass who pays for it all."

—**Mae West**

"Isn't it weird that some small pets make doo doos that look just like the food they eat? I wish I had that talent. Put it back together just the way you found it—incredible."

—**John Mayer**

"Bear costumes are funny. Bears as well."

—**Christopher Walken**

"I've been accused...of loving my dog more than I love the person I'm with. He's really, really cute."

—**Carrie Underwood**

"Before I got Madeline [a dog], I used to see dog people who were so obsessed, and I'd think, 'Oh, that's so sad.' But now, here I am, talking about her all the time. I even dress her up in little outfits."

—**Kristin Chenoweth**

"I'm obsessed with my cat. We have a really strong, really weird codependent, almost Bella/Edward relationship. I'm going to be a crazy cat lady one day, I'm sure."

—**Kristen Stewart**

"I derive a great deal of pleasure from horses and dogs…the ocean…and love."

—**William Shatner**

"I discovered I scream the same way whether I'm about to be devoured by a great white shark—or if a piece of seaweed touches my foot."

—**Axl Rose**

"I hate the ocean. It's all whale sperm. Everybody google it, because that's why the water is salty."

—**Snooki**

"I'm just different. I have a different constitution, I have a different brain, I have a different heart. I've got tiger blood, man."

—**Charlie Sheen**

HOME, STRANGE HOME, PART I

When an animal builds itself a home, it looks for a lot of the same things humans do: a safe neighborhood, room to spread out, a place to slow its bodily functions almost to the point of death. Ahhh, welcome home.

SELLING SPIT BY THE POUND

The edible nest swiftlet lives in Southeast Asia, where the male builds a small cupped nest. This wouldn't be so strange if he didn't use long strings of his own thick, sticky saliva as his building material. The saliva hardens when exposed to air and can stick to the walls of the high, dark caves where swiftlets like to raise their young. For centuries, these odd nests have been valued by the Chinese as the most important ingredient in bird's-nest soup. Traditionally, the dish is considered an aphrodisiac, an energy tonic, and a cure for respiratory ailments. Though there's no scientific proof that these health claims are true, swiftlet homes can sell for thousands of dollars a pound. Wild swiftlets are often in danger from nest poachers, and raising the birds for their nests of spit is now a billion-dollar business.

WHO NEEDS CENTRAL HEAT?

The eastern wood frog is the only frog that can make its home north of the Arctic Circle. When winter comes and it's time for hibernation, the frog doesn't even seek out a warm burrow. It simply slips under leaf litter and freezes. The little guy stops breathing, its blood stops flowing, and its heart stops beating, as its tissues and more than 50 percent of its body fluids turn to ice. The eastern wood frog survives this strange process because it produces lots of proteins and glucose (sugars) that prevent the fluid inside its cells from freezing. When the temperature rises, the leaf litter warms and the frog thaws out, quickly coming back to life.

FASHION FORWARD

The golden orb weaver spider of Madagascar creates a web of spider silk that's one of the largest and strongest in the world, so strong that it can even can catch small birds. And webs can last for years because the silk is so durable. Scientists are trying to duplicate spider silk in the laboratory so they can use it to make everything from parachutes to bulletproof vests. But textile experts use the actual thread because it's so beautiful. They milk the golden orb weaver spiders for their silk (which doesn't harm them) to create a golden cloth. In 2012 a golden cape made from the silk of more than a million golden orb weaver spiders went on display at London's Victoria and Albert Museum.

HIGH-RISE HOTELS

Sociable weavers in Africa are small birds that work together to weave one nest for their entire colony—as many as 100 families. The nests include strong roofs made of twigs, and nesting chambers that are separated and insulated by grass walls to keep the birds cozy in winter and cool in the summer. Sociable weavers keep their nests in such good condition that they can house bird families for more than a century. In fact, the homes are so comfortable that everybody wants to live there: Small birds like finches often move into the nesting chambers, while owls, eagles, and vultures have been known to take up residence on the roof. Fortunately for the squatters, sociable weavers don't mind communal living, and other birds keep them safe from predators.

THOSE DARN DAMS

When it comes to messing with the environment, the beaver is second only to humans. A beaver family fells up to 400 trees a year to do all their building and to supply themselves with food. But chopping trees is just the beginning of the beavers' impact. When they build their home, or lodge, they require it to be at the edge of a lake that's deep enough to store a winter's supply of trees for food. To get the proper depth (four to six feet on average), busy beavers build strong dams across waterways, dig out the bottoms of streams, and flood nearby fields and forests—often damaging farms, timber lots, and suburban homes in the process. Their "dam damages" cost millions every year in the United States alone. Yet beavers are also a boon to conservation—their dams protect wetlands, prevent flash floods, and fight drought.

For more odd animal homes, turn to page 118.

A VERY DIRTY STORY

The dirt beneath your feet is a direct or indirect source of food for all life on Earth. So stop treating it like dirt! Your life may depend on it.

THE DIRT ON DIRT

Earth is the only planet in our solar system with a skin of dirt, which is why it's also the only planet that supports life as we know it. For most of Earth's 4.6 billion years, there wasn't any soil at all—the surface was just bare rock, sand, and dust. Geologists have found no evidence of life on land until about 460 million years ago, when some life-forms (like bacteria, seaweed, and lichen) in seas, rivers, and lakes started colonizing the shoreline. Over eons, their lives and deaths created the organic matter necessary for the creation of dirt, which led to the spread of life on land.

Most people don't think much about dirt until they have to clean it up, but it's essential to the world's survival. It doesn't just grow food; dirt filters the planet's water to make it drinkable and adds oxygen to air to make it breathable. Dirt is so important that there's a problem getting enough of the filthy stuff to go around. That's right: the world is running out of dirt.

IT'S ALIVE!

Earth's dirt isn't easy to create. Some scientists estimate that it can take 500 years for nature to form an inch of soil, and 3,000 years to grow the six inches needed to support plant life. The process starts with rocks. After centuries of wind, rain, heat, cold, and all sorts of chemical reactions, the rocks break down into the tiny particles of sand, silt, and clay that give soil its texture.

But turning these particles into soil takes one more ingredient: organic matter called *humus*. One small teaspoon of healthy soil teems with billions of microscopic creatures, many of which are "detritivores," which means they eat dead things. These microbes devour the bodies and waste products of dead leaves, plants, insects, and animals. With the help of other creatures that also live in soil—like earthworms, for example—detritivores turn carcasses and waste into humus. It's this humus that combines with the weathered rock to create fertile soil capable of growing plants.

The Sahara was once grassland, most likely turned to desert by overgrazing.

THE LAYER CAKE OF SOIL

Once soil is formed and begins to age, its particles settle into layers called *horizons*. The top layer is where rotting leaves, branches, animals, and other waste litter the ground. Next comes topsoil, which is humus mixed with minerals. These two top layers are where seeds germinate and plant roots begin. Plants also send roots down one more layer, to the deeper subsoil containing sand, silt, clay, and mineral deposits. Below that is a horizon of weathered, broken rock with very little organic matter, and many feet down is the solid bedrock that made the dirt to begin with.

Understanding the makeup of these simple layers can sometimes mean life or death. From 1958 to 1962, during its "Great Leap Forward," China tried to modernize agricultural practices on communal farms. Unfortunately, the Chinese used agricultural ideas given to them by Soviet advisors who didn't know about the horizons in dirt. The Chinese authorities forced farmers to adopt farming methods like deep plowing, because they believed that soil brought up from way below the surface was more fertile. Instead, the fertile soil got buried, and the farmers tried to grow plants in soil that had little or no organic matter, contributing to the worst famine the country ever experienced.

ALL DIRT ISN'T CREATED EQUAL

Although all soils are formed the same way, they don't all end up alike because they're made from different rocks, contain different microbes, and experience different climate challenges. So each type of soil has its own unique properties. For example...

- **Aridisols** are dry, desert soils.
- **Oxisols** are found in rain forests where rain leaches out the organic matter.
- **Mollisols** are on grasslands and prairies like the American Great Plains.

Of these three types of soil, only the mollisols are very fertile because their topsoil is fertilized by decomposing plant roots. The other two (because of either too little or too much water) don't contain as much organic matter. Fertile topsoil is precious not only because it feeds the world and takes a long time to create, but also because there's a limited amount of it on the planet's surface.

The only apple native to North America is the crabapple.

DISAPPEARING DIRT

Scientists consider the loss of soil second only to population growth as the biggest environmental problem in the world today. More fertile land is needed to feed the world's growing population, but topsoil is being blown and washed away faster than it's being replenished—10 times faster in the United States and 30 to 40 times faster in China and India. According to a study at Cornell University, each year our planet loses an area of fertile soil that's about the size of Indiana—more than 36,400 square miles. In the last 40 years, the planet has lost 30 percent of its productive topsoil. Eroded topsoil often ends up in waterways, making them more prone to flooding, and the dust created by erosion carries infectious disease organisms like anthrax and tuberculosis.

One of the main culprits in the loss of topsoil is factory farming, where too much plowing and overcultivation leaves the soil bare and open to erosion from wind and rain. To try to solve the problem, scientists are working with farmers to create farming techniques that are more soil-friendly. This includes "no-till" farming, which means no machines plowing big furrows into the land. Instead, seeds are simply planted into topsoil without plowing, and cover crops such as grasses and clover are planted at the end of the season. This type of farming leaves no bare soil to get blown off in the wind or washed away in the rain, and the groundcover crops provide organic matter as the plants rot and die. Instead of destroying topsoil, no-till farming improves it.

In 2011 the United Nations Food and Agriculture Organization recommended that more than $100 billion be spent on an effort to reclaim damaged soil with replanting and restoring organic matter that could make lost farmland fertile again in 10 years or so. If it doesn't happen, scientists fear that the planet's growing population will lead to mass famine by 2050—a tragedy that can be prevented if the world finally starts thinking dirty.

* * *

10 TYPES OF GRASS

1. barley; **2.** wheat; **3.** rye; **4.** rice; **5.** corn; **6.** pampas grass; **7.** common wetland reed; **8.** fescue; **9.** sugarcane; **10.** bamboo.

A baby dolphin must learn to hold its breath while nursing.

BUMPER STICKERS ...AU NATUREL

Toyota be a law Datsun the books about bumper stickers. Honda other hand, Renault said and done, Volkswagen their bumpers around Audi have rights, too! (Lamborghini!)

I Stop For Moose! (usually with a sickening thud)

GEOLOGISTS MAKE THE BED ROCK

STOP CONTINENTAL DRIFT!!!

I Like Big MUTTS And I Cannot Lie

Sorry Earth: I Can't Afford a Hybrid

DO MOLECULAR BIOLOGISTS WEAR DESIGNER GENES?

Chipmunks: Nature's Speed Bumps

You're just jealous the trees won't hug *YOU*!

DO RADIOACTIVE CATS HAVE 18 HALF-LIVES?

MAY THE FOREST BE WITH YOU

Animal testing is wrong. The animals always get nervous and give the wrong answers!

KEEP EARTH CLEAN—IT'S NOT URANUS!

SUBURBIA: Where They Tear Down the Trees and Name Streets After Them

ICO2

A barrel full of monkeys would not be fun—it would be horrifying!

BE KIND-ER TO ANIMALS

I love defenseless animals—especially in a good gravy

COMPOST: A RIND IS A TERRIBLE THING TO WASTE

Schist Happens!

Schist is a geological term for a type of rock. (We had to look it up, too...)

I CAMPED, I SAW, I SKEDADDLED

Humorist Dave Barry once said, "Camping is nature's way of promoting the motel business." Whether you agree or not, we've got some scary stories you can tell next time you're gathered 'round the campfire—or tucking the kids in at Motel 6.

• In 2004 a black bear at Baker Lake Resort in Washington State was discovered sleeping it off in a heap of beer cans. He'd stolen the brews from campers and came back the next day looking for more. The bear was lured away by promises of more beer—and doughnuts—and was eventually captured.

• Yellowstone National Park is a haven for grizzly bears, but no one had been killed by one in 25 years until it happened twice in 2011. In one case, a couple tried to walk away but looked back to see the bear running toward them. One person survived, the other didn't.

• Your fellow campers can be disturbing in all sorts of ways. Take the guy who sleepwalked his way into a nearby lake and had to be dragged out of the water by the people who were camped next door.

• Nothing spoils a camping trip like an old-fashioned cyclone. In the case of one veteran camper, a cyclone sent him running to his car. The next morning, he discovered his tent dangling from a tree.

• Some humans crave adventure to an extreme. The riskiest camping location *ever* may be 4,000 feet up a cliff face hanging vertically in a tent in a stiff Arctic breeze on Great Sail Peak on Canada's Baffin Island. That's what sport climbers did in 2011, as the occasional rock or chunk of ice—one the size of a sedan—fell from above them.

• When Michael Stipe of the rock band REM was 14, he went missing during a mountain camping trip with his Boy Scout troop. His family had given up hope of his survival, but he was finally found—showing signs of hypothermia and experiencing hallucinations, but happy to be alive. He now says he has a profound fear of the outdoors.

When pill bugs are sick, they turn blue.

WHAT'S THE DIFF?

Have you ever wondered about the difference between…?

STALAGMITES AND STALACTITES. Also called "dripstone," both develop in limestone caves when groundwater drips through cracks in the roof and deposits minerals in column formations. Stalactites hang from the cave's ceiling like icicles. As the stalactites drip down, stalagmites build up from the ground underneath them.

A BUTTE, A MESA, AND A PLATEAU. The main difference is size. A plateau is a large, flat-topped hill or mountain; a mesa is medium-sized. When a mesa erodes away into a smaller structure, it becomes a butte (pronounced "beaut"), a small hill or mountain that's either pointed or flat on top.

A SWAMP, A BOG, AND A MARSH. All three are types of wetlands. But a bog is on high ground, so water drains away from it and is replenished only by rainfall. Bogs are covered in peat moss, which makes it difficult for aquatic animals to breathe or survive there. Swamps are low, flat areas where slow-moving water from rivers collects; they're usually muddy and are home to trees and fish. A marsh borders a lake, ocean, or other large body of water; it's got grasses and reeds (but not trees or peat) and lots of underwater life and birds.

A MUSHROOM AND A TOADSTOOL. Scientifically speaking, they're the same. In general, though, people refer to edible fungi as mushrooms and nonedible fungi as toadstools. (But don't assume that you can eat just any mushroom—some are poisonous!)

APES, MONKEYS, AND LEMURS. All are primates and have five digits on each hand and foot. Lemurs are nocturnal and have snouts they use to smell and detect food. Monkeys and apes, on the other hand, are active during the day and have smaller noses because they rely on their better sense of vision. The difference between apes and monkeys: Apes are tailless and have longer arms than legs; monkeys' arms are equal to or shorter than their legs—and most have tails.

ENDANGERED AND THREATENED SPECIES. Either may refer to plants or animals. An endangered species is on the brink of extinction throughout most of its natural habitat. Threatened species are at risk of becoming endangered in the near future.

HURRICANES, TYPHOONS, AND CYCLONES. A cyclone is any type of circular windstorm. Hurricanes and typhoons are cyclones that develop over water. Hurricanes are what we call them when they form in the Atlantic or the eastern Pacific Ocean; typhoons are what they're called in the northwestern Pacific.

A STORM WARNING AND A STORM WATCH. During a tornado, thunderstorm, or hurricane watch, weather conditions are ripe for the storm to develop. When the National Weather Service issues a warning, the storm has already formed in the area.

FROGS AND TOADS. Both are species of amphibians. Frogs spend their lives close to water, but toads are able to venture farther onto dry land. Toads are often brown and have dry, bumpy skin. Frogs are mainly green and are wetter and smoother to the touch.

A SHRIMP AND A PRAWN. Some people think the difference is that prawns are larger, but that's not necessarily true. Instead, look at the body, which is divided into three segments. In a shrimp, the middle section overlaps both the head and tail. The middle segment of a prawn's body overlaps only the tail. Foodies take note: Though prawns are generally larger, the two taste pretty much the same.

A DOLPHIN AND A PORPOISE. Dolphins have a slender body, a long pointed snout, and a curved dorsal fin. Porpoises are chubbier, with rounded mouths and a sharp, triangle-shaped fin like a shark's. Also, dolphins are chatterboxes, but porpoises don't make sounds (not ones that humans can hear, anyway).

A Mayan weapon: A "hornet bomb," an actual hornet's nest thrown at enemies during battle.

A PUMA, A COUGAR, AND A PANTHER. In North America, cougars and panthers are both types of mountain lions, also called pumas. Cougars are tan and live in the western states, including California and Arizona; panthers have reddish fur and live only in Florida.

RABBITS AND HARES. Rabbits are born helpless, blind, and without fur. They hide in underground burrows, emerge to eat grasses and veggies, and live in colonies. Hares are tough, solitary creatures that can survive on their own an hour after birth, live aboveground, and eat bark and twigs. Hares also have longer ears and hind legs than rabbits do.

GOPHERS, GROUNDHOGS, AND WOODCHUCKS. A gopher is squirrel-sized and doesn't venture far from the tunnels it burrows. A groundhog is just another name for a woodchuck. It's larger than a gopher, so the tunnels it digs are wider. A groundhog forages for food on the ground's surface and hibernates in winter. Gophers don't.

A PIG AND A HOG. This one can get confusing. Pigs are usually domesticated or farm animals, but the term "pig" can also refer to any small, young swine, even a wild one. A hog is a feral pig or the name for any adult swine, domestic or not. Got it?

FRUIT FLIES AND GNATS. Gnats are black and feed on plants, algae, and mold. Fruit flies are twice as big as gnats, have red eyes and brown heads, and raid your bananas and fresh produce. The buzzing of both is equally bothersome, however.

SNAKES AND LEGLESS LIZARDS. When a legless lizard slithers around, curls up, and sticks out its forked tongue, it looks like a snake. But you can tell it's a lizard if it has eyelids and ear openings. Also, a legless lizard can't unhinge its jaw to eat prey larger than its head like a snake can. It can, however, detach and regenerate its tail like other lizards do.

Dogs with pointed faces typically live longer then dogs with flat faces.

MOMS GONE WILD

Some mothers in nature are doting, some neglectful... and some are downright deadly.

• Some stats: A female oyster can produce up to 100 million eggs *every year*. A termite queen can pop out an egg every three seconds. A tiger shark can deliver up to 80 pups from one pregnancy. As for rabbit moms, they can have as many as 200 babies per year.

• Science is only starting to understand how embryonic stem cells fix damaged tissues in the body, but for baby mice the process comes naturally. If a pregnant mouse has a heart attack, her fetuses send their own stem cells into her heart. The cells repair and replace the damaged heart tissue to save the mother's life.

• Siberian tiger moms take over large blocks of land as their territory, more than they actually need, so they can give a piece of it to their daughters. That way, young female tigers can start their families without having to worry about fighting to protect hunting areas.

• A queen bee can lay up to 2,000 eggs a day, but she knows how to delegate. Thousands of worker bees care for all her needs: they bring her food, dispose of her waste, and look after the eggs until they hatch and populate the hive.

• The sea louse is a parasite that attaches itself to salmon and other fish and feeds off them. It is one of fishing's greatest pests, but also one of the world's most sacrificing moms. A sea louse's babies come into the world by eating their way through their mother from the inside and splitting her apart.

• A rabbit gives birth in less than 10 minutes and then leaves the den, deserting her newborns. She returns for only a few minutes of nursing once or twice a day. On day 26, she abandons the nest and the little ones hop out to meet the world on their own. Efficient rabbit moms can raise new litters seven times a year.

• Orangutan moms have just one baby at a time, and they carry and nurse the youngster until it's at least six years old. Sons stay with Mom for another two years, but daughters sometimes stick around until they're teens so the mother can share her devoted parenting skills.

• Chimpanzee mothers can have such a close relation with their babies that, if a baby chimp dies, the mother will sometimes refuse to let it go. Instead she grieves by grooming the corpse and continuing to carry it as if it were alive. Some chimps have carried their babies until they were mummified before finally leaving them behind.

• Female alligators can be ferocious, but not to their young. Alligator mothers gently break open their eggs to free the hatchlings, pick up the newborns with their mouths, and then carry the babies to water. They also build nests out of rotting vegetation. Why? So that the nest heats up like a compost pile and incubates the eggs.

• Nurse sharks have two uteruses with 20 fetuses in each one. The baby sharks hatch from their eggs and, as soon as they have teeth, nourish themselves by eating each other. At the end of a nurse shark's pregnancy, she delivers two baby sharks, one tough survivor from each womb.

• Adult koalas survive on highly poisonous eucalyptus leaves because they have a digestive tract that can detoxify those leaves. Koala babies aren't born with the ability to eat eucalyptus, though, so Mom builds up their tolerance by feeding them her feces. (Really.) It's filled with predigested, detoxified Eucalyptus leaves.

• With its many tentacles, the giant Pacific octopus doesn't look cuddly, but it's one of the most dedicated mothers around. In a rocky den, the octopus lays about 57,000 eggs, which she weaves, with saliva, into 200 egg strings that she attaches to the roof of her cave. For more than six months, Mom doesn't even eat as she constantly tends to the eggs, keeping them clean of algae and bacteria and blowing water on them to make sure they're getting enough oxygen. By the time the eggs hatch, the mother is starving and exhausted…and she dies.

For the skinny on animal dads, turn to page 114.

UNCLE JOHN'S PAGE OF LISTS

Some random tids of listy bits from the BRI's bottomless trivia file.

7 SPECIES OF SEA TURTLES

1. Leatherback
2. Green turtle
3. Loggerhead
4. Hawksbill
5. Kemp's ridley
6. Olive ridley
7. Flatback

8 TYPES OF BIRD BEAKS

1. Shredder
2. Cracker
3. Probe
4. Spear
5. Tweezers
6. Chisel
7. Strainer
8. Swiss army knife

5 ANIMALS IN CHINESE MARTIAL ARTS

1. Tiger
2. Crane
3. Leopard
4. Snake
5. Dragon

5 KINDS OF FLIGHT

1. Falling
2. Parachuting
3. Gliding
4. Flapping
5. Soaring

13 KINDS OF WIND

1. Breeze
2. Gale
3. Gust
4. Headwind
5. Mistral
6. Monsoon
7. Prevailing wind
8. Sirocco
9. Tailwind
10. Tornado
11. Trade wind
12. Whirlwind
13. Zephyr

4 TYPES OF MAMMAL TEETH

1. Incisors
2. Canines
3. Premolars
4. Molars

7 TYPES OF FEDERALLY PROTECTED AREAS

1. National park
2. National wild and scenic river
3. National wildlife refuge
4. National forest
5. National grassland
6. National marine sanctuary
7. National trail

3 MAIN TYPES OF SOIL

1. Sand
2. Silt
3. Clay

4 KINDS OF ESTUARIES

1. Drowned river valley
2. Bar-built estuary
3. Tectonic estuary
4. Fjord

Biologists have found that wolves will answer humans imitating their howls.

FROM SEAL GUANO TO CATERPILLAR FRASS

Animal poop has an awful lot of names. Here are the ones we could dig up.

Bodewash: The word, pronounced "BOHD-wash," was used by settlers of both the Canadian and American West as a more "proper" name for dried bison droppings (aka "buffalo chips"), which were regularly used as fuel. Bodewash is a corruption of *bois de vache*, or "wood of the cow," the name given by French explorers in Canada in the 1700s.

Dirt: This isn't used as often as it once was, but you still sometimes hear people refer to dog poop as "dog dirt." It also refers to flea poop, aka "flea dirt." (If it looks like someone sprinkled a pepper shaker on your pet, that's probably flea dirt, and a sign the pet is infested with fleas.)

Dung: A general name for the feces of animals other than humans, but especially in reference to cattle, the word "dung" has its roots in the Proto-Indo-European prefix *dhengh*, meaning "covering"—referring to the ancient custom of covering thatch-roofed homes with dung for insulation.

Excrement: Derived from the Latin for "discharge," *excrement* used to refer to discharge from any orifice. It once would have been entirely appropriate to say, "Hey, you've got some excrement coming out of your nose" to someone with the sniffles. Since the 1700s, though, it's been used more specifically to refer to poop.

Feces: From the Latin *faeces*, meaning "sediment" or "dregs," *feces* refers to the droppings of any kind of animal, including humans, fish, and insects. The singular in Latin: *faex*. The singular in English? There is none—the word is always plural in English.

Frass: This is the poop of plant-eating insects. (Meat-eating insects, such as spiders and mantises, don't have a special name for theirs.) It comes in many forms: Termites leave piles of dry pellets that sort of look like wood shavings; bees poop a thick yellow liquid that looks like mustard; and if you spend some time watching a beetle feeding on a leaf, you might be lucky enough to see it leaving a little green, tubelike trail behind it. That's beetle frass.

Guano: The name comes from *huano*, the South American Quechua people's word for the droppings of seabirds. For centuries the Quechua harvested nutrient-rich huano, which accumulates in huge amounts on what is now the Peruvian coastline, for use as a fertilizer. When European and American scientists discovered in the mid-1800s just how good a fertilizer guano is, it became one of the most important trade commodities in the world. The name's meaning grew to include other types of nutrient-rich droppings that tend to accumulate in large amounts, including bat guano (in caves) and seal guano (on rocky islands where seals congregate). Artificial fertilizer brought about the end of the major guano industry, but it is still valued as a fertilizer today, especially by organic farmers.

Meconium: This is the fecal discharge of a newborn mammal, which is produced for just a few days after birth. It's the poop produced from the stuff that the newborn "ate" via its umbilical cord while still in its mother's uterus. The name comes from the Latin term for "poppy juice" or "opium." Etymologists say this is because human meconium, which is thick, dark, and tarlike, looks a lot like opium.

The same term is also used for the poop of insects whose life cycle includes a pupal stage and refers to a type of poop produced after that stage is completed. A butterfly, for example, upon leaving its chrysalis and first emerging as an adult, will poop a red fluid—that's butterfly meconium.

Muck: Often used today to refer to any "mucky" substance, such as mud, its primary meaning, according to the *Merriam-Webster Dictionary*, is "soft moist farmyard manure." (Manure itself is farmyard poop mixed with decaying organic material, usually straw.)

Ordure: Another name for feces, first recorded in English in the 14th century, it was derived from the Latin *horridus*, for "dreadful" (*horridus* is also the root of the word "horrid"). The word is still used today, especially in literature—eg, "In the madhouse the walls reek with the odors of filth and terminal ills they've soaked up these hundred years. Stains from the rusted plumbing, the ordure slung by irate imbeciles." (From *Suttree*, by Cormac McCarthy.)

Pellet: The feces of many creatures, including rabbits and deer, are called *pellets* because of their shape. And why are they pellet-shaped, you might ask? It has to do with the *peristalsis* action of these animals' colons, which separates fecal matter into fairly equal-sized chunks as it pushes it along with the animals' anal muscles, which clamp down and cut off pellet-shaped pieces of poo as they exit the animals' bodies.

Scat: This refers to animal feces, most commonly the poop of wild animals, and is a relatively new word—it's been around only since the 1920s. Its origin is uncertain: etymologists say it may have come from the word *scatology*, referring to works of art, especially literary, that are deemed obscene…or to the scientific study of feces. (A *scatologist* is a scientist who studies scat.)

Slop: Commonly used to refer to pig feces, this goes back to the Old English word *sloppe*, which literally meant "dung." On a related note: the flower known as the cowslip got its name from *cow sloppe*—or "cow dung"—because it was often seen around pastures.

Spraint: This is used primarily in Great Britain, but it does find its way to North America now and then in literature and film. And what is it? River otter poop. To those in the know, spraint is an especially odoriferous kind of poop; its powerful smell is variously described as similar to the odor of fish, lavender, and/or freshly cut grass.

*   *   *

A BEAVER FACT

Animal Planet lists beavers at number two on its list of the top 10 animal troublemakers, because they cause some $100 million in property damage every year.

BETTER THAN YOU!

Feeling superior? Well, back off a bit. There are plenty of creatures that can do things a lot better than you can.

• The klipspringer, a small antelope found in Africa, can make vertical jumps up to 30 feet. Africa's impala can leap 40 feet horizontally without breaking a sweat. And kangaroos can jump more than 30 feet in one leap.

• Has anyone ever called you lazy? The koala is a champion sleeper, resting for up to 20 hours a day.

• Humans are heavier than water, which means that most of your body will be below water if you're floating. Fire ants, on the other hand, usually sink if put in water...unless they cooperate with their fellow ants. In fact, they often survive floods by holding on to one another and forming a living raft that floats nicely on the water's surface.

• Humans have 206 bones in their bodies, but dogs have more than 300...and snakes can have more than 500 vertebrae in their spines.

• Hummingbirds need to eat at least half their body weight in insects and nectar each day. That would be like a 180-pound human chowing down on 90 pounds of food daily.

• On the other hand, you probably have a better diet than the northern pika, the ringtail possum, and the chinchilla. Those animals regularly eat their own feces.

• At a maximum of 19 feet tall, the giraffe towers over the average woman (5'4") tall and the average man (5'10") tall.

• You have 200,000 receptors per square millimeter in each eye to allow you to see, but buzzards have a million...and squids have a billion.

• The average human has 5 million scent receptors in his nose. A bloodhound has 60 times that many.

The box jellyfish has 24 eyes.

THE BIRTH OF WEIRD

Two interesting things you may not have known about human pregnancy.

THERE'S AN ALIEN IN ME!

In 2003 researchers in Denmark published a study that said mothers whose firstborn children were male rather than female had a much greater chance of having miscarriages in future pregnancies. Why? Because when a woman becomes pregnant for the first time with a boy, the developing baby triggers an immune system reaction in the mother's body—because the developing baby is male, and is seen as foreign by the mother's obviously female body. (A first pregnancy that results in a female fetus does not trigger such a reaction, the researchers said.) During a first pregnancy, the reaction isn't strong enough to harm the fetus, because it starts too late in the pregnancy. But during future pregnancies, the immune system kicks in earlier and, whether the child is male or female, is more likely to cause a miscarriage. The researchers said the study will hopefully lead to the development of medications that can counter the reaction.

PREGNANCY IS FOREVER

It's been known for decades that cells from a developing embryo can detach from said embryo and make their way into a mother's body by traveling the "wrong way" up the umbilical cord. In the 1990s, Dr. Diana Bianchi of Tufts University in Massachusetts proved that those fetal cells can survive in a mother's body for decades. In 2004 Dr. Bianchi took this knowledge one step further when she discovered that the cells can also do something extraordinary: If a mother is injured or becomes ill, the fetal cells—cells from a baby she had many years earlier—can migrate to the injured or diseased site and, once there, divide and change into whatever cells are needed to fix the problem. Just how all this works is a mystery that is still being studied. "A pregnancy lasts forever," said Dr. Bianchi, "because every woman who has been pregnant carries these little souvenirs of the pregnancy for the rest of her life."

LOST CONTINENTS

How do you lose something as big as a continent? Well, they didn't disappear overnight.

THAT SINKING FEELING

Ever since Plato told the world about Atlantis in 360 BC, legends about once-thriving continents that have sunk into the ocean have been proposed and debated. According to Plato, Atlantis was "larger than Libya and Asia together" and was ruled by monarchs who wielded "great and marvelous power." Amid earthquakes and great floods, Plato argued, it "was swallowed up by the sea and vanished." Skeptics think the Atlantis story was pure fiction, but since Plato's time, scholars and archaeologists have spent their entire careers on Atlantean treasure hunts. In the 19th century, new legends began circulating about other continents that also sank beneath the ocean and are waiting to be discovered.

Take the tale of the continent called Mu, another supposedly great and wise civilization that suddenly disappeared into the Pacific. And Lemuria, whose gentle, intelligent people went down in the Pacific or Indian Ocean (depending on the source) and are said to have somehow wound up living in tunnels in California's Mount Shasta. Since no known continent has ever disappeared in a cataclysmic event like Plato described—an earthquake and tsunami—Mu and Lemuria have been pretty much dismissed by science. And though the search for Atlantis goes on, it's now generally thought to have been an island or coastal civilization rather than an entire continent (some archaeologists now believe it's under mudflats in Spain). Meanwhile, as searchers and skeptics wrangle, science is exploring two actual continents that really did sink beneath the waves.

LOST AND FOUND

The Joint Oceanographic Institutions for Deep Earth Sampling (JOIDES) helps geologists better understand the earth's formation by drilling for samples of rock on the seafloor. In 1999 a JOIDES research vessel was extracting samples in a remote part of the southern Indian Ocean, about 1,800 miles southwest of Australia, when the researchers made an amazing discovery. Lying a mile underwater was what some in the media described as a "lost continent."

Now known as the Kerguelen Plateau (named for an 18th-century French explorer), the submerged landmass is nearly three times the size of Japan. Some of the plateau remains above sea level, making up the Kerguelen Islands (also known as the Desolation Islands), Heard Island, and the McDonald Islands. Located in the remote Indian Ocean, closer to Antarctica than any other landmass, and now populated mainly by sea mammals, resting birds, and about 100 human researchers, the islands are the highest points of the drowned land.

After drilling into the Kerguelen Plateau, geologists found buried seeds, spores, pollen, and pieces of wood, showing that the plateau was above sea level for millions of years. Then, about 20 million years ago—without any known catastrophic earthquake or tsunami—it just slowly sank into the ocean.

LIFE ON KERGUELEN

The reasons the Kerguelen Plateau sank have to do with the way the land was formed. At one time, Kerguelen was above a hot spot, a fissure in the floor of the southern Indian Ocean where molten rock bubbled up from inside the earth and erupted underwater. Like the Hawaiian Islands, which were created by a hot spot in the Pacific, Kerguelen is made up mostly of volcanic rock. After dating segments of the rock, scientists discovered that Kerguelen formed about 110 million years ago when a series of massive volcanic eruptions exploded out of that hot spot.

Geologists once believed it would take tens of millions of years for a volcano to create such a large piece of real estate, but the eruptions that created the Kerguelen Plateau were so massive that it took only 4 million years. And what was life like on this volcanic land? Wood and coal residues indicate that it was covered with conifer forests about 100 million years ago. There's also evidence that small dinosaurs populated the place 50 million years ago, as it was lush then with ferns and foliage.

CONTINENTAL DRIFT

But continents don't stay in one place—they're carried by huge, slow-moving slabs of rock called tectonic plates. The drowning

Prairie dogs are popular pets in Japan.

process for Kerguelen began after it was carried northward, leaving behind the oceanic hot spot that created it.

Normally, the outermost layer of a continent, which scientists call the crust, is light and buoyant, even though it's made of rock. It floats on the earth's mantle (the semimolten rock just beneath it) because the mantle is much denser and heavier. But as Kerguelen floated away from its source of lava, its crust cooled and the volcanic rock became denser, heavier, and less buoyant. No longer able to float, the continent began sinking into the mantle. In a process that took millions of years, the land sank lower and lower, and the waters of the Indian Ocean eventually closed over Kerguelen.

WELCOME TO ZEALANDIA

Another sunken continent lies under the Pacific Ocean where Mu and Lemuria were said to have gone beneath the waves. Best known as Zealandia, it's about half the size of Australia, and almost all of it lies underwater. Only 7 percent of the continent is still above sea level: New Zealand on the southern end and New Caledonia to the north.

Zealandia is a microcontinent, meaning that at one time it was part of a larger continent. About 130 million years ago, it was attached to both Antarctica and Australia. First, the forces of continental drift separated it from Antarctica, and then about 80 million years ago, Zealandia left Australia behind as the movement of the tectonic plates pushed it out to sea.

The southerly drifting continent of Zealandia remained above water for millions of years, and like Kerguelen, it was home to trees, flowers, and ferns. Scientists also believe that the ancestors of some of the unique plants and wildlife found in New Zealand once happily thrived on Zealandia, including New Zealand's national symbol, the flightless, long-beaked kiwi bird.

YOU CAN BE TOO THIN

With more than 4 million people now living atop the sunken continent, there have been plenty of people wanting to know why Zealandia went down. Geologists generally agree that Zealandia is underwater primarily because its shape is unusually long and thin. Continents are often compared to ice cubes because they "float" on the heavier mantle like ice cubes float on water. Thicker ice cubes float higher above the water, thinner ice cubes float lower. Similarly with continents, thicker, buoyant landmasses float higher on the earth's mantle, keeping the continent well above sea level.

The crust of most continents ranges from 16 to 43 miles thick, but Zealandia's ridges of continental rock are only about 12 miles thick. So as Zealandia drifted over the ocean, it eroded, thinned even more, and began to sink. The details of exactly how and why the continent are still being explored. Some scientists think that, at one point, New Zealand and New Caledonia were also underwater. Others disagree. However, they all agree that during the Ice Age, Zealandia had more land above sea level. But as the glaciers melted and the seas rose, most of it was covered with water.

DROWNED WORLDS

The Kerguelen Plateau and Zealandia aren't in the running anymore as mysterious lost continents, but they are considered hidden treasures. Natural gas deposits on Zealandia provide much of New Zealand's power, and the continent is rich in valuable minerals. The Kerguelen Plateau is also being explored as a source of oil, gas, and minerals. And there's still a lot to learn from studying Kerguelen and Zealandia. Finding out how these great landmasses sank can help modern humans cope with changes from volcanic eruptions, tectonic plate movements, rising seas, and slowly sinking lands.

*   *   *

ALOHA MEANS "GOOD-BYE," TOO

The Hawaiian Islands are part of a long chain of volcanoes that rose from a hot spot on the floor of the Pacific. Like Kerguelen, they are being carried northwestward away from that hot spot by the movement of the Pacific Plate on the ocean floor. They're also eroding, losing a bit of seashore every year. After leaving their hot spot, they will slowly begin to sink, and eventually, they'll vanish beneath the waves...but not for another 80 million years or so.

SEABIRD FACTS

Unless you're a fish, the open ocean isn't the easiest place to live. But dozens of species of birds spend most of their lives at sea. Terrestrial birds wouldn't last very long away from dry land, but seabirds have some specialized adaptations to help them survive.

SALT GLANDS. Most animals can't drink seawater because of its high salt content. (A shipwrecked sailor in a life raft can die of thirst in just three days even though he's completely surrounded by water because the salt in seawater can cause dehydration faster than drinking nothing at all.) But seabirds have special glands just above their eyes that absorb the salt from their bloodstream and then excrete it through their nostrils in the form of a concentrated liquid—which gives these birds the appearance of a runny nose.

SPECIAL FEATHERS. Seabirds have to deal with being wet all the time, and also with being cold. To accommodate these conditions, they have more feathers than their terrestrial counterparts, and those feathers are densely packed on their bodies. This specialized plumage traps small pockets of air that act as insulation. The feathers are also especially waterproof. (Penguins, for instance, actually have a gland near their behinds that secretes oil the birds use to coat their feathers and provide extra waterproofing.) On top of that, seabird feathers typically follow a basic color scheme that acts as a camouflage: dark on top, so they blend into the surface of the sea when viewed from above, and light on the bottom, so they blend in with the sunlight when viewed from below.

PURSUIT DIVERS. Many seabirds can swim, some remarkably well. Biologists call these birds *pursuit divers*, because they swim underwater to catch food. Some—like penguins, auks, and petrels—use specially adapted wings to do it. Others—cormorants, loons, and some ducks—use powerful legs and webbed feet. Penguins are the most extreme example. They have short, stubby wings that make them incapable of flying, but which are perfectly adapted as flippers underwater. (Some types of penguins can swim as fast as 30 miles per hour and dive 300 feet deep.)

DIVE-BOMBERS. Some birds—among them certain pelicans, gannets, and boobies—manage to catch fish underwater without the benefit of swimming. They do this by dive-bombing out of the sky into schools of fish, hitting the water so hard that their momentum carries them to their prey. Northern gannets are a particularly spectacular example. Large birds with wingspans nearly six feet across, they fold their wings into such a streamlined position that they barely slow down when they strike the water. They can plunge from 90 feet high, hit the water at 60 mph, and dive another 50 feet under the surface.

GREAT MIGRATORS. Certain species of seabirds cover more distance over the course of their lives than any other animals in the world. The long-distance champion is the Arctic tern, which migrates almost the entire distance from the Arctic to Antarctica and back again every year. And they don't even fly in a straight line. They meander around the globe taking advantage of whatever air currents are headed vaguely their way. Arctic terns routinely log more than 40,000 travel miles each year. Another great traveler is the aptly named wandering albatross. They have among the longest wingspans (more than 10 feet on average) and life spans (60 years or more) of any birds on earth. Their broad wings are designed for "no-flap" flying, and they ride thermal updrafts without expending too much energy. Wandering albatross have no set migration route. Instead, they just wander and forage over vast expanses of open ocean, often seeing land only once a year or so when they visit their breeding grounds.

* * *

GRAB A LINE

Cormorants are so good at swimming underwater for fish that people once used them as fishing tackle. It's a simple enough process: Train the animal to come when called, tie a small band around the base of the bird's neck to trap fish in its throat, and let it go. When you get the cormorant back to the boat, you simply have to pull out the fish it's caught from its throat. (Cormorant fishing is still practiced in some places, including parts of Japan and China.)

YOU DUNG GOOD

Pull up a stool and learn about the ways that your poop can help the world.

PROFITABLE POOP?

First, the bad news: About 2.6 billion people around the world have nowhere to "go," so they leave their waste on the ground, where germs spread and cause millions of cases of sanitation-related diseases every year. In developed countries like the United States, animal waste is the problem. Livestock and poultry are confined in such large numbers that their urine and excrement spill into and pollute streams, rivers, and groundwater.

But there's good news on the horizon—more scientists and inventors are returning to an ancient idea of turning dangerous waste into wealth. For thousands of years, the Chinese considered sewage a valuable product that fertilized their fields. Dung traders made lots of money by gathering up sewage and transporting it by boat for sale. In 1908 a visiting American was amazed when he learned that a contractor was paying the city of Shanghai $31,000 in gold to buy the residents' "night soil."

Using raw human sewage on farm fields isn't really an option anymore because it spreads disease. But there are other ways that human and animal waste, even when it isn't made into manure, can be surprisingly beneficial...and even profitable.

THE HOUSE AT POO CORNER

For thousands of years, humans have insulated buildings with a dung-and-mud mixture called *daub* that's plastered over cracks between the logs in log cabins, and the spaces between wooden planks in outbuildings and homes. There's also something called "wattle-and-daub" construction. The *wattles* are vertical wooden stakes woven with thin twigs and branches to make a lattice that's *daubed* with a mixture of clay or mud, straw, and animal dung. People still live in wattle-and-daub structures in Europe, Asia, and Africa, and the homes are not just for people too poor to afford something else. The dried dung doesn't smell, and a well-built wattle-and-daub house can be comfortable, durable, and even

The energy given off by an electric eel could start 50 cars.

beautiful. Tudor architecture, a popular style for modern mansions, was originally done in wattle and daub.

As the world tries to get greener—or browner—there's been a revival of interest in using dung as a building material. In Indonesia, a company called EcoFaeBrick has turned cattle dung into bricks that are 20 percent lighter and stronger than regular bricks. The dung bricks look exactly like traditional bricks and can be used in traditional building—no one can tell that they are made out of poop.

POOP POWER

Cooking with dung has also been around for ages. You might think it's gross, but even the Bible mentions it: In a directive from the Old Testament, God gave the prophet Ezekiel a recipe for bread and ordered that it be baked using dung. American pioneers also cooked with buffalo dung, or "chips," in the Old West. One traveler crossing the Great Plains declared that buffalo chips "burn fiercely" and cooked as well as wood. They also seemed to affect the flavor of food, because he said, "It is a common joke on the Plains that a steak cooked on these chips requires no pepper."

Today, in highly populated areas, burning dung (or any smoke-producing fuel) has big disadvantages. In India, where cow dung typically heats up the cooking stove, the smoke these fires produce can harm people's eyes and lungs, and the flies that are attracted to the drying cow patties can spread disease. That's why, beginning in the 1960s, India became a pioneer in turning dung into a fuel called biogas.

Human and animal manure, as well as kitchen waste, fuel about 2.5 million rural homes in modern India. The waste goes into an airtight concrete tank called a biodigester, where bacteria slowly eat and digest all the waste and then turn it into gases. The result is a gas that can directly power cooking stoves, lamps, and heaters, and it can run generators to create electricity. The gas doesn't smell, it burns without creating pollution, and it doesn't harm humans' eyes or lungs. The residue left in the tank is also useful as a safe, enriched fertilizer for farming.

Whether it's animal or human, poop is (obviously) a renewable energy source, and we'll never run out of it. So the West, which is

Most common rock on earth: basalt.

always in need of fuel, has also started turning to biogas. Google and Duke University recently pooled their resources and invested in a waste-processing plant for hog manure that generates enough electricity for 35 homes. Pacific Gas & Electric in California used waste from a 5,000-cow dairy farm to power 1,200 homes, and a sewage plant in Oxfordshire, England, turns sewage into electricity for 200 homes. Even U.S. astronauts are contributing to the idea of toilets as a source of energy. An in-space experiment used astronaut waste mixed with special microbes to create hydrogen gas. The hydrogen then generated electricity in fuel cells.

"GAS" FOR YOUR CAR

And what about those ever-polluting automobiles? Since 2009 in Oslo, Norway, 80 buses have been running on biomethane, a clean-burning fuel that's made from the methane gas generated from human sewage. Cheaper than diesel, biomethane replaces 52,500 gallons of polluting diesel a year.

Meanwhile, in Orange County, California, where car fumes create the dreaded smog, there's a big need for clean-burning fuel. So companies are using a system that takes the methane gas from sewage and processes it into hydrogen gas that's then sent to a fuel cell to create electricity. The electricity powers the sewage facility, and any remaining hydrogen goes to a fueling station to power hydrogen cars.

Orange County's sewage plant is the world's first fuel cell and hydrogen energy station. By 2015 major auto manufacturers hope to have hydrogen cars on the market, and there will be plenty of demand for this clean-burning fuel. If California, with all its cars, can already produce cheap, clean fuel from sewage, maybe, like the ancient Chinese, we've really found a way to turn poop into gold.

*   *   *

THEY'LL NEVER KNOW THE JOY...

Mayflies are tiny insects, the adults of which have incredibly short life spans—some live for just a few minutes, others for just a few hours or days. They live for such a short amount of time, in fact... that they never poop or pee in their entire lives.

A FISH CALLED...

...Lepidocephalichthys zeppelini—*after the English rock band Led Zeppelin. And a few other creatures with equally unusual scientific names.*

ELECTROLUX ADDISONI. A type of fish known as a ray (like a manta ray), the first *Electrolux addisoni* specimen was captured off the coast of South Africa in 2003 by a diver named Mark Addison. South African scientists based the species name (the second part of the two-part scientific name) on Mr. Addison, and the genus (the first part of the name) after the vacuum cleaner brand Electrolux in honor of the "vigorous sucking action" the ray uses to feed off the ocean floor.

NABOKOVIA. English entomologist Francis Hemming named this butterfly genus in 1960 for Russian novelist Vladimir Nabokov, who authored *Lolita*, among other classics, and who was himself a *lepidopterist* (a person who studies insects like butterflies). Nabokov specialized in a subfamily of butterflies in what is now known as the *Nabokovia* genus.

AHA HA. This Australian wasp was named by scientist Arnold Menke in 1977. When Menke received specimens of the wasps from a friend, he opened the package, saw them, and said, "Aha!"

SPONGIFORMA SQUAREPANTSII. San Francisco State University researcher Dennis Desjardin gave this mushroom species its name in 2011 because the mushroom not only resembled a sea sponge, but when viewed under a scanning-electron microscope, it looked like the ocean floor where TV cartoon character SpongeBob SquarePants lives.

CALLICEBUS AUREIPALATII. This monkey species was discovered in Bolivia's Amazon jungle in 2004. Rather than naming it themselves, the scientists who made the discovery auctioned off the naming rights to the highest bidder. The winner, online casino company Golden Palace, paid $650,000 to name the monkey *aureipalatii*, a Latinized term meaning "Golden Palace." (The $650,000 was donated to FUNDESNAP, the nonprofit organization that maintains the park where the monkey was found.)

LEPIDOPA LUCIAE. American crustacean biologist Christopher Boyko named this marine crab in 2002. At first he wanted to name it for Charles Schulz, the creator of the *Peanuts* comic strip. But when Boyko contacted the famous cartoonist, Schulz's wife suggested he name it after *Peanuts* character Lucy instead… because she's known for being crabby.

YTU BRUTUS. The genus name for this aquatic beetle, *Ytu*, comes from a native Brazilian word meaning "waterfall." *Ytu brutus* got its name in 1980 from Smithsonian entomologist Paul J. Spangler, a Shakespeare fan.

COLON RECTUM. This beetle was discovered in the American Northwest by Melville H. Hatch, a highly respected scientist who was also known for his mischievous sense of humor. He named *Colon rectum* ("Colon" had already been a beetle genus for some time) in 1933, because he thought it was funny. Over the years, he named several other beetle species in the genus, including *Colon monstrosum*, C. *grossum*, and C. *horni*.

ERECHTHIAS BEEBLEBROXI. This moth species has a bump near its head that gives it the appearance of having two heads, just like Zaphod Beeblebrox—the two-headed character in Douglas Adams's *The Hitchhiker's Guide to the Galaxy*.

STRIGIPHILUS GARYLARSONI. A species of louse that feeds off owls, it was named in 1989 by owl expert Dale H. Clayton, in honor of Gary Larson, creator of the cartoon series *The Far Side*. Clayton wrote Larson about the naming, thanking him for "the enormous contribution that my colleagues and I feel you have made to biology through your cartoons." Larson said, "I considered this an extreme honor. Besides, I knew no one was going to write and ask to name a new species of swan after me."

DISTORSIO GRACEIELLAE: German marine biologist Manfred Parth named this sea snail species in 1989. He explained his choice this way: "I dedicate the name to my first wife Graziella Pierantoni (Milano, Italy) and to my future wife Grace Marcos (Palawa, Philippines)."

IRRITATOR CHALLENGERI: A 25-foot-long dinosaur similar to *Tyrannosaurus rex*, *Irritator challengeri* is known from only one fossilized skull. British paleontologist Dave Martill, who studied the skull for years before helping to name it in 1996, said the species name was chosen in honor of Professor Challenger, the lead character in Sir Arthur Conan Doyle's 1912 dinosaur-themed novel, *The Lost World*. The genus name, Martill said, came "from irritation, the feeling [they] felt when discovering that the snout had been artificially elongated." (It turned out that the person they had bought the fossil from had tampered with it.)

IBYKA. Paleobotanists Judith Skog and Harlan Banks named this extinct plant genus in 1973 after the ancient Greek poet Ibykos, who lived in the sixth century BC. The connection: According to legend, Ibykos was murdered, and his killers were found out with the help of birds, specifically cranes. Skog and Banks explained that the first fossils of this extinct plant were discovered with the help of cranes, too—but in this case, the mechanical kind—ones that were used in the construction of a dam in New York State.

LEPIDOCEPHALICHTHYS ZEPPELINI. Auburn University graduate student Justin Havird was studying this new fish species in 2010 when he noticed that the fish's pectoral fin looked like the double-neck guitar played by Led Zeppelin guitarist Jimmy Page. Havird was listening to Led Zeppelin at the time and, you know, one thing led to another.

FUNKOTRIPLOGYNIUM IAGOBADIUS. This mite species is found in rain forests in Queensland, Australia. The origin of its genus name, *Funkotriplogynium*, coined in 1985, is unknown. The species name, *iagobadius*, however, was chosen in 1997 by Australian scientists Owen Seeman and Dave Walter, who thought that the funky genus name deserved a funky species name: *iago* is the Spanish equivalent of "James"—and *badius* means "brown."

CARMENELECTRA SHECHISME. Dr. Neal Evenhuis, entomologist at the Bishop Museum in Honolulu, Hawaii, named this extinct species of moth in 2002. It's pronounced "Carmen Electra She Kiss Me." Dr. Evenhuis said he tried to contact Ms. Electra, best known as a *Playboy* centerfold and *Baywatch* actress, but was unable to reach her. The good doctor hasn't given up: "I'll be willing to meet her," he told the *Chicago Tribune* in 2008.

Citronella, catnip, rosemary, and marigold all repel mosquitoes.

LOOK BEFORE YOU LEAK

Be cautious while doing your business in the wilderness.

IN THE JUNGLE, THE MIGHTY JUNGLE...

In the summer of 2009, two residents of India's Chandrapur district went outside to relieve themselves. Unfortunately, they weren't alone. Forest officer S. L. Thavre explains, "A leopard was seen on the outskirts of Khedmakka village in the wee hours of August 19. It attacked two persons who had gone to answer nature's call." The cat then roamed into nearby communities, pouncing on a total of five people. Luckily, all survived.

DO NOT DISTURB THE ANIMALS

A Texan named Andrew Dales was allegedly drinking up a storm in Cancún, Mexico, in 2009. The 20-year-old stopped to urinate in a lagoon behind a disco club, ignoring signs warning of crocodiles. Although crocs in that area are considered "nonaggressive," they may lash out at humans when provoked. Sure enough, Dales disturbed a sleeping crocodile, which knocked him over and chomped on his leg, arms, and neck. With a head injury and multiple bite wounds, Dales managed to fight off the reptile until he could make it to safety.

TROUBLE DOWN UNDER

In 2008 a carpenter named Daryl Zutt was hunting wild pigs in Australia with a friend when he made a pit stop by the side of the road. Little did he know that he was crouching directly over an eastern brown snake, one of the world's most venomous species. Midway through taking care of his business, Zutt saw the snake slither between his legs and then felt a stabbing pain. The reptile had bitten him in... well...the most delicate place imaginable. (On examining the wound, he said, "I saw fang marks and a bit of blood come out.") Both he and the snake fled the scene. Zutt's friend drove to the hospital, and certain that he would die, Zutt called his mother to say his good-byes. But at the hospital, doctors discovered that the snake hadn't actually released any venom into Zutt's system. And that's a good thing—it would have taken only 0.00007 ounce to kill him.

Bess beetles can make 14 distinct sounds.

LAKE FAQS

There are more than 304 million lakes on earth. Here we'll tell you everything you ever wanted to know about those bodies of water... and some things you didn't know you wanted to know.

WHY DO LAKES MATTER?

Sure, they're pretty, but lakes are functional too. They hold about 87 percent of the world's fresh surface water. (Rivers hold 2 percent, and swamps 11 percent.) Lakes supply crucial drinking water, irrigate farmland, and generate electricity.

WHAT MAKES A LAKE A LAKE?

Each lake has qualities that make it unique. Some have fresh water; some are filled with brine and salt. They have various shapes and colors (some are even pink). What makes them all lakes is that they're all surface bodies of water surrounded by land—and they're bigger than ponds. Although there's no official number to dictate the size of a lake or pond, there is a way to tell them apart. Because lakes are larger and deeper, they have different temperatures at different levels. Ponds are the same temperature all the way through.

HOW ARE LAKES BORN?

Lakes form in basins, hollows in the earth's surface. Over time, a basin fills with water from rain, ice, snow, groundwater, or streams and rivers, and a lake is born. Many natural forces create lake basins—for example, Chubb Lake in Canada formed in a meteorite crater. But most lakes have nothing to do with debris from outer space.

• **Glaciers** created most of the world's lakes. The northern United States, all of Canada, northern Europe, and Asia were all covered with glaciers during the last Ice Age. These heavy masses of ice expanded during the coldest times on earth, and then retreated as the weather warmed. As they grew, the edges of the glaciers gouged deep depressions in the earth's surface that were filled by melted water when the Ice Age ended. For example, the Great Lakes were carved out by a glacier about two miles thick.

Canada has an estimated 2 million lakes, more than any other country in the world.

• Earth movement along the edges of two **tectonic plates** (large slabs of rock that make up the earth's crust) can push those plates farther apart, leaving a deep chasm called a rift valley, which then fills with water. Example: Lake Tahoe in California and Nevada.

• **Landslides** create lakes by damming up a river and flooding the river valley. Example: Derborence Lake in Switzerland.

• **As a river twists and winds** toward the ocean, it sometimes overruns its banks at a bend and can close up, forming an "oxbow lake." Oxbow lakes (called billabongs in Australia) are so named because their U-shape looks like the yokes that were once used to harness oxen. Example: Lake Chicot in Arkansas is the largest oxbow lake in the United States—it was once a part of the Mississippi River.

• **Sinkholes** form when groundwater dissolves rock beds that are made of porous rock like limestone. Example: Red Lake in Croatia is in a sinkhole that's more than 1,700 feet deep.

• **Volcanic eruptions** sometimes leave behind craters that can fill with water. Example: Lake Toba in Indonesia, the largest volcanic lake in the world.

HOW DO LAKES GET THEIR WATER?

There are several classifications:

• **Drainage lakes** are fed by incoming river tributaries, streams, rain, or snow. They also have an outlet where the excess water leaves the lake as a stream. Artificial drainage lakes (caused by damming a river) are called impoundments.

• **Spring lakes** are fed by an underground spring, and their outlet carries away the excess water as a stream. Spring lakes are found at the headwaters of streams.

• **Seepage lakes** don't have an inlet or an outlet—they're filled with rainwater, groundwater, and runoff, and are the most common lakes in North America.

• **Endorheic lakes** don't have an outlet to take water out, so the water leaves through evaporation, leaving behind its salt and minerals. This creates salty lakes like the Caspian Sea in Russia and Turkmenistan.

First YouTube video: The site's cofounder, Jawed Karim, discussing elephants...

WHY ARE LAKES DIFFERENT COLORS?

It all has to do with which substances are suspended in the water. Sediments cause brown water, and algae usually make it green. Tannic acids leached from leaves can make water look black. Minerals, like the reddish brown tint from iron, can affect a lake's color. And some lakes are famous for the color of their water:

• **Deep blue:** Crater Lake in Oregon gets its deep blue color because its water is so pure and deep. Sunlight penetrates very deep into the clear water, and the depth absorbs the sun's longer rays like red and yellow. It also reflects the shortest rays...like blue and violet.

• **Turquoise:** Peyto Lake in Canada is glacier-fed. Nearby glaciers erode the bedrock, grinding it up into bits of rock and sediment called *glacier flour*. The flour then tumbles into the lake, where it makes the waters turquoise.

• **Pink:** The nearly dry Owens Lake in California gets its rosy pink color from the millions of halobacteria that feed on its shallow, salty brine. These bacteria carry a pigment that turns them pink or red.

• **Multicolored:** The three Kelimutu Lakes in Indonesia each filled up a separate crater of the same volcano...and they change color. Sometimes one lake will be blue while another is green and another is red or brown. Then they swap. The lakes' colors are triggered by changing minerals and acids from volcanic activity.

DO LAKES EVER DISAPPEAR?

Over thousands of years, lakes fill up with silt and mud that washes in from the surrounding land. The lake becomes smaller and shallower, and islands can form. Reeds begin to grow, and plant life spreads, creating swamps. As the swamp expands, the lake begins to dry out until it finally disappears.

For the world's largest, deepest, hottest, and most buried lakes (and other extremes), swim over to page 345.

MAN, THAT STINKS!

If animals could wear perfume, would they? Well, if you asked these critters, they might say they already do.

• The **binturong**, a small carnivore from tropical Southeast Asia, smells like buttered popcorn. The scent comes from an area beneath the animal's tail.

• The eucalyptus leaves that **koalas** eat give them a medicinal smell—like cough drops and cold remedies.

• Bacteria of various sorts (and yeast) are the reason some **dogs'** feet smell like crunchy corn snacks.

• If you were to swallow a lot of stinky **skunk** spray, you could become temporarily blind, nauseous, or unconscious. (A skunk's spray, by the way, is *phosphoric*, which means it glows in the dark.)

• When they sting, **bees** release pheromones that can sometimes smell like bananas.

• Africa's version of the skunk is the **zorilla**, or striped polecat. The method of defense is the same, but the zorilla is said to be even smellier than a skunk.

• When threatened, the **tamandua**, a type of anteater found in South America, releases a smelly spray to scare off predators.

• The male **musk ox** uses his own urine to mark his trails and himself, dousing his long, thick, woolly hair with it—especially during mating season.

• **Bull elephants** go through a periodic condition called *musth*, a surge in testosterone that lasts about a month. One of the hallmarks of musth is a secretion that comes from a gland between the animal's eyes and ears: in young elephants, the musth smells like honey and will attract bees. But the older the elephant, the funkier and muskier the secretions become.

• The **crested auklet**, a seabird that lives mainly along the coast of Alaska, gives off a citruslike smell that resembles tangerines. Researchers believe the scent is used for bonding, mating, and to repel parasites.

World's longest horse mane: 18 feet, grown by a mare named Maude.

THE REAL VAMPIRES

These bloodthirsty creatures could drink Dracula under the table.

THE WORLD'S DEADLIEST VAMPIRES

Adult male mosquitoes typically feed on nectar and juices from plants—it's the females that need to feed on blood to get enough protein for their eggs. Both male and female mosquitoes feed through a *proboscis* (a slender tube protruding from an animal's head), but female mosquitoes have "cutters" at the ends of theirs to break into a capillary blood vessel and suck up about twice their weight in blood.

When the mosquito bites for blood, she injects chemicals to prevent the blood from clotting and to relieve pain so the host won't notice the bite. Those chemicals are what make the bite itch later. But what's far worse is that the mosquito may have transmitted a disease at the same time. Female anopheles mosquitoes live all over the world and they transmit malaria, infecting millions of people every year with a disease whose symptoms include fever, sweating, muscle weakness, nausea, vomiting, and even death. In fact, more than 650,000 people (mostly children in Africa) died of malaria in 2010. And if that's not bad enough, mosquitoes also carry the West Nile virus, yellow fever, and other deadly diseases.

SOME VAMPIRES ARE ALL WET

Lampreys are three-foot-long fish that look sort of like eels. Known as the "vampire of the seas," lampreys have no jaws. Instead they have a circular, funnel-shaped, tubelike mouth filled with hooklike teeth—and they have even *more* of those teeth on their tongues. This enables them to latch onto a fish and then use the tongue teeth to open a hole in the fish's scaly skin. Lampreys swim along with their host as they suck out its blood. They mostly like fish, but if they're hungry enough, they will attack people.

There are two types of lampreys—sea and freshwater—and the freshwater type have been in North America for ages. But sea lampreys were accidentally introduced into the Great Lakes in the early

1900s, after they made their way up shipping canals. By the 1960s, they'd killed off 98 percent of the lakes' trout and driven some other fish to extinction. A special fishing unit was set up to reduce the lamprey population, but no one knew what to do with them after that. Although they used to be considered a great delicacy—England's King Henry I was so fond of lampreys that he died after gulping down too many of them at once—no one these days finds them appetizing, so they're mostly used as bait or fish food.

THE GREEDIEST VAMPIRES

Ticks are arachnids like scorpions and spiders—they have eight legs and can be as big as an apple seed or smaller than the period at the end of this sentence. But they all feed on blood. They find their hosts by *questing*, which means they pick spots in the grass where a warm-blooded animal is likely to come along, and then they climb on board. After finding a place where the skin is thin, a tick will grasp it, cut into the skin's surface, and insert a feeding tube. A cementlike substance keeps the tube attached, and painkillers keep the host from noticing as the tick feeds over several days. No other creature has a greater blood thirst—ticks have been known to drink 600 times their own weight in blood.

Like mosquitoes, ticks have been spreading illness for thousands of years. DNA analysis revealed that a 5,300-year-old mummy known as Ötzi suffered from Lyme disease, a bacterial disease spread by ticks. Lyme causes fever, muscle aches, and neurological problems, and is just one of the many diseases spread by ticks. Others include Rocky Mountain spotted fever and a severe skin rash called STARI.

VAMPIRES HATE SUNLIGHT

Bedbugs are tiny, wingless insects with rust-colored oval bodies that feed on warm-blooded animals. When they're after birds, they hide in birds' nests; when they're after bats, they hide in bats' roosts. When they're after humans, they hide in our beds and furniture, in any dark crevice they can find. In the 1940s, bedbugs were eradicated with pesticides that were so toxic that they're now banned. That's one reason the nasty little insects have made a comeback in big cities. Another is that females can lay as many as 500 eggs during their year long life.

Bedbugs wait to attack until people are deeply asleep, usually about an hour before dawn. Then they climb onto your body and pierce your skin with a proboscis containing two hollow tubes. One tube injects saliva that contains painkillers and anticoagulants, while the other tube sucks up blood. The anticoagulants keep the blood flowing freely, and the painkillers keep the host unaware of what's going on. Within five minutes, a bedbug can consume seven times its weight in blood. Then it quickly returns to its dark hiding place, leaving behind small red, itchy bumps.

To learn about bats (the bloodsucking and non-bloodsucking kinds), flap over to page 367.

* * *

SEVEN TYPES OF SPIDER SILK

1. Swathing: Wraps up and immobilizes prey.

2. Webs: Sticky; used for building webs that capture prey.

3. Draglines: Like a safety line, this connects the spider to the web. This is the strongest type of spider silk because it must carry the spider's weight.

4. Parachuting/ballooning: Adult spiders attach this silk to their young and set the babies free. The wind picks up the young spiders and then deposits them in new places, where there are (presumably) new and plentiful food sources.

5. Shelter: This silk is used to create nests or burrows where the spiders live.

6. Eggsac: Well…it makes the sacs that hold a female spider's eggs.

7. Mating: Some spiders spin silk that they then coat with pheromones to attract mates. In other cases, male spiders deposit sperm on this type of silk in preparation for impregnating females.

Limestone neutralizes acid rain.

V IS FOR VENOM

Everything we hope you'll never need to know about venom.

AT LEAST IT'S NOT POISON

First, let's clear up the difference between poison and venom. A poisonous frog and a venomous snake can both kill, but they do it differently. The poisonous frog's victim has either touched or eaten the frog. Venomous animals, on the other hand, apply their toxins directly under their victim's skin by biting, stinging, slashing, or harpooning—anything to get the venom into the bloodstream. If the venom were to go into the victim's stomach instead, the toxins would be broken down by stomach acid and not fatal.

Another thing: Poison is a defense mechanism—other animals will avoid one that's poisonous. But venom is more often a predator's tool. For example, a wasp stings with venom to paralyze an insect so it can fly the creature back to the wasp nest, where the insect is then placed next to an already-laid egg...so that when the wasp's baby hatches, the little darling has a fresh, live meal waiting. Predators also use venom if they're smaller or weaker than the animal they want to kill, and they can use it to tenderize the prey and make it more digestible. Only rarely is an animal both poisonous and venomous.

HERE, HAVE A COCKTAIL

Every venomous organism sports a different mix of toxins. Most deliver a cocktail of complex chemicals, enzymes, and proteins that cause all kinds of things to go wrong for the victim.

• **Neurotoxins** attack the nervous system. They stop the brain's ability to communicate, paralyze muscles, and cause suffocation by shutting down the respiratory system. Neurotoxins can also overload the nervous system with too many signals and cause massive seizures.

• **Cytotoxins** attack cells, causing them to explode and die, pretty much predigesting the victim.

• **Hemotoxins** attack the blood. Some kill the red blood cells that deliver oxygen; others stop blood from clotting, causing internal bleeding. Still others create massive blood clots that prevents blood from flowing through the heart.

- **Cardiotoxins** attack the heart directly so it stops pumping.

Today, a lot of people think that only snakes or spiders are venomous, but fish, insects, lizards, and even mammals kill with venom, too. Don't be afraid, though—most venomous creatures aren't dangerous to humans because their toxins are geared toward incapacitating insects or very small animals. Even so, some of the exceptions to the "not-dangerous-to-humans" rule are the stuff of nightmares.

BRAZILIAN WANDERING SPIDER

The Brazilian wandering spider goes hunting at night for its prey: insects and even small lizards and mice. Brown with red fur covering their fangs, the world's most venomous spider hides during the day, which is when people usually come across them accidentally in the dark corners of their houses or (living up to their nickname of "banana spiders") hiding inside a bunch of bananas at the supermarket.

If simply disturbed, the Brazilian wandering spider might bite and not release venom, but if it feels threatened for any reason, its fangs will release a neurotoxin. Fortunately, it can take days to incapacitate and kill, and there's an antivenin available, so banana shoppers have plenty of time to get treatment. But if left untreated, a bite—especially to a child or an elderly person—will lead to paralysis and death through asphyxiation.

CONE SNAIL

Some of those pretty cone-shaped shells that beachcombers search for were once home to deadly predators. Large cone snails, found in reefs in the Indian and Pacific Oceans, hunt small fish by shooting a tubelike extension from their mouths. Attached is a tiny harpoon tooth that injects a deadly combination of neurotoxins into a victim, instantly paralyzing the fish so it can't get away before the snail slowly crawls toward it—and eats it.

The deadly geographic cone snail, which also lives in the Indo-Pacific region, has been known to kill swimmers and divers who unknowingly pick one up. The conotoxins release a powerful

Whale tails move up and down; fish tails move from side to side.

painkiller so the victim doesn't know that a harpoon has entered its skin. Within minutes, the speedy venom shuts down the nervous system and causes heart failure. (That's why the geographic cone has been nicknamed the "cigarette snail"—because a victim just might have the time to smoke one last cigarette before dying.) So far, there's no known antivenin.

INLAND TAIPAN SNAKE

The nine-foot-long inland taipan is the most venomous of all land snakes. A native of central Australia, it has the nickname "fierce snake," but it's the venom that's fierce. The snakes are pretty shy and reclusive.

Drop for drop, the inland taipan's venom is particularly deadly to humans—one drop can kill 100 people. One of the venom's components is a powerful hemotoxin that causes massive hemorrhaging. It also can cause muscle destruction, paralysis, and death. Fortunately, an antivenin has been developed, so the bite doesn't have to be fatal.

DEATHSTALKER SCORPION

When a regular scorpion spots its prey, it grabs with its claws and uses the stinger on its tail only if the prey is strong and resisting. But the deathstalker scorpion of the Middle East is small with narrow claws, and has a harder time overpowering its prey. So it makes up for that deficiency with more powerful venom in its tail. The deadliest of all scorpions, the deathstalker packs a neurotoxin that causes swelling, numbness, paralysis, and convulsions. Without immediate medical attention, victims will die of heart or respiratory failure. And because these creatures don't mind living indoors, they move into people's homes where they can be deadly. Their venom can cause extreme pain, fever, convulsions, paralysis, and has been known to kill children, the elderly, and people suffering from heart disease.

* * *

If you hear a toad croaking, it's probably a male. The females of most toad species can't croak.

LIFE'S A BEACH

Who needs a zoo when you can just go to the beach?

BACKGROUND
We tend to think of beaches as big, empty places full of nothing but sand, but there's a lot going on that we don't see, and we don't mean in the water. The creatures that live on beaches are some of the most unique on earth—in some cases a combination of marine and terrestrial, and in all cases built for what is a constantly changing environment. Here are a few examples.

BEACH HOPPERS. If you go to a beach with a flashlight at night and look under some rotting seaweed, you might find some small (about ¼ inch long), buglike creatures hopping around. Those would be beach hoppers, also known as "sandhoppers" or "sand fleas," and believe it or not, they're crustaceans and closely related to shrimp. Beach hoppers spend the day burrowed several inches below the surface of the sand to protect themselves from birds and waves; at night they come up to feed on rotting seaweed.

SEA SLATERS. Also known as "sea roaches," sea slaters are burrowing crustaceans like beach hoppers, but they're larger—up to an inch or more in length—and they'll eat any dead matter. You don't have to look under rotting seaweed to find them: they'll be scurrying across the sand in search of a meal after dark. (They're also known as "beach pillbugs," because they resemble the little garden pests you might know as pillbugs, which, by the way, are crustaceans, too.)

SAND CRABS. Dig a hole in the sand about a foot deep, let a wave fill it up, and look for these little guys. Also known as "mole crabs," they grow up to an inch in length, have barrel-shaped bodies, and they are excellent diggers: they can disappear under the sand—tail first—in less than two seconds. Sand crabs feed by sticking their feathery antennae up out of the sand when waves come in, filtering out plankton. Sand crabs spend the early stages of their lives drifting through the oceans as plankton, until they finally wash up on a beach, molt, and become adults.

Squids have three hearts—two for the gills, one for the rest of the body.

GIANT BEACH WORMS. If you're strolling down a beach in Australia, there might be huge carnivorous worms right under your feet. Giant beach worms spend their lives in the sand right at the shoreline, popping up when a wave recedes to search for whatever new organic matter the sea has brought in. If you watch closely, you can sometimes see their white, grublike heads—with little black legs attached to them—pop up out of the sand to grab something. By now, you may be wondering, how big is "giant"? They've been known to grow to more than six feet in length—and there can be tens of thousands of them right under the sand on any given beach.

BLOOD WORMS. Australia isn't the only place that's home to carnivorous beach worms; there are other kinds all around the world. One of the most common is the blood worm, so called because of its red color. They're smaller than the giant worms—a measly 12 inches or so in length—but like the big guys they live under the sand at the water's edge. And like the Aussie worm, wherever they're found, they're a favorite bait of local fishermen.

BEACH BIVALVES. Bivalves are creatures that have two hinged shells, like clams and oysters (the word *bivalve* refers to the two halves of those shells). Some live far offshore, or attached to rocks or piers, but plenty of them live right under the sand. Beach bivalves have tubelike siphons that they use to suck or squirt water, and a "foot" (like a snail's foot); they use both to dig down into sand, which some of them can do remarkably fast. The razor clam, for instance, can dig a lot faster than any human trying to catch it. When it's feeding time, beach bivalves send one of their siphons up to the surface and feed on tiny organisms brought in by waves. The most remarkable bivalve by far is the *geoduck* (pronounced "gooey duck"), a clam that can grow to nearly eight inches across. Found mostly on beaches in Washington State and British Columbia, its name comes from a Native American word meaning "dig deep." Geoducks live as long as 160 years, but remain in one spot for their entire lives, using their three-foot-long siphons to troll for food. Speaking of which, a lot of people (especially fans of Asian cookery) find geoducks a true delicacy, either cooked in a hot pot or stew, or served raw as sashimi.

Largest family of birds on earth: The Tyrannidae, or flycatchers, with over 400 species.

WEIRD (AND AWESOMELY WRONG) THEORIES

We humans are often a bit desperate to claim we "know" things about the world and how it works, when we actually have no idea what we're talking about. Here are a few examples.

RAIN FOLLOWS THE *WHAT* NOW?

In the 1870s a "scientific" theory became popular in the United States: It said that, when humans planted crops in dry, previously unsettled regions, moisture was released into the air, with the result being a change in climate and more rainfall. This became known as the "rain follows the plow" theory, and it was pushed by scientists, and then the press, just as the government was trying to get people to settle the Great Plains—a region long known as a dry and barren wasteland. (The fact that the region happened to be experiencing a rare wet spell in the 1870s helped the theory take hold.) The theory comforted the millions of people who over the following decades moved to the Plains and built farms. No need to worry, promoters said—build it and the rain will come! It didn't. Millions of acres of farmland were subsequently wiped out during the repeated droughts that followed, culminating in the devastating Dust Bowl years of the 1930s.

ORIGINAL ICE CAPADES

Hans Hörbiger was a successful and wealthy Austrian engineer who had lots of time to gaze at the sky through his telescope and develop weird theories about things. In 1913 the weirdness peaked when he published *Welteislehre*, or the "world ice theory." Hörbiger explained that while staring at the moon one night, he realized it was made of ice. But wait, there's more! That was followed by a vision in which Hörbiger learned great truths regarding the formation of the universe...and it all had to do with ice. Hörbiger promoted his theory relentlessly, and even though most serious scientists dismissed it, by the late 1920s the world ice theory was very popular in Germany—largely because many Nazis had taken

In 1979 polar bears at the San Diego Zoo turned green because of algae in their enclosure.

it up. (Heinrich Himmler, one of Hitler's commanders, became a major supporter of the theory, based on the idea that the "ice" somehow related to the Nazi fantasy of the "white Nordic race," which purportedly originated in icy regions of northern Europe.) Hörbiger died in 1931, but his theory remained popular and retained supporters right through World War II...until Germany's defeat and the war's end, when it quietly melted away.

THE ISLAND OF DR. D'OH!

In 1625 respected British mapmaker Henry Briggs published the most detailed map of North America to date. It became one of the most respected New World maps in Europe and helped to promote a theory that prevailed for more than a century: that California was a long, narrow island off the west coast of North America. (The error stemmed from Briggs trusting an earlier and equally wrong Spanish map.) And even though it was soon contested by explorers to the region—and by the early 1700s was *proven* to be wrong by people who actually went overland to California—the "California is an island" theory persisted well into the 1700s. It was finally dealt a death blow in 1747 when King Ferdinand VII of Spain formally decreed that California was *not* an island.

HOW TO BUILD A SCORPION

For thousands of years people believed that living things could grow out of nonliving things. Aristotle, for example, believed that oysters grew out of slime, and eels out of mud. Known as spontaneous generation, this was treated as fact for ages—and even persisted until fairly modern times. In the 17th century, for example, Flemish chemist Jan Baptist van Helmont, one of the most respected scientists of any era (he was the first to show that air was composed of different substances, and even coined the word "gas") believed that you could create animals by following simple recipes. Van Helmont's notes, for example, contain a recipe for making mice: Put some wheat on a dirty cloth, let it sit for 21 days and—voilà!—mice will be created. Another: Put some basil between two bricks in sunlight. Then…scorpions. It wasn't until the mid-1800s that scientific progress finally saw spontaneous generation spontaneously combusted for good.

HE AIN'T HEAVY, HE'S MY WHALE

In which we weigh in on what happens when creatures large and small—and animal and human—step on the scales.

• The blue whale, the largest living creature on earth, can weigh 200 tons. Compared to that, the sperm whale is tiny, just 45 tons.

• The largest dinosaur was believed to be the Argentinosaurus, which weighed somewhere around 100 tons. (That's equal to about eight school buses!)

• A walrus can weigh more than 1.5 tons.

• The average dairy cow weighs about 1,200 pounds.

• Polar bears can tip the scales at 1,700 pounds.

• Though they look bigger, porpoises weigh in at just over 120–135 pounds on average.

• They look delicate, but giraffes can weigh 1.5 tons.

• The largest spider: the goliath bird-eating spider, at a whopping...6 ounces.

• The stomach of a female hippopotamus accounts for about 25 percent of its weight.

• At more than three ounces, the goliath beetle is the world's heaviest insect. That doesn't sound like much...until you consider that a housefly weighs about 0.03 ounce.

• The world's largest human (Jon Brower Minnoch from Seattle) weighed about 1,400 pounds—an approximation because he was too big to get on a scale. He had a disease called massive generalized edema, which made him gain excessive amounts of weight.

• The world's heaviest horse was a Shire named Samson, who tipped the scales at more than 1.5 tons.

• The largest seeds on earth come from the coco-de-mer palm...and can weigh 40 pounds each.

THE LIMNOLOGY QUIZ

Uncle John always thought "limnology" was the study of bathroom floors—so we thought a "Fields of Research Under the Enormous Umbrella of Biology" quiz might be a good idea for this book. Match the field of study on the left with the object of study on the right. (Answers are on page 430.)

1. Anatomy
2. Biochemistry
3. Biogeography
4. Botany
5. Carcinology
6. Cytology
7. Developmental biology
8. Ecology
9. Entomology
10. Ethology
11. Genetics
12. Geobotany
13. Herpetology
14. Histology
15. Ichthyology
16. Limnology
17. Mammalogy
18. Marine biology
19. Microbiology
20. Morphology
21. Mycology
22. Neurology
23. Ornithology
24. Palaeontology
25. Pathology
26. Pharmacology

a) Insects
b) Microorganisms
c) Disease
d) DNA
e) Ecosystems
f) Sea life
g) Inland waters
h) Drugs and their effects
i) Crustaceans
j) Mammals
k) Birds
l) Chemistry of living things
m) Cells
n) Tissues of living things
o) Extinct life
p) Amphibians and reptiles
q) Distribution of life on earth
r) Nervous system disorders
s) Fungi
t) Growth of organisms
u) Distribution of plants on earth
v) Plants
w) Animal behavior
x) Structure of organisms
y) Structure of internal organs
z) Fish

DA BEARS

Q: What happened when the panda had an accident in the sticky tape factory? A: He became a gummy bear. (We promise there are no more jokes like that in this article about bears. Maybe.)

BECOMING BEARS

Starting around 65 million years ago, small marmotlike mammals called *miacids* took advantage of the extinction of the dinosaurs, and started to rapidly expand their territory and evolve into a wide variety of new and very different animals. About 55 million years ago, these new creatures grew into what scientists now classify as a new mammal order: Carnivora. The name means "meat-eating," but they were actually omnivorous—they ate all sorts of foods, including meat, fish, insects, and fruit. They got the "meat-eating" name because they were developing characteristics that were making them into better and better killers—like longer, stronger, and sharper claws and teeth.

Around 40 million years ago, Carnivora split into two distinct lines, Feliforma, or "cat-like," and Caniforma, or "dog-like." All modern cats (as well as many related animals, including hyenas and meerkats) are descendants of those first Feliforms, and they all share many common characteristics, such as short snouts and, in most cases, retractable claws. All modern dogs (as well as several related animals like badgers and raccoons) descended from those first Caniforms, and they share their own characteristics, including long snouts and, in most cases, nonretractable claws.

Then, about 20 million years ago, a new type of creature split away from the Caniforms to produce its own family, with its own unique characteristics. These would become bears.

BEAR NUMBER ONE

Paleontologists say the first true bear was *Ursavus elmensis*, which appeared about 16 million years ago in what is now Europe. *Ursavus elmensis* was the size of a small dog, and it still kind of looked like a dog. But it had also already developed some the characteristics common to all bears today, including the thick, stocky body, the shortish legs, the short tail, and the bear style of walking.

Bug rule of thumb: If an insect has wings, it's an adult.

Another interesting characteristic of bears: While dogs and cats went on to become true carnivores, meaning they eat almost nothing but meat, bears remained omnivores—with plant-based food making up a large portion of their diets.

Several million more years passed, during which *Ursavus elmensis* spawned more new bear species that spread all over Europe and Asia. Some later went extinct, but eight still survive today: the giant panda, the spectacled bear, the sloth bear, the Malayan sun bear, the Asiatic black bear, the American black bear, the brown bear, and the polar bear.

And some of them became world travelers.

COMING TO AMERICA

Fossil evidence shows that over millions of years, bears migrated from Asia to North America via the land bridges that periodically appeared between the two continents as sea levels rose and fell with the comings and goings of ice ages. The first bear to make it over was the short-faced bear, which arrived about 15 million years ago. It evolved into several different species that spread all over North America and into South America. (The most impressive of them was the giant short-faced bear, the largest bear that ever lived, which stood 11 feet tall and weighed up to 3,500 pounds.) All the species of short-faced bears in the Americas went extinct except one: the spectacled bear, which still lives in the mountains of western South America.

The other bear species that made North America home was the American black bear, which arrived around 5 million years ago, the brown bear (200,000 years ago), and the polar bear, an even newer arrival (in the last 150,000 years or so).

HOW TO BE A BEAR

As different as the various bear species are from one another, all bears have some things in common, including...

- Relatively short legs, rounded ears, long snouts, and short tails.
- Broad, flattish molar teeth, which are good for grinding down fibrous plant matter. (This is not true of dogs and cats, which eat almost no plant matter at all. Canines and felines have stout, jagged molars that are especially good for crushing bones.)

Tarantulas are considered a delicacy in Venezuela and Cambodia.

• Broad, flat feet, and the use of *plantigrade locomotion* to get around, meaning that all the bones in their feet touch the ground while walking. (This is as opposed to the *digitigrade* locomotion of dogs and cats.)

• Being primarily *diurnal*, meaning they're naturally active in the daytime, rather than *nocturnal*, or active at night—again, the opposite of most dogs and cats.

THE ELITE EIGHT

Here are the eight bear species that can be found on earth today, and a few of the things that makes each of them unique:

Giant pandas. Known by their distinctive black and white coloring, pandas once inhabited a huge area of eastern Asia, but today can be found only in a few mountainous regions in central China. Males usually reach about 300 pounds on average and, as is true of all bear species, are larger than the females. Pandas are the only bears that are almost exclusively vegetarian: 99 percent of the giant panda's diet is bamboo. They will eat some meat if the situation arises, but since they spend most of their time either sleeping or sitting around eating bamboo, the situation doesn't arise very often. Bear experts say that both of these odd characteristics—the diet and the sedentary lifestyle—came about simply because of the conditions in their habitat: mainly the abundance of bamboo, and the absence of predators. (Bonus: Pandas need huge jaw muscles to grind up bamboo, which is where they get their distinctive round faces.)

Polar bears. On the opposite end of the dietary scale from pandas, polar bears are the only bears that are nearly 100 percent carnivorous. Their diet consists almost exclusively of ringed seals, the smallest and most common seals in the Arctic. Polar bears inhabit a circle of territory around the entire Arctic region, and the theory of how they became the unique Arctic bears they are—and when that happened—is fascinating. The idea is that some brown bears in the far northeast of Asia became isolated by expanding glaciers, and found themselves stuck in the icy, cold, nearly plantless world of the Arctic. But instead of dying out, they went through an incredibly rapid set of evolutionary changes in color, body size and shape, fur characteristics, diet, and more—all of which allowed them not only to adapt to this strange new environment but to thrive. This transformation took place just 150,000 years ago, a blink of the eye in evolutionary terms.

Sloth bears. Found in southern Asia, primarily India, these bears are pretty small, averaging about 200 pounds, and have their own distinctive look: skinny torsos; long, messy black coats that are longer around their shoulders; and whitish snouts. Their mouths—with no upper incisors, a hollowed-out upper palate, and a protruding lower lip—are specially adapted to forming a vacuum with their mouths to suck up termites, their favorite food. (They can be heard "hoovering" up the insects from hundreds of yards away.) Their diet consists primarily of termites, but also includes honey, fruit, yams, leaves, and occasionally meat. They have the longest tails of all bears, at about seven inches long.

Sun bears. Found from Bangladesh to Southeast Asia, including on the islands of Sumatra and Borneo, this is the smallest of all bears; the largest males tip the scales at about 150 pounds. They have very short, sleek, and dark brown fur, except for an orange-yellow U-shaped mark on their upper chest, which is said to resemble a rising or setting sun, and which is the source of their name. They eat mostly fruit and insects, but will eat most anything if they are hungry enough. They are also excellent climbers, and spend most of their time in trees, on nestlike platforms they make from broken-off branches and leaves. They spend days on end on these platforms, just eating and sleeping.

Spectacled bears. These descendants of the short-faced bears live in the Andes of South America. They're black, with beige markings on their chests, and also on their faces—often in a way that makes them look as if they're wearing glasses, hence their name. They weigh about 340 pounds on average and their diet includes fruit, nuts, honey, berries, corn, and cactus flowers (a particular favorite that they have to climb cactuses to reach). They eat some meat, most often in the form of rabbits, rodents, birds, and occasionally llamas. Like sun bears, spectacled bears spend a lot of time on platforms they construct in trees.

American black bear. Found throughout Canada (except on Prince Edward Island), in 32 American states, and in far northern

Frogs eat their skin after they shed it.

Mexico, this is the most common bear in the world. Males can reach about 550 pounds. Even though they're called black bears, their color ranges from shades of blond to brown to dark black. Their diet consists primarily of grasses, roots, berries, and insects, but they are the most opportunistic of all the bears, and they'll eat just about anything—including a lot of the stuff you put in your trash. They also eat fish and mammals, especially young deer and moose.

Asiatic black bear. Also known as the "moon bear," these bears are a bit smaller than American black bears, and have black fur, except for a white V-shaped patch on their chests. They are found in Iran, Afghanistan, Pakistan, northern India, Nepal, Myanmar, throughout most of Southeast Asia, up to northern China and far eastern Russia, North and South Korea, Japan, and Taiwan. Like spectacled and sun bears, they spend a lot of time on tree platforms. Their diets are similar to the American black bear's, but with more meat on the menu, including monkeys, wild boars, and even the occasional water buffalo.

Brown bear. Found in northern Europe, all across northern Asia, throughout Alaska, through all of western Canada, and across some of the northern United States, these are what we regularly call grizzly bears. They range from cream-colored to black, and are easily distinguished by their massive heads and their prominent shoulder humps (a sign of the well-developed muscles they use for digging and turning over rocks). They average about 1,000 pounds, but some have weighed in at more than 2,000 pounds. They are the absolute top of the terrestrial food chain wherever they live, and will hunt and kill deer, elk, musk oxen, moose, salmon, and even bison. Their fearsome reputations aside, depending on their location and the time of year, up to 90 percent of the brown bear's diet is plant-based, and includes huge amounts of berries, roots, and mushrooms.

Bear right…to page 381…for more fascinating facts about bears.

LEAVE IT TO MOM

Does your stuff need cleaning, fixing, or general spiffing up? Mother Nature offers these household hints.

VINEGAR. You can throw away all those chemicals under the sink because vinegar is a miracle cure for many household dilemmas. Undiluted vinegar cleans chrome and porcelain, disinfects the toilet bowl, and kills mildew. It can remove grease, candle wax, bad smells, and bumper stickers. Mixed with water, it can get stains off of aluminum pans. You can use it to control dandruff, soothe a bruise or sore throat, and take the sting out of a sunburn. Bugs and weeds both hate it, too.

WALNUTS. Get rid of scratches on dark furniture by rubbing them with a piece of walnut meat and then polishing as usual. The scratches will almost completely disappear. (Another hint for furniture: Toothpaste, rubbed in, will remove white rings made by wet or hot glasses or mugs.)

TEA. It's not just for drinking anymore. Tea can be used as conditioner for your hair or for a refreshing (and odor-killing) foot bath. Rub a damp teabag over your face for a free skin toner. The next time you get a flu shot or your child gets a booster shot, lay a wet tea bag over the injection site—the tannic acid helps to relieve soreness.

SALT. Remove a fresh grease stain by covering it with salt—let the stain dry and then brush away the salt. Salt also makes an excellent scrub, both for dirty dishes and dirty skin. Use a pinch of salt as a temporary toothpaste substitute, or mix it with water and gargle with it. Salt is a great deodorizer for smelly sneakers and garbage disposals. It will also kill those irritating weeds that grow through your patio.

LEMONS. There's a reason so many commercial cleaners smell like lemons: It's a great natural deodorizer. You can use lemon juice to pretreat rust-stained clothing before washing, or mix lemon juice with an equal amount of water and scrub perspiration stains away. And when you've used up the lemons themselves, try burning lemon peels in the fireplace to eliminate bad smells around the house.

BAKING SODA. Fishermen and fisherwomen take note: Cleaning your hands is easy with a couple of teaspoons of baking soda and plain old water. Just wet your hands, rub in the dry stuff for a minute, rinse, and the fishy smell should be gone. This trick works well with cutting boards, too, especially if you add a little salt to the mix.

APPLES. If your almost-new bag of brown sugar has gotten hard as a rock, soften it by putting a slice of apple in the bag or container with the brown sugar. In a day or so, you should be able to use the sugar again.

ASPIRIN. Got pimples? Get rid of them by crushing an aspirin, mixing in a little water, and applying the paste. Wait a few minutes, wash it off, and repeat if necessary. The aspirin will take away the pain that can accompany pimples and help dry them up.

SHAVING CREAM. If you don't have this stuff around, you'll want to go get some. Work it in the carpet to banish a stain (test it on a hidden spot first to make sure the color isn't affected). When redoing a room, use a little spritz of shaving cream to remove latex paint and soften your hands. Tuck it in your camping supplies, too, because it cleans hands without water.

CHALK. Don't throw out those little nubs of chalk left over after a craft project. Instead, tie them in the bottom of a pantyhose leg and hang it in a closet to help eliminate dampness. Or put a small piece in your jewelry box or silver chest to prevent tarnish.

CLEAR NAIL POLISH. Use clear nail polish to coat the undersides of aerosol cans to prevent rust rings. Dab a little on the front of buttons to keep the thread from fraying. Slap a coat around a loose screw, reinsert, and tighten for a new fit.

...can split into two cells in about 20 minutes.

WHAT'S THE WORD, BIRD?

In some cases, the origins of bird names can be self-explanatory—a yellow-rumped warbler, for example, is named for its warbling song and…well…its yellow rump. But what about the less-obvious species names that we take for granted?

• Early settlers in North America simply called the **cardinal** a "redbird." When it was later classified by naturalists, it was dubbed "cardinal" in reference to the high-ranking officials of the Catholic church who traditionally wore bright red vestments.

• The **cormorant**, a sleek, black marine bird that looks a little like a cross between a crow and a small pterodactyl, got its name from a corruption of the Latin *corvus marinus*, literally, "raven of the sea." Its scientific family name is *Phalacrocoracidae*, from a Greek—and much less poetic—term that translates to "bald raven."

• The **flamingo** was originally called *flamenco* by Spanish explorers. The word comes from the Latin *flamma*, meaning "flame," in reference to the bird's hot-pink coloring. (The origin of this bird's name is not to be confused with that of the gypsy music known as flamenco, which is a corruption of "Flemish," the once-presumed ethnic origin of gypsies.)

• Which came first, the fruit or the bird? The **kiwi**, a plump flightless bird found exclusively in New Zealand, was named by the Maori in imitation of its shrill cry: *kee-wee, kee-wee*. The kiwi*fruit*, also known as just plain "kiwi," has gone by a variety of names, including macaque peach, Chinese gooseberry, and the (less-appetizing) hairy bush fruit. The berry grows in countries all over the world, but for commercial reasons, New Zealand growers and exporters dubbed them "kiwifruit" because, like the birds, they are fuzzy, round, and brown.

• Henry David Thoreau once described the distinctive call of the **loon** as "demonic laughter." But the word *loon*, in this case, isn't connected to "crazy as a loon" insanity, which derives from "lunatic." The bird's name comes from the Scandinavian word *lom*, meaning "lame," because loons, although excellent swimmers and divers, appear helpless when they move around on land.

• The **ptarmigan**, a member of the grouse family, gets its name from *tarmachan*, a Gaelic word meaning "croaker," after the bird's hoarse cry. In the late 1600s, Scottish naturalist Robert Sibbald added the silent "p" in an article he wrote, under the mistaken impression that the term was Greek in origin.

• The **American robin** was misnamed by European settlers who saw the red breast and assumed the bird was related to the European robin. It's actually a member of the thrush family, though. As for the European robin, the theory goes that a British naturalist, following a trend in giving human names to familiar species, named the sociable little bird the robin (back then a diminutive form of Robert).

• The **swallow** got its name from the Anglo-Saxon *swalewe*, which itself comes from the Old Norse *svala*, meaning "cleft stick," referring to the bird's distinctive forked tail.

* * *

WHY ARE FLAMINGOS PINK?

Surprisingly, they're not always. Young flamingos have gray plumage, and an adult flamingo can be white, orange, red or pink. A flamingo's coloring depends on its habitat and food. Flamingos live at the edge of very salty lagoons (they can even drink salt water, excreting the salt through glands near their beaks) where they feed on brine shrimp and algae. These foods contain a high amount of *carotenoids*, the organic pigments that produce color in plants and animals. The brine shrimp and algae contain high amounts of a particular carotenoid called *canthaxanthin*, which turns things pink and orange. In the past, when zoos didn't know the secret of flamingo coloring, they didn't feed their flamingos the right carotenoids and their captive flamingos were often white.

WEATHER GONE WEIRD

The forecast for tomorrow is "mostly light with a chance of dark toward evening." Now that we've gotten that out of the way, it's time to look at some serious weather.

• Lightning can heat the air around it to temperatures of more than 50,000ºF.

• Even if the sky overhead is clear, lightning from a storm as many as 25 miles away can still strike you. And thunder always comes with lightning; it just might be too far away for you to hear.

• During a "superstorm" in March 1993, more than 44 million acre-feet (an area of volume defined as one acre to the depth of one foot) of snow and rain fell on the East Coast of the United States.

• 90 percent of avalanches happen within 24 hours of a snowstorm. An avalanche can send millions of tons of snow down a hill at speeds of 200 miles per hour.

• One of the worst droughts ever recorded occurred in Sichuan Province in China in 1936. Five million people died and more than 30 million farms were destroyed.

• Although it's rare, large fires can cause thunderstorms if the heat from the fire collides with cool temperatures in the upper atmosphere.

• An unusual phenomenon called a "heat burst" happens when a small downdraft of warm air blows straight from above and replaces the cool air beneath, raising the temperature for just a few minutes. One heat burst in Kimberly, South Africa, boosted the atmospheric temperature 43ºF in just five minutes. Forty minutes later, the temperature had dropped back to normal.

• Temperatures in Oymyakon, Siberia, sometimes dip to an incredible low of -96°F, making it the coldest place on earth. At that temperature, a person's breath freezes in midair and hangs there as a foggy vapor trail.

• If you're at a high enough elevation, it can snow on the equator.

BAD*SS BEASTS

You know all about lions and tigers and rhinos that will charge at you like a locomotive, but prepare yourself for a few tough buggers you may not have heard of before.

ANIMAL: Giant Amazonian centipede

BACKGROUND: Found in northern South America and on some Caribbean islands, this centipede species can grow to 12 inches in length and can be as big around as your thumb. Like all centipedes, they have on their first body segment a modified pair of claws called *forcipules*...through which they can deliver a potent venom. Most centipedes use that venom to kill insects, but the giant Amazonian centipede takes it to another level—it will capture, envenomate, kill, and eat insects, lizards, frogs, and even mice.

BAD*SS! If that isn't enough, the giant Amazonian centipede has another favorite prey. If it comes across a suitable cave, it will crawl up the walls to the ceiling, attach itself there with its strong rear legs, and let its body hang down. Why? So it can catch passing bats...which it will then kill and eat.

ANIMAL: Shocking pink dragon millipede

BACKGROUND: Just over an inch long, covered in tiny spikes, and bright pink in color, the shocking pink dragon millipede was discovered in 2007 in Thailand.

BAD*SS! The scientists who discovered these millipedes said they spend most of their time foraging for decaying matter (millipedes, unlike centipedes, are not carnivores) right on top of leaf litter, where their bright pink color makes them very easy to spot. This is odd behavior for millipedes, which are usually found under rocks, fallen logs, leaves, and the like because they're a common food for a wide variety of predators. But the shocking pink dragon millipede doesn't care about that because, if something comes along and tries to eat it, it will activate special glands in its body, produce some cyanide gas, and shoot the gas right out of its mouth at the predator. Whatever predator made the mistake of messing with the millipede will be quickly on its way, and the millipede will go

Rats can tread water for up to three days.

back to its shocking pink business. (Bonus: Shocking pink dragon millipedes smell like almonds. That's because of the cyanide, which occurs naturally in almonds and gives them their distinctive odor.)

ANIMAL: Gaur
BACKGROUND: Gaurs (rhymes with "powers") are enormous, the largest of all wild cattle. Found in India and Southeast Asia, the biggest of the bunch have weighed in at more than 3,000 pounds, reached 10 feet in length, and stood more than seven feet tall at the shoulder. Their smaller young are commonly taken by a number of predators, but the only animals that have been known to kill adult gaurs are especially large saltwater crocodiles and tigers.
BAD*SS! Tigers are arguably nature's most ferocious terrestrial killing machines, but that doesn't mean they always succeed when attacking guars. There have been numerous reports of tigers going after gaurs and being killed themselves, usually as victims of the gaur's long and very sharp horns. In one exceptional case, rangers in Nagarahole National Park in southern India came across the carcass of a large adult male tiger. An examination of hoofprints and other signs in the area told them the tiger had been in what the rangers called a "prolonged" battle with a gaur, during which the gaur repeatedly gored the tiger, trampled it with its hooves, and, for good measure, picked it up and slammed it into a tree several times (possibly even after it was dead).

ANIMAL: Honey badger
BACKGROUND: A relative of the American badger, the honey badger makes its home in Africa, the Middle East, and India. It's a solitary creature, spending several hours of the day and night roaming the area around its burrow searching for food. It will eat almost anything, including fruit, vegetables, carrion, rodents, eggs, lizards, frogs, and snakes.
BAD*SS! Honey badgers especially like to eat snakes—and not just any old snakes. If one comes across the scent of even a highly venomous snake like a king cobra or puff adder, it will track it relentlessly, and upon finding it will attack it without hesitation. If a deadly snake bites the honey badger, the animal will continue

The faster a kangaroo hops, the less energy it burns.

to fight the snake. Biologists still can't explain it, but honey badgers appear to be immune to snake venom. From *National Geographic* magazine:

> One night we saw a young male [honey badger] collapse. He'd been struck in the face by a puff adder just before he bit its head off. We expected that he would die. But after two hours he woke up, groggily finished his meal, and later trotted off into the sunrise.

Honey badgers have also been known to stand up to—and scare off—jackals, hyenas, leopards, and even lions. And if a honey badger comes across a turtle or tortoise, it will eat it, shell and all. (Oh yeah, they like honey, too.)

ANIMAL: Blue sea slug

BACKGROUND: This species of small sea slug can be found floating on the surface of temperate and tropical oceans all over the planet. Their bodies—two to three inches long, pale, and dark blue in color—have several dark, spiky "fingers" growing out of them. To tell the story of this sea slug, we first have to tell the story of another nasty oceanic creature: the bluebottle jellyfish. A bluebottle's body is several times larger than that of a blue sea slug, and its venom-carrying tentacles can reach 30 feet in length. Contact with the tentacles causes severe pain in humans (but only rarely sickness and death). Bluebottles use that venom to paralyze their prey, usually fish.

BAD*SS! Blue sea slugs eat bluebottle jellyfish—venomous tentacles and all. Not only are they completely impervious to bluebottle venom, blue sea slugs somehow select the most potent venom they find on a bluebottle victim's tentacles—and save it in sacs on the tips of their aforementioned spikelike fingers. This way, they can use the venom they stole from a bluebottle against future predators or prey. Not only that, but because blue sea slugs manage to concentrate the most venomous venom from bluebottles they eat, they're actually *more* venomous than bluebottles.

About 11 percent of the earth's surface is used to grow food.

STAY-AT-HOME DADS

It's pretty well known that male sea horses deliver that species' babies, but there are some other exceptions to the "love 'em and leave 'em" rule most male animals live by.

• The male giant water bug has a toxic bite—but he doesn't use it on his babies. His mate cements about 150 eggs to his back, and then he lugs them around for three weeks until they hatch. Dad also does push-ups in the water several times a day to aerate the water and make sure the eggs get the oxygen they need.

• In addition to handling a harem of up to 12 females, the male rhea—a South American flightless bird that resembles an ostrich—raises the chicks. After he builds a nest, Mom lays the eggs, and Dad sits on the nest to incubate and defend the eggs while she moves on to mate with other males. A male rhea will hatch up to 60 chicks, protect them from predators, and teach them the skills they need to survive.

• The female Australian marsupial frog lays her eggs on the ground, and when the tadpoles hatch, they climb up their father's body and wriggle into pouches (called "hip-pockets") on either side of his groin. He then carries them for 10 weeks until they're fully developed.

• After a hardhead catfish fertilizes a female's eggs, he pops up to 50 of them in his mouth—but instead of eating them, he lets them hatch and mature in there. The process takes two months, and during that time, the male catfish doesn't eat *anything*.

• Newborn marmosets are big, usually a pair of twins weighing almost a quarter of their mother's weight. (That's like a 120-pound human mother giving birth to 30 pounds of kids.) Dad takes over within 24 hours of the birth, protecting them, grooming them, and carrying them through the trees. He returns them to their mother only for feeding.

• When wolf cubs are young, Mom stays with them while Dad goes looking—sometimes as far as 20 miles away—for food. He

Genetic studies show that fungi are more closely related to animals than to plants.

chews the meat and vomits it up for his pups until they're old enough to chew it themselves. And when he's not hunting, Dad plays with his brood, bringing them bones or pieces of hide while teaching them to hunt and how to be part of a pack.

• When a red fox female is nursing her pups, the male brings fresh food to her four to six times a day. He helps raise the pups, too, teaching them how to sniff out food and how to defend themselves.

• A burying beetle lives on the corpses of other insects and small animals, so the male first finds a carcass to attract a mate. Then he and Mom prepare the carcass, bury it, and use it to feed their little larvae. (They do kill some of the larvae to ensure that they have enough food to raise their young to maturity, but they try to feed as many as they can.) If something happens to Mom, Dad keeps feeding the troops until they crawl off on their own.

• The male goby fish isn't as conscientious: After the female lays thousands of eggs under a shell or rock, the male guards them for one to two weeks until they hatch. The catch is that he'll eat the larger eggs that take longer to hatch. With those eggs gone, he can get off guard duty faster and go back to mating—an occupation he seems to prefer.

• A male pipefish has a built-in pouch to carry eggs that are deposited by a female. He nourishes his eggs with resources from his own body, but—oops!—sometimes he absorbs the eggs as food. Turns out that male pipefish prefer their mates on the large side and will eat some of the eggs if the mother was small. When they meet a big female pipefish, they'll carry all the little ones safely to term.

To read about animal moms, turn to page 64.

* * *

FLIPPER THE BIRD?

The squeaky, chattery "voice" of the dolphin on the television series *Flipper* (1964–67) wasn't a dolphin: It was the doctored song of the Australian kookaburra.

HAPPY ARBOR DAY

For Christmas, millions of people cut down trees. For Arbor Day, they plant them. Here's the story of an original American holiday.

A TREE-MENDOUS PLAN

After graduating with an agriculture degree from the University of Michigan in 1854, Julius Sterling Morton moved to a small settlement called Nebraska City in what would a few months later be called the Nebraska Territory.

Morton faced a problem shared by many settlers in the territory: It was a treeless plain. That meant no trees for building materials, to burn for fuel, or to use as shade for crops. But Morton was one of the New World's first "tree huggers," stating, "We ought to bequeath to posterity as many forests and orchards as we have exhausted and consumed." So he started bequeathing trees, beginning with his own land. By 1860 Morton boasted a lush orchard of more than 300 trees. A few years later, he had more than 1,000.

TREE-DING BOLDLY

As the orchards grew, so did Morton's influence in Nebraska, which became a state in 1867. Morton was the founder and editor of the *Nebraska City News*, the state's first newspaper, in which he frequently wrote editorials about the benefits, practical and aesthetic, of tree planting. He also organized the Nebraska State Horticultural Society and served on the Nebraska State Board of Agriculture.

While serving on the board, Morton came up with an idea to spread his belief in tree planting statewide (and eventually worldwide). On January 4, 1872, Morton drafted a resolution that April 10 be "set apart and consecrated for the planting of trees in the State of Nebraska, and to urge upon the people of the State the vital importance of tree planting." Morton called the special event Arbor Day (*arbor* is Latin for "tree").

The state legislature agreed and on April 10, 1872, the first unofficial Arbor Day was celebrated throughout Nebraska. Prizes were awarded to counties, cities, and individuals who planted the largest number of trees. That day, an astounding one million trees took root in Nebraska—an average of more than six for every man, woman, and child in the state. By 1885, Nebraska had planted more than 700,000 acres of trees, earning it the nickname "the Tree Planters' State."

Arbor Day became a legal civic holiday in the state in 1885. It was held on April 22—Julius Morton's birthday. In addition to a parade in Nebraska City, Morton introduced what has since become a long-standing Arbor Day tradition: Schoolchildren went outside and planted trees together. Morton left Nebraska in 1893 when he was appointed secretary of agriculture by President Grover Cleveland.

HAPP-TREE HOLIDAYS

In 1970, nearly a century after Arbor Day was first celebrated, President Richard Nixon declared the last Friday of every April to be observed as National Arbor Day. The day often coincides nicely with Earth Day, which is held every April 22.

All 50 states recognize the April observance, although many hold an additional state Arbor Day in a month more suited to local tree planting. For example, Florida and Louisiana have theirs in January, Hawaii's is in November, and South Carolina's is in December. Countries the world over, including Australia, Brazil, China, Iceland, Japan, Scotland, and Yemen, also observe civic tree-planting days.

Today, tree-planting events are organized and promoted by the National Arbor Day Foundation, which was created in 1972. In addition to increasing the number of thriving trees in the United States, it saves older trees around the world with its charity, Rain Forest Rescue. To date, the foundation has saved more than two billion square feet of rain forest in North, South, and Central America.

Morton nicely summed up the unique nature of his creation: "Arbor Day is not like other holidays. Each of those reposes on the past, while Arbor Day proposes for the future."

The red varnish used on many violins is sap from the dragon blood tree.

HOME, STRANGE HOME, PART II

Who wouldn't want to live among toxic chemicals or in a pile of dung? Here we introduce more odd abodes and the animals that inhabit them. (Part I appears on page 54.)

HORRIBLE LIVING CONDITIONS?

Who'd want to live in a place filled with toxic chemicals and total darkness? Giant tube worms, that's who. At the bottom of the ocean there are breaks, or "fissures," in the earth's surface where hydrothermal vents can be found. From these vents, molten rock bubbles up from inside the earth and emerges onto the dark ocean floor, creating smoke and boiling ocean water that's filled with dissolved minerals and chemicals. The mix is so toxic that scientists thought no creature could survive near it…until they found thriving colonies of giant tube worms. These worms are about eight feet long and attached to the ocean floor. They have white tubular bodies, with red tips filled with blood. Inside the worms' bodies are bacteria that convert the hydrothermal vents' chemicals into food. The toxic soup is so essential to them that if a geothermal change causes the vents to disappear, the tube worms die.

THIS QUEEN HAS A CASTLE

In parts of Africa termite mounds can reach 30 feet high. While the queen busily produces eggs, worker termites mix mud, saliva, and dung to form a cementlike substance that they use to build soaring towers. Some towers house indoor fungus gardens that provide food, others are nurseries for the young, and of course there's a royal chamber for the queen. If termites were the size of humans and the mounds were enlarged to scale, they'd be taller than the Empire State Building.

SAFETY IN A DANGEROUS NEIGHBORHOOD

Ovenbirds get their name from their nests, which are built with a domed top that looks like a Dutch oven. The songbirds build their "ovens" on North American forest floors, and because the nests are on the ground, marauding chipmunks often make off with the eggs. So before it chooses a nesting site, the bird becomes a spy. It eavesdrops on chipmunk calls to determine where the chipmunks' homes are. Then the ovenbird builds its own nest as far away as possible.

THAT JUST STINKS!

In Sri Lanka, an elephant researcher has found three types of frogs that live in elephant dung. No one knows why the frogs do this, but there are some guesses: Dung piles are also home to beetles, ants, spiders, and other insects, so it could be an easy way for the frogs to get a quick meal without much effort. Elephant feces also provides moisture in a dry area. Finally, the dung provides shelter—even if it's stinky—in an area where there's not much leaf litter that a frog might normally call home.

HOME INVASION

Prairie dogs build underground burrows that can run for miles in all directions. They're well constructed with mounds of dirt at the entrances for sentries to use to watch for danger. The homes also have underground chambers for sleeping, nurseries for the babies, and even bathrooms for waste. A black-footed ferret, on the other hand, doesn't build anything. Instead, it invades the burrow of a prairie dog, kills the original inhabitants, and moves its own family in. Taking over all those nice underground rooms, black-footed ferrets eat, sleep, raise their young, and spend most of their time underground…except at night when they're hunting prairie dogs.

* * *

TWO PROVERBS ABOUT GRASS

- "Customers are jade; merchandise is grass." (Chinese)
- "When you have a good government, the grass will grow over your troubles." (Japanese)

The world's only known koala bear twins were born in 1999.

RANDOM ORIGINS

A few origin stories of things you're probably familiar with.

THE HAVAHART LIVE TRAP

In the 1930s the Allcock Manufacturing Company in Ossining, New York, made laxative pills. But when World War II came along, everything changed—even laxative pill makers—and Allcock started manufacturing bullet casings and aircraft fuel tanks. That twist of fate met another: One of Allcock's employees was German-born inventor Rupert Merkle, who had an idea for a animal trap that captured animals without harming them. (One of his earlier inventions was a pair of inflatable boots used to walk on water, which he had tried out, unsuccessfully, on San Francisco Bay.) Merkle knew Allcock had large amounts of metal on hand, and he showed company owner Fox Brandreth Conner his idea: a box-shaped trap with wire mesh sides and bottom, a sheet-metal top, and two sheet-metal doors that were held open at either end of the trap. When an animal was enticed into the trap with bait and stepped on a small trip-platform, the doors fell closed, and sturdy wire clips fell with them, locking them in place—and locking the animal in the trap. Brandreth loved it, and he and Merkle came up with the name "Havahart," for "have a heart." The traps were so popular that by the late 1940s they were all Allcock sold, and today Havahart traps are by far the most popular live animal trap in the world. (Today they come in many sizes, from small ones to catch mice, to large ones to catch mountain lions.)

THE FISH FINDER

In the early 1950s, fisherman Carl Lowrance of Joplin, Missouri, had an idea: What if someone developed a small, portable sonar device that could help fishermen like himself locate small schools of fish in lakes? Commercial marine fisheries were already using sonar by this time, but the devices they used were huge and delicate, and they could detect only very large schools of fish—no help to the average fisherman on a relatively small lake. Lowrance, without any experience in the field (he owned a banana distribution business), decided to invent the thing himself. Carl's sons Arlen and Darrell were enlisted to help, and the Lowrances quickly became convinced they could use emerging transistor technology to make a small, sturdy, and fairly precise sonar unit. After a few years of trial and error, they did it: In 1957 they sold their very first "Fish Lo-K-Tor," an underwater sonar unit about the size of a fisherman's tackle box. Turn it on, and it would tell you how deep the water was beneath you and would indicate if you were over even a pretty small fish school. Improvements were made over the years, and before long the "Little Green Box," as it became known (because the unit came in a metal box painted in a green design), was a hit. By the 1980s, more than a million had sold, and "fish finders," as fish-locating sonar units are commonly called today, are now standard equipment for serious fishermen all over the world. (And Lowrance Marine Electronics still makes them.)

ANTIVENIN

In the 1890s French doctor and scientist Albert Calmette made a medical discovery based in part on Louis Pasteur's then-recent breakthroughs in vaccination. First, Calmette showed that vaccination applied to snake venom: if an animal is given diluted doses of snake venom, it will produce antibodies to fight that venom and thereby become immune to it. That's straightforward vaccination science—but Calmette went one step further. He showed that the antibodies produced in a vaccinated animal could be harvested (via the animal's blood) and then used to save another animal that had *not* been vaccinated, but had been bitten by that same kind of snake. And it applied to nonvaccinated humans who had been bitten, too. Calmette had invented *antivenin*. In the years since, antivenins to treat the bites of many different venomous creatures (each one requires its own specific antivenin) have been developed, including several venomous snake, spider, scorpion, and even tick species, and more are being developed all the time. They have saved the lives of tens of thousands of bite victims. And the process Calmette came up with is basically the same one used to make antivenins today: Animals, primarily horses, but also sheep, goats, and rabbits, are vaccinated with venom, and the antibodies they create are taken from their blood and saved, waiting for the next victim. (Hey...what's that by your foot?)

Tongue-twisting trivia: Saw-scaled snakes make a sizzling sound.

IT'S NOT A MOUSE

Nine out of ten dentists surveyed said 95 percent of people would call almost any small, furry, scampering creature they came across a "mouse." But in a majority of those cases, they'd be 100 percent wrong!

BACKGROUND

The small, gnawing rodent most of us think of as a mouse is a "house mouse," better known to scientists as *Mus musculus*, and by far the most common mouse species in North America (and most of the world). But there are a bunch of other critters out there that are very mouselike in appearance: They have small bodies carried very low to the ground, their movements are quick and scampery, and they have pointed snouts adorned with prominent whiskers. So you can see why someone untrained in *Mus musculus* specifics might mistakenly call one of those creatures a "mouse." The next time you're out in the garden or cleaning up behind the shed—take this handy "not-a-mouse guide" with you so you can properly identify your squeaky little friends.

MOUSE MIMIC: Vole

INFO: Voles are small rodents found in 23 species over much of North America. They grow from three to five inches long (not counting the tail), range from gray to dark brown, and look a lot like mice. The easiest way to tell them from mice: they have small, fur-covered ears, as opposed to the large, bald ears of mice. They also have fur-covered tails, as opposed to the mouse's bald tail, and smaller, beadier eyes. And they're herbivores, eating only plants, whereas omnivorous mice will eat almost anything. Voles don't like to be out in the open, so the most likely place to come across them is under dense leaf litter or in thick grass, where they forage for their plant-based foods.

MOUSE MIMIC: Shrew

INFO: Shrews are found in more than 30 species over much of North America, and are a bit smaller than voles, growing from two to six inches in length. They are also very mouselike in

A dragonfly nymph can live underwater for more than five years before becoming an adult.

appearance, but are actually only distantly related to mice—and they're not even rodents. The best way to tell if you've found a shrew is by its nose: shrews have very elongated and pointed noses, much more so than mice or voles. After that, look for the ears—in all shrew species they're small, and in many they're so small that you can't even see them. They also have extremely tiny eyes and short, fur-covered tails. Another big difference: shrews have sharp, pointed teeth, rather than the "buck teeth" incisors of rodents. That's because shrews are insectivores, and although they eat some plants foods, their diet is made up of primarily of insects, worms, snails, grubs, amphibians, small voles, mice, and even other shrews. Most shrews prefer to be underground, and, like voles, are most often seen under litter or in thick grass.

MOUSE MIMIC: Mole

INFO: Seven species of moles are found in the United States and Canada. Like shrews, they are not part of the rodent family, and they are unique little creatures. The first thing to look for when trying to identify a mole is their eyes—because you won't find them, or you'll have a hard time trying. Moles have extremely tiny eyes mostly hidden by fur, and they are nearly blind, relying on their sensitive noses to get around. The next thing to look for is their characteristic front feet: they have long and very stout claws, and the feet themselves stick out from their bodies like little clawed paddles. They also have cylindrical, tube-shaped bodies, flexible noses, and short tails. Moles spend virtually all their time underground, hunting for grubs, worms, and insects, and the most common way to come across them is while digging in your garden.

MOUSE MIMIC: Pocket gopher

INFO: Many of us "know" gophers from the 1980 film *Caddyshack*, and therefore "know" that gophers are relatively large, robotlike, and surprisingly witty rodents. But believe it or not, they're not really like that at all. Pocket gophers, known as the "true gophers," come in many species, and range from about 5 to 14 inches in length. The smaller one, especially can seem very mouselike. What to look for: Gophers have stockier bodies than mice, voles, and shrews, their noses are less pointed, and their two top incisors are exposed and easy to see. Also, they have expandable cheek pockets

In ancient Greece, killing a dolphin was punishable by death.

that are often stuffed with food. (Those are the "pockets" for which pocket gophers are named.) Pocket gophers are herbivores and are, of course, fantastic burrowers, leaving mounds of dirt outside the many entrances to their deep and extensive burrows. The most likely place to see them and their dirt mounds: in our lawns and gardens. (Grrrr.)

MOUSE MIMIC: Kangaroo mouse (and rat)

INFO: There are two species of kangaroo mice and 19 species of kangaroo rats, all of them found in desert regions of the American West. Their names aside, they are not true mice or rats. At first glance, they look the same: They have mouselike bodies, ranging from 2½ to 6 inches in length; long tails; big ears; and big, round eyes. But look closer: They also have short, stumpy front legs and very large hind legs and hind feet. And they're bipedal, getting around by hopping on their hind feet—just like kangaroos. They also have cheek pockets that they use to hold food, just like gophers. Kangaroo mice and rats live mostly on grass seeds, and occasionally eat insects and carrion, and you're only likely to see them if you enjoy hiking in the desert.

MOUSE MIMIC: Pika

INFO: You'll find these guys only at high elevations—between 8,000 and 13,000 feet—in the American and Canadian West. Scampering across the rocky terrain, they really can look like mice or rats. Pikas grow from 5 to 12 inches long, and have mouselike bodies and large, round ears. But if you look closer, they kind of look like rabbits. Pikas tend to sit hunched up like rabbits, they have no visible tail, and they have somewhat broad, rabbitlike noses. That's because pikas, as mousy as they may seem, are actually part of the rabbit family, and are closely related to rabbits and hares. If you're ever hiking at high altitudes out West, look for pika "haystacks": pikas spend the summers gathering grasses and other vegetation into large piles out in the open. When it dries out, they carry it into their dens to use as bedding and food to get them through the long mountain winters.

The word "squash" comes from the Native American word *askutasquash*...

SCRABBLE ANIMALS

A few words you might want to use during your next game of Scrabble.

AI (Brazilian sloth species)

ADDAX (Saharan antelope)

AGOUTI (burrowing rodent found in the Americas)

BANTENG (Asian wild cattle)

BHARAL (Tibetan wild goat)

CHEVROTAIN (deer found in Asia and Africa)

CHUCKWALLA (lizard found in Mexico and Southwest U.S.)

COYPU (South American rodent)

DEGU (South American rodent)

DOWITCHER (wading birds)

EYAS (falcon chick)

FOSSA (Madagascan mammal)

GERENUK (African antelope)

GRIVET (African monkey)

HYRAX (mammal found in Africa and Asia)

JACANA (wading bird found in many parts of the world)

JUNCO (North American bird)

KAKA (New Zealand parrot)

LECHWE (African antelope)

LEVERET (a young hare)

NILGAI (Asian antelope)

NYALA (African antelope)

ORYX (African antelope)

OUZEL (European blackbird)

PACA (South American rodent)

QUELEA (African weaverbird)

QUOKKA (Australian kangaroo-like marsupial)

QUOLL (Australian marsupial)

RORQUAL (type of whale)

SKUA (seabird)

SORA (North American marsh bird)

TRAGOPAN (Asian pheasant)

TROGON (bird found in tropics worldwide)

UNAU (Sloth of Central and South America)

VISCACHA (South American rodent)

WIDGEON (Eurasian duck)

YABBY (Australian crayfish)

ZOOPHILE (someone who loves animals)

BIRTHWRONG

On page 97, we brought you the stories of some odd and obsolete scientific theories about our often confounding world. Here are a few more...this time concerning how babies are made.

SUNSHINE OF MY LOVE. The ancient Greek mathematician and philosopher Pythagoras (570–495 BC) is known for formulating one of the earliest recorded theories on human reproduction that included the idea of a human "egg." Remember: Human egg cells couldn't be seen before microscopes were invented, but lots of animals, including birds and turtles, laid large eggs, so the idea of humans also coming from eggs wasn't that farfetched. And how did Pythagoras think an egg was activated, so to speak? He believed that during sex (or even without sex, but just closeness), something radiated from the brain and nerves of the man into the woman and stimulated an egg into developing. Also, he said that the brain and "higher" parts of the body were formed by the man's radiation; the "lower" parts were formed from the woman via menstrual blood. Pythagoras' egg and radiation theory was very popular in the ancient world.

GENDER BENDER. The ancient Greek physician Hippocrates (460–370 BC), known as the "Father of Medicine," put forth the idea that no egg was involved at all, but rather that embryos were created as a mixture of semen—both Dad's *and* Mom's—inside the uterus. More than that, he believed that if both parents contribute *strong* semen—spiritually speaking—during sex, the resulting child will be male. If both contribute *weak* semen, it will be female. If they each provide semen of different strengths, whichever parent provides the stronger batch wins the baby gender battle.

ORIGINAL CHEESEHEADS. The ancient Greek scholar Aristotle (384–322 BC) also believed that no egg was involved, but he had a different view about conception. He believed that a man's semen carried *pneuma*, a Greek word meaning "soul." During sex, he said, this magical liquid made its way to the woman's uterus, where it caused the woman's menstrual blood to coagulate—like "milk into cheese," he said—forming an embryo. The embryo then went through several "soul" stages until it finally became a little human and was born. Aristotle had such an enormous influence on the Western world that this was the prevailing theory on human reproduction for the next 2,000 years.

THE EGGISTS. In 1651 the English physician William Harvey proposed that not only birds, turtles, lizards, and other large, egg-laying animals came from eggs, but that *all* animals—even humans—did, too. Harvey was hugely respected by this time (he had been personal physician to English kings for decades), but such an idea had to be squared with the religious doctrine of the era, which still held that all living things were initially created by God. This led to a school of thought known as *ovism* (from *ovum*, Latin for "egg"). It said that every human egg cell held, basically, a whole, if not fully grown, human being inside it—which had been created by God. It simply needed semen to "activate" it into developing fully. Ovism soon became the prevailing theory on human reproduction.

THE SPERMISTS. In 1677, thanks to the development of powerful microscopes, human sperm cells were observed for the first time—tiny heads, lashing tails, and all. This led the Dutch scholar Nicolas Hartsoeker, one of the first sperm cell viewers, to propose that there were actually fully formed tiny humans in the head of every sperm. (That's a copy of one of Hartsoeker's actual drawings—of a tiny man in a sperm cell—on the right.) This led to the birth of a movement known as *spermism* (really). It and ovism remained the foremost theories on human reproductions for another hundred years.

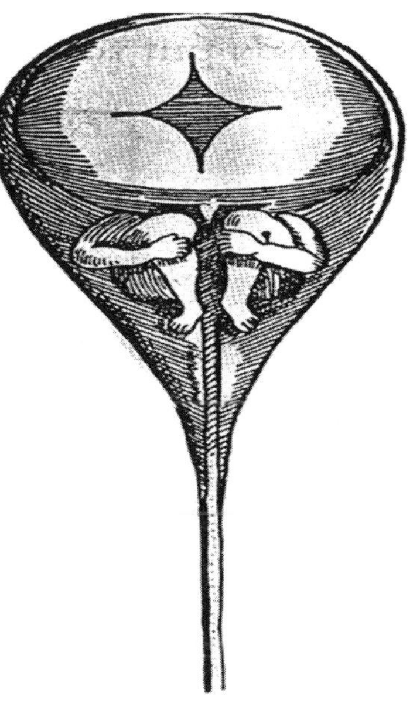

WHEN MEN GAVE BIRTH. In 2008 doctors removed a growth from the brain of a newborn baby boy in Colorado. The growth had two tiny feet and one tiny hand in it. It was the result of a phenomenon known as *fetus in fetu*, in which an undeveloped fetus is absorbed by its twin. We know this *now*, but imagine if you lived in ancient times and found a growth like that—especially in a boy. People thought they were fetuses, and that led to some interesting ideas: One was that the human race used to be a single-sexed race of beings that had babies via virgin birth and that the race split into the two sexes in the distant past. Women ended up with the child-bearing role, but men retained "vestigial birthing equipment" (that's why men have nipples!) that once in a while produced a partially formed fetus—like the one found in the baby boy in Colorado. And this wasn't something that was believed only in ancient times: members of the Theosophical Society, founded by famed occultist Madame Blavatsky in 1875, believed this well into the 20th century.

JUST THINK IT? There weren't just odd theories on the nature of conception—there were also equally odd beliefs about the development of fetuses after conception. In the 1800s, for example, "maternal impression" became a widely respected medical theory. It said that a pregnant woman's thoughts, fears, excitements, and so on could physically affect the child in her womb. From an 1869 article by a doctor in Philadelphia's *Medical & Surgical Reporter*, titled "Maternal Impressions":

> I once had a case in which the child was born with very little cutaneous covering, all raw and in horrible condition, the mother having been frightened by a man coming into her house with a bleeding, lacerated foot and ankle from a wound on the railroad.

And in 1903, the *American Textbook of Obstetrics* even cited maternal impression as the probable cause of the deformities of John Merrick—the "Elephant Man"—the reason being that Merrick's mother likely saw and was frightened by elephants while she was pregnant with him. This bogus theory remained common well into the 1900s, and it wasn't until proper knowledge of genetics came along that it was finally (we hope) discredited.

Highly volcanic areas have some of the most fertile farmland in the world.

ANIMAL ACTS, PART I

Some of us love reading about the private lives of celebrities (admit it!), but what about those movie and TV stars who aren't human?

ARNOLD ZIFFEL. With two PATSY Awards (like the Oscars, but for animal actors) to his credit, and one of the few animal actors important enough to play an animal with an actual last name, Arnold the pig was one of TV's most popular stars in the mid-1960s. To land his role on *Green Acres*, Arnold had to learn to open doors, carry objects, pull a wagon, play the piano, and fetch the mail. He could grunt on command and "deliver newspapers," and got sacks and sacks of fan mail. The first Arnold, a Chester white, came from Mooresville, Indiana. Subsequent Arnolds—and there were several—were Yorkshire pigs.

BENJI. The adorable Benji was a mix of schnauzer, cocker spaniel, and poodle. Those who knew him off-screen called him "Higgins." Adopted from an animal shelter in Burbank, California, in 1960, Higgins's first big-time role was on *Petticoat Junction* from 1963 to 1970. His next big break was the title role in the 1974 film *Benji*. Higgins died the next year, so when the first of the *Benji* sequels went into production in 1977, his daughter, Benjean, took over.

TOTO. Dorothy's male dog in 1939's *The Wizard of Oz* was played by a female Cairn terrier with the unoriginal name "Terry." But that would change, like many things do, with fame. *Oz* was Terry's seventh film (she went on make seven more before she retired), and she was paid $125 a week during filming, which was more than the Munchkins' salaries. The film made her such a star that her owner officially changed her name to Toto. Terry/Toto died in 1945, age 11. Her "autobiography," *I, Toto*, was published in 2001.

SMOKEY THE BEAR. The cartoon bear was based on a real bear that was found as a cub and badly burned after a five-day forest fire in New Mexico in 1950. Smokey was rescued and adopted by the Forest Service and went to live at the National Zoo in Washington, D.C. His name was copyrighted by Congress in 1952 and, from then until his death in 1976, Smokey the Bear earned more than a million dollars for the Forest Service.

BEN. The bear who played Ben in the film and TV versions of *The Life and Times of Grizzly Adams* was actually a female grizzly bear named Bozo who, according to her bio, was discovered working in a circus. She reportedly became so enamored of her costar, Dan Haggerty (who played Grizzly Adams), that her trainers allowed her to work with no restraints at all—including none on her diet. During the first 13 weeks of production, Bozo gained 100 pounds, which makes her the only network star to put on that much weight and still keep her job.

CLARENCE. Originally named Freddie the Freeloader and raised first in a Los Angeles apartment, then at a compound north of the city, Clarence the lion was taught his bag of tricks through "affection training." He first appeared in the 1965 movie *Clarence, the Cross-Eyed Lion. Daktari* the TV show that sprang from the movie, was set in Africa but filmed north of Los Angeles, and featured Clarence as an easygoing big cat who had a fondness for children. (Not to eat them, he just liked them.) The real Clarence did most of the close-ups and all of the action with his costars, both human and chimpanzee. Four other lions doubled for him in situations where Clarence, who really was cross-eyed, couldn't see well enough to perform. Clarence died in 1969 at the age of seven.

FLIPPER. And they say there are no good roles for women in the movies. The dolphin known as "the King of the Sea" was played by a total of six female dolphins. In the two feature films (*Flipper* in 1963 and *Flipper's New Adventure* in 1964), Mitzi the dolphin played Flipper. On the TV show, from 1964 to 1968, Suzy and Kathy (on loan from the Miami Seaquarium) did most of the grunt work, along with occasional appearances by Patty, Scotty, and Squirt. Female dolphins were preferred because they're less aggressive than males (no kidding) and therefore their skin is more likely to be free of scars. The only time a male dolphin was called in was to perform one show-stopping stunt: the tail walk.

For more Animal Acts, turn to page 191.

A dog's shoulder blades are not attached to the rest of its skeleton.

WELCOME TO AMERICA

Twelve thousand years ago, if humans or animals felt like walking from Asia to North America, all they had to do was head over the Bering Land Bridge. (It's a little harder now.)

A MYSTERIOUS, DISAPPEARING BRIDGE

From the edge of Alaska's Seward Peninsula, Siberia is just 53 miles away. And at a point just south of the Arctic Circle, the two continents are separated only by a narrow channel of water that links the Arctic Ocean to the Bering Sea. That channel is called the Bering Strait, and scientists long wondered if primitive people used it to cross from Asia to North America.

But frequent, severe storms and massive ice floes would have made it difficult for primitive people to make their way across the Bering Strait by boat. And so, for centuries, archaeologists speculated that perhaps there had once been a piece of land that stretched across the strait. If so, people could have walked from one continent to the other in less than three days.

The idea first appeared back in 1590, when a Jesuit priest named Jose de Acosta noticed a resemblance between the native people of South America and those of Asia. He was the first to propose that the first people in the Americas had traveled there from Asia—he just didn't know how. In the 1800s, archaeologists expanded that hypothesis, saying that at least some of the indigenous people of North and South America had migrated from Asia to America over the Bering Strait, walking on a bridge of land that was above sea level. They called the theoretical region the Bering Strait Land Bridge, or "Beringia." And unlike many early theories of how the world worked, the land bridge idea has held up against modern scientific examination.

THE WIDEST BRIDGE EVER

Beringia existed during the Pleistocene epoch, which lasted from about 2.5 million years ago to 11,500 years ago. At times during the Pleistocene, the earth was going through ice ages, and its water was frozen in massive glaciers. Since the planet has always had the same amount of water on it, what was trapped in glaciers meant there

A palm tree's long, bare trunk is adapted to survive tsunamis intact.

wasn't as much in the oceans. Water levels during the Pleistocene were about 300 feet lower than they are now, and the Bering Strait is only 165 feet deep at its lowest point. So when there were large glaciers on the continents, the bottom of the Bering Strait was well above sea level, and it connected Alaska to Siberia.

Beringia is called a "land bridge," but it wasn't a narrow path. The ocean around the Bering Strait is so shallow that when water levels fell, they exposed a landmass with a width of about 1,000 miles, almost the distance from San Francisco to Denver.

Russian and American scientists have studied the Bering Strait shoreline and dated *sea cores* (long cylinders of sediment) from the ocean floor. Traces of pollen, plant material, and insects in the cores help them date when Beringia existed as dry land. That happened at various times for more than two million years, and the land bridge stayed above water for thousands of years at a time. During one of the more recent appearances, the land bridge popped up about 30,000 years ago, staying above water for at least 15,000 years. It was during that time that humans living in Siberia had the opportunity to walk over into the Americas.

THOSE RESTLESS BERINGIANS

The sea cores also give clues about what Beringia was like: flat, dry, treeless tundra, where the soil was frozen much of the year. It had little rain, bitterly cold winters, and a thin cover of snow that melted in the cool, dry summers. Since it was too dry to have glaciers (which covered much of North America at the time), Beringia would have seemed like a comparatively good place to live. It was cold and harsh, but it still had grasses, herbs, and shrubs that could support wildlife. Caribou evolved on the land bridge, and woolly mammoths and mastodons grazed there...so did some yaks, musk oxen, bison, deer, rabbits, camels, and horses. Predators followed the grazing animals, and soon saber-toothed tigers, bears, and wolves were also living and drifting between the two continents. And humans would likely have followed the animals.

Research shows that many indigenous peoples in North and South America share DNA, physical characteristics (a similar formation of teeth and jaws), culture, and even language with Siberian natives of northeastern Asia. Instead of a mass migration, though, it's likely that small bands of hunters and their families fol-

There are no known paintings or drawings of giant pandas from before the 20th century.

lowed prey animals from Asia into Beringia and then onto the North American continent. Then when the climate began to change and the water rose, access to Asia disappeared and the people who had crossed the bridge were "stuck" in America.

Or so the scientists believe. Studies of the first humans in the Americas are still ongoing, and so far, only sparse evidence exists about their migrations. There are also some pretty big problems the migrants would have had to overcome. For one thing, when the land bridge was exposed, much of what's now Canada and the United States were covered with glaciers. People would have had trouble actually moving into North and South America. However, there were two ice-free "corridors" that might have provided pathways for migration southward. An inland corridor ran from Alaska along the eastern side of the Canadian Rockies to Montana. And a coastal corridor lay in the Pacific Northwest. When one corridor was iced over, the other was usually open. So most archaeologists believe that the first people in the Americas traveled along the West Coast and continued south, always looking for new opportunities in various parts of the new continents.

THANKS FOR JOE CAMEL

The human mysteries may still be hard for archaeologists to piece together, but they do know that Beringia was important to wildlife. Many animals—including dinosaurs, rabbits, and bears—moved from continent to continent, making each a more diverse place. And when it came to saving wildlife from extinction, Beringia made a big difference. For example, camels, which have adapted so well to the deserts of the Middle East, had forebears that lived in North America. Most of the animals that made their way across Beringia came from Asia to America. But the camels went the other way—from America into Asia and then to the Middle East. In the Americas, camels became extinct. Only the ones that crossed into Asia survived.

Horses also evolved in North America, and they also went extinct on that continent. Had prehistoric horses not crossed the land bridge into Asia and kept traveling until they reached the plains of Mongolia, the animals might never have survived to become human companions.

Only mammals whose males don't have nipples: rats and horses.

YOU'RE *HOW* OLD?

Nothing lasts forever, including earth's plants and animals. On the other hand, there might be a plant capable of breaking that rule…

• **2 days:** The life span of the gall midge (a kind of gnat) after emerging from its nest.

• **14 days:** The average life span of a mosquito, assuming you don't squash him on your arm first.

• **25 days:** Roughly the amount of time an adult housefly could buzz around your house before you found it dead—of natural causes—on the windowsill.

• **18 months:** The life span of a bedbug without a food source. If bedbugs can't readily feed, they go into a state of dormancy for as long a year. With food (like your blood or skin), they live about nine months.

• **4 years:** The life span of a black widow spider in captivity. In the wild, it's one to three years.

• **5 years:** The life span of a pet gerbil, if he or she is especially healthy.

• **16 years:** The record for a chicken's life span—its normal life span is seven to eight years.

• **28 years:** The record life span for the queen of an ant colony. During her lifetime, a queen ant could become the mother of about 32 million baby ants.

• **29 years:** The record age for a dog, although most large breeds live only seven or eight years and smaller breeds generally live into their early teens.

• **30 years:** The approximate age at which scientists believe Tyrannosaurus rex was ready to go to that great Jurassic Park in the sky.

• **40 years:** The life span of a sloth in captivity. (No surprise, really, since he does nothing but take it easy all day.)

• **48 years:** The record age for a cow—in this case, a cow named "Big Bertha" of County Kerry, Ireland.

• **62 years:** The record held by Old Billy, a horse that

pulled barges up and down canals, born in 1760 in England.

• **60–70 years:** The average life span of an elephant. (The record holder lived to be 86.)

• **122 years:** The record human life span, held by France's Jeanne Calment, born in 1875.

• **200 years:** The average life span of a saguaro cactus. (By the way, saguaros don't begin to grow arms until they're somewhere around 50 years old or more).

• **226 years:** The age of the world's oldest koi fish, a female named Hanako, who spent her life swimming in a pond in central Japan.

• **700 years:** The life span of a saw palmetto tree.

• **2,230 years:** The average age of a giant sequoia tree.

• **9,550 years:** The age of a Norway spruce discovered in Sweden.

• **Immortal:** The theoretical life span of the hydra, a genus of simple freshwater animals. Scientists have discovered that the creature is able to renew its own tissues and does not seem to age or die.

* * *

SEAL-YA LATER!

In July 2009 a juvenile sea lion at Newport Harbor in Orange County, California, started acting aggressively, so harbor patrol officers decided it had to be removed. They guided the young sea lion onto their rescue boat, planning to take him out to a rocky island where sea lions regularly hang out. On the way there, the animal jumped into an auxiliary driving seat...and took over control of the boat. It used its flippers to hit the throttle, and turned the wheel back and forth, sending the boat on a lurching course. It even turned the boat's lights on and off. (People watching from shore couldn't tell what the heck was going on.) Finally, the officers got the sea lion out of the seat and went back to the dock. An hour later—having had its fun—the sea lion jumped into the water and swam away.

According to legend, Egypt's first pharaoh, Menes, was killed by a hippo.

THE WORLD'S MOST ELIGIBLE BACHELOR

He's a worldwide icon who's been waiting for his soul mate for about 90 years, during which time he's attracted a huge fan base that's fascinated by every little detail of his sex life. Meet Lonesome George.

LONE SURVIVOR

The story of Lonesome George begins on the isolated Galápagos Islands in the Pacific Ocean about 525 miles west of Ecuador. The islands are well known as the home of giant, land-based tortoises that weigh hundreds of pounds and can live for more than 100 years. Both the islands and the big reptiles made their mark in history when Charles Darwin's ship, the HMS *Beagle*, stopped at the Galápagos in 1835.

On that visit, Darwin learned that it was easy to identify which island a tortoise was from simply by looking at the creature. The tortoises from wet Santa Cruz Island, for example, were large with domed shells. On dry Española, where there's little vegetation, tortoises were smaller with saddle-shaped shells that flared upward to allow their long necks to reach high-growing plants. These adaptations, along with the tortoise's development into different subspecies on different islands, helped Darwin formulate his theory of evolution.

HELLO PEOPLE, GOOD-BYE TORTOISES

Darwin not only studied the Galápagos tortoises, he also ate them. Ships like the *Beagle* captured tortoises and took them aboard as prized edible livestock that needed very little care and could go long periods without food or water. On top of that, human visitors brought in other animals like goats and pigs that trampled and ate tortoise eggs, competed for food, and destroyed trees and grasslands. Before the islands were invaded by humans, they were home to more than 200,000 tortoises. Today, even after repopulation efforts, there are only about 20,000 in all. When Darwin and the *Beagle*

About 90 percent of the world's opals come from Australia.

visited, there were 15 subspecies of tortoises. Today there are 11. Well, 11 plus one—the solitary member of the *Geochelone nigra abingdoni* subspecies of tortoise: Lonesome George.

A CAUSE IS BORN

On the tiny volcanic island of Pinta—whose ecosystem had been devastated by pirates, whalers, and fishermen, and whose tortoises had been considered extinct for decades—a healthy, five-foot-long, 200-pound tortoise was discovered in 1971. He was immediately taken to Santa Cruz Island and the Charles Darwin Research Station, a scientific center dedicated to conservation in the Galápagos. Scientists were ecstatic when they realized that the reptile was a surviving member of the Pinta Island subspecies, and they began searching Pinta and zoos around the world for other survivors. But the tortoise appeared to be the last of his kind, so someone named him Lonesome George, reportedly after 1950s TV comedian George Gobel, who had given himself that same nickname.

Because he's the last remnant of his subspecies, Lonesome George has made it into *Guinness World Records* as the world's rarest living creature. A symbol of the fragility of life on earth, he's also become a star in the struggle for conservation and preservation of the world's wildlife—and the archipelago has become the world's leading ecotourism destination. More than 100,000 people visit each year, and many of them are there to see Lonesome George.

THE NEXT BEST THING

Humans are also intent on meddling in George's sex life. Soon after his discovery, a reward of $10,000 was offered for a Pinta Island female that could mate with George and produce offspring. When the technology became available, DNA scans were made of tortoises all over the world, but no match for George was ever found. Scientists and conservationists didn't want the subspecies to die out with George, so they persisted in their tries to make him a father. After all, tortoises can live for 200 years, and although no one knows George's exact age—as of 2012, he's believed to be between 90 and 100, a mere youngster in his sexual prime. If he couldn't mate with a pure Pinta female, perhaps he could mate with a tortoise who was a close relative and at least some of his genes would be passed on to future generations.

Only two mammals native to Hawaii: the hoary bat and the monk seal.

For years, George shared his life and his pen with two female tortoises from nearby Isabela Island, yet he wouldn't mate with any of them. Zoologists suspected that years without companionship were probably to blame, but they refused to give up and were willing to try some pretty…revolutionary things. A Swiss zoologist, for instance, coated her hands with the genital secretions of female tortoises, and manually massaged George's genitals. These ministrations succeeded in getting George interested in the females in his pen and in trying to mate, but he still seemed unsure of how to go about it. So younger tortoises were brought to the enclosure to teach George about the turtle "birds and bees," and eventually, George figured things out. In 2008 headlines proclaimed: "Lonesome George the Galápagos Tortoise Finally Mates!" But all the excitement turned to disappointment when the eggs found with George's two lady friends proved to be infertile.

CAN SCIENCE EVER UNLONESOME GEORGE?

Scientists have considered cloning George, but the technology hasn't yet been developed and would be expensive to create. What may help in the meantime is the study of DNA. In 2011 George's female companions of 20 years were replaced by Galápagos tortoises from the nearby island of Española, a group of bachelorettes whom scientists, after some DNA testing, found to be much closer to George genetically than his previous gal pals. So there's still some hope he'll be able to produce offspring.

In the meantime, Lonesome George continues to serve as a warning of all that humans can lose by disregarding their effect on the environment. Posted on the tortoise's enclosure is a sign that reads: "Whatever happens to this animal, let him always remind us that the fate of all living things is in human hands."

* * *

HEADS UP!

"I ask people why they have deer heads on their walls. They say, 'Because it's such a beautiful animal.' There you go. I think my mother's attractive, but I have photographs of her."

—Ellen Degeneres

FLYING FISH

And we mean low-flying, dangerous flying fish...

FLYING MACKEREL. In April 2007 Floridian Josh Landin was fishing with friends off Florida's central east coast when he hooked a small fish. He leaned over the side of the boat to grab it...and a 5-foot-long, 51-pound king mackerel jumped out of the water, hit him square in the chest, knocked him back into the boat, and proceeded to attack him. His friends finally got the fish off of him, killed it, and rushed Landin to the hospital. He needed 105 stitches to close the cuts on his hands and legs.

FLYING BARRACUDA. Koral Wira, 14, was on her family's 21-foot cabin cruiser in the Gulf of Mexico in June 2010 when a 4-foot-long, 30-pound barracuda jumped from the water and landed mouth-first on her left arm. The barracuda—a fish renowned for its razor-sharp teeth—badly mangled the girl's arm ("It looked like raw hamburger!" her mother said) before flopping to the deck, where it thrashed around madly until Koral's father killed it with a stab to the eyeball. The injured teen was rushed to the hospital (but not before Dad made her pose for a picture with him and the fish), where she needed 51 stitches to close up her wounds.

FLYING STURGEON. Beauty shop owner Dawn Poirier, 32, of Kenneth City, Florida, was boating with her boyfriend on Florida's Suwanee River in 2006. They were doing about 30 mph down the river when a sturgeon about 5 feet long leaped from the water, smashed into Poirier's face, knocked off part of the boat's motor, flopped back into the water, and swam away. Poirier was in a coma for more than two weeks, needed surgery to repair the entire right side of her face, and ran up medical bills totaling more than $130,000. "It was like I was in a really, really bad car accident," she sid later. "My entire life was changed because of a fish."

FLYING EAGLE RAY. A spotted eagle ray, a species known for making spectacular leaps from the water, did just that one afternoon in March 2011 off the Florida Keys. Unfortunately,

Cats have only about 473 taste buds; dogs have about 1,700.

40-year-old Illinois native Jenny Hausch, on a guided boat tour with her family, was in its flight path. The blow knocked Hausch to the deck—with the 5-foot-long, 175-pound ray on top of her, pinning her down. As her children screamed in the background, Hausch's husband and the boat's crew worked to get the ray off of her. It took nearly four minutes, but when they finally did, Hausch was—amazingly—completely free of injury. They even finished the day's tour. "The kids were pretty shaken," Hausch said, "but we didn't want them to be too scared of the water."

FLYING NEEDLEFISH. In June 2009, a 29-year-old man was fishing in the Mediterranean Sea off the coast of Israel when a needlefish more than a foot long sailed out of the water, coasted through the air...and impaled the man's face with its long, hard, and very pointed snout. The fish—a couple inches of it embedded just below one eye in what must have been a very surprised face—flapped like crazy until the tip of its snout broke off in the man's face. The doctors who performed the surgery to remove it said that the tip had pierced the man's nasal cavity and sinus—and stopped just short of his eyeball. The victim went on to make a full recovery.

FLYING GREAT WHITE SHARK. South African shark researchers were in an 18-foot boat off the country's southeastern coast in July 2011. One of the crewmembers was dropping chopped-up sardines into the water in hopes of attracting the great white sharks they'd been studying for the past three years. "Next thing I know I hear a splash," leader Dorien Schröder told the *Guardian*, "and see a white shark hovering, literally, over the crewmember" who was dropping the fish into the water. Schröder pulled the man out of the way just before the 10-foot-long, 1,000-pound flying shark landed in the back of the (18-foot!) boat. The shark thrashed and smashed things to bits, even breaking the boat's fuel lines. Fortunately, it got stuck between some equipment and couldn't move. The terrified crew un-terrified themselves, radioed for help...and began pouring water over the shark's gills to increase its chances for survival. Soon the boat was towed to the harbor, and the shark was lifted from the boat with a crane. It was lowered into the water, released, and amazingly, it swam away, apparently no worse for the wear.

THE WONDERFUL WORLD OF WEEDS, PART II

On page 15, we introduced you to some weeds that might deserve to live. Here are a few more.

MULLEIN

A member of the snapdragon family, mullein (pronounced MULL-in) made a handy torch during medieval times; the flower at the end of its tall stalk was dipped in wax and set aflame. Centuries before that, women in ancient Rome used golden mullein flowers as a hair dye.

How to find it: Easily recognized because it's much bigger than other weeds at full maturity—as high as eight to ten feet tall—mullein is normally found growing wild in ditches, loves sunshine, and needs open ground to germinate. Its stalk, covered with yellow-gold flowers, looks a little like a gladiolus plant.

What it's good for: According to folklore, mullein leaves were the go-to plant for reducing swelling. In the old days, the fuzzy mullein leaves were gathered and boiled or steeped and then wrapped around the swollen extremities of patients. It's also believed to be an effective remedy for congestion and coughing. The flavors of lemon and honey complement mullein leaf tea. Some smoke it in a pipe or homemade cigarette. One remedy in particular, according to Native Americans, is to combine mullein with a flowering plant called *lobelia*. This combination is smoked from a special pipe and is believed to relieve pneumonia and other lung issues.

Internal medicine: If you were to dry a bunch of leaves in a brown paper bag for two weeks, and then crumple them and add hot water, you'd end up with a tea that treats internal swelling in the ears, lungs, and liver.

Nutrients: Mullein has lots of vitamins (B2, B5, B12, and D), minerals (including iron, potassium, and magnesium), and other good stuff like natural mucilage, a gooey, gummy substance often used to treat congestion and coughing.

...A. One theory: So they appear taller to the next dog that sniffs there.

MILK THISTLE

A member of the daisy family, milk thistle is a Mediterranean native that now grows all over the world. This particular thistle was named for the white, milky sap that's produced when its leaves are crushed.

How to find it: Once you know what you're looking for, it's hard to miss. A milk thistle plant can grow up to 10 feet tall, flourishing best in a sunny, dry environment. The flowers are reddish-purple, and the wide leaves contain white "veins."

What it's good for: Known mostly for its use in cleansing and strengthening the liver, especially one that's been weakened by hepatitis or liver disease, milk thistle also has cholesterol- and cancer-fighting properties. Plus, according to animal studies, if milk thistle extract is provided within 10 minutes of ingesting the poisonous *Amanita phalloides* mushroom, the thistle acts as an antidote to the toxic effects. Even if it takes up to 24 hours to get ahold of the milk thistle extract, it will still greatly reduce risks of liver damage—and possibly death—that comes from eating the mushroom.

Internal medicine: Milk thistle roots can be eaten raw or boiled. If you remove the little spikes from the stems, the stems can be eaten like celery stalks. And like spinach, you can steam or wilt the leaves. (The seeds should not be eaten.)

Nutrients: The primary component that makes milk thistle nutritious and medicinally beneficial is *silymarin*, an antioxidant that reduces inflammation and can block or remove liver toxins. It also contains *linoleic acid* (a type of omega fatty acid), an anti-inflammatory agent that promotes skin, hair, and bone health.

CURLY DOCK (ALSO CALLED "YELLOW DOCK")

Curly dock started out in Europe and western Asia, but long ago made its way to North America, where the Native Americans put it to good use as a treatment for boils and cuts. In times of great need (like famine), they used the seeds to make a kind of porridgy mush—but only in times of *great* need, because you have to make sure to boil it long enough to get rid of the oxalic acid, which can be poisonous if you eat too much.

Note: The ASPCA also lists curly dock as being toxic to dogs.

How to find it: If you live in the country, you can probably find curly dock growing by the side of the road, in a nearby field, or even in your backyard. Look for it wherever there's rich, moist, heavy soil, or close to the seashore. The leaves are long and wavy. Curly dock can grow up to five feet tall by mid-spring. It produces small green flowers and hard red fruit.

What it's good for: Curly dock has been used to treat jaundice, scurvy, and rheumatism. It's also said to be a powerful blood purifier and a laxative. Some herbalists say that, used long term, it will even cure skin problems like acne.

Internal medicine: Curly dock's young, springtime leaves can be eaten fresh or cooked. They work best when mixed with other greens (like dandelion, watercress, and baby spinach leaves). The long, yellow taproot can be boiled and drunk as a tea to help treat skin problems and for liver detoxification.

External medicine: The perfect remedy for the sting of stinging nettles, curly dock can easily soothe the inflammation. Just roll a fresh green leaf between your thumb and forefinger to crush it, then rub the juicy pulp on your burning skin. It is also used topically to treat rashes and sores.

Nutrients: Curly dock leaves contain vitamins A and C, and are a good source of protein, iron, beta-carotene, potassium, and calcium.

The fine print: *The information in this article isn't meant to diagnose, treat, or cure. As always, talk to your doctor before making abrupt dietary changes and/or consuming home remedies in any form—especially if you're pregnant, nursing, and/or taking prescription medications.*

* * *

TWO USES FOR DUNG

• In the 17th century, a Persian shah made courtiers smoke camel dung as a punishment for smoking tobacco.

• In 2011, in Middlesbrough, England, pig manure was spread over the forest floor to keep teenagers from using the woods as a place to drink and do drugs.

HORNYWINKS, SHAGS, AND STINKPOTS

All right, folks, let's try to keep the snickering to a minimum, especially while you're telling the kids about these animals with giggle-inducing names.

• The **Andean cock-of-the-rock** lives in the high-altitude forests of the Andes and is the national bird of Peru. The male of the species has a striking head crest and bright scarlet plumage that he shows off during his courting of the (sorry, ladies) relatively drab females. This elaborate and colorful courtship display is how the species got its name.

• The **bushtit** is among North America's smallest birds. The tiny gray tit (for short) is often seen hanging out with mixed-species flocks, foraging for small insects with a crowd of chickadees, kinglets, and warblers.

• The **dik-dik** is a small antelope, roughly the size of a terrier, that lives in the bush of eastern and southern Africa. Its name is said to be an imitation of the female's high-pitched alarm call.

• **Goatsuckers** are a family of birds that includes nightjars, nighthawks, and whip-poor-wills. All members of this family hunt at night by flying with their beaks open to snare insects midair. Their name comes from an old (but mistaken) belief that the birds used their wide mouths to suckle milk from the udders of goats.

• About the size of a turkey, Europe's largest land bird, the **great bustard**, is a game bird that generally keeps its feet on the ground but is capable of quick and powerful bursts of flight. It's thought that the name "bustard" is from the Latin *avis tarda*, which means "slow bird," but that's the opposite of this bird's behavior. All the same, that "tarda" sticks like glue: The great bustard's Latin name is *Otis tarda*.

• Sounding a bit like a bad memory for a swingin' Londoner after a long night on the town, the **rough-faced shag** is actually a cormorant (as all shags seem to be, and vice versa). This one is unique to the shores of New Zealand. The "rough-faced" appellation probably comes from the fact that this particular shag has yellow-orange swellings that look like big warts above the base of its bill.

• **Hornywink** is an archaic Cornish term for the lapwing, a crested wading bird. "Horny" may have originated as a reference to the hornlike crest on the northern lapwing (which is also called a "peewit"); "wink" may simply be a corruption of "wing."

• The **slippery dick** is a striped, cigar-shaped fish of the wrasse family. It lives in coral and rocky reefs throughout the Caribbean, the western Atlantic, and along the shores of Mexico. All the other fish in its genus have names like black wrasse, pinkbelly wrasse, and even Mardi Gras wrasse, but there's no telling what makes this guy more slippery (or dickish) than the other wrasses in its family.

• The **stinkpot turtle** is a small turtle that lives in the eastern half of the U.S. and southeastern Canada. Also known as the common musk turtle, this reptile is named for its skunklike ability to release a foul-smelling odor to ward off predators.

• The **blue-footed booby** is a duck-sized shorebird that lives off the western coast of Central and South America, with the greatest population on the Galápagos Islands. The word "booby" is a corruption of *bobo*, a Spanish term meaning "fool," in reference to the way the bird walks on its large, striking, blue webbed feet.

• An ancestor of the domestic donkey, the **African wild ass** looks a little like a gray zebra with stripes only on its legs. Although the donkey is common all over the world, only 600 African wild asses live in the wild today.

• There are roughly 30 different varieties of **titi monkeys** (including the ornate titi, the coppery titi, and—are you ready for this?—Barbara Brown's titi), all of which make their home in South America. The cat-sized primates live in densely forested areas, high up in the branches of trees, where they dine on fruit, leaves, and insects. And where they don't appreciate being laughed at, thank you very much.

A tarantula can live for more than two years without food.

GOOD BOY, MAX!

They're cuddly, they're good listeners, and they keep you healthy. Why wouldn't *anyone want a house pet?*

PSYCHIC PETS

Reward: Better health and safety for diabetics and epileptics.

How: By detecting an insulin attack or seizure before it happens.

Story: One former disabilities specialist credits her cats—Prissy and Chili Bean—for warning her before she had seizures. A half-hour before the onset of an attack, Prissy would start pawing at her, and Chili Bean would nudge her as if to say, "It's time to lie down." There are similar stories of dogs who can identify changes in blood glucose levels that signal an impending insulin crash. How animals predict these incidents is a mystery. It's possible they're detecting either chemical changes (perhaps with their noses, which smell 50 times better than ours) or electrical impulses in the body that precede a seizure.

DOGS HELPING VETS

Reward: Therapy and physical assistance for traumatized patients.

How: By alleviating anxiety, and lowering blood pressure and heart rate.

Story: When Army Staff Sergeant Brad Fasnacht was injured by a bomb in Afghanistan in 2009, he suffered a broken back and two broken ankles, and sustained a traumatic brain injury. After overcoming the immediate effects of his physical injuries, he had to face post-traumatic stress disorder (PTSD), which made him terrified to leave his apartment. He recovered thanks to his dog, Sapper, a one-year-old Australian cattle dog mix who accompanies Fasnacht whenever he leaves home. Before Snapper, Fasnacht says, "I'd just freak out, getting really uneasy. But not anymore." Sapper keeps his owner functioning in the world, licks his face when he has nightmares, and even helps him with his remaining physical disability: "I've lost some of my hearing," Fasnacht explains, "but Sapper alerts me if someone is coming up behind me."

ONLY THE LONELY

Reward: Unconditional love.

How: By simply wanting to love and be loved.

Story: Pets are so beneficial that some nursing homes have loosened their "No Animals" rules. Marie was one resident who needed a furry visitor. With no surviving family, she had lost interest in life and just lay in the fetal position scratching at sores on her legs. She ignored people, but brightened up when a staff member brought her a Persian cat named Handsome. Right from the start, Handsome gave Marie lots of love and distracted her from her ailments. Within a month, Marie's sores healed, and she began to interact with nurses and other residents, mostly discussing her new pet and inviting them to come play with him.

RESCUE MISSION

Reward: Being saved by Fifi and the gang.

How: By being kindhearted (or warm-blooded) in the face of danger.

Story: One blisteringly cold January in Massachusetts, Nina Sweeney woke up in the middle of the night, bedridden with a paralysis she'd never experienced before. On top of that, the fire warming her home died out. As the temperature dropped below zero, Sweeney and her pets (one dog and seven cats) were stuck in bed for two days without heat before they were found. But they didn't freeze: The dog slept on Sweeney's stomach, one cat was along each of her sides, another around her neck, one on her chest, one under her arm, and two under the blanket with her. Their body heat saved her life.

Want to know how pets are bad for you? (Yikes!)
Turn to page 252.

* * *

DID YOU KNOW?

Catfish have taste receptors all over their bodies. That means a catfish can taste anything that comes into contact with its skin, including chemicals in the water.

HOW TO BUILD AN OUTDOOR FIRE

We know, we know—Og and Gog had this one figured out a million years ago. But just in case you haven't…

IT WILL HAPPEN

There is a very good chance that at some point in your life—even if you're the most home-loving, easy chair–sitting, gelatinous blob of a human that ever lived—you're going to have to make a fire outdoors. The kids will demand it. Or the spouse will kick you out of the cabin one night while you're staying in the mountains on a winter vacation. With this in mind, you're going to need some tried-and-true tips for starting a fire in the great outdoors. So here you go.

BURN, BABY, BURN

If you're at a campground that provides a fire pit, you should use it, as this is the safest and easiest way to go. If none is available, you're going to have to build a fire ring or pit yourself. Here's how:

• Pick a flat spot with little or no vegetation, and be sure to look out for any low, overhanging tree branches. Clear all debris around the fire area to a diameter of 10 feet.

• For a fire ring only: Collect several rocks—brick-sized or larger and flat or flattish on two opposite sides. Arrange the rocks in a ring in the center of your clearing. The ring doesn't have to be big—just a few feet across is fine—although it can, of course, be bigger in you want a bigger fire.

• For a fire pit: A fire pit is the ideal choice because it's less likely wind will carry any flaming material out of the fire. Dig a pit three or four feet across (larger for large fires), and six to eighteen inches deep, depending on the tools you have available and the amount of work you're willing to do. (A tire iron works pretty well to break up packed dirt, which you can then scoop out by hand.) Then place the same kind of rocks collected for the ring around the pit.

Some common mushroom odors: candy, fruit, licorice, seafood, gasoline, and burned rubber.

WHAT YOU'LL NEED

Water. It's the last thing you'd think, right? But it's the first thing to make sure you have handy, not only to douse any flames if the fire jumps and spreads, but to put the fire out completely when you're done for the night. No fire should be left burning with nobody awake and in attendance. Most experts recommend at least a bucket of water for this purpose. Others recommend a bucket of water *and* a fire extinguisher.

Fire starter. Matches, lighter, flint and striker stone, magnifying glass—whatever you've got.

Tinder. This is the very flimsy stuff that you light first to get the fire started. It can be any number of things, including pine needles, grass, wood shavings, or paper; the important thing is that it must be very dry.

Kindling. This is the slightly larger stuff that the flames from the tinder will light. Most people just use dead, dry twigs from trees, one to two feet in length, but you can also make kindling yourself by chopping larger pieces of wood down to very thin pieces.

Fuelwood. This is the heavier wood that will be lit by the kindling, becoming the actual fuel of the fire once it gets going. It doesn't have to be huge—anything about the thickness of your arm will do, although you can of course use big, bulky logs once the fire really gets going.

Important tip: Stack your tinder, kindling, and fuelwood in separate piles, not too close to the fire ring.

START 'ER UP

Now throw all the tinder, kindling, and fuelwood into your fire ring, douse that sucker with a whole can of lighter fluid, and toss a match in there.

Most people are familiar with the "tepee" method of fire building, but there are actually several other methods, some of which you may not have heard of. We'll start with the tepee style, then give you some info on a few of the others.

Tepee: Make a pile of loosely assembled tinder in the center of the fire ring. The size of the pile depends on the size of the fire you want: For an average fire, make a pile about the size of half a

Daddy longlegs are arachnids, but they're not spiders. They have no venom or silk glands.

basketball. Now stand pieces of kindling—thinnest pieces first—around the tinder, with their top ends meeting above the pile, forming a tepee shape. Don't stack the wood too densely. Fire feeds on oxygen, so you want air to be able to move freely through the structure. Make sure you leave an opening that you can reach your fire starter through—and if it's not too windy, make it on the windward side: The wind will help spread the fire through the structure. Use gradually thicker pieces of kindling as you add layers to the tepee, and then finish with four or five pieces of fuelwood about as big around as your wrist. Now light the tinder. Monitor the fire's progress—be ready to throw more kindling on the fire if it seems like it will be used up before the fuelwood catches. Add larger pieces of fuelwood when the fire gets going. As it burns, the tepee will eventually collapse into a layer of coals. Once the fire is burning strongly, add fuelwood by laying it on the fire, preferably in crisscrossed layers, to allow plenty of air to feed the fire.

Log cabin: For this one, build a tepee just like above. Then take two pieces of fuelwood about as big around as your arm, and lay them at the base of the tepee on either side of it. Then lay two more across them, making a square shape around the tepee. Then add two more across those two pieces, again on either side of the fire. Continue building up like this, building a "log cabin" around the tepee. When you've gone high enough, build a roof on the cabin by placing a layer of relatively thin fuelwood across its top. Light the tinder (you may need to fashion a torch of sorts with rolled-up paper or a long piece of tinder to get to it). Add larger fuelwood when the fire gets going.

Lean-to: Stick a pointed piece of thin fuelwood or stout kindling into the ground at an angle, so that just two to four feet of it sticks out of the ground. Make a tinder pile underneath it, and then lay a small tepee of kindling directly on the tinder. Next, lay larger pieces of kindling so they lean on either side of the stick you've stuck in the ground. Add a few layers of thicker and thicker kindling over the first layer, and then a final layer of thin fuelwood. (Remember to not pack it too densely.) Light the tinder, let the fire get burning, and slowly place more fuelwood in the fire, building it up until it's the size you'd like.

A hyena's front legs are longer than its back legs.

Parallel: Also called a "hunter's fire," this is a small, simple fire built between two logs placed on the ground just six inches or so from each other. The logs protect the small fire from wind—and provide a surface for pots and pans.

Council fire: This one's a biggie, requiring a good supply of large logs, the largest a foot or more in diameter and four to six feet long. Place four or five of the largest logs parallel on the ground, and a foot or so apart from one another. Make a second layer by laying several slightly thinner logs across these. Make a third by placing several still thinner and shorter logs atop and across the second layer. Repeat this process using smaller and smaller logs, until you have a pyramidal structure four or five feet high. The last layer should consist of fairly thin pieces—just an inch or so in diameter—and should make a platform at least a couple of feet across. Build a tepee fire on top of this last layer, and light it. The fire will burn from the top down, lighting each new layer as it goes. Council fires are slow, steady burners that last a long time. So they're often the choice for large groups performing ceremonies, and also a favorite for scouting groups.

* * *

THE HOAX IS ON YOU!

In 1799 a sea captain sent George Shaw, curator of the Natural History Department of the British Museum, an animal carcass supposedly found in Australia. It appeared to be a mole with a bird's bill and beaver's tail attached. Shaw suspected a hoax and thought that "there might have been practiced some arts of deception in its structure." He wondered if swindlers had merged animals together and passed the whole off as a new species. His peers were equally skeptical.

But as more specimens turned up, scientists were forced to believe in and categorize the new animal…and that's how the duck-billed platypus became legendary for being *real*.

THE CRITTERS ARE COMING!

What happens when the delicate balance of nature tips in such a way that a particular animal population spikes to unsustainable levels? Pretty much what you'd expect: chaos...famine...and critters out the wazoo.

THE 48-YEAR CURSE

The wild bamboo forests in northwest India and parts of Burma are home to an odd curse: Every 48 years, like clockwork, they produce an army of hungry rats that devour the local rice crop. The phenomenon is called *mautam* (which translates to "bamboo death") and is caused by the life cycle of melocanna bamboo, the local variety. The plants live for exactly 48 years, at which point entire forests die off simultaneously. But before they die, they produce a tremendous amount of seed-filled fruit. The fruit will replant the next generation of bamboo, but in the meantime, it also provides a huge increase in the amount of food available to the local black rat community.

The sudden food surplus sets off a population boom. For as long as the good times last, the rats breed continuously. It takes only about 11 weeks for the baby rats to reach maturity. That means, during the year that the forest fruits, the rat population jumps exponentially every couple of months—from as few as 100 rats per acre to as many as 12,000 per acre. And at just about the time that the rat population is hitting its peak, the bamboo fruit runs out.

When that happens, millions of starving rats swarm the countryside, eating everything in their path...which spells disaster for the local rice farmers. In the past, without advance planning and no ability to bring in extra food from outside the region, the rat plague could lead to famine and political upheaval. As for the rats, once they've decimated the rice crop, they starve to death en masse. Their population numbers crash back down, but everyone knows they'll be back...in 48 years.

Most vocal of all wild North American mammals: coyotes.

THE HOUSE MOUSE INVASION

For more than a century, Australians have been at war against what they call the "mouse plague." Once every four years on average, somewhere in Australia, vast stretches of farmland are devastated by millions of hungry mice. Why are Australian mice so hard to control? Probably because they aren't natives—they're an invasive species.

The mice that cause such destruction Down Under actually belong to one of the most common mouse species in the world: the house mouse. Native to Asia, these mice abandoned foraging in the wild in favor of scavenging in human settlements nearly 10,000 years ago. And as human agriculture and civilization spread across the globe, the house mice spread too. They most likely arrived in Australia as stowaways aboard the first ships that brought settlers there in the 1780s.

House mice are among the fastest breeders in the world. A female's pregnancy lasts just 19 days and produces five to ten baby mice. Those baby mice start having their own babies when they're only six weeks old. Oh, yeah—and females can get pregnant again just one to three days after giving birth. This means that one female mouse can produce 500 new mice in less than six months.

THE ORIGINAL AND STILL THE WORST

Desert locusts are the granddaddy of all animal plagues. Ancient Egyptians wrote about them 3,500 years ago, and they've been menacing much of North Africa and the Middle East ever since. For thousands of years, no one had any idea where they came from. Most years, there were no locusts at all. In a bad year, though, they showed up by the billions, in huge clouds dense enough to blot out the sun. The clouds swept across the countryside, eating every bit of vegetation in their path and leaving farm fields stripped bare. It wasn't until the 1920s that scientists uncovered the secret of the locusts' mysterious appearances.

It turns out that locusts are just regular grasshoppers driven crazy by overcrowding. The desert is a harsh environment, and there's usually not enough food to support a large grasshopper population. To ensure survival of the species, female grasshoppers lay as many as 150 eggs just under the surface of loose, sandy ground. Ordinarily, not all of the eggs hatch—and not all of the ones that hatch survive. But when a particularly wet winter comes along, two things happen: First, more of the eggs hatch. And second, the extra moisture means that extra vegetation grows, providing enough food to support the extra population…at first.

Scientists aren't exactly sure why, but overcrowded conditions cause grasshoppers to change both their appearance and their behavior. Their color morphs from green to a yellow-and-black pattern. More importantly, their personalities change—from solitary individuals to being clustered together in an organized mob that moves across the landscape as one giant, food-frenzied unit. Weird but true.

Bonus: The swarm, American-style. For the first three or four decades of settlement on the Great Plains, American farmers regularly had their crops wiped out by the Rocky Mountain locust. In 1874, a swarm of locusts estimated at a size of 198,000 square miles—about twice the size of Colorado—swept through Nebraska. By the early 1900s, the Rocky Mountain locust had disappeared from the landscape, apparently gone extinct. The only explanation scientists have come up with for why this happened is that the settlers may have plowed up the locusts' breeding grounds without even realizing it.

* * *

THREE DINGO FACTS

1. Dingoes were first brought to Australia around 6,000 years ago by Indonesian sea traders.

2. They're not just in Australia—dingoes are still found in the wild in parts of Southeast Asia, especially in northern Thailand.

3. Dingoes are unique among canines in that they have rotatable wrists...as people with domestic dingoes find out when dingoes learn to use those wrists to open doorknobs.

THE ANIMAL TOE QUIZ

Toes—where would be without 'em? (We don't know, but we'd certainly be no-toe-rious, woudn't we?) P.S. You are not actually expected to answer these questions correctly…just have a toe-rific time trying. (Answers on page 430.)

1) Pigs are *ungulates*—or hoofed animals—with their hooves split into separate toes. How many toes do pigs have on each foot?'

2) How many *total* toes does the two-toed sloth have?

3) Parrots have four toes—the equivalent of your big toe and the next three. How many of those toes face forward and how many face backward? And which ones do which?

4) How many toes on the feet of cormorants and boobies are webbed? How many on the feet of ducks and geese?

5) What is the only existing bird with two toes on each foot?

6) What are the only mammals with just one toe?

7) Kangaroos, wallabies, possums, koalas, wombats, and other marsupials in the order Diprotodontia have a common characteristic concerning the second and third toes on their hind feet. What is it?

8) In 2011 a stray cat helped raise $110,000 for a Wisconsin animal shelter. How many toes did it have?

9) All *tetrapods*—creatures with four limbs (like us)—around today either have five toes (or toes and *fingers*, if they have them) on each limb, or they descended from creatures that had five toes and lost them. *Acanthostega* was a salamanderlike creature that lived about 365 million years ago and, paleontologists say, was one of the earliest tetrapods to appear on earth. How many toes did *Acanthostega* have?

10) Name three famous *humans* with webbed toes.

11) In December 2011, a Scottish fisherman had his missing thumb replaced with what?

12) Cats have five toes on their forepaws and four on the rear. Name three other animals with this toe configuration.

13) Name 10 animals with "toe" or "toed" in their names.

OH, BABY!

Birds do it. Bees do it. Here's how the rest of the animal world does it. (And what happens after that.)

• Female mayflies of the *Dolania americana* species have five minutes after their final molting stage to zoom out of the water, find a mate, do the mating, and then fall back into the water to lay their eggs. After that, they die.

• The longest gestation period for any animal is the alpine black salamander, which can be pregnant for more than three years.

• A newborn blue whale calf is about 23 feet long, weighs up to four tons (slightly less than an adult elephant), and can swim within 10 seconds of being born.

• Elephant calves are the largest infants on land, weighing as much as 300 pounds.

• The gestation period for the American opossum is just 13 days.

• Kangaroos are born extremely premature and hairless, and are only about an inch long. Immediately after birth, they crawl up their mother's fur (she licks a path) and into her pouch, where they attach to a teat and stay for several weeks. Mother kangaroos come back in heat almost immediately after giving birth, so any new embryos go temporarily dormant until the first baby can live on its own and there's room for a new one in the pouch.

• Rabbits can have a litter of babies every 30 days or so.

• Female alligators lay their eggs in a compost pile to keep them warm. If the temperature in the compost stays at or below 86°F, the eggs will hatch female gator babies. If it gets to 93°F or hotter, the embryos will turn out to be boys.

• Hibernating female bears often sleep through their babies' births.

Longest human pregnancy: 375 days, almost 100 days past the normal 280.

STORYTIME WITH ABRAHAM LINCOLN

These true accounts of President Lincoln's animal encounters show that the Great Emancipator's compassion wasn't limited to humankind.

LITTLE ABE AND THE WILD TURKEY

Lincoln learned at seven years old that he was different when it came to animals. Most boys his age didn't think twice about hunting wild game during the frontier days of the early 19th century. But one day, young Abraham Lincoln shot a turkey on his family's farm. According to biographer Thomas Keneally, "The experience of destroying animal life, of seeing the gush of blood, repelled him, and he would never become the dead-eye frontier marksman of American myth."

WHAT THE SHELL?

When Lincoln was a teenager in the 1820s, a common pastime among his classmates was to catch terrapins (freshwater turtles) and then turn them over on their backs to watch them try to right themselves—usually unsuccessfully. Lincoln would have no part of such games.

And when those games took a more sinister turn, the teen refused to stand idly by. This story comes from the 1909 book *The Heart of Lincoln*, by Wayne Whipple:

> One day Abe Lincoln came and caught a group of mischievous boys putting live coals on a poor mud-turtle's back. The lads, and several girl friends, laughed to see the turtle moving slowly and aimlessly about in its surprise and misery. When Abe saw what was going on he dashed into the group in a frenzy of wrath, snatched the shingle from the ringleader's hand, dashed the burning coals off the poor turtle's back, then began beating the boys with the thin board. When he had scattered them right and left, according to one of the girls who witnessed the sudden scene, "He preached against such cruelty" and, with angry tears in his deep, gray eyes, told the snickering offenders that a terrapin's or "an ant's life is as sweet to it as ours is to us."

A group of porcupines is called a "prickle."

FEATHERED FRIENDS

This anecdote comes from Lincoln's friend Joshua F. Speed, who was traveling with the future president in 1839:

> We were riding along a country road, two and two together, some distance apart, Lincoln and Jon. J. Hardin being behind. We were passing through a thicket of wild plum and crab-apple trees, where we stopped to water our horses. After waiting some time, Hardin came up and we asked him where Lincoln was. "Oh," said he, "when I saw him last" (there had been a severe wind storm), "he had caught two little birds in his hand, which the wind had blown from their nest, and he was hunting for the nest." Hardin left Lincoln before he found it. He finally found the nest, and placed the birds, to use his own words, "in the home provided for them by their mother." When Lincoln caught up to the party they laughed at him. Said he, earnestly, "I could not have slept tonight if I had not given those two little birds to their mother."

THE GOAT KEEPER

Lincoln's White House years were mired by family tragedy and the nation in turmoil. His menagerie of animals helped keep him grounded during those troubled times. The Lincolns owned dogs, cats, rabbits, and turkeys. But the president had a special fondness for his two pet goats, Nanny and Nanko. The First Lady's seamstress, a former slave named Elizabeth Keckley, recounted this story in her 1868 book, *Behind the Scenes, or, Thirty Years a Slave, and Four Years in the White House*:

> One Saturday afternoon I went to the White House to dress Mrs. Lincoln. I had nearly completed my task when the President came in. It was a bright day, and walking to the window, he looked down into the yard, smiled, and, turning to me, asked: "Madam Elizabeth, you are fond of pets, are you not?"
>
> "O yes, sir," I answered.
>
> "Well, come here and look at my two goats. I believe they are the kindest and best goats in the world. See how they sniff the clear air, and skip and play in the sunshine. Whew! What a jump," he exclaimed as one of the goats made a lofty spring. "Madam Elizabeth, did you ever before see such an active goat?" Musing a moment, he continued: "He feeds on my bounty, and jumps with joy. Do you think we could call him a bounty-jumper? But I flatter the bounty-jumper [men who enlisted in the Union or Confederate

Opossums, moles, and hedgehogs all have a natural immunity to snake venom.

armies during the Civil War just to collect the $300 incentive offered to new recruits; then they'd desert]. My goat is far above him. I would rather wear the goat's horns and hairy coat through life, than demean myself to the level of the man who plunders the national treasury in the name of patriotism."

THE CAT'S MEOW

This final—and perhaps most touching—account of the 16th president's love of the animal kingdom is retold here in Carl Sandburg's 1939 book *Abraham Lincoln: The War Years*:

Near the end of the Civil War, Abraham and his family had been invited to visit General Ulysses S. Grant's headquarters at City Point, Virginia. The trip took place in late March of 1865 about three weeks before the assassination. During his visit to City Point, the president happened to be in the telegraph hut on the day that Grant's army began the final advance of the Civil War. In the hut the president came upon three tiny kittens. They appeared to be lost and were wandering around and meowing.

Abraham picked up one of the kittens and asked, "Where is your mother?" A person standing nearby said, "The mother is dead." The president continued to pet the little kitten and said, "Then she can't grieve as many a poor mother is grieving for a son lost in battle." Abraham picked up the other two kittens and now had all three in his lap. He stroked their fur and quietly told them, "Kitties, thank God you are cats, and can't understand this terrible strife that is going on." The Chief Executive continued, "Poor little creatures, don't cry; you'll be taken good care of." He looked toward Colonel Bowers of Grant's staff and said, "Colonel, I hope you will see that these poor little motherless waifs are given plenty of milk and treated kindly." Bowers promised that he would tell the cook to take good care of them. Colonel Horace Porter watched the president and recalled, "He would wipe their eyes tenderly with his handkerchief, stroke their smooth coats, and listen to them purring their gratitude to him."

* * *

"All my life I have tried to pluck a thistle and plant a flower wherever the flower would grow in thought and mind."

—Abraham Lincoln

WEIRD (HUMAN) NEWS

In these three stories, there's nothing too out of the ordinary about the animals—it's the people that are a bit loony.

WEAR A SUIT TO WORK

In a nature reserve in China's Sichuan province, biologists wear full-body panda suits whenever they interact with a group of orphaned baby pandas. Their goal: To raise the young bears free of human influence before they are released into the wild. The suits are bulky, and the scientists aren't nearly as graceful as real giant pandas. (It looks like a scene from a cheesy movie.) The scientists admit that they have no way of knowing whether the young pandas are fooled.

SLEEPING WITH THE FISHES

A reporter in Tripura, India, went undercover as a fish trader in 2007. His trail led him to the morgue at the local hospital, where he made a shocking discovery: Local fish sellers were storing hilsa, a popular fish in India, with dead bodies. Why? Because private freezer space is expensive to rent, so the sellers bribed hospital employees to let them store their hilsa in the morgue for much cheaper. When the story broke—and consumers learned that the fish they bought from the market had spent the night with dead bodies—they were angry. So was India's health minister, who vowed that the fish sellers and hospital staff would be punished.

FLY AWAY HOME

The Roman poet Virgil (70–19 BC), best known for the *Aeneid*, once held a lavish funeral on his land. Senators and noblemen attended. The poet himself read a long eulogy for the deceased. An orchestra played solemn music as the tiny coffin was placed in its tomb. What was Virgil burying? His beloved pet...housefly. But there was a method to the poet's madness: He did have a fondness for flies, but he also hated paying high taxes on his land. So, after noticing a loophole in the Roman tax code that excluded mausoleums from paying up, Virgil deemed his land a mausoleum. And he had the tomb of his beloved fly to prove it.

Q & A

Wherein we answer some of your most burning nature questions.

CAN TREES TALK?

A. "Talk" may be too strong a word, but many scientists do believe that trees communicate with one another. Oregon physicist Ed Wagner says, "If you chop into a tree, you can see that adjacent trees put out an electrical pulse [like a] cry of alarm. People have known there was communication between trees for several years, but they've explained it by the chemicals trees produce. I think the real communication is much quicker and more dramatic than that...This is an automatic response."

The chemical theory is worth mentioning too, though. In 1979 Davey Rhoades, a chemist and zoologist in Seattle, did an experiment on willow trees. He set up two plots of trees near each other. One group was infested with caterpillars, the other was not. After about two weeks, Rhodes found that, as a way of protecting themselves, the willows in the caterpillar plot had started to produce a chemical that was distasteful to the insects. Not surprising. The amazing part was that the untouched trees, the ones that hadn't had any caterpillar attacks at all, started producing the *same* chemical... as though the affected trees had somehow warned their neighbors.

Q. WHY IS ICE SLIPPERY?

A. The simple answer is...because there's water on it. But where that water comes from is the source of much debate. For decades, the accepted explanation was that putting pressure on ice (like a person standing on it) lowered its freezing temperature, thus causing a thin layer of water to form. When the pressure was removed, the theory went, the water refroze. But most scientists now believe this to be totally wrong.

These days, there are two dominant theories. The first isn't new—it was proposed in 1850 by British physicist Michael Faraday. He believed that the surface of ice, by its nature, just always includes a very thin layer of water. In 1996 University of California–Berkeley chemist Gabor Somorjai claimed that he'd proven Faraday's assertion with an experiment that measured how electrons bounced off of ice. (They bounced differently if there was water than when the solid's surface was dry.) But Miquel Salmeron, another UC Berkeley chemist, was quick to disagree. He did his own experiment, dragging a tiny needle across the surface of a piece of ice and finding that there was actually a great deal of resistance. This led him to conclude that ice, on its own, isn't really that slippery after all. Instead, Salmeron proposed, it is friction, or movement, that causes a slight rise in temperature and creates a thin layer of melted water on the surface of ice. The tip of his needle was so small that it did not cause much friction, explaining why it met with resistance. The blade of an ice skate, however, would cause a great deal more friction, melting the ice and allowing the skater to glide along. Salmeron was quick to note, though, that his explanation should not be taken as fact—it's just a theory. And so it seems that even the scientists are stumped by this question. As one chemist from Lawrence University said, ice is "a very mysterious solid."

Q. WHY IS THE SKY BLUE?

A. The short answer: It's not. The longer answer: It's all about light. The earth's atmosphere is made up of all kinds of things: mostly oxygen and nitrogen gases, but also water vapor, dust particles, bits of salt from the ocean, and more. All light includes a variety of colors that travel from the light source to our eyes in waves. All the colors combined look white to us, and as light from the sun travels through open space without any obstructions, it maintains that white color. But as soon as the light hits the earth's atmosphere, the various waves start bumping into things: gases, dust, salt, and so on. Each substance affects the light differently, absorbing or reflecting the colors at different rates and speeds. The gases in the earth's atmosphere absorb the blue light and reflect it all around, giving the impression to our eyes that the sky is blue. In realty, however, it's black...which you can see at night when there's no sunlight.

Cool fact: On earth, the sun looks yellow (if you look at it at all, which you shouldn't do!). But that's because yellow is one of the waves of light that doesn't get scattered by the atmosphere. If you were in space, the sun would look white, because its light includes all the colors and there's no atmosphere to get in the way.

MEET THE BURROWERS

You'll have to dig deep to figure out some of the answers to this burrowing critter quiz. *(Answers on page 432.)*

1. According to American and Canadian folklore, on February 2, if this animal comes out of his burrow and sees his shadow, he'll go back underground and nap through six more weeks of winter.

a. meerkat

b. prairie dog

c. groundhog

d. ferret

2. In a classic 19th century children's story, a little girl has a series of fantastic adventures after she falls into this animal's burrow.

a. mole

b. rabbit

c. badger

d. armadillo

3. In North America, otters build burrows or dens, but where do they spend much of their time hunting and traveling?

a. rivers

b. deep caves

c. sand dunes

d. swamplands

4. What small burrower is so fierce that its name became a term for a woman with a violent, scolding temperament?

a. bilby

b. coypus

c. kangaroo rat

d. shrew

5. Why does the burrowing owl collect mammal dung?

a. To seal the burrow when it's nesting

b. As an aphrodisiac for a mating ritual

c. To keep predators away

d. To attract tasty dung beetles

6. What pink, wrinkled animals have no fur, but use their sensory whiskers to help them navigate through their underground homes?

a. voles

b. guinea pigs

c. naked mole rats

d. ferrets

7. What was the name of the Animal Planet television series filmed in Africa that captured the communal, burrowing life of Flower and the Whiskers mob?

a. *Meerkat Manor*

b. *Prairie Dog Place*

c. *Badger Burrow*

d. *Hamster Hall*

8. What food do moles collect in their underground burrows?

a. apples

b. worms

c. bird eggs

d. nuts

9. Which of these sea creatures burrows into the ocean bottom and, when it washes up on the beach, is usually dead and picked up by shell collectors?

a. sand dollars

b. mussels

c. sea anemones

d. coral

10. This little desert burrower goes beneath the surface to survive the fierce heat of the Sahara. (It also inspired a wise character in the novel *The Little Prince.*)

a. pika

b. desert tortoise

c. fennec fox

d. aardvark

* * *

THE WORLD'S DEADLIEST...

• **Twister:** A tornado that ripped through Missouri, Illinois, and Indiana on March 18, 1925, killed nearly 700 people.

• **Hurricane:** At least 300,000 people were killed when a hurricane hit Bangladesh on November 12, 1970.

• **Hailstorm:** This took place on May 22, 1986, in Sichuan, China, killing 100 people and injuring 9,000 others.

• **Avalanche:** The Wellington, Washington, avalanche in the Cascades killed 96 people on March 1, 1910. Some of the dead included passengers and employees on two trains that were waiting at the Wellington depot when the wall of snow came roaring down Windy Mountain and pummeled them.

"Dumbledore" is an Old English term for a type of bee.

BIG BOTTOMS

Where can you find the world's tallest mountains, most active volcanoes, and deepest canyons? Hold your nose and jump in, because they're all on the ocean floor.

WATER WORLD

According to the United States National Oceanic and Atmospheric Association, about 95 percent of the ocean floor remains unmapped. And since the world's five oceans cover nearly 140 million square miles, that leaves a whole lot left to explore. Earth's oceans are…

• **The Pacific** is, by far, the world's largest ocean. With an area of more than 60 million square miles, it covers about 28 percent of the earth's surface, making it nearly equal in size to all of the landmasses on the planet combined.

• **The Atlantic** is the second largest, covering about 21 percent of the earth's surface with an area of 41.1 million square miles.

• **The Indian Ocean** comes in as the third largest ocean, covering roughly 26.5 million square miles.

• **The Southern, or Antarctic Ocean** was once considered part of the Pacific. Now it's the fourth largest ocean with its southern boundary on the freezing coast of Antarctica. It covers an area of roughly 7.8 million square miles.

• **The Arctic** is the world's smallest ocean and the one that is the farthest north. Most of it lies above the Arctic Circle, covering 5.4 million square miles.

HOW LOW CAN YOU GO?

If you were to step off the land of any continent where it meets the ocean, you'd step onto the "continental margin," the shallowest part of the ocean floor. It includes these three areas:

• **The continental shelf** is a section of land that's connected to the rim of a continent. It slopes downward gradually at an angle of one to three degrees. Some continental shelves are narrow, some are wide, and they can stretch for miles. Continental shelves make only 8 percent of the ocean floor, but they're the part that fishermen and geologists know best. They have lots of sunlight and fertile soil deposited by rivers, streams, and coastal currents. Seaweed, plankton, and microbes grow there and feed the fish that exist in greater numbers and varieties on the continental shelf than anywhere else in the ocean. There are also often minerals, gas, and oil found in the rocks that form continental shelves.

• **The continental slope** starts at about 450–650 feet below sea level. Where the shelves end and the continental slopes begin, the land drops off steeply. Continental slopes fall away so quickly that the ocean becomes thousands of feet deeper within a couple of miles. Here, the water is much colder. It has less oxygen and is home to less marine life.

• **The continental rise** lies just below the continental slope and forms the end of the continental margin. The continental rises are created from the mud, silt, and sand that are deposited on the continental shelves by streams and rivers. Currents pick up the sediment and send it tumbling down the steep sides of the continental slopes until it lands in the continental rises.

For more about the ocean's deep, dark depths,
swim over to page 246.

* * *

BEHOLD...THE TURTLE

"All the thoughts of a turtle are turtle."

—Ralph Waldo Emerson

"There is a fine line between the perseverance of the courageous tortoise and the habit of the stubborn donkey."

—Jonathan Lockwood Huie

"Aesop was writing for the tortoise market. Hares have no time to read."

—Anita Brookner

THE TIDES

Trying to explain the tides to a non-astronomer is kind of like trying to explain the infield fly rule to a non-baseball fan: It's going be confusing, but once you get it, the whole thing seems obvious.

SWING YOUR PARTNER

The tides rise and fall because of the way that the Moon orbits Earth. To understand how it works, we're going to have to play with water balloons. (WARNING! This could get messy. Young readers who don't want to get into trouble should ask their parents for permission before performing this experiment. It's also probably a good idea to do it outside.)

First, fill a balloon with water and tie it to one end of a string. Hold the other end of the string in one hand. Now swing the balloon in a big circle over your head. Pretend that the balloon is Earth and your hand is the Moon. The string represents the gravitational force that holds the two together. Notice that both your hand (the Moon) and the balloon (Earth) are moving in circles.

Most illustrations of the Moon's orbit make it look like Earth sits still while the Moon does all the work. But actually, Earth and the Moon are equal partners. In the case of our experiment, the balloon is pulling on your hand, and your hand is pulling on the balloon. Now take a closer look at the "Earth" balloon. As it swings, the weight of the water inside pulls it into an oblong shape. Scientists call that *centrifugal force*. The same thing happens to the actual Earth.

BIG, BLUE, DISTORTED MARBLE

The reason that the Moon's orbit can distort Earth's shape has to do with the nature of gravity and distance. The strength of the gravitational force that exists between any two objects decreases with distance. This is important because Earth's diameter is so big that one side of the planet is always about 8,000 miles closer to the Moon than the other. That means gravity pulls harder on the side of Earth that faces the Moon than it does on the side that faces open space. But the side that faces away from the Moon also has centrifugal force acting on it. So the Moon's gravity pulls harder on one side of Earth, and centrifugal force pulls harder on the other. Result: The planet gets stretched.

On land, this stretching effect is so small that we don't notice it. But two-thirds of Earth's surface is covered by ocean, and it's a lot easier to move water than it is to move land. So as the ocean on Earth's Moon-facing side stretches out toward the Moon, the ocean on the opposite side stretches out toward open space. Scientists refer to the stretched-out areas as *tidal bulges*. Wherever the two bulges are on the planet at any given time are the areas at high tide.

AS THE (DISTORTED) WORLD TURNS

Now that we know how the gravitational and centrifugal forces between the Moon and Earth cause the two tidal bulges, let's look at what happens when you stand on one spot on Earth. The planet spins on its axis, giving us the appearance of the Sun and Moon going around us once each day. (The Moon actually takes a little longer than the Sun—about 24 hours, 50 minutes—but that's not important right now.) The two tidal bulges don't spin with the planet, though—they stay in line with the Moon. So if you stand at one spot on Earth, those two bulges will pass by you two times. And the most stretched-out, low spots will also pass by two times. That's why we have two high tides and two low tides every day.

BUT WAIT...THERE'S MORE!

People who live near the ocean know that not all high and low tides are exactly the same—some are higher or lower than others. Why? The main reason is that the Moon sometimes gets interference from the Sun. Everything we've told you about the forces between Earth and the Moon is also true of the forces between Earth and the Sun. The Sun creates its own tidal bulges, but the difference is that the Sun is about 92 million miles farther away from Earth than the Moon is. So solar bulges are about half the size of lunar bulges.

When the Sun and Moon are in a straight line with Earth, their tidal bulges work together to create extra-high (and extra-low) tides. These are called *spring tides*, though they don't have anything to do with the season. When the Moon moves out of alignment with the Sun, the solar bulges work against the larger lunar bulges, creating milder tides. These are called *neap tides*. (Nobody actually knows the origin of that word.)

It's easy to predict spring and neap tides by observing the different phases of the Moon. The full moon and the new moon—which happen when the Sun and Moon are aligned with Earth—accompany spring tides. The first and last quarters of the Moon—which show up when the Sun and Moon are most out of alignment with Earth—accompany neap tides.

GOODNIGHT, MOON

The shape of the Moon's orbit also affects the severity of tides. The Moon doesn't orbit Earth in a perfect circle—its orbit is elliptical, or oval-shaped. Over the course of that orbit, the distance between Earth and the Moon varies by as much as 30,000 miles, which has a marked effect on both the gravitational and the centrifugal forces. That means, when the Moon is at its closest to Earth, the tides are at their highest and lowest. When the Moon is farther away, the tides become milder. Remember all that the next time you go to the beach and the tide comes in and wrecks your sand castle.

* * *

AN OLD JOKE

A couple at the Smithsonian's National Museum of Natural History were looking at some dinosaur bones. The wife asked the guard, "Can you tell us how old these dinosaur bones are?"

The guard said, "Sixty-five million, six years, and six months old."

"That's awfully exact," said the husband. "How do you know their age so precisely?"

"Well," the guard answered, "the dinosaur bones were 65 million years old when I started working here, and that was six and a half years ago!"

EAT OR BE EATEN

Here we examine the never-ending battle between predator and prey. Bon appétit!

"Edible: Good to eat, wholesome to digest, as a worm to a toad, a toad to a snake, a snake to a pig, a pig to a man, and a man to a worm."

—Ambrose Bierce

"The scientific name for an animal that doesn't run from or fight its enemies is 'lunch.'"

—Michael Friedman

"Fear is the venom impact of predator sting, causing prey not to focus on survival."

—Toba Beta

"In nature, there is less death and destruction than death and transmutation."

—Edwin Way Teale

"A lion's work hours are only when he's hungry; once he's satisfied, the predator and prey live peacefully together."

—Chuck Jones

"The apple tree never asks the beech how he shall grow, nor the lion the horse, how he shall take his prey."

—William Blake

"The real terror of beholding sharks feeding is that may be all there is to life...A frenzied churning of flesh into flesh of another kind."

—Johann Wolfgang von Goethe

"A hungry wolf at all the herd will run; In hopes, through many, to make sure of one."

—William Congreve

"Nature reserves the right to inflict upon her children the most terrifying jests."

—Thornton Wilder

"Nature is not cruel, only pitilessly indifferent. This is one of the hardest lessons for humans to learn."

—Richard Dawkins

"Honey badger's really pretty badass. No regard for any other animal whatsoever. Look at him just grunting and, ew, eating snakes? Oh, they're so nasty. Oh, look! It's chasing things and *eating them*!"

—Randall, "the honey badger guy"

A starving mouse will eat its own tail.

XTREME EARTH

It seems that no one's ever suggested to Mother Nature that she do anything in moderation...sort of like how Felix the Dog gobbles up treats at the BRI.

LIGHTNING ALWAYS STRIKES THE SAME PLACE

The Catatumbo River in Venezuela is the site of a continual lightning storm. More than 160 nights a year there's a light show in the sky above the spot where the river empties into Lake Maracaibo. On those nights, thousands of lightning bolts flash 16 to 40 times a minute for 10 hours at a time. And it's been that way for centuries.

Throughout history, sailors have relied on the lights for navigation. Called the "Beacon of Maracaibo," the storms can be seen as far as 200 miles away. In 1595, they revealed the presence of Sir Francis Drake's ships trying to sneak up on the Spanish garrison at the city of Maracaibo. Venezuelans even credit the lightning with guiding their navy when they fought against Spain for independence in the early 19th century.

So what accounts for these near-constant lightning storms? For one thing, the area is ringed with mountains that trap warm rising winds that are filled with moisture collected from the evaporating waters of the river and the lake. As the winds rise, it puts them on a collision course with the heavy, frigid air coming down from the high Andes. It's a type of wind collision that's a typical recipe for thunderstorms. Some scientists have added another element to the mix: the theory that ionized gases rising from decaying matter in marshes and oil deposits also encourage the lightning in the storms because they give off electrical discharges.

QUIT BLOWING YOUR TOP!

Stromboli is one of the eight Aeolian Islands, a chain of volcanic islands that lie just north of Sicily. The island is home to about 500 residents as well as the most active volcano on earth: Mount Stromboli, which has been erupting pretty much nonstop for more than 2,000 years (making it the longest-erupting volcano on earth). Just over 3,000 feet above sea level, the volcano has been nicknamed the "Lighthouse of the Mediterranean" because its fiery eruptions can be seen for miles.

Mount Stromboli typically explodes every 15 minutes, ejecting lava sprays, "lava bombs" (blobs of lava), and hot rocks. Its eruptions are so famous that when other volcanoes explode in a similar way, it's called a "Strombolian" eruption: a mild explosion that produces molten rocks and ash. But don't be lulled into a false sense of security. Tourists who come to enjoy the fireworks have been—on occasion—injured or killed by sudden violent explosions, flying rocks, or cave-ins.

Some of the more violent eruptions cause landslides along the southeastern slope of the volcano, which is called La Sciara del Fuoco ("stream of fire"). In 2002 an explosion sent such large amounts of rock into the sea that it caused two tsunamis. Buildings on the island were damaged, but luckily there were no fatalities. Geologists warn that someday—though they don't know when—La Sciara del Fuoco could collapse. If that happens, the tsunami will be so large that the island will be completely destroyed.

PRAYING FOR RAIN

The driest nonpolar desert on earth—the Atacama Desert—stretches 600 miles north to south along the coast of Chile between the Pacific Ocean to the west and the Andes Mountains to the east. The Andes prevent rain clouds from reaching the Atacama; in fact, some places in the central desert haven't seen even a drop of rainfall since records have been kept. On average, though, the desert gets an average rainfall of a measly ½ inch or so.

Geological and mineralogical studies show that the Atacama has been arid for more than 20 million years, which makes it the world's oldest stretch of desert. In fact, in many spots the Atacama is so barren that there aren't even any flies because there's nothing for them to eat. Some moisture—in the form of fog from the Pacific Ocean—does reach parts of the Atacama. There, cacti and desert animals survive by taking in the droplets of liquid formed by the fog.

But this driest desert may eventually lose that distinction due

Beavers have a set of transparent eyelids to protect their eyes underwater.

to climate change. In 2012, for the first time since weather records have been kept, the Atacama was hit with four days of rain so heavy that it caused floods and mudslides.

SOME THINGS JUST MAKE YOU SEE RED

In the summer of 2001, people who were out in a rainstorm in Kamala, India, found themselves drenched in what looked like blood. The red rains lasted until September, when they simply disappeared. Scientists, of course, got busy looking for an explanation. The first theory they came up with was that the rain had been tinted by a meteor explosion in the upper atmosphere that created red dust. That theory died out when no meteor debris was found in rain samples. Then in 2006 physicists theorized that biological material from outer space could have been swept into the atmosphere via a comet. Headlines like "Rain Could Prove That Aliens Have Landed" filled the international press.

But an Indian government analysis ultimately discovered the real—and less dramatic—culprit: algae spores. A type of algae (part of the *Trentepohlia* genus) creates a red-orange lichen that grows on Kamala's trees, and in 2001 weather patterns caused a profusion of them. The spores were probably carried into the rain clouds in a warm updraft of air—it's estimated that a ton of them fell to earth again in Kamala's rain of blood.

THAT'S ONE GNARLY WAVE

Lituya Bay is a nine-mile-long fjord on the Alaskan panhandle, about 120 miles from Juneau. Part of it sits above the Fairweather fault, one of the world's most active. On July 9, 1958, a powerful earthquake struck Alaska along that fault line, the effects of which were felt for 400,000 square miles—even as far south as Seattle, about 900 miles away. The epicenter of the quake was only 13 miles from Lituya Bay in the state's southeast corner.

At the head of the bay is Gilbert Inlet, surrounded by high cliffs and glaciers, and that's where the earthquake caused a landslide that sent 40 million cubic yards of rock and glacier ice into the water some 3,000 feet below. The massive landslide triggered a huge tsunami…the largest wave in recorded history. It was 1,720 feet high—taller than the Empire State Building. The crashing wave ripped out all the vegetation, including millions of trees, in its path. Fortunately the area was isolated at the time, and the bay was used mainly by fishermen as a temporary harbor. So only five people died in the disaster.

STRIPED ICEBERGS?

In 2008 Norwegian sailor Oyvind Tangen posted several photographs on the Internet that he had taken while aboard a ship in the Southern Ocean, about 1,700 miles south of South Africa. The images showed large icebergs with one or more striking, colorful bands—including blues, greens, yellows, and reds—striped across the icebergs' curving contours. At first, people thought Tangen had doctored the images, but the phenomenon has since been confirmed and explained. The bands are formed when the ice is still part of an ice shelf and are caused by the layered buildup of dead marine life (plankton, krill, etc.), each of which forms its own unique colored layer. When a chunk of ice breaks off a shelf and becomes an iceberg, the cross-sectioned layers appear as colorful stripes.

Extra: The photos of the striped icebergs made the rounds of the Internet again starting in 2010, only this time they were accompanied by messages that said the photos were taken on Lake Michigan. Not true! There are no icebergs on Lake Michigan or any of the other Great Lakes.

* * *

THE TULIP BUBBLE

Tulips were first introduced into Europe by the Ottoman Empire in the 1550s. The flowers became enormously popular among the upper classes in the Netherlands—so much so that the price of a single bulb reached the modern equivalent of more than $1,000, and they were sold and resold by traders like today's stocks. The tulip market collapsed in the winter of 1636–37, when interest simply dried up and several people lost fortunes to the suddenly worthless tulip trade. Many historians call the "Tulip Mania" era, as it is known today, the first economic bubble—and burst—in modern history.

THE HAIR OUT THERE

The facts—some of them hair-raising—about hair.

• If you're average, you have 120,000 hairs on your scalp. Natural blondes have slightly more (140,000); redheads have slightly fewer (90,000). Women have more hair on their heads than men do.

• Fur is just another word for hair. Whiskers, on the other hand (the kind that cats and dogs have), are special. These ultrasensitive hairs help animals navigate.

• What manufacturers call "hair care" can actually damage your hair. Shampoos, combing, brushing, dyeing, and using dryers and other styling tools can cause split ends. Other culprits: poor diet, excessive sun exposure, and chlorine. By the way, split ends can't be repaired—the only way to get rid of them is to cut them off.

• There was a time when Disneyland prohibited men with long hair from entering the park, and until 2000, Disney's male "cast members" couldn't have facial hair.

• An average man's beard will grow between five and six inches in a year. Men who prefer not to sport facial hair spend about five months of their lives with a razor in hand.

• African American hair is less dense per square inch than Caucasian hair (190 hairs versus 227 hairs per square inch). Afro-textured hair also grows more slowly.

• Humans' head hair rarely grows much longer than 28 inches.

• The hair on your arms and legs, however, is genetically programmed to stop growing when the hair reaches a half inch to two inches in length.

• Hair grows faster in warmer weather.

• Hair does not continue to grow after death, but because the skin shrinks, it sometimes looks like it does.

90 percent of plants depend on fungi for their survival.

• *Trichophagia* is the term for compulsively eating your own hair. The disorder is sometimes accompanied by *trichotillomania*, obsessively pulling your hair. Unlike cats, humans aren't able to cough up a hairball—human "hairballs" (called "bezoars") have to be removed surgically.

• The shape of your hair follicles determines how curly or straight your hair is. Curly hair follicles are oval; straight hair follicles are round and tube-shaped.

• Hair holds its natural color for years, so the only way your hair can "turn gray overnight" is if you dye it.

• The hair on your head grows in a *whorl*, a circle that grows either clockwise or counterclockwise. Just 5 percent of people have two different whorls (known as "double whorls"); an even smaller percentage have three.

• At six months in utero, humans have all the hair follicles they'll ever have on their entire bodies.

• If you're average, you'll find 550 eyebrow hairs above each eye. Why do you have eyebrows at all? To keep sweat out of your eyes.

• Hair has a growth stage of two to six years. The follicle rests for up to three months, then allows the hair to fall off, and starts the process again.

• Humans have about the same number of hair follicles as horses, chimpanzees, and mice.

• When in a growth phase, a rat's whisker will grow one millimeter per day, or about 1.2 inches a month.

• The hair on a polar bear's body is hollow and translucent to better trap warmth and to take advantage of whatever sun the animal might soak up. That means, technically speaking, that polar bears aren't white—they just look like they are. Their fur is actually colorless, but looks white in the sunlight…and their skin is black.

Elephants can stop and start their digestion at will.

NATURE GOES TO WAR

Most people think biological warfare is a modern phenomenon created by scientists in a laboratory, but it's actually been in use for centuries. From ancient times, whenever humans needed help defeating their enemies, they drafted Mother Nature into their army.

SNEAKY TRICKS WITH SNAKES

In the fifth century BC, Scythian archers (who lived in what is now the Crimea near the Black Sea) dipped their arrows into viper venom mixed with blood and animal dung. They were crack shots, the Scythians, and already famous because each archer could fire off about 20 arrows per minute, but the arrow mixture made them even more formidable. The venom contained toxins that destroyed red blood cells and caused a lot of pain; a wounded man would suffer until his eventual death from heart failure or respiratory paralysis. If, by chance, the venom didn't work, the infection caused by the blood/feces combination would do the job.

Then there was Hannibal, the ancient military commander best known for the elephants he brought along when he led his Carthaginian army over the Alps to attack Rome—but elephants weren't the only trick he had up the sleeves of his tunic. In 190 BC, when his navy fought against King Eumenes of Pergamon (now in Turkey), Hannibal stocked his ships with clay pots filled with venomous snakes. When the ships came within range of Eumenes' navy, Hannibal's men hurled the pots at their enemies. The pots smashed on the decks, and the snakes slithered out, throwing Eumenes's sailors into a panic. Hannibal's forces easily won the battle.

YOU CATCH MORE ENEMIES WITH HONEY

When the ancient Greeks besieged the town of Krissa in the sixth century BC, they poisoned the local wells with the toxic hellebore plant, a flowering perennial. The enemy was knocked out with extreme stomach distress, diarrhea, and—in strong enough doses—death.

Another case of mass poisoning took place in the first century

Species in the orchid family outnumber mammal species four to one.

BC. Knowing that rhododendron was poisonous and that when bees made honey from rhododendron nectar, the honey contained alkaloids that could severely sicken humans, the Heptakomotes (who lived in what is now Turkey) used it to defend themselves against the Roman legions led by Pompey the Great. They left batches of the toxic honey near the path of Pompey's advancing troops, and the soldiers, who thought they'd found abandoned spoils of war, ate it all. The fierce Roman soldiers—now suffering from delirium, vomiting, and diarrhea—were easily defeated by the weaker Heptakometes.

TUNE IN, TURN ON, DROP OUT

In the sixth century BC, the Assyrians poisoned the wells of the Israelites and other enemies with a fungus—rye ergot—that caused hallucinations and, in strong enough doses, could kill.

During World War I, Britain started dropping cigarettes and propaganda leaflets from planes to try to persuade the Ottoman Turks to drop their alliance with the Germans, but the Turks would smoke the cigarettes and throw away the propaganda. Just before the Battle of Beersheba, a British intelligence officer decided to drop cigarettes laced with opium. When the British attacked the next day, the Turks were so high that they had trouble standing, let alone fighting. Needless to say, the British were victorious.

SMOKING CAN BE DANGEROUS

The Chinese had lots of recipes for cooking up military victories. In the fourth century BC, they used an ancient version of a poison gas to defend a fortress against a besieging enemy. When enemy soldiers tried to tunnel into a citadel, the Chinese defenders "smoked them out" by burning toxic substances like sulfur, which creates poisonous sulfur dioxide when burned. The Chinese soldiers directed the smoke into the tunnels with a long pipe and a bellows. Clouds of poisonous smoke and gases overwhelmed the enemy in the small underground space—they dropped where they were and died of asphyxiation.

BEE BOMBS AND SCARY SCORPIONS

In the days of high-walled castles and fortresses, bee hives and hornet nests were used as weapons—hurled via catapults over town and castle walls. The Romans especially liked to use bees and other stinging insects in their naval battles. They'd catapult the nests and hives onto ships and wait for chaos to break out and the sailors to jump overboard.

In the second century BC, the Romans found themselves the victims, though. When they tried to climb the walls of the ancient fortified city of Hatra in Iraq, the defenders threw clay pots at them containing not just bees or wasps but—some historians believe—venomous scorpions.

Centuries later, the Vietcong also used scorpions against American troops during the Vietnam War. Because the North Vietnamese often operated out of a network of underground tunnels, any U.S. soldier unlucky enough to have found one of the tunnels might be surprised by trip wires and booby traps. If a tripwire was hit, a grenade might go off...or a box filled with stinging scorpions might fall on the soldier's head.

GERMY WARFARE

What is believed to be history's first use of a plague as a weapon took place in 1346 when Mongol emperor Janiberg Khan's troops held the town of Kaffa (now Feodosiya, Ukraine) under siege. Bubonic plague had broken out among the emperor's troops, so he had the corpses of his soldiers catapulted over the walls of Kaffa in an effort to spread the disease. It worked, and the locals got sick. But Khan wasn't able to take advantage of Kaffa's suffering: He had to retreat anyway because so many of his own men were dying. Once the Mongols were gone, the residents of Kaffa (many of whom were traders from Italy) tried to escape the contagion by fleeing back to Europe on flea-ridden, rat-infested ships. Some historians believe that Khan's use of biological warfare launched the Black Death, the plague epidemic that hit Europe in the 14th century and killed about 25 million people.

TROJAN HORSE, AMERICAN-STYLE

In the 18th century, Native Americans were giving the British all sorts of trouble during the French and Indian Wars, so in 1763 Sir Jeffrey Amherst, commander of the British forces in North America, ordered that the blankets of smallpox patients (which were usually burned) were to be given to the Delaware Indians to "reduce them." Blankets and a handkerchief that had been used by smallpox patients were passed to the tribe leaders during a meeting to discuss peace terms. Like most Native Americans, the Delaware had no natural antibodies to protect them from diseases like smallpox, and were decimated by the disease.

* * *

FANTASTIC FISH

Some fish do really amazing things.

• **Breathe with lungs:** Scientists believe that the first fish to take to land millions of years ago was related to today's eel-shaped African lungfish. Why? They come up to the water's surface about every 30 minutes to breathe air through actual lungs. In the dry season, when their lakes or streams can dry up, they burrow into the mud and make an airhole to breathe through. They stay dormant for months until things get wet again.

• **Change their sex:** Clownfish are all born male, and in a school of clownfish, all stay that way except one dominant female. When she dies, the dominant male of the group changes his sex and becomes the dominant female.

• **Skip:** Mudskippers live in Africa and Polynesia, where they spend time out of the water feeding on small animals and insects in the mud. Using their large pectoral (front) fins like crutches, they sometimes curl their bodies sideways and spring forward in a type of "skip."

• **Hide in trees:** The mangrove killifish of Florida and Central and South America live in small pools of water that often dry up. When that happens, these little (two-inch-long) fish alter their gills to hold water inside them. The water provides them with oxygen while they flop into the cracks of trees and logs waiting (sometimes for more than 60 days) for their pools to return.

Scientifically speaking, only insects belonging to the order Hemiptera are considered "bugs."

SCENTS AND SENSIBILITY

Today, most perfumes and colognes are synthetic, made in laboratories. But in the old days, they came from natural substances... like flowers, tree resin, or sperm whale vomit.

MUSK

From: Musk deer

Smells like: Warm and earthy

Story: By far, one of the most common ingredients in perfumes throughout history, musk has long been considered an aphrodisiac. In fact, musk is so popular that the word has become a general term to describe any earthy, sensual scent. Even a very small amount of musk can permeate a room, and it has a tendency to cling to anything that comes in contact with it. In the 18th century, the East India Company banned the substance from ships carrying tea, because when the tea arrived, it tasted like musk. And Josephine, wife of Napoleon, supposedly loved it. Even 40 years after her death, the smell lingered in her dressing room.

AMBERGRIS

From: Sperm whale intestines

Smells like: When it's fresh, ambergris smells like...well...fecal matter. But after it ages for a few months, it takes on a sweet, earthy smell, like seaweed and roses.

Story: Ambergris is a growth that forms in a sperm whale's gut around bones and other undigested pieces of fish. The sperm whale's stomach secretes a waxy bile that coats the irritant. Then, when the mass gets too big, the whale either passes it through its intestinal tract or spits it back up.

During the 19th and early 20th centuries, sperm whales were hunted almost to extinction by whalers who made a lot of money selling their highly prized blubber and ivory-like teeth. But even in those days, ambergris was considered a special find. Sailors who discovered masses of it floating in the ocean (weighing up to 100 pounds and looking like huge sponges) were considered extremely lucky because ambergris was rare and prized for use in expensive perfumes. Because so many sperm whales were killed, they are now

Archaeologists have found the ruins of a perfume factory on Cyprus—from 4,000 years ago.

a protected species, so almost no modern perfumes are made with natural ambergris.

CIVET

From: The perineal (anal) glands of civets, nocturnal foxlike mammals from Africa and Asia

Smells like: Deer musk

Story: The civet's perineal glands produce a yellow, fatty substance that both sexes use to attract mates. It became very popular as a perfume component in the 17th and 18th centuries because it was similar to the prized deer musk smell. In particular, English dandies (essentially, 18th-century metrosexuals) often wore civet-scented gloves and handkerchiefs. Because it can be harvested without killing the animal, it's still available today.

FLOWERS

From: Various types of flowering plants—rose, orange, jasmine, and gardenia are among the most popular scents.

Smells like: Well…flowers

Story: Floral scents are probably the most recognizable perfume ingredient. But not all florals are created equal, and some have baffled perfumers for centuries. The earliest known method for collecting floral oils was simply to press the flowers, like squeezing an orange. But that method only works for scents that have lots of oil in them, like citruses. So eventually, perfumers began using a process called distillation, putting the botanical mass in water and boiling it. Distillers then collected and condensed the steam to produce a concentrated solution of floral oil.

This method works on many flowers, but the heat destroys some scents. So in the 19th century, a Frenchman named Jacques Passy came up with another method to capture flowers' smells. His method, known as *enfleurage*, pressed flowers between layers of fat, resulting in a scented substance called a *pomade*.

But there were still flowers whose scents couldn't be captured by any of these methods. Freesia, gardenia, honeysuckle, lilac, lily of the valley, orchid, tulip, and violet especially evaded perfume makers because the complex and fragile molecules that make up those scents are destroyed in the extraction process. When syn-

Grinning or pulling on their lips is a sign of aggression in monkeys.

thetics came along in the 20th century, scientists were finally able to capture the scents in a bottle—or rather, a rough approximation of the scent. A really discerning nose, for instance, can tell the difference between a synthetic lilac scent and that from the flower itself.

FRANKINCENSE

From: Tree resin, specifically from the *Boswellia sacra* tree found mostly in Africa and Asia

Smells like: Exotic, spicy, smoky, and sweet

Story: Frankincense—one of the gifts offered at the birth of the baby Jesus in the story of the nativity—was among the earliest, most prized, and most expensive components of perfume. According to the ancient Roman historian Pliny, only men from certain families were allowed to gather frankincense. And while they were harvesting it, they were required to remain celibate and not attend funerals, so their spirits (and the scent) would remain pure.

* * *

THE ANT DRIVER

Deep in the jungles of Thailand lives a parasitic fungus that can get ants to do its bidding. The unfortunate insects inadvertently pick up the fungal spores on the forest floor. The fungus quickly spreads throughout the ant and starts to take over its muscles and brain. The ant stumbles as if drunk—that's the fungus learning how to "drive" the ant. Once the fungus has gained control, the ant awkwardly finds its way to a tree trunk, climbs up, and starts wandering around on the undersides of the tree's lowest leaves (not normal ant behavior). Once the infected ant finds a suitable leaf, which for some reason always occurs at around noon, the fungus forces the ant's powerful mandibles to chomp down hard on the leaf's main vein. Then the fungus turns off the mechanism that allows the ant to open its jaws. The ant can't let go. But the fungus doesn't kill the ant immediately. It waits until sunset. Then, as night falls, fungal cells burst out of the ant's head and send out a stalk. New spores erupt from the stalk and drift to the forest floor...where they will await the next unfortunate ant.

Without the atmosphere, the average temperature on earth would be just 5°F.

YOU KNOW THE "RACCOON"...

...but do you know the other *raccoon? The pygmy one that lives only on a Mexican island? Here's that story, and the stories of some other little-known cousins of animals we "know" so well.*

YOU KNOW: The wolf

SPECIFICS: The iconic, night-prowling, howling dog that most of us think of as the wolf is the species *Canis lupus*, which we know most commonly as the gray wolf. It can be found in parts of the continental U.S., most of Canada and Alaska, Asia, and eastern Europe (where it's known as the "Eurasian wolf").

YOU MIGHT NOT KNOW: The red wolf (*Canis lupus rufus*). There are 39 recognized subspecies of *Canis lupus*, each with its own unique characteristics. One of the most interesting: the red wolf, which once roamed all over the eastern U.S., but primarily in the Southeast. Unfortunately, they went extinct in 1980. Fortunately, a captive breeding program was already underway by that time. In 1987 the red wolf was reintroduced into the wild in northeastern North Carolina. And even though they're still critically endangered, it was a success—red wolves can be found there today. Red wolves are smaller and more slender than gray wolves, reaching about 80 pounds (grays can reach 175 pounds). They have larger ears and more red coloring in their coats.

YOU KNOW: The fox

SPECIFICS: What most of us know as the fox is either the red fox (*Vulpes vulpes*) or the gray fox (*Urocyon cinereoargenteus*). They're an interesting story in their own right, as they're not closely related. The gray fox first appeared in what is now North America, making an evolutionary split from an earlier canine species more than 3 million years ago. Its range today extends from southern Canada to northern South America. The red fox first appeared in Eurasia, also more than 3 million years ago, and it didn't make it to North America until 300,000 years ago. Its

Other names for the gray wolf: timber wolf, Arctic wolf, tundra wolf, and Plains wolf.

modern range still runs through Eurasia, as well as Alaska, most of Canada, and the northern half of the United States.

YOU MIGHT NOT KNOW: The island fox (*Urocyon littoralis*). This is a fox species that split from the gray fox after becoming isolated on six of the eight Channel Islands of Southern California about 15,000 years ago. Scientists think they got to the islands by natural rafts. At the time, sea levels were much lower, and gray foxes are believed to have been caught on floating debris and carried to the islands. Since then, they've changed: Island foxes have much of the grizzled-gray, reddish-brown, black, and white coloring of gray foxes, but these guys are tiny—the size of house cats. Five pounds is an average weight, where grays easily run to 15. (This is the result of a natural phenomenon called *insular dwarfism*, which sees animals shrink in size over time when they are subjected to a geographically small environment, like that of an island.)

YOU KNOW: The raccoon

SPECIFICS: The inquisitive, "masked," nighttime raider of garbage cans and occasional mangler of pets is the raccoon species *Procyon lotor*. They are enormously successful animals, and are found virtually everywhere in North America (except for the very far north), in wilderness regions, towns, and cities.

YOU MIGHT NOT KNOW: The Cozumel pygmy raccoon (*Procyon pygmaeus*). It's found only on Cozumel, a small island off the east coast of Mexico's Yucatán Peninsula. Rising sea levels isolated it there roughly 26,000 years ago, and it has since then evolved into its own species. Pygmy raccoons have the mask and overall raccoon appearance, and their diet is roughly the same: they'll eat almost anything, but primarily crayfish, insects, and fruit. But the Cozumel pygmy raccoon is, as the name implies, quite small (another result of insular dwarfism), topping off at around nine pounds—about half the weight of its cousin to the north. Other differences: they have a black throat band; they lack a thick underfur, which they don't need in the warm climate on Cozumel, and which makes them look "skinnier" than the northern raccoon; and the fur on their tails is golden-yellow. Males also have orange fur on the scruffs of their necks. (There is actually one other raccoon species: the crab-eating racoon, *Procyon can-*

Female fireflies can't fly—their wings are too short.

crivorus, is native to Central and South America. The name is deceiving, though, as they will eat almost anything, and they look a lot like the northern raccoon.)

YOU KNOW: The skunk

SPECIFICS: Americans and Canadians of a certain age know their skunks—because we watched *Pepé Le Pew* cartoons on TV every Saturday morning! Pepé was a striped skunk (*Mephitis mephitis*), the most prevalent species in North America. They're shiny black, with bright white on the tops of their heads and necks that breaks into two white stripes that run down their backs, meeting again at the tail. They also have a thin white stripe between their eyes, pointed snouts, and very small ears.

YOU MIGHT NOT KNOW: The American hog-nosed skunk (*Conepatus leuconotus*), native to the American Southwest and Mexico. These skunks have solid black faces with no white stripe between their eyes. Also, the white on their backs is often solid rather than striped. But most significantly, they have broad, hairless, flat-nosed snouts like pigs. They use those snouts as pigs do—to root in the earth for insects, grubs, and other foods...which is why they're called "rooter skunks" in Texas.

YOU KNOW: The crow

SPECIFICS: The large, black, inquisitive bird you think of as the crow is very likely the American crow (*Corvus brachyrhynchos*), which can be found virtually everywhere in the continental U.S., as well as in the southern half of Canada and into Mexico.

YOU MIGHT NOT KNOW: The northwestern crow (*Corvus caurinus*) and the fish crow (*Corvus ossifragus*). If you live in coastal regions of the Pacific Northwest, the far west of Canada, and Alaska; or in the coastal regions of the American Southeast, you may think the crows you know are just plain old crows, but they might not be. In those regions, populations of crows long ago developed into their own unique species. Today they overlap with the American crow—and they are very hard to tell apart. The most noticeable physical difference: both species are a fair bit smaller than the American crow. The most noticeable *behavioral* difference: While the American crow will eat just about anything,

A baby mouse is called a "kitten," a "pup," or a "pinkie."

including fruit, insects, carrion, eggs, frogs, crabs, and a lot more—both the northwestern crow and the fish crow have adapted to coastal living. They feed primarily on fish, shellfish, crabs, and mussels they capture in coastal waters. (And the Southeast's fish crow has a unique call: The American crow makes the raspy "krahw," or "caw caw caw" call, but the fish crow gives what is described as a very nasally "nark" or "nyuh ur ur ur.")

YOU KNOW: The rabbit

SPECIFICS: North America is home to a lot of rabbit species. The most well known is the eastern cottontail (*Sylvilagus floridanus*)—the one with the iconic white tail—which lives all over the eastern half of the U.S. Out West, there are jackrabbits. They're actually hares, the most prevalent being the black-tailed jackrabbit (*Lepus californicus*), which is much larger than the cottontail and has much more pronounced and powerful hind legs, as well as longer ears. And if you're way up in the very far north of Canada, the "rabbit" you know is probably the fluffy white arctic hare—*Lepus arcticus*.

YOU MIGHT NOT KNOW: The swamp rabbit (*Sylvilagus aquaticus*). This is a species of cottontail that lives in the American South from Georgia to Texas. And not only can they swim, they actively seek out water. Swamp rabbits regularly cross creeks and ponds in search of marsh plants to eat. And to escape a predator they often jump into water and sit very still with just their little noses exposed—like alligators. This, not surprisingly, makes one of the swamp rabbit's chief predators…the alligator.

BONUS: In 1979 President Jimmy Carter was in a small boat, fishing on a pond at his home in Georgia, when a swamp rabbit jumped off the shore and swam toward the boat. Carter had to use one of his oars to keep what he called an "enraged" rabbit from climbing into the boat. The story became an international sensation the next day, when the *Washington Post* ran a front-page story under the headline "President Attacked by Rabbit."

LET'S DO A STUDY!

Want to get a handle on money matters, lose weight, live longer, or make those selfish jerks in your life a little nicer? Well, there's a study for that.

MONKEY BUSINESS

At Yale University, seven capuchin monkeys were trained to use 12 small silver disks to "buy" either Jell-O cubes or grapes. Once the monkeys knew how to spend and budget their money, researchers put some treats on sale. The researchers found that, just like humans, when a treat like Jell-O was suddenly cheaper, the capuchins bought more of it.

Capuchins also shared human tendencies when it came to the kind of gambling they preferred. In the "winning gamble game," they started with one treat and had a chance to win one more. In the losing game, the monkeys began with two treats, but ran the risk of winding up with only one treat. In each case, about 70 percent of the monkeys preferred to play only the winning game...just like most people.

COUCH POTATO MICE GET THINNER ON FAT

That "exercise in a bottle" pill could be closer than ever thanks to a hormone called *irisin*. Harvard University researchers discovered that irisin can be found in human muscle cells, that it increases when people exercise, and that it triggers calorie-burning. Irisin also converts white fat, which stores energy and can lead to chronic illness, into brown fat, which burns energy and helps keep people fit. Brown fat is better known as "baby fat," and it generates heat to keep babies' small bodies warm. Adults have brown fat too, and slender people have more, which may help them burn calories.

The Harvard scientists injected mice on a high-fat diet with irisin. The mice were obese and had blood-sugar problems that indicated future diabetes. But within 10 days, the mice started losing weight, and their blood-sugar levels came closer to normal. Their muscles also consumed more oxygen, as if they had spent time exercising. Researchers say irisin's ability to stimulate brown fat might one day help people lose weight and might even prevent blood-sugar problems and diabetes.

MILE-HIGH HAMSTERS

In an Argentine study, hamsters were given a laboratory simulation of a six-hour time change. The hamsters, accustomed to 14 hours of light and 10 of dark, suddenly had the lights going on early. Their pattern shifted, just as day and night would shift if they'd flown from New York to Paris. During the simulation, the hamsters had trouble getting their body clocks to adjust and they stayed off their exercise wheels. But hamsters who'd been given small doses of *sildenafil*—the generic name for Viagra—were back on their wheels up to 50 percent faster than their drug-free laboratory companions.

LIVE LONGER, BUT YOU WON'T ENJOY IT

In 2007 a good news/bad news study came out of the University of Buffalo. The good news was that researchers had found a way to make rats live as much as 40 percent longer and to slow down the disabilities normally caused by aging. The bad news? To get those results, the researchers had to cut the number of calories the rats consumed by 40 percent. That finding wasn't new. Since the 1930s, studies have shown that caloric restriction can increase rodent life spans. But this study provided some clues as to why: The restricted diet reduced the rats' amount of *visceral fat* (abdominal fat), which can cause inflammation that in turn causes chronic conditions like heart disease, diabetes, and some cancers. The rats eating fewer calories also stayed fitter. Aging rats on a normal diet lost lean muscle mass, but rats on calorie restriction maintained it.

DYING STINKS

Researchers have found that fruit flies lived nearly 20 percent longer than normal if they had no sense of smell. Even flies that were on calorie-restriction diets, which normally prolonged their lives, had a shortened life span…just from being able to smell yeast (which for hungry fruit flies is a real treat). To further test whether odors affected fruit fly longevity, scientists put flies on a regular diet and then eliminated their ability to smell carbon dioxide. (People can't smell the gas, but fruit flies can.) Fermenting foods, like rotting fruit or yeast, give off carbon dioxide. Female fruit flies that couldn't smell it lived 30 percent longer than the ones who could. But scientists still have a puzzle to solve: Being smell-deprived when it came to carbon dioxide didn't help male fruit flies live longer at all.

SELFISHNESS VS. MOTHER LOVE

Duke University scientists made selfish monkeys more generous with a hormone called *oxytocin* (not to be confused with the painkiller oxycotin), nicknamed "the love hormone" because it builds bonds between mothers and babies. Researchers tested rhesus monkeys—a species known for being competitive, surly, and uncooperative—while having them breathe oxytocin through a nebulizer. In the study, two monkeys were seated next to each other and trained to select symbols from a screen that allowed them to deliver juice to themselves or their neighbor. Then they were each given a choice (different monkeys got different choices): 1) They could get juice for themselves only or get no juice at all. 2) They could get juice for themselves or for their neighbor. 3) They could get juice for their neighbor or throw the drink away.

Usually, the monkeys given the third choice would rather have no juice than give any away, but that changed after they inhaled oxytocin. While on the hormone, they were more likely to give rewards to their neighbor. The monkeys also paid more attention to each other, making eye contact and becoming more social. Scientists hope that oxytocin therapies will eventually improve the social skills of people suffering from disorders like autism and schizophrenia.

* * *

A GROANER

Q: Why do seagulls live near the sea?

A: Because if they lived near the bay, they'd be called bagels.

ANIMAL ACTS, PART II

If it's animal actors you want, it's animal actors we've got.
(Part I appears on page 129.)

PETE THE PUP. It's hard to pin down just one Pete the Pup from the *Our Gang/Little Rascals* series because there were so many of them over the years, but it's safe to say they were all American pit bulls and all sported a man-made black ring around one of their eyes. Pal the Wonder Dog originated the role of Petey in 1927, and according to Hollywood insiders, Pal's starting salary for the *Little Rascals* series was $125 a week—only Allen Hoskins, who played Farina (the most popular character), made more. Pal died in 1930 and was succeeded by his son Pete, who played Petey until 1932.

MORRIS. Morris the Cat became a star when he was cast as the spokescat for Nine Lives cat food. Morris (original name: Lucky) was lucky indeed because he was discovered at a Chicago-area Humane Society and was adopted on the day that he was scheduled to be euthanized. The original Morris made more than 50 commercials and performed in the movie *Shamus*. Since his death in 1978, there have been at least three more Morrises.

SKIPPY. The title role in the Australian TV show *Skippy the Bush Kangaroo*, was mainly played by a small kangaroo named Josephine, but each show required more than a dozen stand-ins and doubles because kangaroos are basically untrainable. Unlike highly intelligent pigs (see Arnold Ziffel in part I), the kangaroos couldn't even be trained to stay on set, so an off-camera assistant had to hold onto the tail of the star or stand-in so the animal didn't run away. The amazing things that Skippy supposedly did, like open doors or serve tea, were done by a human holding sticks with kangaroo paws on the end. But the fans didn't know that...or care: The show, which first aired in 1966, made Skippy a megastar in 84 countries before its run ended in 1969. It's claimed that Josephine lived not like the star she was, but was kept in a cloth sack, probably so she couldn't escape back to the bush.

TRIGGER. Roy Rogers's palomino horse, Trigger, was sired by a Thoroughbred and a palomino mare. He was still using his original name, Golden Cloud, when he made his movie debut in *The Adventures of Robin Hood*, playing Maid Marian's (Olivia de Havilland) horse. When Rogers bought him in 1938 for $2,500, he renamed the animal Trigger and began to train him immediately to do tricks for the more than 100 movies he would appear in (though stunt doubles were used for hard or dangerous work). A huge TV star in the 1950s, Trigger died in 1965, at which point Rogers had his old friend stuffed and mounted. The taxidermied horse sold for $266,500 at an auction in 2010.

* * *

45 ANIMALS NAMED AFTER ANIMALS

Antelope squirrel
Ant lion
Bee wolf
Bird snake
Bull shark
Buffalo carpet beetle
Butterfly fish
Cow ant
Crocodile fish
Deer fly
Dolphin fish
Elephant bird
Fish crow
Flea beetle
Gnu goat
Goat antelope
Grasshopper mouse
Hog badger
Horse mackerel
Leopard frog
Leopard tortoise
Lizardfish
Mackerel tabby
Magpie goose
Mole cricket
Mosquito fish
Mouse deer
Opossum shrimp
Otterhound
Oyster crab
Peacock goat
Porcupine fish
Rabbit bandicoot
Rhinoceros auklet
Sable antelope
Salamander mussel
Sloth bear
Sponge oyster
Squirrel monkey
Stag beetle
Swan goose
Turkey vulture
Vulture bee
Whale shark
Zebra turkeyfish

EUREKA! THE DISCOVERY OF PHOTOSYNTHESIS

It took two centuries and scads of ingenious experiments, but eventually some smarty-pants scientists figured out how plants grow.

BACKGROUND

Imagine that you lived in ancient times and wanted to answer some of life's big questions: How did we get here? What are those lights in the sky at night? Why do I poop? And, for our purposes here: How the heck do plants grow out of the ground?! Well, that kind of grandiose pondering eventually produced some answers. Today, most of us are at least somewhat familiar with *photosynthesis*, the process by which plants use energy from the sun to survive and grow. But it took us a really long time to get here.

The first popular theory on plant life came from one of the most important scholars in history, the ancient Greek philosopher Aristotle. He wrote, in the fourth century BC, that plants derived nourishment by absorbing nutritional soil through their roots. His work was so influential on Western thought that this was the prevailing theory on plant growth for 2,000 years—never mind that it was completely wrong. It wasn't until the 1500s, when the Scientific Revolution began in Europe, that people began to try, at least, to apply rational thought to the great questions of the day. And the life of plants finally got a much closer look.

PLANTING THE SEEDS

In the early 1600s, Flemish chemist Jan Baptista van Helmont performed an experiment he believed would prove Aristotle's theory wrong—an almost sacrilegious thing to do at the time. Van Helmont dried a large amount of soil in an oven (to get all the water out of it so he could weigh just the soil itself) and put 200 pounds of it (exactly) into a large pot. Then he planted a sapling willow tree, which he had also carefully weighed, into the pot.

He kept the tree in a controlled environment to ensure that it got no nourishment from any outside sources. He watered it with distilled and pure rainwater and kept the soil covered so no foreign substances could fall into it. After five years he removed the tree from the pot, redried the soil, and weighed both the soil and tree. Result: The tree had gained 164 pounds—and the soil weighed almost exactly the same as it had five years earlier. If Aristotle's theory was true, the soil should have been very much depleted.

Van Helmont had not only shown that Aristotle was wrong, he had also proven his own theory: that plants grow by sucking water up through their roots and converting that water into plant tissue. Except that van Helmont's theory was wrong, too. But never mind: Someone had kicked the great Aristotle to the curb, and by doing so had ushered in an entirely new era of botany.

Bonus: In 1630, in another experiment, van Helmont burned 62 pounds of charcoal made from wood in a closed container. Afterward, he weighed the ash: It weighed just one pound. Where had the other 61 pounds gone? Van Helmont concluded that some of the charcoal had become a "wild spirit," or "gas," a word he coined from the Greek word for "chaos." And although he called it "wood gas," van Helmont had in fact discovered carbon dioxide, or CO_2. And that discovery was going to prove to be especially valuable to scientists in the future.

AIR TIME

News traveled more than slowly in those days; it took 50 years to prove van Helmont's water-into-plants theory had been misguided and another 50 years after that before the next great leap in plant science took place.

In the 1720s, British physiologist Stephen Hales, who had already made a name for himself in the study of animals, started performing experiments with plants. In one of them, Hales attached long glass tubes (¼-inch in diameter) to the ends of cut-off branches of plants, and measured how far sap could be pushed up the tubes (it was found, for example, that a grapevine could push sap to a height of nearly 25 feet). But Hales noticed something else during his experiments: Bubbles often appeared in the sap—meaning that the cut-off branches were emitting air as well as sap. This, along with other evidence he had accumulated in years of experiments, led Hales to believe that plants absorbed and expelled air—they did, in fact, "breathe" in their own way. It was not the first time the idea was proposed, but it was the first time such an eminent scientist proposed it. Other scientists worked on the theory over the next decades, but with little success.

Another 50 years passed. Then, in the 1770s, British scientist Joseph Priestley decided to carry on where Hales had left off—and made one of the most important discoveries ever in the science of botany.

GAS ATTACK

It was by this time known that a lit candle with a jar placed over it would soon go out (due to lack of oxygen, although this wasn't understood then). Priestley expanded on the experiment, and found that a *mouse* with a jar placed over it would soon lose consciousness and, if left in the jar too long, would die. The theory that explained this phenomenon at the time was that fire, and the breathing mouse somehow "dirtied" the air, making it progressively less pure.

But much more important was Priestley's next discovery. If he put a living plant under a jar with a lit candle, the candle burned longer than it normally would. And if he placed a plant under a jar with a mouse in it, the mouse would survive. This, as you can imagine, was an *astounding* discovery. Without realizing it, Priestley had discoverered that plants emit oxygen. (Though, in fact, oxygen was not properly identified until a few years after Priestley's experiments.)

HERE COMES THE SUN

Priestley's experiments proved that plants did *something* to air. Nobody knew what, but it was an enormous step forward, and just a few years later, in 1778, Dutch physician Jan Ingenhousz repeated Priestley's experiments, but this time with an added, and ingenious, element: He kept some of the jars and plants in darkness, and exposed others to sunlight. Through those experiments Ingenhousz discovered that a candle would burn longer, and a mouse would be revived by having a plant in the jar...only if the plant was exposed to direct sunlight. What this proved was that

Dam squatters: Muskrats sometimes move into occupied beaver dams.

plants did something to air—but only with the help of the sun. Science was, once again, turned on its head.

Ingenhousz followed up his brilliant experiment by attempting to reconcile his conclusions with a not-so-brilliant theory that had been around since the mid-1600s. What the plants in his experiment were doing, he said, was cleansing the air of an impurity known as *phlogiston* (FLOW-jiss-ton), which was supposedly produced by fire and breathing creatures, among other things. (The phlogiston theory was posited to explain oxidation processes such as fire and rust.) So once again, a supersmart (for his day) scientist was wrong. It took Antoine Lavoisier, the French chemist who had earlier identified oxygen as an element, to disprove the phlogiston theory, proving instead that what plants were in fact doing was emitting oxygen into the air.

ONE OUT OF TWO AIN'T BAD

It had been nearly 2,000 years since Aristotle had made the first scientific attempt to understand plants, and nearly 200 years since Jan Baptista van Helmont had debunked Aristotle and ushered in the modern era of botany. At this point, the final steps toward understanding at least the rudimentary science behind photosynthesis were just around the corner. And from here on in, things began to move pretty quickly.

The next big question to answer was: If plants were emitting oxygen, where was it coming from? That question was answered in 1782 when Swiss botanist Jean Senebier, while expanding on Ingenhousz's experiments, proved for the first time that plants absorb CO_2 from the air and break it down. That, he said, was where the oxygen came from. (Wrong again, but it was a really long time before this particular theory was disproven.) On the plus side, Senebier was also able to show that it was the *green* parts of plants, rather than the not-green parts, such as flowers, that did this. This was the part he got right.

So: Plants absorb CO_2, use energy from the sun to break it down, convert the carbon in the CO_2 into plant tissue, and emit the oxygen.

EUREKA!

The last really big piece in the photosynthesis puzzle finally

Makeup of air on Earth: 78% nitrogen, 21% oxygen, 0.93% argon, 0.039% carbon dioxide.

arrived in 1804, courtesy of Swiss chemist Nicolas de Saussure, who proved that the carbon a plant got from absorbed CO_2 could not possibly be enough to account for the growth of plant fiber. There had to be something else involved—and he proposed that it was water (which botanists already knew was absorbed by plants through their roots). He was right.

The centuries of questions, experiments, failures, and successes had finally paid off, and the basic process by which plants attain nourishment and grow was finally understood. There were many details to flesh out over the ensuing years (especially the discovery of *chlorophyll*—the stuff inside plant cells that does the actual conversion of sunlight into energy—and which makes plants green), but the basic process had finally been found out.

PHOTOSYNTHESIS

Ladies and gentleman, how plants do it:

• Plants absorb CO_2 from the air via tiny pores in their green parts, most especially their leaves.

• Water (H_2O) is absorbed through the roots.

• Sunlight on plants' green parts induces chemical reactions that break down molecules of H_2O and CO_2. More technically: Photochemical reactions caused by sunlight striking chlorophyll in plant cells releases adenosine triphosphate (ATP), the energy "currency" of cells, which is used to fuel the breakdown H_2O and CO_2.

• Some of the carbon and oxygen from the broken-down CO_2 combines with hydrogen and oxygen from the broken-down H_2O to produce glucose, the "food" the plant uses both as a source of energy and to make plant fiber.

• The only thing left over is oxygen, which is emitted from pores in the green parts of the plant.

• And we get to breathe. Thanks to plants…and photosynthesis. (And thanks to all those guys who worked so hard over all those centuries so you could read about it today!)

NATIONAL ANIMALS

Here in the United States, we have the bald eagle as our national bird. Other countries have these animals.

Australia: Emu, kangaroo, and (unofficially) koala

Bahamas: Blue marlin, flamingo

Bangladesh: Royal bengal tiger

Belgium: Lion

Bermuda: Humpback whale

Botswana: Zebra

Canada: Beaver

Ivory Coast: African elephant

Croatia: Dalmatian

Cuba: Cuban crocodile

Denmark: Mute swan

Finland: Brown bear

Germany: Black eagle

Greece: Dolphin, phoenix

Iceland: Falcon

Ireland: Irish wolfhound

Israel: Israeli gazelle

Italy: Italian wolf

Kuwait: Camel

Mauritius: Dodo bird

Mexico: Xoloitzcuintli (the Mexican hairless dog...not to be confused with Mexico's national dog, the chihuahua)

New Zealand: Kiwi

Peru: Vicuna (a hoofed mountain-dwelling mammal)

Russia: Russian bear

Rwanda: African leopard

South Korea: Tiger

Spain: Bull

Tanzania: Giraffe

Thailand: Thai elephant

Togo: Hippopotamus

JIMMIE'S ANGEL FALLS

You've probably heard of this waterfall. It's less likely, however, that you've heard the story of its introduction to the outside world, and how it got its name.

ANGEL EYES

In November 1933 a small, single-engined aircraft flew over a high and enormously broad tabletop mountain in a remote region of eastern Venezuela. Over one of the mountain's very steep sides tumbled a waterfall—the likes of which the pilot, a 33-year-old American named Jimmie Angel, had never seen before. On his return to the Venezuelan capital of Caracas, Angel told anyone who would listen about the "mile-high waterfall" he had seen, but, he wrote later, "Nobody would believe me."

Jimmie Angel was born near Springfield, Missouri, in 1899. How and when he learned to fly remains a mystery. What is known is that in the late 1920s, after years of working as a barnstormer, movie stunt pilot, and flight instructor in the States, he flew to South America. Somewhere along the line he got a job flying to remote regions of Venezuela hunting for potential sites of gold mines.

ANGEL DESCENDS

It was on one of those searches in 1933 that Angel spotted his waterfall. He vowed to get back to it—and he did, although it took him four years. In 1937, this time accompanied by his wife and two friends, Angel flew back to the waterfall, and actually landed his plane on top of the mountain it fell from. Unfortunately, in doing so, he wrecked the plane, and the group had to make its way down the mountain on foot. It took them 12 days. When they finally made it out alive, word of the waterfall spread around the world, and the waterfall was officially named Angel Falls in Jimmie Angel's honor. At 3,212 feet in height, it remains the highest waterfall in the world.

Bonus: Angel's plane sat atop the mountain, not far from the top of the falls, for the next 33 years. It was finally taken away in pieces in 1970, and reassembled. It can be seen today outside the airport in the nearby town of Ciudad Bolívar.

For more waterfall information, plunge on over to page 299.

PREDATORY PLANTS

Hey, wait a minute...is that plant eating your gerbil?

FLESH-EATING FLORA

Carnivorous plants developed a taste for flesh over 200 million years of evolution. Here's how it happened: All over the world, in areas where the soil is low in nutrients (particularly swamps and marshes), some plants had to make up for the nutritional shortfall. So they developed the ability to capture and eat insects, fish, small reptiles, and even the occasional small mammal. Here are some of our favorites.

SNAP TRAPS

These plants have jawlike, hinged leaves that act like a trap. The leaves are lined with rows of fine trigger hairs that, when touched by an insect, cause the lobes of the leaf to close, capturing the prey inside. The two lobes then form a seal to create a temporary "stomach," where the hapless bug is digested over a couple of weeks. When consumption is complete, the lobes reopen to set another trap. The leaves repeat this cycle three or four times and then become inactive as new leaves sprout and take over.

The best known in the snap-trap category is the Venus flytrap, native to the Carolinas in the United States. Another member of the family, the waterwheel plant (named for its shape), lives in the waters of Europe, Asia, Africa, and Australia.

LOBSTER-POT TRAPS

These predatory plants have a complicated underground leaf chamber that, for microscopic organisms, is easy to enter but impossible to escape. The best example of this category is the corkscrew plant, which has a Y-shaped leaf filled with twisting corridors that lead to a final stomachlike chamber, where tiny protozoan creatures are digested.

PITFALL TRAPS

These grow in the rain forests of South America. The most prominent member of this group is the pitcher plant. Its leaves curl inward, like a piece of paper that's been rolled into a cone. Insects (and in some cases rodents) climb into the pitcher's "mouth" only to find they can't get out. The walls inside are slippery, and the cavity is filled with a liquid that drowns and digests any critter unlucky enough to venture in.

FLYPAPERS

As their name suggests, these plants use sticky stuff—a gluelike substance known as *mucilage*—to trap their prey. The leaves of the plants are studded with fine glandular tentacles that secrete the mucilage. Once an insect comes into contact with the gumminess, there's no escape. A trapped bug eventually dies from asphyxiation or the exhaustion of flailing around trying to free itself.

The most widely distributed flypaper plant is the sundew, which includes almost 200 species across every continent except Antarctica. Their beautiful glistening leaves make them a favorite ornamental plant, though they're difficult to keep alive in a home garden—no matter how many bugs you feed them.

Another flypaper plant is the butterwort, which produces an antibacterial enzyme that prevents its captured prey from rotting during digestion. Hundreds of years ago, farmers in northern Europe started using this enzyme to heal sores and wounds on their cattle. Butterwort is also used in Norway to make *tjukkmjølk*, a thick curdled milk.

SUCTION TRAPS

These come in just one variety: the bladderwort. But more than 200 species of bladderwort grow in either water or wet soil and can survive almost anywhere fresh water can be found. The plants feature bladders that pump out liquid, which in turn creates a vacuum whereby prey, mainly insects, are sucked in through a sort of trapdoor on the bladder. (Larger species of bladderwort are big enough to capture and digest fish and tadpoles.) Scientists consider the suction trap one of the most sophisticated structures in the plant kingdom.

The instrument used to measure movement along fault lines is called a "creepmeter."

YOU SHOULD'VE ASKED YOUR MOTHER, PART II

More innovations inspired by Mother Nature.
(Part I appears on page 51.)

A BUNCH OF BIRD TRAINS

One of the fastest trains in the world is Japan's Shinkansen bullet train, which opened in 1964 and travels between Hakata and Tokyo at 200 mph. In its early days, the bullet train had a problem with the amount of noise it created. As it sped along, air hit the train's metal pantographs, which collect the electricity from the overhead wires, and made really loud sounds. Fortunately, Eiji Nakatsu, the chief engineer for the Shikansen bullet train, was also a member of Japan's Wild Bird Society. Nikatsu started studying owls because he knew they flew quietly. He discovered that small serrated (sawtooth) feathers on the owl's wings changed its reaction to air currents and allowed the bird to swoop down silently on its prey. After engineers serrated the train's pantographs in a similar pattern, the train ran with much less noise.

A second problem occurred when the train rushed through narrow tunnels. As the train exited the tunnels, it pushed out compressed air that expanded with a huge boom, making a racket that disturbed residents and wildlife. Nakatsu believed the "boom problem" was caused by changes in air resistance, so he studied the kingfisher, a bird that dives soundlessly from air, where resistance is low, into water, where resistance is high. Nakatsu found that the bird's ability to dive without making a splash was due to the "keen edge and streamlined shape" of its long beak. When the Shinkasen train was designed so that its front had a shape like a kingfisher's beak, the booming stopped.

FLOWER POWER

Though lotuses grow in the mud, these plants have developed a way to keep their leaves clean. Instead of absorbing water like most leaves, lotus leaves have a rough surface structure that pushes water away. As water rolls off the surface, it takes dirt and dust with them.

Lotusan paint produced by a company in Georgia imitates the cleanliness of the lotus. The paint has a similar molecular structure and mimics the lotus leaf's roughened surface. Buildings painted with the Lotusan paint stay cleaner and are better protected from mold than those sealed with ordinary paint because when water hits them, it picks up dirt and carries it away.

COCKROACHES HAVE HEART

More people die of heart disease than any other ailment, so scientists are always trying to create affordable and safe artificial hearts that can permanently replace a failing ticker. Indian biomedical engineer Sujoy Guha has designed one that he calls the "biventricular pump." Though it still needs more testing, Guha and his team believe the biventricular pump could revolutionize heart care because it's based on the inner workings of a very hardy-hearted creature… the cockroach.

Human hearts have four chambers, but only one, the left ventricle, actually pumps blood throughout the body. This pumping system can put stress on the heart's chambers, and if one them fails, the heart's owner dies. Cockroach hearts, however, have as many as 13 chambers, and each one gently pumps blood into the next, gradually building the pressure until there's enough to pump blood throughout the body. Not only is there less pressure on the heart valves, but if one heart chamber fails in the insect, the rest of them keep working and the roach lives on.

Guha's synthetic heart device has two pumps and multiple, interconnected diaphragm chambers that allow the pressure to build up gradually until the blood is pumped throughout the body, like the slow buildup of pressure in a cockroach heart. The graduated system of pressure puts less stress on the artificial heart's pumping mechanisms, so they're less likely to fail. The cockroach-inspired heart has another striking advantage: It costs about $2,500…compared to more than $50,000 for other artificial hearts. Someday the biventricular pump may help people live longer, and then we'll all owe a big debt to biomimicry—not to mention the cockroach.

Turtles are the only animals whose hips and shoulder blades are inside their rib cages.

THE CHIMP LADY SPEAKS

Jane Goodall's five decades of work with chimpanzees taught her a thing or two...about human nature.

"There are different ways of looking out and trying to understand the world around us. There's a very clear scientific window. And it does enable us to understand an awful lot about what's out there. There's another window, it's the window through which the wise men, the holy men, the masters, of the different and great religions look as they try to understand the meaning in the world. My own preference is the window of the mystic."

"What I have learned from [chimpanzees] has shaped my understanding of human behavior, of our place in nature."

"Anyone who tries to improve the lives of animals invariably comes in for criticism from those who believe such efforts are misplaced in a world of suffering humanity."

"Only if we understand can we care. Only if we care will we help. Only if we help shall they be saved."

"The least I can do is speak out for those who cannot speak for themselves."

"The greatest danger to our future is apathy."

"How we humans came to be the way we are is far less important than how we should act now to get out of the mess we've made."

"As views are becoming more polarized, we must work to understand each other across political, religious, and national boundaries."

"Compromise is all right, as long your values don't change."

"One thing that I had learned from watching chimpanzees with their infants is that having a child should be fun."

"We have so far to go to realize our human potential for compassion, altruism, and love."

"I wanted to talk to the animals like Dr. Doolittle."

It takes about 100 years for a cave stalactite to grow 1 inch.

ANIMAL AMBASSADORS

Move over Kardashians, these media darlings not only knew how to build a huge fan base that lasted more than a few TV seasons, they also helped to change humans' view of the animal world.

ELSA THE LIONESS (1956–61)

Elsa was one of three orphaned cubs rescued in the 1950s by George Adamson, the senior game warden of Kenya's Northern Frontier District. (Adamson and a scouting party had been called out to capture a lioness that was attacking people. When the lioness charged, the men killed her in self-defense... and only discovered her cubs, Elsa among them, afterward.) Two of the cubs went to a zoo, but George's wife Joy insisted on keeping Elsa to raise, an idea that was unheard of then because, at the time, lions were just considered to be mindless killing machines.

Not Elsa, though. She was playful, loving, and devoted to the Adamsons. When she reached three years old, however, she'd grown so large and strong that the couple decided she couldn't continue being a pet. So George began taking Elsa out to the bush, helping her learn to stalk animals, kill her own food, and fend for herself. Eventually, Elsa became the first captive lion successfully returned to the wild.

Elsa retained her affection for George and Joy, always returning home to visit. When she arrived one day with three cubs, it was clear she'd adapted to her new world. But life in the wild was hard—Elsa died of a blood disease before her cubs were grown. So the Adamsons raised them, too, and then set them free on the African plains.

Claim to fame: Joy Adamson wrote *Born Free* about raising Elsa and returning her to the wild. The book became a best seller and was made into a film in 1966. George trained the captive, but not-quite-tame lions that starred in the movie, and the natural charm of the lions helped make the film an international hit.

Legacy: Elsa's love and loyalty changed an entire generation's view of wild animals. For the first time, lions were seen as individuals with differing personalities, instead of brutes just to be hunted. The success of Elsa's release into the wild also sparked a new movement to help captured animals to be returned to an environment that was as close as possible to what nature intended. When Elsa was returned to the wild, most people considered it a novel and even crazy idea, but today, returning animals to their native habitat is an important part of conservation.

After Elsa's death, Joy established Elsa Wild Animal Appeal to aid in the preservation of animal habitats. She also became a founder of the World Wildlife Fund. George founded the George Adamson African Wildlife Preservation Trust and worked full time teaching orphan and captive lions how to survive in the wild. And the actors who played Joy and George Adamson in the 1966 movie founded the Born Free Foundation to aid wild animals in captivity.

CHI-CHI THE GIANT PANDA (1957–72)

In 1958 Communist China was filling its formerly neglected Beijing Zoo with African animals, and Heini Demmer, an Austrian animal dealer, took Chi-Chi the panda in exchange for bringing giraffes, rhino, hippos, and zebras to China. Demmier planned to sell Chi-Chi to the Chicago Zoo, but the Cold War was raging and the United States was boycotting "communist goods," so Chi-Chi was unable to enter the United States. Instead, she moved to the London Zoo, where she was supposed to stay just a few weeks because the organization had a policy of not buying endangered pandas. However, Chi-Chi was such a hit with visitors that the zoo decided to keep her anyway and give her a home.

Chi-Chi enjoyed being with humans and playing games, which immediately endeared her to the English public. A trip to Moscow to mate with the giant panda An An made daily, international headlines as hopes were high—but were dashed when the two animals didn't get along. In London Chi-Chi was a star and indulged. She preferred human foods to bamboo, and got them, even chocolate treats. That poor diet was a likely reason that she died at only 15. (Today pandas can live more than 30 years in captivity.) Her stuffed body is now in London's Natural History Museum.

Claim to fame: Chi-Chi was the first giant panda to arrive in Europe after World War II, and the first to cause "pandamania" in the Western world. With her entertaining and charming personality, Chi-Chi was often a headliner in international news, and she became a TV star after appearances on a live show called *Zoo Time*.

Legacy: In 1961 Chi-Chi's image became the logo for the new World Wildlife Fund (WWF), which is now one of the world's largest independent conservation organizations. The use of a panda mascot influenced the WWF to pursue a partnership with China to research the animals. That research has helped biologists and conservationists better understand how to protect the beloved giants in the wild and in captivity.

ECHO THE AFRICAN ELEPHANT (1945–2009)

Born in Kenya's Amboseli National Park, Echo lived in a close-knit family unit with her mother, sisters, cousins, siblings, and children. Grown male elephants typically leave the family herd and live mostly solitary lives, but a female elephant can become a herd's leader if she assumes responsibility for the group's survival. In her mid-20s, Echo became the leader of her herd.

Echo dealt with the kind of challenges and tragedies that defeat many humans. When her calf was born with a crooked leg and couldn't stand, Echo didn't abandon him—she nurtured and encouraged him until he was finally able to walk. Years later, when another calf was abducted by a rival herd, Echo organized her largest elephants into a posse, charged the kidnappers, and took back her daughter. Echo also comforted her older daughter who lay dying after being shot by a hunter, and then took on the care of her orphaned grandchild. Under Echo's leadership, her herd thrived and multiplied.

Claim to fame: In 1990 naturalist Sir David Attenborough made a documentary about Echo for the BBC. Over the next 20 years, as other films were made about Echo's life and millions of TV viewers watched her work hard for the well-being of her family, Echo became the most admired elephant in the world.

Legacy: Watching happy elephants living in a close-knit family brought support to a movement to free the big animals from the circuses and zoos where they were solitary and confined. The Echo documentaries were also used by wildlife protection organizations to gain public support for preserving elephants in the wild. Plus, Echo's famous herd still brings many tourists to Amboseli, and conservationists hope that the money made will help the Kenyans save their disappearing wildlife.

KOKO, THE GORILLA (1971–)

Born at the San Francisco Zoo on the Fourth of July, Hanabi-Ko, or "Koko," is a female lowland gorilla whose name means "fireworks child" in Japanese. In 1972 Stanford University graduate student Francine Patterson wanted to see if gorillas could communicate with humans. So she initiated Project Koko at the San Francisco Zoo and began teaching the young gorilla three words in sign language: "eat," "drink," and "more."

Within weeks, Koko was signing. She and Patterson eventually moved to the Gorilla Foundation in Woodside, California, where they're still working on Project Koko. To date, Koko has learned more than 1,000 signs, understands about 2,000 words, and has invented her own signs (a mask is an "eye hat," for instance, and a ring is a "finger bracelet.") Koko can even signs lies—she once pulled a sink out of its mooring but told Patterson that one of the zoo's employees had done it. Most touching is Koko's ability to use sign language to express her emotions of love and grief. She still signs about missing her kitten All-Ball, who died in 1984.

Claim to fame: "This fine animal gorilla" (as Koko has described herself) has starred in documentaries on PBS, been featured in *National Geographic*, and appeared on *Mister Rogers' Neighborhood.* With Patterson's help, she's had "conversations" with Betty White, Leonardo DiCaprio, Robin Williams, and even fans on AOL. The children's book *Koko's Kitten*—published in 1987 about her relationship with All-Ball, whom she named because he didn't have a tail—became an international best seller.

Legacy: Before Koko and Patterson worked together, no one had tried to teach gorillas how to communicate; many people believed the animals were bad-tempered and unintelligent. And even though there is still some debate in the scientific community over whether Koko can really communicate as well as Patterson claims she does, Koko's documented abilities have helped humans recognize that gorillas are actually pretty smart. Koko's life story is also being used in Africa by conservationists because she helps convince locals that gorillas and their habitat should be saved.

Insect with the most toxic venom: the harvester ant.

NATURE FILMS: BEFORE COUSTEAU

Have you seen The Cheese Mites? *No? How about* Ingagi? *Not that one either? Well, sit back and read the story of some nature films that are even older than Uncle John.*

BACKGROUND

When Jacques Cousteau burst into international fame in 1956 with *The Silent World*, his documentary about the stunning world beneath the ocean's surface, he introduced millions of people to a whole new aspect of the natural world that they knew almost nothing about. And he introduced them to a genre of filmmaking that few at the time were aware of. The public's love affair with the genre has never subsided, as the blockbuster successes of films like *March of the Penguins* and Disney's *Earth* clearly show. But Cousteau was not the first filmmaker to use wildlife and the natural world as the principal "actors" in a film—that actually goes back to the very beginning of filmmaking. Here are a few of the milestone moments (and some just plain bizarre ones) in the early history of capturing nature in film.

• ***The Horse in Motion*** (1878). In 1878 American photographer Eadweard Muybridge invented the *zoopraxiscope*, a device that could project images of still photographs in quick sequence, giving the illusion of movement. Film historians call it the first prototype film projector. (Thomas Edison copied aspects of it for his much more famous Kinetoscope.) The first movie the zoopraxiscope ever projected: *The Horse in Motion*. It was just three seconds long, and consisted of 12 stills of a horse taken along a length of track at different stages of its stride, in the hopes of learning whether horses' feet all leave the ground at the same time while galloping. (They do.) So what was perhaps the very first film ever made was, in its way, a nature documentary.

• ***Cockfight*** (1894). On April 14, 1894, the world's first commercial "movie house" opened in New York City. It had 10 of Thomas

Edison's Kinetoscopes—peep-show devices, basically, that you had to peer into to see a short moving picture. One of the pictures available that first day: *Cockfight*. It was a 40-second silent film of two roosters fighting each other, with two men behind them pretending to bet and be excited. Not exactly a "nature" film, it nonetheless was an early example of a filmmaker using an animal as a movie's subject.

• ***Rough Sea at Dover*** (1895). This 39-second film (also silent, as all the films listed here are unless otherwise noted) was made by early film pioneers Birt Acres and Robert Paul. It had two shots: The first showed waves crashing against a long pier in Dover, England. The second (location unknown) was taken from a riverbank and was of a swiftly moving river. *Rough Sea at Dover* showed in 1896 at London's Royal Photographic Society, making it the first projected film ever shown in Great Britain. It went on to make several showings in the United States.

• ***The Cheese Mites*** (1903). In this minute-long film, a man notices something funny about the cheese he's eating. So he looks at it through a microscope. The remainder of the film shows tiny mites scrambling around, as seen through an actual microscope, and the man being disgusted and storming off. Made by American Charles Urban, it was shown at London's Alhambra Music Hall in August 1903. It was so popular that it caused a boom in the sale of cheap microscopes in the city. When London's Science Museum showed *The Cheese Mites* in 2008, it called it "the world's first science and nature documentary."

• ***With Roosevelt in Africa*** (1909). British wildlife photographer Cherry Kearton made this film showing former American president Theodore Roosevelt on his famous safari trip to East Africa in 1909. It had several city scenes and scenes of rural native peoples, but it also had a big focus on African animals in their native habitat, which it showed to American audiences for the first time. And Kearton was one of the rare filmmakers adamant about authenticity when it came to nature scenes: "There is no excuse for nature faking," he said. "The truth about birds and beasts is far stranger and more interesting than anything that the faker can imagine." Kearton went on to make several more nature-themed films, which he starred in and narrated himself, becoming an

Porcupines can learn complex mazes and remember them for up to 100 days.

international star. His biggest hit: 1930's *Dassan: An Adventure in Search of Laughter Featuring Nature's Greatest Little Comedians*—a humorous look at the penguins on Dassan Island, South Africa.

• ***The Grand Canyon*** (1911). In 1904 brothers Emery and Ellsworth Kolb set up a photography studio right on the rim of Arizona's Grand Canyon. In 1911 they boated the Green River south from Wyoming to the Colorado River, then through the Grand Canyon—and filmed the journey, becoming the first to do so. They traveled the country showing the film, and started showing it daily at their Grand Canyon studio in 1915. Until 1932, Emery showed the film and sat in the room giving live narration. You can still see it in the revamped studio today, making it very likely the longest continuously running film in history.

• ***Nanook of the North*** (1922). American gold prospector and amateur filmmaker Robert J. Flaherty made this film while living with Inuit villagers on Hudson Bay in northern Quebec, Canada, in 1920 and 1921. The film focused especially on one family—"Nanook" was the head of the household—going about their daily lives in the frozen north. It included fishing and hunting scenes, and even the building of an igloo. Several aspects of the film were entirely fake, however: for example, Nanook's real name was actually Allakariallak, and the hunting scenes were staged. But it became the first internationally successful feature-length documentary and is heralded today as the film that started modern documentary filmmaking. Flaherty developed each day's footage and showed it to the Inuit people taking part in the film, asking them what they thought and taking their suggestions—in an attempt to make the film as true to life as possible. It's a documentary filmmaking technique still honored today.

• ***Ingagi*** (1931). In this feature-length film, an intrepid British explorer in the jungles of the Congo comes across a tribe of people who sacrifice their "naked ape-women" to gorillas. And the "naked ape-women" have sex with said gorillas. The film even showed a child with tufts of curly hair taped to his body who was supposed to be the progeny of such an encounter. *Ingagi* was marketed as a straight documentary by RKO Radio Pictures, one of the most respected film companies of the day, and it smashed several box office records for a few months before it was revealed as a fraud and theaters stopped showing it. (One scene showed the discovery an entirely new species of animal called a "tortadillo." It was later revealed to be a turtle with wings, scales, and a tail glued to it.) The film was of course a precursor to RKO's ultra-mega-smash hit of 1933—*King Kong*. (This is the first film listed here that had sound—as it was just becoming common in films—in the form of the now ubiquitous documentary narrator.)

• ***The Private Life of the Gannets*** (1934). Famed British naturalist Julian Huxley directed this 10-minute film on the gannet, a seabird, on its breeding island off the Welsh coast. The film featured aerial shots of the bird-covered island, very crisp and clear closeups of bird anatomy, and brisk and compelling—if a bit stilted in a 1930s way—narration explaining to the viewers what they were seeing. For example: "What excitement! A mating pair express their emotion by billing. The long beaks click against one another like rapiers." *The Private Life of Gannets* had a profound effect on nature filmmaking—as it became the first such film to win an Oscar, netting the 1938 prize (four years after it was made—the rules were different then) for Best Short Subject.

• ***Zoo Quest to Sierra Leone*** (1954). In 1954 Jack Lester, curator of the reptile house at the London Zoo, invited a 28-year-old producer from the BBC to accompany him to Sierra Leone to film him and his staff capturing animals for the zoo. The show was to be presented by Lester, but he became ill, so the young producer took the job. His name: David Attenborough. The combination of vivid footage from the field and Attenborough's obvious skills as a presenter made the show a enormous hit, and it created a template for nature documentaries that lasted for decades. *Zoo Quest* ran seven episodes over the next 10 years, and Sir David Attenborough, of course, went on to become one of the most famous presenters in television history.

* * *

DOWNSIZING

The weirdest small animal prize goes to the paradoxical frog from South America. The tadpole it comes from starts out being up to 10 inches long...and shrinks to a fifth of that size, before turning into a 2-inch-long frog.

HODGEPODGE

Quick! Some animal facts.

• Snails have thousands of teeth, but they're unlike any you've seen before. Nearly all snails have what are called *radulas*, which are hard, ribbonlike organs that look like tongues and contain rows of tiny teeth. Some snails have thousands of these tiny teeth because they're replaced by new ones as they wear away.

• The chameleon and American woodcock each have a 360-degree field of vision, allowing them to see what's in front of and behind them... and even over their heads.

• Goats can also see almost everything around them, without ever moving their heads.

• Bats can hear at 120,000 Hertz, the highest frequency of all animals.

• Large land mammals such as giraffes, elephants, and cows sleep less than four hours a day. Giraffes can actually go without sleep for weeks at a time.

• Elephants can smell water from up to three miles away.

• A cricket's ears are not connected to its head—its ears are located on its front legs, beneath its knees.

• Crested auklets and whiskered auklets, types of seabirds that roam the North Pacific, seem to be the most fragrant creatures around. Emitting a pleasant citrus scent, they're known as "tangerine-scented birds."

• Snails breathe through their feet.

• An ostrich's eye is larger than its brain.

• There are white horses, but no albinos. A true albino horse would have pink skin and red eyes.

• Contented elephants purr.

• Newborn bats are a quarter of their mom's weight. That's like a human mother giving birth to a first-grader.

***Euhirudinea*—the "true" leeches—have suckers at both ends of their bodies.**

HAVE A HEART

It's only a pump, but if you didn't have one, you wouldn't be here.

THE HEART OF THE MATTER

In a cave in Pindal, Spain, there's a surprisingly well-drawn wall painting of an elephant made some 50,000 years ago. In the chest area is a red mark that some people argue is the creature's ear, a handprint, or a mistake on the artwork. But others say it's the animal's heart.

Of course, ancient hunters would have noticed a dying heart in a fresh kill. Ancient Egyptians knew about hearts (which they removed and stored in jars alongside their wrapped, entombed dead). Early Chinese medical practitioners knew it as part of the circulatory system. And the centuries-old sacred Hindu text, the *Atharvaveda*, included chants for heart health. The Greeks were also aware of a beating heart in the body, but thought it was the home of the soul. The brain, many of them believed, was what kept us alive. By about the 16th century, humankind had a pretty good idea what the heart looked like and what exactly it did, thanks to increasingly sophisticated scientific methods and public acceptance of dissection for the sake of information.

THE FOUR OF HEARTS

The human heart can be broken down into four anatomical parts: the left and right ventricles and the left and right atria. As the heart muscle contracts, both atria contract, forcing blood into the ventricles, which then contract to force blood out of the heart. Then, while the heart rests a beat, blood fills the organ again. It might seem as if the right and left sides are redundant, but that's not so. The right side of the heart sends blood to the lungs for oxygen collection; the left side collects the oxygen-laden blood from the lungs and sends it to the cells and other organs.

IS YOUR HEART IN THE RIGHT PLACE?

It's a myth that your heart is on the left side of your chest—it's actually more in the center of your body, slightly more to the left than the right. That "rule" doesn't apply for all humans, though.

Science has found instances in which the heart is in the opposite position, as in the case of "mirror-image twins," identical twins whose body parts are mirrored, as if they're facing each other through a mirror. In that rare situation, one twin's heart is to the left, the other's is to the right. At any rate, no matter where it lies in your chest, if you're an adult, your heart is about the size of your two fists together.

THE HARDWORKING HEART

In humans, fetal hearts start beating at about four to five weeks and continue to do so, over and over, about every eight-tenths of a second for your entire life. Your heart beats more often when you exercise, get angry, become excited, are frightened, or are otherwise flooded with heart-speeding adrenaline.

If you're average, your heart will force about a million barrels of blood through your body in your lifetime, and it will beat almost three billion times. If your heart were to stop for even a few seconds, you'd lose consciousness. If it stopped for six minutes or more, you'd die.

I *HEART* YOU

The Romans were the first to propose that the heart was a person's emotional center, so it didn't take much to make the connection between the heart and love. The physical reactions we have when we fall in love—that heady rush, the flip-flop in the midsection, the increase in pulse—probably led to that belief. The ancients also thought that there was a vein that ran from the fourth finger of the left hand directly to the heart (there isn't), which is why we wear wedding rings on the left "ring finger."

(NOT) COMPLETELY HEARTLESS

Like humans, most other creatures need hearts to stay alive—the exceptions are jellyfish and coral, which don't have hearts. But that doesn't mean that all other hearts work like ours do:

• Instead of circulating oxygen-rich blood back to the lungs, a fish's heart sends the blood to its gills.

• Frogs have three-chambered hearts: two atria and just one ventricle.

Aptly named: The screaming hairy armadillo is known for...its loud screams.

• Insects have hearts (of sorts), but their circulatory system is open. This means that bug blood (called hemolymph) flows throughout the insect's body—not in arteries and capillaries like ours—propelled by a vessel in its abdomen that functions as a heart.

• The blue whale is the largest creature on earth, so it stands to reason that the whale's heart is the largest, too. A blue whale's heart can weigh 1,300 pounds…about half the size of the average compact car.

• A hovering hummingbird's heart flutters at 1,200 beats a minute or more.

• The giraffe has the highest blood pressure in the animal world because its heart must pump blood with extra force to overcome the gravity associated with a head so high. That doesn't mean the giraffe is a big-hearted fellow, though—its heart is as big as any animal its size. Instead, the walls of a giraffe's heart are thicker and more powerful. And to accommodate all that extra pressure, the giraffe's blood vessels also thicken as the animal (and its neck) grows and ages.

• During hibernation, a bear's heart rate drops to about 22 percent of the number of beats it needs when it's active—about 19 beats per minute in hibernation versus the normal 84 beats per minute while it's doing things like raiding your campsite looking for marshmallows.

• The average pig heart is close in size and output to the average human heart, which is why researchers are looking for ways to genetically modify entire pig hearts for use in human chests. At the moment, though, only pig heart valves—stripped of their genetic material to avoid tissue rejection—are used in human heart surgery.

• The first successful human heart transplant was performed in 1967; the patient lived less than three weeks. Today, the first-year survival rate for cardiac transplant patients is 90 percent.

SCAT-CAN-DOO

It's happened to all of us—you're walking down the street or in the woods and you step in something that you wish you hadn't. But what kind of scat is that?

THE PROOF IS IN THE POOPING

Looking closely at an animal's droppings can tell you a lot. Good scat readers can not only identify an animal by examining its excrement, they can also determine its sex, health, and age, and what it recently ate. And it's not that hard. First, narrow down the possibilities by noting where you are: You won't see cow scat, for instance, on a city street. If you're on safari in Africa, you most likely won't see (or step in) skunk doo. Next, check out the scat's shape, length, and width: Is it round, square, tapered, or blunt-ended? What color is it, and is there anything in it, such as hair, grass, or berry seeds? Then, compare it with the following:

• Fox scat almost always includes hair and is almost always tapered on both ends. Foxes often leave their droppings on stumps or logs to mark their territory. Coyote and wolf scat is similar in shape and content, but larger.

• What an elephant leaves on the ground depends on whether it lives in the wild or in a zoo, what it eats, and how much. On average, elephants poop every six hours and leave around 200 pounds of scat per day. Wild elephants eat branches, grass, and roots; zoo and circus elephants eat branches, too, and also hay, straw, and some vegetables and fruit. Elephants don't digest their food as well as humans do, so what goes in looks a lot like what comes out. Grass, branches, roots, and leaves will create scat that looks like it contains roughage. Vegetables and fruit, because of their higher water content, don't show up as much on the back end.

• The general shape of cow poo is round and flat (hence the term "cow pie"). The average cow will give back approximately 20 times its own weight in manure in a year.

• Most of the time, beavers go to the bathroom in the water, but their scat can sometimes be found on the edges of lakes and ponds. Made mostly of wood chips and sawdust, beaver pellets are oval and rather large, a little more than an inch long and nearly an inch wide.

• In the spring, moose scat might look like a cow patty because the animals are eating new plants. But in the fall, moose poo comes out in oval pellets.

• Porcupine scat is made mostly of wood fibers. Up to an inch long each, the droppings may be left in a chain connected by those fibers.

• Like most cats, lynxes and bobcats leave scat that is blunt-ended and segmented. Also like most housecats, both big cats often bury their scat beneath dead leaves and forest detritus.

• Wombat feces are cube-shaped. Strange as it sounds, scientists believe the shape is to keep the scat from rolling off logs and hills, since the wombat is extremely territorial.

• It's not exactly true that rabbits eat their own poop. Rabbits (and hares) produce a material called *cecotrope*, which is filled with digestible and beneficial dietary nutrients, but happens to come from the bunny's butt. Cecotropes are not feces; in fact, if a rabbit doesn't get its daily dose, the animal may die. Cecotropes, which don't smell very good, look like a tiny cluster of dark brown grapes. Rabbit and hare feces are a different matter. Those are made up of undigestible plants and grasses, and are small and round. Pet rabbit droppings tend to be left in a pile, whereas wild rabbit scat may be scattered, since the animal moves more widely while it defecates.

UNCLE JOHN'S NOTE: If we've convinced you to give scatology a try, here's one important bit of info: Never handle scat with your bare hands. Animal poop, even when dry, can contain bacteria and other nasty stuff that can be deadly to humans.

* * *

The Great Elephant Poo Poo paper company in Thailand turns elephant dung into decorative, no-smell stationery. The dung is collected from conservation parks, and some of the profits go back to the parks to protect and care for the elephants. One piece of elephant dung can produce 25 pieces of writing paper.

MYTHCONCEPTIONS

You may not have known it, but there's a myth out there about arachnid urine. We looked into that—and some other animals myths, too.

Myth: Peonies need ants to open their flowers.

How it spread: This is a popular myth among gardeners. It spread because it's common to see ants swarming peony buds in the morning, and before and while they're opening.

The truth: Peonies can open just fine without ants. Ants swarm the flowers because peonies secrete a nectar that ants love to eat. (The same myth is also associated with hibiscus flowers—and it's untrue in that case, too.)

Myth: Elephants love peanuts.

How it spread: Peanuts became a popular food in the United States in the mid-1800s, and they became a staple treat at the many circuses traveling the country at the time. Around this same time, elephants started being introduced to circuses. People walking around with bags of peanuts naturally tried to feed them to the elephants, and the elephants often ate them. So the idea spread: Elephants really like peanuts!

The truth: Elephantologists say elephants have no particular affinity for peanuts—they eat them simply because they're offered. Elephants much prefer the foods they eat in the wild—primarily grasses, leaves, shrubs, fruit, and especially tree bark.

Myth: Camels store water in their humps.

How it spread: This myth is thousands of years old, and probably came from a simple mistaken inference made by people observing some obvious camel characteristics: 1) camels can go for a long time without drinking water—about seven days on average; 2) when they finally get water they can drink enormous amounts—up to 30 gallons in one go; and 3) they have humps. Combine these things and it's not too hard to see how this myth came to be.

The truth: Camels' humps don't store water, but are made up primarily of fat, which allows for another camel characteristic that you rarely hear about: they can go for just as long, or longer, without eating as they can without drinking—all because of that extra fat stored in their humps. The real reason they go so long without water is because their liver and kidneys are extremely efficient when it comes to water usage, which also accounts for the fact that camels can go many days without urinating. When they finally do go, their urine is as thick as syrup. Plus, camels' red blood cells are oval, rather than circular, like most other mammals. This more streamlined shape allows the vital cells to continue to circulate even in a very dehydrated state, making them yet another key characteristic regarding the camel's ability to go so long without water.

Myth: Elephants are afraid of mice.

How it spread: This is another very old myth, with its first recorded mention going all the way back to AD 77, when Roman scholar Pliny the Elder wrote, "The elephant hates the mouse above all other creatures." Pliny's work was read and respected for centuries in the Western world, and the elephant and mice myth became "common knowledge," even to this day.

The truth: Modern biologists have tested this myth numerous times, and elephants appear little more than bored at the sight of a mouse. Experts say the myth may come from the fact that elephants have poor eyesight and usually barely notice something as small as a mouse until it's right on top of them, at which point they may be surprised by the tiny creature's smell.

Extra: It should be noted the Jamie Hyneman and Adam Savage of the Discovery Channel show *MythBusters* also tested this myth in 2007. The two elephants they observed actually seemed putoff by the sudden appearance of a white mouse and went out of their way to walk around it. So maybe this needs more testing after all?

Myth: Some spiders have 10 legs.

How it spread: This has probably been around as long as people thought to count spider legs, and it's still something that arachnologists are regularly asked about.

The truth: All known spider species—all 40,000 and more of them—have eight legs. The answer to why some people think they're seeing 10 legs lies in basic spider anatomy: All spiders have *pedipalps*, a pair of appendages that grow from the front of their heads and are segmented in roughly the same way spiders' legs are. Except they're not legs—they're mouthparts. Pedipalps are used for holding prey, not for walking. They're also usually very short, much shorter than legs, though in some species, especially the tarantula, pedipalps can be as long or longer than the spiders' legs. So sometimes it looks like spiders have 10 legs.

Myth: Spiders can cause skin ulcerations similar to those caused by bites...just by peeing on you.

How it spread: According to Rod Crawford of the Burke Museum of Natural History and Culture at the University of Washington, this myth started in Central America, and in recent years has made its way to the United States. And it originally had to do with horses, not humans. Crawford wrote:

> In Guatemala this myth (still going strong in 2008) centers on a tarantula species locally called *araña de caballo* (horse spider), which is said to cause severe hoof and leg trouble in horses and other livestock by urinating on them.

The truth: For starters, spiders don't urinate in the way we think or urination—they actually combine urine and fecal matter inside their bodies and emit it as one fairly solid mass. And, says Crawford, it can't cause skin ulcerations. It's made primarily of guanine, which, as one of the main ingredients in DNA, is actually present in every single cell in your body.

Myth: Wolves howl at the moon.

How it spread: People all over the world developed myths involving wolves and the moon. (In Norse mythology, for example, the wolves Skoll and Manegarm chase the sun and moon around the sky, and will do so for eternity.) It's not hard to see why such myths came to be: Wolves are nocturnal, doing their hunting—and howling—at night. Over the eons people came to associate these feared and respected night hunters with that other great symbol of the night, the moon. Not only that, but wolves point their snouts to the sky while they howl, which makes them look like they are "howling at the moon."

The truth: Wolves howl to communicate with other wolves, whether there's a moon out or not. Scientists who study wolves say their howls can mean different things, including a call for the pack to gather, or a message to rival packs to stay away.

Myth: Bees make honey.

How it spread: This one spread because, well, bees *do* make honey.

The truth: However, only a small number of bees make beeswax hives and fill them with honey. In fact, there are only seven species of true honeybees—out of the approximately 22,000 species—on the planet. Several other species not considered true honeybees make and store honey, too, but not in the amounts that honeybees do. Some of the remaining bee species make tiny amounts of honey to feed to their young, but most make no honey at all and don't even live in hives. (Most bees are solitary, and make nests in the ground.)

Myth: Sprinkling salt in your cupboards will keep ants away.

How it spread: The origins of this myth are uncertain, but it is extremely widespread and probably goes back many centuries. The logic behind the salt and ant myth, as explained today, varies. Some say it's because salt is hard for ants to walk on or that ants don't like the smell of salt or that everybody knows ants like sweets—which means they must not like salt.

The truth: There is no proof that salt has any ability to keep ants away. In fact, recent studies have shown that ants living in areas where there is not a lot of natural salt in the soil actually *like* salt, and will go out of their way to find it. So if you sprinkle salt in your cupboards, you may actually be attracting ants.

Bonus: If you have an ant problem and were just about to try some salt—don't worry! You can still try some of the other substances that loads of people swear will keep them away. These include pepper, cinnamon, chili powder, coffee, talcum powder, rice, vinegar, mint apple jelly, tea bags, soapy water, grits, Bounce fabric softener, and ground unicorn horn. We should note that, as with the salt myth, there is no proof any of these actually work. (Except the ground unicorn horn, of course…)

Black bears have been known to open door latches and unscrew jar lids.

13 WAYS TO DIE... BY ELEPHANT

Elephants can weigh up to eight tons, their trunks are 40,000 muscles strong, and they know how to hold a grudge. So it shouldn't come as a surprise that every year they kill hundreds of people...like these unlucky folks.

DON'T BE CRUEL. In 2000 a "taxi" elephant that transported tourists around Bangkok gored a man to death after he offered the animal food...and then took it away.

CAMERAS ROLLING. Three kids escaped unharmed while 38-year-old TV show host Anton Turner was mauled to death by an elephant in 2009. They were all in Tanzania filming the BBC children's show *Serious Explorers* about the adventures of David Livingstone (of "Dr. Livingstone, I presume?" fame).

UNCEREMONIOUS. In 2001 in Kathmandu, Nepal, an elephant used in a religious ceremony went wild and charged a woman, killing her. Despite that, the proceedings continued. When the pachyderm refused to cross a river as part of the ritual, it broke free again and almost stomped on several dignitaries.

ISN'T IT IRONIC? Don Hornsby, a wildlife conservationist, was trampled to death when he tried to photograph an elephant while vacationing in Zimbabwe in 2010.

JUST TRYIN' TO HELP. A zookeeper was treating a female elephant at a zoo in the Czech Republic in 2001. While he was giving her an injection, she jerked away, he tripped on her chains, and she gored him in the chest.

SERVES 'EM RIGHT. In 2007 an elephant gave South African hunter Christo Kaiser a taste of his own medicine. Kaiser's Unico Hunting Safaris group was prowling around northern Botswana, but they didn't notice an elephant that had creeped up on them. At the last moment, the elephant charged, and Kaiser was killed. His companions narrowly escaped.

FASHION TRAGEDY. Gianpaolo Tarabini, cofounder of the Italian fashion house Blumarine, was on a 2008 safari in the Zambezi Valley of Zimbabwe when his group was attacked by two elephants and he was fatally injured.

MOST EVIL USE OF ELEPHANT. The Mughals used elephants to commit executions, sometimes attaching blades to their tusks before letting the animals loose to attack enemies. In the 16th century, the Mughal emperor Humayun sentenced an imam to be crushed to death by elephant for criticizing Humayun.

DEADLY WALK TO SCHOOL. In 2009 an elephant in Kenya went berserk at the sound of a frightened schoolgirl's screams, trampled her, and threw a man in the air. The man survived; the girl didn't.

IGNORING RED FLAGS. At a 1994 circus performance with hundreds in attendance, an elephant (who had endangered people three times the year before) killed trainer Allen Campbell. The African elephant, named Tyke, also seriously injured another circus employee before escaping the arena. As she ran amok for 30 minutes in downtown Honolulu, police fired more than 80 shots and finally felled her. Tyke later died of her injuries.

ELE-FIGHT! In southern Thailand, a 63-year-old Swiss tourist was killed and four others were injured (one of them ended up with 12 broken ribs) when two male elephants they were riding got into a tiff over a female and bucked off their riders.

DRUNKEN RAMPAGE. In 2010 several elephants raided an East Indian village's stash of rice-based alcohol meant for an upcoming festival. The creatures quickly turned belligerent and raged for four days in Orissa and West Bengal, flattening 60 homes and killing three villagers.

Female poison dart frogs care for any red or green young. Males look after yellow babies.

UN-EXTINCT

On page 373 we'll tell you some stories about animals that have gone extinct in relatively recent times. Well, for a little happy balance, here are some animals that were once believed to be extinct—but aren't.

LA PALMA GIANT LIZARD

In 2007 biologist Luis Enrique Mínguez, working on La Palma in the Canary Islands off the coast of northwest Africa, took a photograph of a reptile about a foot long and resembling a monitor lizard. In December of that year, after the photo had been studied for months, it was announced that it was a La Palma giant lizard, which had supposedly been extinct for 500 years. The lizards were known from writings going back to the ancient Romans, but were believed to have been decimated by rats and cats that were introduced into the island's population, as well as by humans who had hunted them. They were thought to have gone extinct by the early 16th century. How the lizards survived unseen on the island—which has a population of about 86,000 people—for so long is a mystery. How many of the lizards are on the island is still unknown; biologists say there may be as few as 50.

TAKAHE

Geoffrey Orbell was a doctor and hunter on New Zealand's South Island. In the 1940s, he heard stories about the takahe—a turkey-sized flightless bird distinguished by its bright orange-red beak and legs—that had been native to the island for millions of years, but which had been wiped out in the 19th century. (The last known takahe was seen in 1898, when a dog was found with one in its mouth.) Orbell began collecting stories about the bird and became convinced that it might still exist. In November 1948 he and three companions were searching for signs of the bird in a remote region in the island's far south when, according to Orbell, "suddenly, a large blue-green bird stepped out from among the snow tussock." It was a takahe. And there were more. Orbell and his friends caught two of the birds, and took several photographs of them. In the following days the photos made the front pages of newspapers all over the world. The takahe is still rare and endangered; only about 200 are alive today. But thanks to Orbell and the serious conservation efforts spawned by his successful quest, they're still around, and hopefully will be for a long, long time.

CAVE SPLAYFOOT SALAMANDER

A species found only in remote caves in the central Mexican state of Hidalgo, the cave splayfoot salamander is brownish in color and has webbed feet. And that's about all we know. The species was first discovered in 1941, which was also the last time it was seen for decades. It was assumed to be extinct, but in 2010, California biologist Sean Rovito visited the region and rappelled down into a large cave system where he immediately saw the salamander in question, the first anyone had seen in almost 70 years. Soon after that, he saw another, and also saw another species, a bigfoot splayfoot salamander, which hadn't been seen in 10 years. For survival, both species rely on the conditions of the region's caves, which are kept cool and humid by the surrounding pine and oak forests. Their discovery has helped environmentalists in the battle to slow deforestation in the region, and plans are now underway to set aside habitats for both species.

OMANIUNDU REED FROG

In September 2010 Jos Kielgast, a student from the University of Copenhagen, was deep in a reedy swamp alongside a tributary of the Congo River in the Democratic Republic of the Congo. It was the middle of the night. Kielgast heard a frog. He carefully followed the sound through the darkness for an hour, at which point he found and photographed a Omaniundu reed frog. Just over an inch long, and brown with bright, fluorescent green spots; it was the first one seen since 1979. Kielgast was part of an international team that had set out in August 2010 on a five-month search of 21 countries to try to find amphibian species that hadn't been seen for at least a decade and that were all feared extinct. (Sean Rovito, who caught the salamander mentioned above, was also part of that effort.) Most of the searched-for species were unfortunately not rediscovered, but several were, including other frog species—one of them was the Chalazodes bubble-nest frog, which was last seen in India...in 1874.

Swordfish lose their scales and teeth as they reach adulthood.

CAHOW

Cahows are seabirds that travel great distances throughout the year, but nest only in natural crevices on the rocky coasts of the British-owned islands of Bermuda. They once numbered in the millions, but after the introduction of pigs to the islands by Spanish explorers in the 1500s and then British colonization in the early 1600s, their numbers dwindled. By 1630 the cahow was gone. Three hundred years later, in 1951, after a number of reports of possible cahow sightings, an expedition was launched to see if the "extinct" birds could be found. They were: 18 breeding pairs were found on rocky islets. Conservation and breeding programs have since brought the bird's numbers up to the hundreds.

Bonus: The cahow was named onomatopoeically for its eerie call, which it makes only at night. According to legend, the sound scared the 16th-century Spanish explorers, which is why they never settled the islands. Today the cahow is Bermuda's national bird—the country's way of thanking the bird for scaring off the Spanish and leaving the islands to be colonized by the British.

EXTRA

A few more not-so-extinct creatures:

• In September 1981 John and Lucille Hogg were at their ranch in Wyoming when their dog Shep brought a dead minklike creature into the house. A local taxidermist identified it as a black-footed ferret, a species declared extinct two years earlier. Further study found that as few as 18 of the ferrets remained, but—thanks to Shep—today there are more than 1,000.

• The Arakan forest turtle was last seen in its native Burma in 1908, but then, in 1994, a few were seen…at a Chinese food market. Where they came from couldn't be determined. Thank-fully, five more were found in 2009 at a remote Burmese elephant sanctuary. They remain one of the rarest turtles on earth.

• In 1870 a skink (a lizard about 20 inches long with long, curved teeth, and therefore given the name "terror skink") was found on a South Pacific island. It was the only one of its kind ever seen… until another was captured and photographed on the island in 2003. No further sightings of terror skinks have been recorded since then.

GOING VIRAL

Most people think of viruses only in terms of the human illnesses they cause, but there's a lot more to the story than that. Viruses may be one of the key building blocks of life on earth.

GENETIC PARASITES

Without viruses, complex life might never have evolved on the planet at all. Even now, viruses play a vital role in producing things that are as important to life as oxygen. Why are they so important? Well, it has to do with genetics.

A virus is a tiny scrap of genetic material. Think of those science-book illustrations of spiral DNA strands. Now imagine using a pair of imaginary scissors to snip off an infinitesimal piece. Wrap the DNA snippet in a protective shell made of protein material, and you've got a virus. And they're small: The entire genome (or genetic sequence) of a virus might be just a dozen or fewer individual genes. Compare that to DNA in human cells, which are made up of about 20,000 genes. But the bizarre part is that viruses actually enter the cells of larger, more complex beings—like humans—and interfere with the function of the beings' DNA. And that's all they do.

SNIFF, SNIFF, A-CHOO!

Because viruses are so small, scientists couldn't really isolate and identify them until the invention of the electron microscope in the 1930s. Naturally, the first viruses that people studied were the ones that made them sick. Humans suffer from a long list of viral illnesses, such as smallpox, AIDS, influenza, hepatitis, and even some types of cancer. The common cold is also viral and serves as a good case study to explain the basic life cycle of all viruses.

The virus that causes colds is known as human rhinovirus (HRV), and its only purpose is to reproduce itself. It does this by invading the cells that make up the surface of a person's nose, throat, and lungs. Once inside a cell, HRV acts like a computer hacker, plugging scraps of alien DNA into the cell's genetic material and reprogramming it—basically ordering it to reproduce itself and, thereby, produce new copies of the virus. The host cell soon fills with so many new copies of HRV that it bursts and dies.

All the classic symptoms of a cold—stuffy nose, sore throat, cough, and fever—aren't actually caused by the virus. Those are the by-product of the human immune system fighting off the viral attack. Fortunately, the immune system is strong enough to eventually kill off the invaders, but by that time, the HRV has probably moved on, using the runny nose and cough the body produces to spread to another person.

MAJORITY SHAREHOLDERS

The viruses that make people sick, however, make up just a fraction of the millions of different viruses that exist in the world. Scientists say there are viruses that have adapted to invade the cells of nearly every kind of life-form, from large mammals to microscopic bacteria. The oceans alone contain trillions of them. Viruses are likely the oldest and most abundant form of life on earth. Why are they so successful? Mostly because they're so adaptable.

A virus is nothing but a very small piece of DNA that makes copies of itself. Not all of the copies are perfect. Glitches in the replication process—called *mutations*—happen all the time. Some of the mutations are bad copies that are unable to reproduce. Those just die off. Other mutations, however, benefit the virus, enabling it to survive in new environments. Most viruses infect only one species. But mutations make it possible for a virus to jump to an entirely new host species. This is where terms like "swine flu" and "avian flu" come from. Those are versions of influenza viruses that jumped to human populations from pigs and poultry.

THE GENE EXCHANGE

Okay, so viruses are super-small and abundant and have a remarkable ability to survive and spread by adapting to new environments. But how does that support the claim that life as we know it could not have happened without them? Scientists believe that, over the course of billions of years, viruses have acted as a kind of genetic trade network. In adapting to and invading new species, viruses have introduced new types of genes into new types of organisms.

The oldest known traces of life are fossils of single-celled marine microbes that lived 3.5 billion years ago. By about 2 billion years ago, they had begun to evolve into the first multicellular organisms. Evolutionary biologists believe that viruses may have been the agents by which those early microbes communicated and shared genetic information with one another, thereby evolving into much more complex organisms. Without viruses, the theory goes, evolution might have stalled at little specks of bacteria.

Furthermore, in the last few decades, as geneticists have learned to decode the complex DNA of different plants and animals (including humans), they keep finding little sections of DNA that look like certain types of viruses. They think this means that sometimes the virus inserts itself into the full DNA spiral of its host cell...and becomes permanent.

But why doesn't that kill the host cell? Scientists aren't sure, but they say that such viruses might simply have suffered a mutation that made them unable to order a cell's DNA to replicate. The virus just got stuck in the cell's DNA, and when it came time for that cell to reproduce naturally, its DNA—with the new addition of the virus—was copied too. Scientists call this an *endogenous retrovirus*, and have found evidence of them in most types of vertebrates. That means that portions of the human genome may have actually originated as viruses that infected our ancestors millions of years ago.

ENVIRONMENTAL ENGINEERS

Last but not least, we'd like to leave you with this: If all the viruses in the world were to disappear tomorrow, people would no longer have to get flu shots every year...but it wouldn't matter because everyone would be dead. Why? For starters, viruses kill half of all the bacteria in the ocean every day, keeping the microbial life of the seas in balance. That balanced microbial community, in turn, produces about 50 to 85 percent of the oxygen in the earth's atmosphere. What's more, many of those little critters produce that oxygen using photosynthesis genes originally acquired by their ancestors from...that's right...viruses.

So next time you catch a cold, remember: Viruses may be disgusting, disease-causing parasites, but without them we might not even be here to get sick in the first place.

Q. Why do you drool before throwing up? A. To protect your teeth from the acids in vomit.

THROUGH THE KEYHOLE

Here we examine the nature of those who examine nature.

"What is a scientist after all? It is a curious man looking through a keyhole, the keyhole of nature, trying to know what's going on."

—**Jacques Cousteau**

"Those who contemplate the beauty of the earth find reserves of strength that will endure as long as life lasts."

—**Rachel Carson**

"To the dull mind, nature is leaden; to the illumined mind, the whole world burns and sparkles with light."

—**Ralph Waldo Emerson**

"The wilderness and the idea of wilderness is one of the permanent homes of the human spirit."

—**Joseph Wood Krutch**

"Wildlife is a magnet. It's something that I can't help."

—**Steve Irwin**

"We're animals. We're born like every other mammal and we live our whole lives around disguised animal thoughts."

—**Barbara Kingsolver**

"Our ability to perceive quality in nature begins, as in art, with the pretty. It expands through successive stages of the beautiful to values as yet uncaptured by language."

—**Aldo Leopold**

"We should venture on the study of every kind of animal without distaste; for each will reveal to us something natural and something beautiful."

—**Aristotle**

"In the enfranchised mind of the scientific naturalist, the usual feelings of repugnance simply do not exist. Curiosity conquers prejudice."

—**Bruce F. Cummings**

"Study nature, not books."

—**Louis Agassiz**

"As long as I live, I'll hear waterfalls and birds and winds sing. I'll interpret the rocks, learn the language of flood, storm, and the avalanche. I'll acquaint myself with glaciers and gardens, get as near the heart of the world as I can."

—**John Muir**

PHREAKY PHENOMENA

Hold on to your hats! These powerful and mysterious forces of nature are rare...but true.

THE PERFECT FIRESTORM

A fire tornado results when a fire is whipped into a burning frenzy by intense winds. Here's how this rare phenomenon works: First, a strong updraft of hot air hits a wildfire. As the hot air rises, it makes room for outside air to flow in. As that air whips in, it can form a whirlwind that picks up the flames and becomes a swirling column of fire nicknamed a "fire devil" or a "whirl."

Fire devils often range from 30 to 200 feet high and usually last a few minutes. Like regular tornadoes, though, they can reach more than half a mile high with winds of 100 miles per hour...and they can be just as deadly. The worst fire devil occurred in Tokyo in 1923, when 38,000 people were killed in 15 minutes.

UFO LANDING PADS?

In 1985 astronauts made a fascinating discovery: A giant ring of ice had formed on Siberia's Lake Baikal, the deepest freshwater lake on the planet. The ice circle was perfectly round, rotated slowly, and was so huge that it couldn't even be seen from the highest mountaintop. It was only visible from space. Since then, other twisting ice structures, which one scientist calls "very, very rare," have been found on lakes and rivers in Russia, Scandinavia, and Canada. One, nearly three miles in diameter, was spotted from the International Space Station in 2009.

It took more than 20 years, but researchers think they've finally figured out what causes the ice rings: methane gas rising from the bottom of cold bodies of water. Water warmed by the gas hits the ice at the top of the lake and begins to melt it. Then the earth's rotation causes the ice to turn.

WHERE THE OCEAN MEETS THE SKY

Atmospheric gravity waves re-create the motion of the ocean, but in the sky. Waves of air move up and down as they roll through the atmosphere, fueled by buoyancy (the force that makes air rise) and gravity (which makes it fall). Climatologist Tim Coleman explains: "Gravity is what keeps them going. If you push water up and then it plops back down, it creates waves. It's the same with air."

Gravity waves begin when a stable layer of air is displaced by a draft (from a storm, for instance), causing air to ripple across the sky. It's similar to the rings that emanate outward when a stone is thrown into stagnant water. Clouds develop high on the crest of each gravity wave and dissipate near the trough. So, to a person on the ground, gravity waves look like rows of clouds with clear sky between them. Their actual movement across the sky can really only be seen in time-lapse video.

IT'S THE BLOOMIN' ALGAE

A fascinating spectacle sometimes seen in oceans and rivers is a red tide, or more accurately an "algal bloom." The water is tinted a brilliant red color by the overgrowth of an algae species that is normally microscopic. At night, red tide water turns an amazing bioluminescent blue. Why? When waves or boats disturb them, red algal blooms give off a brief flash of blue light. Algal blooms form when too many nutrients like nitrogen and phosphorus collect in water, causing the algae to reproduce so quickly that the ecosystem is overtaken. When these blooms coat the water's surface, they block sunlight, hog the oxygen, and kill off underwater plants and animals. Some red algal blooms also produce toxins that harm aquatic life and humans. Mammals can become ill or die if they swim in the water or eat shellfish harvested there. Algal blooms may hang around for months, wreaking havoc on the environment and the area's tourism trade.

WHO'S THE RAREST OF THEM ALL?

A *circumhorizontal arc* (aka, "fire rainbow") is the world's least common natural atmospheric condition, but it's actually neither a rainbow nor a fire. Although the phenomenon appears as rainbow-colored clouds sporting wisps that look like flames, it is produced by ice crystals, not warmth, and conditions have to be perfect for one to form. Start with cirrus clouds more than 20,000 feet high. Then add the sun also high in the sky, at least 58 degrees above the horizon. The clouds must contain hexagonal ice crystals just the right thickness and aligned horizontally with a flat face pointed at the ground. Similar to a prism, light enters through the vertical side face and exits through the flat bottom, producing an arc of colors that lights up the cloud.

Some of these anomalies cover hundreds of square miles and last for more than an hour. However, due to the specific conditions they require, the arcs are impossible to view in latitudes below 55 degrees south or above 55 degrees north. Sorry, Canada!

IT'S RAINING AMPHIBIANS!

Once in a great while, people are forced to seek cover from a storm that drops not just rain, but...*live animals*. It happened in England in the 1800s, when jellyfish fell from the clouds; then, in the 1930s, frogs followed suit. In 2010 a remote town in Australia experienced showers of hundreds of spangled perch two days in a row. The kicker? The town was more than 200 miles from the nearest body of water.

This phenomenon is truly a mystery. Some scientists theorize that massive evaporation, a strong updraft, or a tornado picks up aquatic life along with water, blows it 70,000 feet high, and carries it many miles before the winds die down and the animals fall with the rain. However, this doesn't explain the situations in which only a single species rains at once (like the perch in Australia), instead of a mixture of different animals.

People in Honduras have a legend to explain this phenomena. Every summer in Yoro, Honduras, fish rain down during thunderstorms. The Hondurans believe it's an answered prayer. Long ago, a Catholic priest prayed for food for the starving natives. Supposedly, that's when the fish rains began. Today, some of the fish fall into waterways and swim off. What do villagers do with the rest? Cook and eat them, of course. Waste not, want not.

* * *

TOOTHY FACTS

A human adult has 32 teeth, each weighing a few ounces. But most marsupials have between 30 and 50 teeth, and a single bull elephant's molar could weigh up to 10 pounds.

THE FROG IN THE MINE SHAFT

When coal mining was in its heyday, miners brought a caged canary into the shaft with them. That way, if the levels of harmful gases grew too high, the canary would drop dead...and the miners would hightail it out of there. For this article, think of earth as the mine shaft, and amphibians as the canary.

PUDDLE OF LIFE

Early one April morning, while walking in the mist-laced cloud forest of Costa Rica, a scientist named Martha Crump rounded a bend and came upon one of the most dazzling spectacles she'd ever seen. In a shallow puddle of rainwater no wider than a kitchen sink, a frenzied mob of golden toads were mating. More than 100 of the creatures—the males brilliant orange, the females blackish and spangled with red—had piled in to form a teeming, splashing, groping mass. Females who wandered into the pool were instantly set upon by a horde of desperate males, each one dead-set on mating with her. After the toads finished the ritual, they hopped off, one by one, into the undergrowth.

DISAPPEARING ACT

As an expert on reptiles and amphibians, Crump knew the importance of what she was witnessing. The golden toad was both an exceptional and rare species, its entire population strung along the narrow spine of a single mountain. Despite their gaudy colors, the toads had escaped all scientific notice until 1966—when they were dismissed by some as a painted hoax—and had rarely been seen since. They were thought to spend the vast majority of their time underground, emerging only briefly after spring thunderstorms to reproduce. This unusual species was literally putting all its eggs into one puddle.

But five days later, when Crump paid the puddle another visit, it was nothing but a dry dimple in the earth. Toad eggs lay in shriveled strands, some already fuzzy with mold. She returned the following spring with high hopes but could find only 10 toads. The next spring, there was only a solitary male, singing in vain. That was 1989—and that male was the last golden toad ever seen.

GLOBAL STORMING

As news of their disappearance spread, other stories emerged of disease, deformities, and sudden disappearances throughout the amphibian family tree. In California, there was the perplexing case of the red-legged frog—the once-familiar species that Mark Twain featured in "The Celebrated Jumping Frog of Calaveras County"—which has now disappeared from some 70 percent of its former range. In Minnesota, a biology class field trip in 1995 turned sinister when students found dozens of frogs with extra limbs, missing eyes, and other freakish mutations.

And in Australia, there was the platypus frog, first documented when it was found in a mountain stream in 1973. Its discoverers placed a few specimens in an aquarium and were stunned when one of the frogs calmly spat out six live tadpoles—from its mouth. The platypus frog turned out to be the first known vertebrate to use its stomach as an incubation chamber, a feat that had never been thought possible. The scientists rushed to plan a research program around the species—only to watch, over the next few years, as it seemingly vanished from the wild.

On the surface, the loss of a few species may not look like a disaster. After all, more than 6,000 species of frogs, toads, salamanders, newts, and caecilians make up the class Amphibia. But that number may have declined by more than 100 over the last few decades, and it's estimated that as many as 2,000 more may be threatened with the same fate. A growing band of scientists are making it their mission to find out why, and what it might mean for the rest of the planet.

A DOUBLE-EDGED SWORD

Amphibians might seem to be unlikely candidates for catastrophe. They've been around for some 400 million years, weathering asteroid strikes and ice ages, and their very name has come to suggest flexibility and adaptation. But scientists have found that some of their greatest assets have now become liabilities.

- One problem is their signature skill, the ability to move easily between land and water. Because their life cycle often hinges on success in both environments, a deterioration in either one can be fatal.

• Their permeable skin is an evolutionary adaptation that allows them to live in the depths of lakes (where the skin acts like a giant gill, absorbing oxygen) as well as in the open desert (where it acts like a sponge, sucking moisture). But a membrane that so easily absorbs the vital stuff of life can also absorb dangerous toxins and pollutants.

• Many amphibians lay their delicate eggs in shallow water, where they can now be scorched by ultraviolet radiation streaming through a weakened ozone layer. And many breed in spectacular, short-lived congregations, where diseases can spread like wildfire.

• They're able to breed and thrive in temporary habitats—but those same habitats are subject to rapid change and destruction.

Case in point: The golden toad—breeding in those barely-there mating pools—painted itself into a climatic corner. According to a University of Miami study published a decade after the toad's disappearance, global warming had spurred a series of exaggerated El Niño currents, which raised the cloud layer and turned the usually mild Costa Rican dry season into a struggle for existence. The toads' eggs dried out as puddles waited for refills that never came, and the toads themselves dried out without the life-giving mist soaking into their skin.

AMPHIBIOUS ASSAULT

But the trouble isn't confined to rare species. The leopard frog remains one of the most widespread amphibians in North America, but in parts of its range (like northern Minnesota, where that school group took its field trip), it's now difficult to find wetlands where many of the frogs are not grotesquely deformed. Science has yet to solve this particular mystery. Many think the culprit may be a wide array of factors, including UV radiation, hormone-mimicking pesticides, tadpole-infesting parasites, and more.

One of the most ominous of the amphibian afflictions is a mysterious fungus called the chytrid. Only recently discovered, it has been implicated in mass amphibian deaths in places as far-flung as Venezuela, Spain, and New Zealand, and is thought to claim its victims by clogging their skin and suffocating them. Although the

Snakes have no taste buds.

chytrid's gruesome effects and sudden global emergence might suggest a sort of amphibian Ebola virus, there is evidence that frogs and toads have actually been living with it for decades, if not far longer, implying that the deadly outbreaks of recent years are a symptom of some deeper disturbance. Some believe the chytrid may have contributed to the extinctions of both the golden toad and the platypus frog and, in at least the former case, may have been accelerated by the changing climate, with subtle shifts in temperature and moisture allowing the fungus to flourish.

But the list of amphibian killers is a long one. There's the disfiguring iridovirus that has devastated tiger salamanders. And there are more general threats, like deforestation and acid rain. And don't forget cars and trucks: One census of road-killed animals in Indiana found that more than 90 percent of the victims were frogs, toads, and salamanders. Scientists have suggested that this plague of troubles is anything but a coincidence. Instead, they may all be symptoms of the same underlying disease: an unsettling of the biosphere.

ACCIDENTAL ASSASSINS

When viewed from the historical perspective, the amphibians' current crisis looks a lot like crises they've weathered before, and they're likely to pull through it. After all, they pulled through the last such event, the asteroid strike that's believed to have killed off the dinosaurs. But the difference this time around is that the trigger may have been technology. One hypothesis for the rash of deformities in Minnesota suggests that farmers have been applying more fertilizer, which has been washing off into wetlands, which has glutted the water with nutrients, which has triggered explosions of algae, which has provided more food for snails, which have served as hosts for parasitic worms, which have then infected the frogs, with ghastly effects.

KERMIT'S DEFENDERS

Scientists and activists worldwide are working together to meet this crisis head-on. An international organization called Amphibian Ark has devised a $500 million plan to rescue the world's imperiled amphibians through captive breeding. But at this point, a huge part of their task is simply to convince people to care. The scientists' answer to that: Amphibians as a class are vital contributors to healthy ecosystems. Some forests hold more than 1,000 salamanders per acre, and one 25-acre wetland can produce more than 300,000 frogs and toads in a season. And each individual eats an enormous amount of insects and plays an integral role in cycling nutrients—functions that would be impossible to replace. Without the amphibians, the entire mix would be thrown out of balance—risking the well-being of animals and humans.

Then there are the possible health benefits that we're just beginning to understand. A chemical produced by the leopard frog has been suggested as a treatment for brain tumors; poison dart frogs produce a painkiller 200 times as potent as morphine; and the platypus frog, with its uncanny ability to "turn off" its stomach acids to protect its developing young, was thought to hold promise as a model for ulcer control…until it went extinct.

Finally, amphibians may be doing us a great favor by giving us a preview of the horrors that environmental disruption could unleash. Could we soon see mutant humans with six eyes and seven limbs? The golden toad and its cousins may be remembered as the canary in the mine shaft, perhaps bringing enough attention to the plight of the ecosystem to make a major difference in their future. And ours, too.

* * *

TWO GREAT VOLCANIC HIKES IN THE CASCADES

• **Bumpass Hell Trail** in California's Lassen Volcanic National Park. Named for an unfortunate settler who nearly lost a leg when he fell through a soft layer of rock into a boiling, acidic pool. Thankfully, there's now a boardwalk that winds through raging fumaroles and incredible volcanic vistas.

• **The Obsidian Flow** trail at Newberry National Volcanic Monument in central Oregon cuts through a giant "tongue" of obsidian that flowed out of a nearby mountain. Hike among truck-sized boulders of volcanic glass.

ANIMAL ORGANS YOU DON'T HAVE

Oh, you smug human, you. You can talk, walk upright, read books, and philosophize. But compared to these animals and their specialized organs, you're nothing!

• Sharks are super-sensitive to electrical fields. When small fish or mammals move, breathe, or swim near a shark, the fish release tiny electrical impulses. By using specialized sense organs around its snout and mouth (called *ampullae of Lorenzini* for Stefano Lorenzini, the scientist who discovered them in the 1600s), sharks can sense the smaller creatures—whether they can actually see the fish or not. And when that happens...*bon appétit*!

• Snakes have a special pit on the roofs of their mouths called the Jacobson's organ that allows them to taste the air. As the snake flicks its tongue in and out, scent molecules are collected and deposited in the pits, giving the snake a good sense of any prey that's around and available.

• Other animals, humans included, also have a Jacobson's organ, in the backs of the noses. But in cats, dogs, horses, painted turtles, elephants, and others, the organ is highly sensitive. Painted turtles use it to smell underwater, and some animals use their Jacobson's organs by curling their upper lips (the way cats "smell" with their mouths open). It's believed that the Jacobson's organ allows animals to determine sexual readiness and to scope out its own—or another animal's—territory.

• Toothed whales (which include dolphins, orcas, and porpoises) are blessed with a unique kind of echolocation. As they swim, they emit high-pitched clicks that bounce off objects and return. This helps the creature determine what it's sharing its water with, including the other animals' size, texture, and edibility. This ability is made possible by a special, fat-filled organ called a *melon*, located in the whale's forehead. The clicks return through the melon to the animal's jaw and then continue on to its brain.

The sun's UV light has antiseptic properties.

EAT YOUR CHILDREN WELL

Fluffy baby ducklings, adorable little puppies, and cannibalistic sharks that eat their siblings while they're still in the womb. You'll find the latter story here along with a few others, all of which involve cute little baby animals.

WOMB WITH AN *EWW!*

Most shark species are *ovoviviparous*, which means that young sharks hatch from eggs inside their mother's body before being born. In most cases this is accompanied by *oophagy*, or "egg eating." In other words, once the little shark embryos are developed enough, they eat their own egg yolks for nourishment. And if they're quick about it, the first one done will then proceed to eat his brothers' and sisters' egg yolks, too. If the lucky winner runs out of eggs, hey, that's no problem: The mother shark continues to ovulate during pregnancy, sending a continuous supply of eggs for her little shark fetus to feed on until it's born. Some species go even further, and practice *adelphophagy*, meaning, literally, "eating one's brother." That means the baby sharks don't just eat eggs—they actually eat each other in savage fetal battles right there in Mommy's womb. The last shark standing in the womb will be a veteran killer even before it's born.

WHAT A CUTE LITTLE DOLPH...OH MY GOD!!!

In the late 1990s, the bodies of dead baby porpoises were found washed up on beaches in both Virginia and on the east coast of Scotland. Biologists from both locations joined forces to study the deaths, which at first were thought to have been caused by undersea blasting or sonar testing. Closer study revealed otherwise: the porpoises had died of internal injuries that could only have been caused by prolonged, focused attacks. When teeth marks in the form of lacerations and puncture wounds on the little bodies were matched to adult dolphins, the authorities had their official suspects. The dolphin theory was backed up over the next few years as videotapes of the attacks started surfacing. They each showed

A box jellyfish sting can kill a person in less than five minutes.

groups of adult dolphins attacking baby porpoises, using their bulbous foreheads to ram the porpoises again and again, even flipping them high into the air and smashing them—with precision timing—when they hit the water. Worse: They weren't doing it for food. Once a porpoise had been killed, the attackers simply swam away. Researchers say the dolphins may have been using the baby porpoises as hunting practice.

THE BOYS ARE BACK IN TOWN...

Langur monkeys inhabit the forests of South Asia, primarily India, living in groups dominated by one older alpha male. He drives out all the younger males in the group, and becomes the only one to breed with the remaining females. The males that have been driven out form bands and roam the forests. When they encounter another alpha male and his harem, they attack, trying to drive the old male away. If successful, the conquering males then grab every last baby monkey—all of them fathered by the old alpha male—from the females, and kill them, usually by smashing their skulls against trees. The leader of the marauders then becomes the new alpha male, the other adult males are driven out, and the cycle of sex, murder, and mayhem begins again.

BYE-BYE, BIRDIES

The wattled jacana, a medium-sized wading bird found in Central and South America, is unusual in that the females, which are larger than the males, take more than one mate at a time, and lay their eggs in up to four different nests at any given time. The females don't sit on the eggs or feed and protect the chicks—that's the males' job. A mother jacana's job is to help protect all the nests from intruders, including other females. That's because unmated females, when given the opportunity, will attack a rival's nests, fight off the protecting male, and kill the chicks by picking them up and smashing them violently to the ground. After killing the chicks, the murderess immediately begins courting the male—whose chicks she just smashed—and the male soon gives in and mates with her. She then makes a new nest and the male takes care of it for her...until another psycho female jacana comes along.

Horses can't see directly in front of themselves.

FROM ALLUVIUM TO ZYGOPTERA

Let's take this opportunity to come to terms with some nature terminology.

Alluvium: Sediment or soil deposited by a river or running water.

Biosphere: The global realm of all living things; in our case, the planet Earth.

Chaparral: A plant community in which shrubs dominate, occurring usually in regions that have from 10 to 20 inches of rainfall annually and with a Mediterranean-type climate: warm, dry summers and mild, wet winters.

Deciduous: Refers to plants that lose all of their leaves for part of the year—like leafy trees that turn colors in the fall (as opposed to "evergreens," which keep their leaves or needles all year-round).

Eider: A large sea duck that flies at speeds up to 70 mph, the eider breeds in the Arctic and other northern temperate zones, lining its nests with "eiderdown"—the soft, warm, fluffy stuff from the female's breast—that's been harvested for ages as a stuffing for pillows and quilts.

Fugu: A highly poisonous puffer fish that's used as food in Japan…after the toxic parts are removed.

Genlisea: Members of the bladderwort family, genlisea are a genus of carnivorous herbs found throughout Africa and Central and South America. Having no roots, they use underground leaves to attract, trap, and digest their itsy-bitsy food, which mostly consists of microorganisms like protozoa. Charles Darwin mentioned genlisea in his 1875 book *Insectivorous Plants*, suggesting that the plant was carnivorous, but his theory—although well-researched for its time—wasn't proven as fact until 1998.

Hibernaculum: In zoology, a shelter used by hibernating animals; in botany, a protective casing a plant uses to survive changing weather conditions during its dormant period.

Igneous rock: The rocks that form when lava or magma cools and then solidifies.

Japonica: Latin for "Japanese," the name refers to all kinds of species and subspecies that include plants, animals, and insects: e.g., the kumquat (*Citrus japonica*), the loquat (*Eriobotrya japonica*), the Japanese tree frog (*Hyla japonica*), Japanese honeysuckle (*Lonicera japonica*), the drone beetle (*Rhomborrhina japonica*), the pagoda tree (*Styphnolobium japonicum*), and last but not least, a sushi lover's favorite condiment…the wasabi, or Japanese horseradish (*Wasabia japonica*).

Kettle: A group of hawks circling together on thermal updrafts (*see "thermal" below*).

Lepidoptera: The order of insects that includes butterflies and moths.

Marshmallow: A pink-flowered medicinal and ornamental plant whose sap was used to make marshmallow candy in ancient Egypt. In the mid-1800s, marshmallow sap was replaced by gelatin, and the modern-day marshmallow industry was born (sans real marshmallow plants).

Neotropics: The geographic region that stretches south from the Tropic of Cancer and includes southern Mexico, Central and South America, and the West Indies.

Owl pellet: The indigestible parts of an owl's latest meal, including the fur, feathers, and bones too large to pass through the animal's digestive tract. These parts are regurgitated as a compact pellet, sort of like the fur balls that cats cough up.

Prehensile: Refers to the body part of an animal that is used to grasp things, like an elephant's trunk, a giraffe's tongue, an octopus's arms, or a howler monkey's tail.

Riparian: Related to, or having a location on, the banks of a natural course of water such as a river or stream.

Staging: In bird migration, it's the act of gathering in large groups at a prime feeding spot at the start of migration; it's also the practice of pausing at places along a migration route to rest and feed before continuing.

The rafflesia (corpse flower) is a bodiless, stemless, leafless, rootless, parasitic flower.

Thermal: A column of warm air that rises when the ground is heated by the sun; one of the many sources of lift that helps birds gain altitude.

Ursidae: The classification family that includes all bears.

Vernalization: The process, natural or artificial, by which plants are readied for flowering through exposure to cold temperatures. For example, some spring plants won't bloom unless they've gone through a period of dormancy in which the temperature falls below 45°F.

Whitewash: A name for the white stains from bird excrement that are usually found where birds perch or nest.

Xeriscaping: Landscaping in ways that reduce or eliminate the need for supplemental water from irrigation, e.g., using drought-tolerant plants.

Yuzu: A citrus fruit that looks like a small grapefruit when ripe, it's thought to be a hybrid of the sour Mandarin orange and an *ichang papeda*, a hardy Chinese citrus plant.

Zygoptera: A suborder of insects (and a clunky mouthful of a word) for what we call the damselfly, a delicate and graceful relative of the dragonfly.

* * *

SACRE BLAH!

After the slaughter of Allied forces at Gallipoli, Turkey, in World War I, thousands of corpses littered the beaches. According to military historian Peter Hart in his 2011 book *Gallipoli*, crabs that were used to feeding on fish and other marine animals that washed onto the shore feasted on those bodies. More: Soldiers of the French Foreign Legion harvested those crabs…and made a "tasty bouillabaisse" of them.

MORE BIG BOTTOMS

On page 165, we began a voyage to the bottom of the sea. Now, let's go even deeper.

THE ABYSS

Beyond the continental rise is the abyss, the lowest part of the ocean basin. Here, the average depth is about 2.65 miles below sea level, and the lowest spot is 6.6 miles deep. The sun can't penetrate to the bottom, so there's no light, and the temperature is close to freezing. Only special submersibles can go down this deep, so the abyss remains one of the least-known parts of the planet. It's also home to some of earth's most extreme and amazing landscapes:

• **The abyssal plains** are formed of basalt rock covered with mud and silt. They stretch for miles out from the continental rise and cover about half of the ocean floor.

• **The mid-ocean ridge** is the longest mountain range on earth. It rises from the ocean floor, snaking its way around the globe to span 40,389 miles. In places like the Mid-Atlantic Ridge, rift valleys (types of depressions) form at the top of the mountain ridges because they are located exactly where two tectonic plates (great slabs of rock that form earth's surface) are slowly moving apart. As the plates pull away from each other, the rifts appear, and molten magma rises from inside the earth to fill in the gaps. As the rock cools, it creates a new and ever-expanding ocean floor.

• **Black smokers** are geysers usually seen at a depth of about 7,000 feet, near the area where the seafloor is spreading. When tectonic plates pull apart, they create cracks and crevices on the ocean floor. Seawater fills the openings and is heated by magma under the earth's crust to temperatures of 700°F or more. When the geyser's hot water erupts into the ocean, volcanic chemicals and metals (mostly iron and sulfides) turn the steam black.

• **Seamounts** are underwater volcanoes—they're usually extinct, but not always. These volcanoes rise thousands of feet from the bottom of the ocean and are usually high enough to reach sunlit waters, where they attract plankton, coral, fish, and other marine

Good advice: To minimize germs, always flush the toilet with the lid closed.

life. When seamounts are still active (and close enough to the surface), they can blast steam and rock debris high above the ocean's surface.

• **Ocean trenches** occur in areas where tectonic plates are pushed together so that one slides under the other. At these spots, called "subduction zones," the ocean trenches make deep and narrow chasms into the ocean floor. These are some of the deepest canyons on the planet. The Pacific Ocean's Mariana Trench is 50 times larger than the Grand Canyon. The very deepest section of that trench—called Challenger Deep—is located about 250 miles southwest of Guam and contains the deepest known point on earth: 6.78 miles below sea level and deep enough to swallow Mount Everest.

EXTRA

James Cameron is most famous as the director of the Oscar-winning film *Titanic* and for directing the blockbusters *Aliens* and *Avatar*. But in March 2012, he made the news for an entirely different reason—he teamed up with National Geographic and launched an expedition to the bottom of the Mariana Trench. Cameron climbed into a submersible and dove almost seven miles down to Challenger Deep, which he described as a desolate landscape "devoid of sunlight, devoid of any heat, any warmth." He saw tiny shrimplike arthropods and giant amoebas in the trench, but very little else in the way of life. One his return, he said, "My feeling was one of complete isolation from all of humanity. More than anything, [it's] realizing how tiny you are down in this big, vast, black, unknown, and unexplored place."

* * *

"My favorite animal is the turtle. The reason is that in order for the turtle to move, it has to stick its neck out."

—Dr. Ruth Westheimer

The yellow-bellied three-toed skink is currently evolving from egg-laying to birthing live young.

GEOLOGY 101

A quick and dirty rundown of how some of geology's most important discoveries changed humans' view of Mother Earth.

NOTHING MUCH HAS HAPPENED SINCE NOAH

In the early 1700s, people had very different ideas about the history of the earth. Most of them had no idea that dinosaurs ever existed, and they believed that mountains had sprouted up like trees. Scholars wrote that the earth was only about 6,000 years old and that its landscape had been shaped by the great flood that Noah survived. This view of the world came from the way people interpreted the Bible, but after 1700, some people (now called geologists) began to study the earth, and what they found changed everything.

1788: BASIC GEOLOGY FOLLOWS A ROCKY ROAD

Some of the most important finds of geology come from the study of plain old rocks. Rocks make up the earth's solid surface, or "crust," but for geologists, rocks are not only clues to the earth's past and how it works now, but also to what will happen in the future. Early geologists placed rocks in three groups:

• **Igneous rocks** are created from magma (molten rock) from inside the earth that has risen toward the surface and cooled. There are two kinds of igneous rocks: intrusive (made of magma that has slowly cooled underground) and extrusive (made of cooled lava that has spewed from volcanoes).

• **Sedimentary rocks** are formed from tiny particles of eroding rocks. The grains are carried away by wind or water and deposited in valleys, riverbeds, or the ocean in horizontal layers called strata. When other strata form above the particles, the lower strata is squeezed and cements together to form rocks. Since sedimentary rock can also hold plant material or marine or animal skeletons, sedimentary rock is where the fossils are.

• **Metamorphic rocks** are sedimentary or igneous rocks that have been subjected to so much heat and pressure that they undergo a chemical change and become a completely different rock altogether. Take limestone, for example, which can transform into marble.

In 1788 James Hutton—who has been called the "father of geology"—pointed out that even though rocks seemed to be just lying around doing nothing, they're actually always transforming. Some of his views came to be known as the "rock cycle." Here's how it goes:

• Molten magma rises and a volcano erupts. The lava cools and hardens into igneous rock.

• Over time the igneous rock erodes.

• Rivers carry its particles to the ocean floor.

• More layers pile on top of these particles until they harden into sedimentary rock.

• The sedimentary rock is at the bottom of so many layers of rock that it's subjected to intense weight and pressure, causing it to go through a chemical change and become metamorphic rock.

• The metamorphic rock gets pushed deep below the crust, where it meets enough heat to melt it back into magma.

• The process begins again.

Hutton's theory was met with strong opposition from the biblical theorists. But his discovery that rocks were always transforming revealed that our planet was in a state of constant change.

1907: WHAT'S THE GEOLOGICAL TIME?

William Smith was a surveyor in charge of constructing canals across England when he began studying sedimentary rocks. He discovered that they were always layered in the same horizontal pattern and that each layer encased the same type of fossils. This led him to the logical conclusion that since the patterns of strata and the fossils inside them never varied, each layer must have been deposited at about the same time. In 1815 he created the first geological map accurately depicting the strata rock across England, Wales, and part of Scotland.

In 1824 a dinosaur fossil of a Megalosaurus was the first to be described scientifically (before this, people thought dinosaur bones came from dragons, griffins, or giants). Scientists began making a time line for when dinosaurs roamed the earth. They could tell which dinosaurs were oldest because their fossils were always in the bottom layers. But then a problem arose from the studies.

In the late 1800s, most people still believed the earth to be just 6,000 years old. Yet the fossils showed the development and extinction of too many plants and animals for such a young planet. In 1907 an American scientist, Bertram Boltwood, discovered how to calculate the age of a rock through a process called radiometric dating, and he proposed that earth was at least 2.2 *billion* years old. Other scientists found other ways to more accurately test rocks, and the earth's age was eventually put at around 4.56 billion years. Here's the timeline:

• **Precambrian era** (4,560–540 million years ago, or "mya"): Oceans and single-celled bacteria developed in an era that accounts for 88 percent of the planet's history.

• **Paleozoic era** (540–251 mya): Various life-forms developed—fish in the sea, and plants, amphibians, and reptiles on land. But the era ended with a mass extinction that killed most life-forms on earth, including many of the dinosaurs. Scientists are still unsure about the cause, but suspect that it was probably a combination of gradual environmental change and a catastrophic event or series of events (an asteroid hitting the earth, enormous volcanic eruptions...that sort of thing).

• **Mesozoic era** (251–65 mya): As life came back from extinction, fish, coral, and mollusks dominated the oceans, and large dinosaurs ruled the land until they all perished in another mass extinction at the end of the era.

• **Cenozoic era** (65 mya–today): This era brought about a rise in flowering plants, as well as an increase in birds, insects, and mammals—including humans.

1911: WE'RE DRIFTING APART

German scientist Alfred Wegener was the first to note that large rock formations in South America matched those of Africa, and that the outlines of the two continents looked like parts of a puzzle that could easily fit together. In 1911 Wegener wrote that the continents were once an enormous supercontinent called Pangaea

(Greek for "all earth"). He explained that, about 300 million years ago, the continents began moving apart...and they still are. Wegener called the process continental drift.

Continental drift got a scientific cold shoulder until the 1950s and 1960s, when exploration of the seafloor proved Wegener right. The continents are always moving in tiny increments—about an inch each year—because the ocean between them is widening. Scientists also discovered that the solid ground beneath our feet isn't solid at all: the earth's surface has cracked into huge slabs of rock called tectonic plates.

Some continental plates are aboveground, like the one that carries Europe and Asia. Others—like the Pacific plate—are under the oceans. Beneath all the tectonic plates, hot magma is always bubbling up from inside the earth. Under the ocean, about halfway between the continents, the plates are slowly pulling apart. As the cracks between the plates widen, hot magma escapes and spreads outward—creating more crust and pushing the plates even farther apart. Meanwhile, at other undersea locations, the tectonic plates are pushed together, and one plate is forced under the other, where heat and pressure transform it into semimolten magma.

The discovery of tectonic plates helped geologists understand some of nature's most powerful events. When continental plates collide, the crust can be pushed up to form great mountains: The Himalayas, for example, were created when India slammed into Asia. At other times, when plates are pushed together, cracks in the crust open up and volcanoes form. And sometimes the earth's plates slide in opposite directions and rub against each other, causing earthquakes.

* * *

PLANT VAN WINKLE

In February 2012 a team of Russian scientists announced that they had grown a small flowering plant known as *Silene stenophylla* from seeds that had been trapped deep in ice...for about 32,000 years. The seeds are the oldest ever successfully grown into plants. (Bonus: Evidence shows that the seeds were orignally buried in the ground by a squirrel.)

BAD BOY, MAX!

They're smelly, they're germy, and some of them lick their own butts. Why would anyone *want a house pet?*

NO KISSY-KISSY!

Risk: Meningitis

How: Giving kisses to your dog

Story: A 44-year-old Japanese woman came down with a high fever, nausea, and headache. It turned out to be bacterial meningitis, a potentially fatal disease that can be transmitted orally. But she hadn't acquired it from a person: Experts say she got it from constantly "kissing her dog's face and feeding it by transferring food mouth to mouth." (Ugh.) But to get meningitis, you don't have to actually kiss a pooch (or kitty or bunny, which are also carriers). One man developed it after his dog licked him on an open surgical wound. Up to 75 percent of dogs host meningitis bacteria in their mouths, which are, despite popular legend, not cleaner than human mouths.

TAINTED TURTLES

Risk: Salmonella

How: Exposure to turtles (also snakes, frogs, and iguanas)

Story: In 2007, more than 100 people across the United States came down with a salmonella infection, including two friends, aged 13 and 15. Both girls were very sick with fever and cramps, and the older one was hospitalized for eight days with acute kidney failure. The cause? The teens had swum in an unchlorinated pool that was sometimes frequented by two pet turtles. Soon after the outbreak, it was discovered that nearly all the victims had been exposed to pet turtles either directly or indirectly.

DANGEROUS TURDS AHEAD

Risk: Giardia, *E. coli*, salmonella

How: Picking up or walking through doggie doo

Story: Just one gram of dog feces has 23 *million* fecal coliform bacteria, some of which can make you ill with fever, nausea, bloody diar-

Britain's largest type of flea lives on Britain's smallest mammal, the pygmy shrew.

rhea, or worse. One infant's *E. coli* infection was traced back to the family dog. The canine, who might have gotten the bacteria from cattle, had pooped on the living room carpet, and the baby got sick after playing on the floor. The infection quickly progressed into a destructive kidney disorder, which the baby luckily survived.

GO EAT WORMS!

Risk: Roundworms

How: Ingesting the eggs, perhaps when a pet licks his nether regions and then kisses your face

Story: Roundworms are intestinal parasites that can be passed to humans if animal feces—or soil contaminated with it—accidentally gets in your mouth. Seem unlikely? Each year, 10,000 Americans are horrified to learn their bodies are hosting roundworms, which sometimes appear as spaghetti-like worms in their stool. In 2010 British toddler Aimee Langdon was exposed to roundworms when she got a bit of dog poop in her eye. She was hospitalized the next day. The good news: Treatment prevented the worms from migrating to her brain. The bad news: Little Amiee was left nearly blind in one eye.

LET SLEEPING DOGS LIE?

Risk: Broken limbs, concussions

How: Tripping over a pet

Story: Every year, 86,000 Americans are injured in falls caused by cats and dogs. The headlines read "Liza Minnelli's Dog Breaks Her Leg" when, in November 2011, the 65-year-old actress tripped over her dog and fell, fracturing her leg in three places. She continued to perform in a concert that month... perched in a wheelchair with her leg in a cast (and she didn't seem to mind being carried on and off stage by two handsome young men). Not so fortunate was British soccer star Liam Lawrence, who missed a few games in 2008 after he tripped over his sleeping Labrador retriever and hurt his ankle. Lawrence said afterward, "The dog's fine."

Want to know how your pets are good for you? (We do!)
Turn to page 146.

A shark vomits by thrusting its stomach out of its mouth...then pulling it back in.

QUANIMALS

There are 18 quizillion different animals in the world. (Okay, we made that up.) Only four have names that begin with Q. (Okay, we made that up, too.) Here's a list of our favorite quanimals.

Quadrate pebblesnail: Small mud snail found in North American rivers.

Quahog: Type of clam found in waters off eastern North America.

Quail: Ground-feeding bird related to the pheasant and found all over the world.

Quarry worm salamander: Species of worm salamander (they kinda look like worms) found in Costa Rica.

Quarter horse: American horse breed known for its short-distance sprinting speed.

Quechuan hocicudo: Mouse-like rodent living high in the Andes Mountains in Bolivia.

Queen snake: Nonvenomous snake related to the garter snake and found in the eastern United States.

Queen Alexandra's birdwing: Huge butterfly species (wingspan as wide as 12 inches) native to Papua New Guinea. Named after the wife of England's King Edward VII.

Queen of Spain fritillary: Butterfly found from Africa to Asia. Named by English botanist Moses Harris in 1775. Just why he named it that...nobody knows.

Quetzal: Brightly colored bird native to Central American rainforests.

Quetzalcoatlus: Type of pterodactyl—flying reptile—that went extinct 65 million years ago. (Its wingspan was over 40 feet.)

Quietschbüker: Fish species related to whitefish found only in Breiter Luzin Lake in northern Germany. (The meaning and origin of the name are unknown.)

Qinghai lake toad: Amphibian found in swamps, marshes, and on land in China.

Quokka: Cat-sized kangaroo-like herbivorous marsupial found in Australia.

Quoll: Another cat-sized marsupial, this one carnivorous and found in Australia and Papua New Guinea.

I FOUGHT THE SNAKE

The trouble with snakes is that, in confrontations with humans, the snake usually wins.

DON'T GO FOR YOUR GUN

Ali-Asghar Ahani was hunting in Iran in the early 1990s when he came across a snake and tried to capture it by pressing the butt of his shotgun behind the snake's head. The snake wrapped itself around the weapon and used its tail to fire a shell into Ahani's head, killing him. Ahani's pal tried to grab the gun, but the snake shot the other chamber off, too. The friend escaped unharmed…so did the snake.

Then there's Florida's Garrett Bauernschmidt, who in 2011 couldn't resist pointing his handgun at a water moccasin lurking outside his front door. The 75-year-old's first shot went wide. When he tried to reload, the gun went off, and a bullet ripped into his hand. The snake slithered away unharmed.

DON'T HANDLE A SNAKE WHILE DRUNK

In September 2011, Dave Senk of Sacramento asked to hold someone's pet python...and then decided to take a bite out of it. Senk says he was too drunk to remember the incident, but he was arrested on suspicion of unlawfully maiming or mutilating a reptile. The snake got stitched up and survived.

The most mythic act of drunken snakebite happened in Australia in 1997: Gordon Lyons was on a road trip when he spotted a snake by the side of the road. He had a beer in his right hand, so he grabbed the snake with his left. Before he could toss it in a sack, the snake bit right through his hand. A little later, Lyons stuck his hand in the bag and was bitten eight more times. At the hospital, the inept snake-wrangler's heart stopped briefly and his left arm had to be amputated. The man later claimed it was a spur-of-the-moment suicide attempt following the breakup of his marriage and a custody battle over the kids.

DON'T LIVE IN INDIA

About 7,000 to 8,000 snakebites take place every year in the

United States, but only five or six prove fatal. Serpent-congested Australia sees only about one snakebite death a year. But then there's India, where every year the deadly Russell's viper kills more than 20,000 people—mostly farmers in rural areas. Another 30,000 Indians are killed by other species of snakes for a grand total of 50,000 deaths a year—as much as the rest of the world combined. The reason? Lack of access to vaccines and quality medical care, and the fact that many bite victims don't get to see a doctor at all.

DON'T BUY YOURSELF A PET SNAKE

Most snakebite victims in the United States are the owners of the snake that ends up biting them. An Indiana man tried to remove the skin growing over the mouth of his deadly rhinoceros viper, was bitten, and ended up in the hospital. Luckily, no venom made it into his system.

Another man from Indiana wasn't as lucky in 2006: He took his sick pet python out to the shed for some medical treatment and was found dead three hours later. The snake had wrapped itself around his owner's chest and neck...and squeezed.

DON'T GO ANYWHERE NEAR A PYTHON

• Speaking of pythons, at least 12 people, including five children, have died in the United States from python attacks since 1980.

• Locals and scientists believe that damage from 1992's Hurricane Andrew released Burmese pythons from pet shops into southern Florida. There's still no clear estimate of how many snakes actually got out, but 20 years later, some people think there might be hundreds of thousands of pythons out there now, slithering around in the Florida wilderness.

* * *

PREPARE EYE-ROLL...

"Two silkworms had a race. It ended in a tie."

—Unknown

HOW DOES YOUR GARDEN GROW?

The way in which plants move and grow has intrigued everyone from the poets of ancient Greece to Charles Darwin, but modern science still hasn't cracked all the secrets.

WHY WOULD THEY DO THAT?

Since ancient times, people have been scratching their heads and wondering why plants grow the way they do. In particular, why do shoots grow up out of the ground, while roots head down into the earth? Particularly intriguing to the ancient Greeks was the question of why plant stems bend toward light, a phenomenon that scientists now call phototropism. The Greeks offered one explanation in a myth about a beautiful water nymph named Clytie, who fell in love with the sun god Apollo as he rode a fiery chariot across the sky. As is usual in myths, things didn't end well: Apollo loved someone else, and when Clytie realized that her infatuation was hopeless, she stood weeping in the same spot without eating or drinking. All she did was watch for Apollo and his chariot. Eventually the grieving nymph transformed into the first sunflower, which turned on its stalk as it followed the sun. Through the centuries, scientists offered more...well, scientific explanations, but it wasn't until the 19th century that people really began to understand phototropism.

TIPSY

In 1809 Swiss botanist Augustin de Candolle discovered that plants turned toward light because was there was more growth on the shady side of the plant (making it longer) than on the sunny side. Then in 1880 Charles Darwin (already famous for his theory of evolution) wrote a book called *The Power of Movement in Plants*, which explained how that uneven growth occurred. Darwin and his son Francis had experimented with the seedlings of canary grass that they grew to feed their birds. They covered the tips of the seedlings with a material that blocked light. This stopped the

A tiger's tongue is so rough that it can lick the paint off of a building.

plants from turning toward the light even though light was still shining on the stems. When the tips of the seedlings were uncovered, the plants went back to bending toward the light again.

Darwin wrote that these and other experiments demonstrated that the grass seedlings had "some matter in the upper part which is acted on by light, and which transmits its effects to the lower part." It wasn't until the 1920s that the "matter" was discovered. Botanist Fritz Went found that it a hormone caused plants to turn toward the sun. He named the hormone *auxin.*

MAKING THEIR MOVE

Today scientists know that not only phototropism, but all "tropisms" (turnings in plants) are affected by auxin. The hormone is produced at the top of the main stem of a plant (just as Darwin thought) and moves downward to the root tips, where it's stored. Auxin stimulates growth because it causes plant cells to get longer. The larger the concentration of auxin in a plant cell, the more the cell lengthens. So when auxin accumulates in certain places in the plant, it causes unequal growth that makes plants bend and turn in certain directions, creating a tropism.

Tropisms are especially important because they help plants reach out and get the elements they need for survival. For example, all green plants need light to produce oxygen and make food, a process called photosynthesis. Since plants can't get up and walk over to the light source, they use auxin to create a tropism (phototropism) that bends toward it. But there are other tropisms out there. Here are the rest:

• **Geotropism** is turning in response to gravity. When a seed is in the ground and a root emerges, auxin collects and works to make the upper side of the root grow longer, turning the root tip down. Meanwhile, auxin collects on the underside of the stem, causing the bottom to grow faster than the top, which pushes the stem upward.

• **Thigmotropism** is turning in response to touch. It causes plants to "feel" their way up walls, poles, or trellises. An example is a vine that coils its tendrils around a trellis for support. The coiling of this tendril is believed to be the result of more auxin in the cells of the outer side of the tendril than on the inner side.

• **Hydrotropism** is turning in response to moisture. Roots grow down toward gravity, but auxin will also collect in root cells and direct their growth toward moisture.

• **Positive and negative tropisms.** Some of the tropisms that plants use are called positive because they turn a plant toward a stimulus like light, moisture, or gravity. Negative tropisms use auxin to bend plants away from that stimulus. These are usually mentioned when talking about gravity: Positive tropisms cause the plant roots to grow down toward gravity. Negative tropisms cause the plant stem to grow upward, away from gravity.

A GARDEN VARIETY MYSTERY

Scientists know a lot about tropisms and auxin, but they have many unanswered questions too. In particular, they still don't understand the mechanisms at work within the plant and how those are able to send out auxin in response to light, moisture, gravity, and touch. But they keep looking...and hoping that the plants will reveal more about their methods.

* * *

BUG THERMOMETERS

• Male crickets chirp by rubbing their front wings together. They chirp faster when weather is warm and slower when it's cold, so you can use them to estimate the temperature. Here's how: Count cricket chirps for 14 seconds, and then add 40 to the total. For example, if a cricket chirps 34 times in 14 seconds, just add 40 and the temperature is 74°F.

• If that seems too easy, you can always listen to katydids instead. Their chirps also vary according to temperature. To use the katydid method, count the chirps for a minute. Then subtract 19, divide the answer by 3, and add 60. The formula looks like this: Temperature = 60 + [(Chirps -19)/3]. That means if the katydid chirps 25 times in a minute, the temperature is 62°F. (It also may mean that it's time to buy an outdoor thermometer.)

• Keep in mind, though: Crickets and katydids stop chirping altogether when the temperature falls below 55°F.

TOP 7 ANIMAL BODY PARTS WE'D LIKE TO HAVE

BRI member Thom compiled this list of really cool body parts that animals have, but we don't. It's just not fair! (He also really loves hockey.)

7. CLAWS: Humans really got ripped off in the whole finger-weapon department. Imagine if we had claws like tigers—then imagine hockey. We rest our case.

6. HORNS: How cool would it be to have a pair of long, sweeping, super-pointy horns growing out of our heads? It might make mosh pits a tad more dangerous, but does anyone really care? (And you'd always have somewhere to hang your coat!)

5. FLIPPERS: Forget swimming ability—can you imagine what it would be like to slap someone with a walrus flipper?

4. EXOSKELETONS: Bones are such trouble. You've got arthritis, hip replacements, and compound fractures that can puncture vital organs—plus, broken bones can stick right out of your skin! That's just tacky! All of this could be solved with a nice hard exoskelton. (Note: This would also be great for hockey.)

3. SPINNERETS: If we could produce webbing like spiders can, we could encase noisy toddlers in soft, soundproof capsules that could then be stuck to the ceiling. I think we've said enough.

2. STINGERS: You're in the bar having a nice cold glass of beer and the guy next to you will not shut up about his job, his car, the Buffalo Bills...and ZAP! You just shot him with 1,000 cc's of nature's most powerful neurotoxin via your flexible, scorpionlike tail. And you never even took your eyes off the hockey game!

1. ESCAS: An *esca* is the thing that grows from the top of the head of an anglerfish and that acts as a lure to attract fish, which an anglerfish then eats in one terrifyingly fast and toothy gulp. If you had one of those...well, we could use it to distract children while we're encasing them in webbing.

WHEN ANIMALS ATTACK!

What are you supposed to do if you encounter an animal in the wild? Fight back, play dead...run? It depends. Uncle John has some tips on how to prevent an attack—and what to do if prevention doesn't work.

MOUNTAIN LIONS

Prevention: Anyone who shares a house with cats knows how much they love to sneak up and ambush their prey. Same goes for mountain lions. Although it's rare for a human to be attacked (rarer than being struck by lightning), mountain lions have occasionally pounced on unsuspecting hikers, joggers, bikers—and children. A mountain lion's prey is usually alone or appears weak. If you're in a rural mountainous area, stay in a group of two or more, especially at dusk and dawn, the animals' favorite times to hunt. Always carry a walking stick or a knife. If you stumble across an animal carcass that's been partially eaten by a large predator, get out of there fast before the killer returns.

If that doesn't work: Scary as it sounds, if confronted by a mountain lion, you should face it and challenge it by looking it right in the eye. Tell it to go away in a firm and confident (gulp!) voice. The goal is to convince the animal that you are a threat, not easy prey. Make yourself appear large—wave your arms around, stand on your tiptoes, open your jacket. Don't ever crouch or bend down. Don't turn your back on it either—mountain lions prefer a sneak attack, and they aim for the spinal cord. It's unlikely that you'd be able to outrun the animal, so if a mountain lion lunges at you, fight back. Try to stay on your feet. Some victims have even fended off an attack by smacking the coming mountain lion with the butt of a gun.

BEARS

Prevention: When hiking in the wilderness, it's a good idea to make some noise as you go along because bears don't like to be startled. Pay attention to signs that warn of bears (both the official kind, like "Watch Out for Bears," and the unofficial—like scat, tracks, or animal carcasses). Keep all your food, wrappers, and garbage locked up and airtight so wandering bears won't smell it.

A camel won't sweat until its body temperature reaches 106°F.

You can even carry bear pepper spray in an accessible place like a holster. If you see bear cubs, move away and keep an eye out for their overprotective mother. When you come across a bear that doesn't notice you or isn't acting aggressively, quietly and slowly back away until it's out of sight. If the animal does spot you, do not make eye contact. Speak in a calm, monotone voice. And if you can, slowly pull on a backpack or coat to protect your back.

If that doesn't work: If a bear charges you, aim your bear spray at its face and shoot when it gets within about 25 feet. Unfortunately, this won't always deter the animal. What to do next depends on the type of bear you've encountered. If it's a grizzly, the best thing to do is lie in the fetal position or facedown, protect the back of your neck with your hands, and don't scream. Play dead during and after the assault, because grizzlies sometimes hang around for a while. For less temperamental species like black or brown bears, stand your ground, yell, and fight back, aiming for the snout and eyes. In no way should you ever run or climb a tree—bears are much better at both than you are. (*For more about the world's different kinds of bears, check out page 101.*)

SHARKS

Prevention: There are fewer than 100 shark attacks a year worldwide. Your risk can be lowered even further by swimming in a group instead of alone, avoiding waters where there are fishermen or fish bait, and staying out of the water at night when sharks are active and hard to see. Be alert near steep underwater drop-offs or between sandbars, favorite shark hangouts. Shiny accessories, brightly colored swimwear, or a bleeding wound can attract a shark's attention—and so can thrashing around in the water. If you spot the dreaded triangular fin, keep track of it so you don't get ambushed from below or behind. Swim quickly to shore without yelling or splashing too much.

If that doesn't work: If a shark approaches you with intent, fight back. The experts recommend whacking and clawing at its eyes and gills. Use whatever's nearby—a rock, a camera, goggles, or even your hands if that's all you've got. Smack the end of the shark's nose, even though this puts you at risk of getting bitten. If its jaws latch onto you and won't let go, there are a couple of options, both equally scary but sometimes effective: You can grab and hold onto its body so it doesn't tear off your limbs as it shakes you from side to side, or you can try to lift the part of your body that's being bitten above the water, where the shark will be unable to breathe and will have to let go. Your next step is to get to shore and apply pressure to your wounds until help arrives.

BEES

Prevention: Honeybees live in colonies and sometimes gang up on humans when irritated. To avoid attracting their attention, don't wear dark- or bright-colored clothing, strong fragrances, or shiny jewelry. Experts recommend that people listen for buzzing and watch for a straight line of bees flying back and forth. If you recognize these signs, leave the area calmly, quickly, and quietly. Don't ever bug bees by making noise, swatting them, or spraying water or pesticides at them.

If that doesn't work: If bees swarm at you, rush to a building, car, or tent while covering your mouth and eyes (it's okay to peek so you can see where you're going). Use your hands or shirt to protect your face. If there's no nearby shelter, run to a dark part of the woods, bearing in mind that you may have to sprint as much as half a mile before they give up the chase. (Jumping into water probably won't help, because the bees can just hover until you come up for air.) Once you're in a safe place, use a fingernail or credit card to scrape out any stingers sideways as quickly as possible, counting as you go because a medical staff may need to know later on. Wash the wounds with soap and water and apply ice for a few minutes. Even though the average person—that is, someone who is not allergic to bee stings—can tolerate 10 stings per pound of body weight, you should seek emergency room treatment if you've been stung more than 15 times, your face swells, or you have trouble breathing.

To learn what to do in case of a snake attack, slither over to page 309.

GENUS & SPECIES

Scientists call it "binomial nomenclature"—the two Latin words that identify animals and plants. The first name is the genus; the second is the species. Can you match each plant or animal (1–23) with its Latin name (a–w)? *(Answers on page 434.)*

1. Adder
2. Atlantic salmon
3. Balsam fir
4. Beet
5. Black rat
6. Bok choy
7. Cat
8. Cedar of Lebanon
9. Chicken
10. Chimpanzee
11. Devil maple
12. Flowering tobacco
13. Red fox
14. Foxglove
15. Horse
16. Komodo dragon
17. Lion
18. Nile crocodile
19. Indian oil sardine
20. Sugar maple
21. Tiger lily
22. Tokay gecko
23. Wolf

a. *Abies balsamea*
b. *Acer diabolicum*
c. *Acer saccharum*
d. *Beta vulgaris*
e. *Brassica chinensis*
f. *Canis lupus*
g. *Cedrus libani*
h. *Crocodylus niloticus*
i. *Digitalis purpurea*
j. *Equus caballus*
k. *Felis catus*
l. *Gallus gallus*
m. *Gekko gecko*
n. *Lilium lancifolium*
o. *Nicotiana alata*
p. *Pan troglodytes*
q. *Panthera leo*
r. *Rattus rattus*
s. *Salmo salar*
t. *Sardinella longiceps*
u. *Varanus komodoensis*
v. *Vipera berus*
w. *Vulpes vulpes*

Good thing it's slow: The slow loris is the only primate with a toxic bite.

TINY BUBBLES

Some animals need bubbles to survive. Yes, that's right—bubbles.

THEY'RE HAVING A GAS

Pacific and Atlantic herring both expel bubbles out of their back ends. When they do, it causes high-frequency noises that sound like a squeaky, high-pitched raspberry (aka, a Bronx cheer or a "zerbert"). Scientists have a technical name for the sounds: "fast repetitive ticks," or FRTs.

This strange little fish characteristic has several unusual aspects. First, the gas bubbles aren't caused by the digestive process. Instead, the fish swallows air from the surface of the ocean and then emits the air through a small opening near its anus, so technically the bubbles aren't flatulence even though they sound like it. Second, the herring only expel these bubbles at night. And finally, *they* can hear these sounds, but other fish can't. Scientists think it's because the bubble sounds have a special use—they help the herring stay safe by telling each other where they are in the dark. The raspberries have such a high-pitched sound that the herrings are able to communicate without other fish overhearing them and snapping them up for a tasty meal.

A SMELLY SECRET

Star-nosed moles are small (about eight inches long), with large, furless front claws for digging and a star-shaped nose that's made up of 22 fleshy pink "tentacles." The animals live in wetlands, mostly in Canada and the United States, where they dig underground tunnels that usually lead into a stream or pond. Living in near-total darkness, star-nosed moles are almost completely blind, but they're also among the world's must successful hunters. The secret? Those tentacles on their noses blow bubbles, and the moles re-inhale them as fast as five to ten times per second. The bubbles travel into the water where the moles live and pick up scents that can be used to locate prey. In addition, the tentacles have thousands of receptors that can touch as many as 12 objects per second, so the moles can swim like lightning through the water. They follow the bubble scent at high speed, eating up insects, mollusks,

Asian water deer are the only deer with tusks instead of antlers.

crustaceans, and small fish along the way. They've even bubbled their way into *Guinness World Records* as the world's fastest eaters.

DON'T READ THIS BEFORE LUNCH

Gray foam-nest tree frogs have disk-shaped sticky pads on their toes to help them climb the branches of trees, where they spend most of their days hiding in crevices. When it's time to make a nest, the female chooses a tree overlooking a pond or stream, and in the evening she climbs the tree and picks a spot on a leaf or branch overhanging the water. Then she uses her urine and secretions of mucus and whips the mixture into a bubbly foam nest with her hind legs. (It may not sound appetizing, but it works.) After the female lays her eggs in the nest and various males fertilize them, the cocoon of foam protects the developing eggs from both predators and the hot sun. The outer edge of the foam develops a crust in the heat, but inside, the eggs stay moist until the tadpoles hatch a few days later and drop into the water.

GONE BUBBLE FISHIN'

Humpback whales grow to be about 52 feet long and weigh up to 50 tons. At that size they need to eat a *lot*—an average-sized humpback whale can chomp down more than 5,000 pounds of food a day. In order to catch enough fish to satisfy their enormous appetites, humpbacks often trap their prey by blowing "bubble nets." When they want to catch a school of fish, they begin blowing bubbles out of their blowholes as they dive about 50 feet down into the water. Then, as they swim back up to the surface in a spiral, they create a circular wall of bubbles 10 to 100 feet wide with a yummy school or two of fish trapped inside. The whales swallow the prey as they swim up through the center of the bubble net. Sometimes humpbacks fish in a group, driving the fish to one location and then working together to surround them with bubbles. When that happens, each humpback takes a turn at feeding inside the bubble net.

For more bubble stories, turn to page 361.

FUNKY MONKEYS

Their scientific name is Chlorocebus aethiops sabaeus, *but the vervet monkeys that populate the islands of the Caribbean are commonly called "green monkeys" because their golden fur has an olive-green tint. They're also called unprintable names because they can be destructive, thieving pranksters...and drunks.*

PIRATES OF THE CARIBBEAN

Vervet monkeys are lively and cute, with a white splash of fur around their black faces and that green-gold fur on their bodies that ends in a perky golden tail. Native to Africa, they're found along the western coast as far north as Senegal and as far south as Ghana. Back in the 1600s, their good looks took them abroad: They were captured, put on slave ships, and sent to the New World to be sold as pets. In the Caribbean, some escaped captivity and went feral, easily adapting to the warm climate and abundant native plants and wildlife. The monkeys reproduced by the thousands, and colonies of them still populate the islands of St. Kitts, Nevis, and Barbados, where they delight the tourists and drive the farmers (and some bartenders) crazy.

Green monkeys are omnivorous; their natural diet includes grasses, fruits, seeds, small animals, and insects. They're also smart enough to avoid poison and traps, so they feast on crops stolen from local gardens and farms. In the Caribbean, they've also adapted to the tourist trade by taking food from unwary vacationers. But on the island of St. Kitts, the monkeys do more than just pilfer food—they're notorious for stealing booze.

YO HO HO!

Most animals don't voluntarily drink alcohol, but the vervet monkeys of St. Kitts are an exception. It all began with sugarcane—the main ingredient in rum and the most important crop on St. Kitts. About 300 years ago, the green monkeys first found overripe, fermented canes in the fields. They chewed on the stalks and got tipsy. Pretty soon, they discovered that rum had the same taste, so they moved on to that.

Today, the liquor-loving monkeys flock to the trees near the beaches and outdoor bars where colorful cocktails are served. Sometimes the bartenders try to scare them away with water pistols, but the vervets are brave and will sneak up to grab any drink that a tourist neglects or abandons. If they like the taste, they keep drinking. By evening, crowds of monkeys gather in the tourist areas, drunkenly squabbling and barely able to stand up. The antics of the St. Kitts "drunk monkeys" have made them a major tourist attraction; visitors seem to love watching the animals get wasted and act like silly, drunk people.

BINGERS VS. TEETOTALERS

In fact, research is now showing that the monkeys have a lot in common with human alcoholics. Beginning in the 1990s, Frank Ervin, a professor of psychiatry at McGill University in Canada, led a series of experiments in which his team offered more than 1,000 St. Kitts monkeys a choice of water, alcohol, fruit juice, or a mixture of alcohol and water (like a scotch and soda). What the scientists found was fascinating. Fifteen percent of the monkeys were teetotalers who didn't drink any alcohol at all. Another 15 percent were steady drinkers who didn't mess around with fruit juice in their drinks and chugged more than five grams of alcohol a day (which may not sound like a lot, but these little guys sometimes only weigh as much as a newborn human baby). Nearly 5 percent were bingers who drank themselves into a stupor. But the vast majority (65 percent) were what the researchers called social drinkers—they drank in social situations, preferred to drink alcohol diluted with fruit juice, and actually didn't drink before lunch.

What made these findings remarkable was that the percentages of teetotalers, social drinkers, steady drinkers, and bingers were similar to percentages in the human population. According to Professor Ervin, there's not much difference between a crowd of soused monkeys and a human cocktail party: "You have one who gets aggressive, one who gets sexy, one who thinks everything's funny, and one who gets really grumpy. The binge drinkers gulp down the alcohol at a very fast rate and pass out on the floor."

WHAT DRIVES A MONKEY TO DRINK?

It used to be thought that alcohol addiction was a combination of environmental pressures and mental or emotional weakness. This theory began to change when scientists found evidence of inherited tendencies toward alcoholism. Researchers think the drinking habits of St. Kitts vervets indicate a major biological component. Green monkeys became alcoholics even on a lush, sleepy island where they had no lack of food or shelter, and their lives were relatively stress-free. As for mental or emotional weakness, many of the alcoholic monkeys are respected leaders in their society. Most of the steady drinkers are young males (another similarity with humans). Professor Roberta Palmour, a McGill University professor of human genetics, found that they are "good alpha males… they keep order well, and they're very dominant...this kind of alcoholic monkey is a very functional animal."

WE HAVE MET THE MONKEYS, AND THEY ARE US

According to the World Health Organization, alcohol abuse is the world's third-leading cause of premature death. Currently, scientists are studying the brain chemistry of alcoholics in hopes of finding medical advances that will make it easier for people to stay sober. The monkeys are helping with that.

Researchers have found that alcoholic green monkeys are biologically different from teetotalers and social drinkers. When steady drinkers in the monkey population are sober, they have problems with their neurological transmitters and don't get enough of the "feel-good" chemical dopamine. When bingeing monkeys are sober, they suffer problems with the feel-good hormone serotonin. Alcohol helps ease these problems temporarily, but makes them worse in the long run. As a result, Ervin and his team theorized that differences in brain chemistry may explain drinking patterns in humans.

Monkeys may also be leading the way in science's search for the human "alcohol gene." If alcoholism is an inherited tendency, then there will be a genetic component. Palmour suspects that genes cause the predisposition to alcoholism in St. Kitts monkeys. Since these animals share about 96 percent of their genetic composition with humans, understanding the liquor-loving St. Kitts monkeys could lead to greater understanding of the human genetics of alcohol abuse. In fact, Palmour believes the monkeys may show science "better ways of intervening and, ideally, preventing problems before they occur in potential human alcoholics."

"MUD-LUSCIOUS AND PUDDLE-WONDERFUL"

The funny title is how poet E.E. Cummings described the natural world. That about sums it up for us, but we thought (this being a nature book) we'd offer a few more perspectives.

"You didn't come into this world. You came out of it, like a wave from the ocean. You are not a stranger here."

—Alan Watts

"Forests, lakes, and rivers, clouds and winds, stars and flowers, stupendous glaciers and crystal snowflakes—every form of animate or inanimate existence leaves its impress upon the soul of man."

—Orison Swett Marden

"To me a lush carpet of pine needles or spongy grass is more welcome than the most luxurious Persian rug."

—Helen Keller

"Nature always tends to act in the simplest way."

—Daniel Bernoulli

"Let us permit nature to have her way: she understands her business better than we do."

—Michel de Montaigne

"Adopt the pace of nature: her secret is patience."

—Ralph Waldo Emerson

"I go to nature to be soothed and healed, and to have my senses put in order."

—John Burroughs

"It seems to me that we all look at Nature too much, and live with her too little."

—Oscar Wilde

"The sun, with all those planets revolving around it and dependent on it, can still ripen a bunch of grapes as if it had nothing else in the universe to do."

—Galileo Galilei

"Nature will bear the closest inspection. She invites us to lay our eye level with her smallest leaf, and take an insect view of its plain."

—Henry David Thoreau

The giant burrowing frog doesn't croak—it hoots like an owl.

"Human subtlety will never devise an invention more beautiful, more simple or more direct than does Nature, because in her inventions, nothing is lacking and nothing is superfluous."

—Leonardo da Vinci

"Nature is an infinite sphere of which the center is everywhere and the circumference nowhere."

—Blaise Pascal

"Until man duplicates a blade of grass, nature can laugh at his so-called scientific knowledge."

—Thomas Edison

"The moment one gives close attention to anything, even a blade of grass, it becomes a mysterious, awesome, indescribably magnificent world in itself."

—Henry Miller

"Look deep into nature, and then you will understand everything better."

—Albert Einstein

"One touch of nature makes the whole world kin."

—William Shakespeare

"All rivers, even the most dazzling, those that catch the sun in their course, all rivers go down to the ocean and drown. And life awaits man as the sea awaits the river."

—Simone Schwarz-Bart

"Look at a tree, a flower. Let your awareness rest upon it. How still they are, how deeply rooted in Being. Allow nature to teach you stillness."

—Eckhart Tolle

"Nature, always inartistic, takes pleasure in creating the impossible."

—Jerome K. Jerome

"If future generations are to remember us with gratitude rather than contempt, we must leave them more than the miracles of technology. We must leave them a glimpse of the world as it was in the beginning, not just after we got through with it."

—Lyndon B. Johnson

"I just wish the world was twice as big and half of it was still unexplored."

—David Attenborough

Some diamonds have been carbon-dated to at least 3.4 billion years old.

ODD COUPLES

And you thought some of your friendships were odd pairings. How about a snake and a hamster? Or a crow and a kitten?

CASSIE AND MOSES

In 1999 Wallace and Ann Collito saw a baby kitten being cared for by a crow. The crow fed the kitten worms and insects, and herded her out of the street to protect her from cars. The pair played all day, and the Collitos began feeding these unlikely pals. They also filmed them because no one believed the story. Eventually Cassie the kitten moved into their home, and Moses the crow showed up every morning at 6:00 a.m., cawing until Cassie came out to play. Bird and cat played together for five years until Moses passed away from old age.

TARRA AND BELLA

In 2003 Tarra, an 8,700-pound Asian elephant, took up with Bella a cute, white mutt. Both lived at the 2,000-acre Elephant Sanctuary in Tennessee, where circus and zoo elephants retire and roam free. Rescued stray dogs at the sanctuary don't usually mix with the elephants, but Bella trusted Tarra so much she would roll over for a belly rub from the elephant's enormous foot. Tarra and Bella ate together, strolled together, and often slept near one another in the elephant barn. When Bella suffered a spinal cord injury, she was cared for in the sanctuary office, and Tarra spent her days waiting nearby. She didn't roam the acreage again until Bella recovered and could go with her. In 2011 Bella was killed by coyotes at least a mile from where she was found. The sanctuary officials believe that Tarra carried her friend home as a final loving gesture.

BALOO, SHERE KHAN, AND LEO

In 2001 an Atlanta drug bust turned up some unusual contraband: a baby bear, baby lion, and baby tiger, each about two months old. The "status-symbol" pets belonged to drug dealers and had been badly neglected. The police sent them to the Noah's Ark Rehabilitation Center in Locust Grove, Georgia, where the animals were given veterinary care and a home. Since the three were already bonded "like brothers from the same litter," the staff at Noah's Ark raised them together, even nicknaming the trio "BLT" (for bear, lion, and tiger). Today, Baloo the bear, Shere Khan the tiger, and Leo the lion share their own clubhouse and a large natural habitat that allows them plenty of room to move around. Of the three, say officials at Noah's Ark, Baloo is the leader, Leo sleeps a lot, and Shere Khan is a playful pest. Despite these personality differences and the fact that any one of the three could easily hurt the others, the animals share a loving bond—all three will snuggle up together if it's cold. It's the only known bear, lion, and tiger friendship in the world.

OWEN AND MZEE

Whena tsunami hit the east coast of Kenya in 2004, a baby hippo lost his family. Conservationists named him Owen and took him to the Haller Park animal sanctuary near Mombasa. Confused and exhausted, Owen ran toward a creature that no one else would have mistaken for a hippopotamus: Mzee, a 130-year-old Aldabra tortoise. The young hippo wouldn't leave Mzee's side. The tortoise not only accepted Owen, he cared for him too. Mzee taught him which leaves to eat, and he nibbled at Owen's feet to steer him in the right direction on walks. He also played with Owen in the water. Eventually, the pals were separated because Owen had grown so much that he could have accidentally harmed Mzee (by falling on him, for example). So Owen moved in with Cleo, a female hippo, and Mzee got a tortoise companion. Both are doing well.

POPPY AND BUTTERMILK

Sometimes you don't know who your friends are until there's a crisis. In Butte County, California, Art Colyer has a small herd of goats and a "cantankerous" donkey named Poppy. One night in 2010, he awoke to a scream, ran outside with a flashlight, and saw a mountain lion attacking his goat, Buttermilk. The big cat had hold of Buttermilk's face and nose, and although Colyer ran forward shouting, the mountain lion paid no attention. It did, however, pay attention when Poppy charged the mountain lion and brayed in its face. Colyer said that the donkey began "running around whooping it up and hitting him with everything she had." After Poppy landed a few well-placed kicks, the mountain lion took off, and the donkey stayed near Buttermilk until the goat was taken away for veterinary care. Since the attack, says Colyer, Poppy is still cantankerous with humans, but not with Buttermilk.

AOCHAN AND GOHAN

In 2006 at the Mutsugoro Okoku Zoo in Tokyo, Japan, Aochan, a two-year-old Japanese rat snake, was being finicky about his food. He refused to eat the frozen mice put in his cage. His worried keeper decided to try to whet the snake's appetite with something a little more challenging—he put a live dwarf hamster that he called Gohan (which is the name of a tasty steamed rice dish) in the cage. To everyone's surprise, the three-foot-long Aochan befriended the 3.5-inch Gohan by snuggling with him instead of eating him. Today, the friends still share the same cage; Gohan even sleeps on the snake's back. As for food, Aochan now eats his frozen mice without hesitation.

SURYIA AND ROSCOE

The Institute of Greatly Endangered and Rare Species (TIGERS) is a wildlife sanctuary for apes and big cats in South Carolina. There, six-year-old Suryia, an orangutan, lives a charmed life that includes elephant rides along the river with his handlers. On one of those excursions, Suryia caught sight of a stray blue tick hound (now known as Roscoe). Dogs and primates don't usually get along, but as soon as Suryia saw Roscoe, he jumped off the elephant, and the pair played like long-lost friends. When Suryia returned to TIGERS, Roscoe followed, and while people tried to find Roscoe's owner, the orangutan fed him some monkey biscuits. No one ever claimed Roscoe, who now lives at TIGERS, where he plays and swims with his new buddy. They sometimes even ride together on the back of Bubbles the elephant. Aww.

* * *

Weighing in at just over an ounce, the black-legged falconet and the white-fronted falconet are the smallest birds of prey.

MISCENATURALLANEOUS

We made that word up. But we did not make up this random collection of cool stories about nature.

IF NESSIE WERE A CARPENTER...

In January 2012, British scientists released the results of a study in which they showed that Scotland's Loch Ness acts as a kind of enormous level—like a carpenter's level. They did this by placing hypersensitive sensors around the lake and measuring the exact water level at each spot for 201 days. Result: The water of Loch Ness moves back and forth along its length, rising and falling slightly at each end about every 12.5 hours. Why? Because the whole of Scotland, and, indeed, all of the island of Britain, is tilted just the tiniest bit by the massive amounts of water around it as the tides change. How much does the lake rise and fall at each end? About 1.5 millimeters. "If you were on a boat in the middle of the loch," said Philip Woodworth, one of the scientists, "you certainly wouldn't notice it."

BAD BOIDS, WATCHA GONNA DO?

In 2011 police in Lower Saxony, Germany, started training their newest recruits: cadaver-sniffing vultures. The reasoning went that vultures, which eat nothing but carrion, or dead flesh, find that food using their incredibly powerful olfactory glands, and the police hoped that they could train the vultures to find the remains of murder victims. The experiment didn't go so well, however, as newspapers reported that the vultures failed to locate a single cadaver laid our for them by their trainers. The "lead" vulture, named Sherlock, the stories reported, didn't like flying and preferred to walk, which, even if he *did* find cadavers, would made him less effective than a sniffer dog. And according to trainer German Alonso (yes, the German trainer's name is German) the other two vultures, Columbo and Miss Marple, don't seem to be able to do anything other than attack each other.

NATURE'S FAITHFUL LAUNDROMAT

You've heard of Old Faithful, the famously regular natural geyser in

Yellowstone National Park in Wyoming. Every 65 to 92 minutes, it sends a plume of water and steam up to 185 feet into the air, each blast lasting from 90 seconds to five minutes. It is an awe-inspiring sight, one that's been viewed by millions of people since the park first opened in 1872. What most people *haven't* heard about the natural wonder is that, in the late 1800s, settlers in the region used Old Faithful as a washing machine. While the geyser was dormant, settlers would throw dirty laundry into the opening through which the geyser erupts. The clothes would be churned about in near-boiling water below the surface, and, when the geyser erupted—the clothes would be shot into the air and finally fall to the ground, steamed and completely washed. The practice was eventually put to an end, as it was not only deemed a bit tacky to treat a treasured national site as a washing machine, but it was exceedingly risky: the enormous amount of water the geyser sprays can reach more than 204°F, and can cause severe burns. Today a fence keeps visitors from getting close to the geyser itself.

I'LL TAKE A NICE COLD ROADKILL OF BEER

In July 2010, Scottish beermaker BrewDog released one of the strongest, most expensive—and tactless—beers ever made. Called the End of History, the beer was 55 percent alcohol (most beers are 3 to 6 percent) and cost $765 a bottle. But strangest of all, the bottles that hold the beer are encased in the bodies of actual dead animals found on roadsides. Just 12 bottles of the bizarre brew were made, and they were housed in four squirrels, seven weasels, and a hare, each one configured by a taxidermist so the bottles' openings stick out of the animals' mouths. Replying to public outcry that the roadkill-encased beer was degrading to animals, BrewDog owner James Watt said, "We think to use dead animals in this way is much better than for them to be left to rot on the roadside." Within just four hours of its release, all 12 bottles had been sold to wealthy (and deranged?) customers around the world.

NO MORE CROCODILE TEARS

To cry "crocodile tears" is to give an insincere display of grief because supposedly, crocodiles, being the primitive and cold-blooded killers they are cannot shed real tears. The saying, which dates to at least the 13th century, comes from a myth that crocodiles cry while eating their prey. In more modern times, "experts" have helped spread this myth by continuing to claim that it's true. Crocodiles have tear glands near their eyes just as we do, the story goes, and they can discharge tears out of their eyes, or back into their mouths just as we can. According to the myth, because crocodiles don't chew their food, but simply swallow huge chunks of it, they actually need those tears to flow back into their mouths to moisten the pieces of food in order to help them swallow. The fact that some of those tears also spill out of the crocodiles' *eyes* while they're eating makes it look like they're crying. *Actual* crocodile experts, however, say this is a bunch of hooey. Crocodiles do have tear ducts to keep their eyes moist, but they are not used to moisten food. For one thing, crocodiles live in water, and their food, like everything else about them, is already pretty moist. Not only that, but crocodiles regularly stash prey they've captured and killed in underwater caches, where they let it rot until it is soft and easy to eat.

WALK LIKE...A GRAND CANYON?

On April 5, 1909, the front page of Arizona's *Phoenix Gazette* newspaper ran a story saying that an expedition funded by the Smithsonian Institute had uncovered hidden caverns in the Grand Canyon. Inside the caverns, the article claimed, were ancient Egyptian temples. They contained statues, friezes, jewelry, and other artifacts covered in hieroglyphs. There were even mummies. The discoveries had been made by "Prof. S. A. Jordan" and explorer "G. E. Kincaid," both, the story said, Smithsonian employees. The story caused an enormous sensation, as you might expect, but the Smithsonian responded by saying it had never heard of either Jordan or Kincaid. That didn't quite do the trick: To this day, the institute receives letters asking about the story, and conspiracy theories concerning the troves of ancient Egyptian treasures found in the Grand Canyon still thrive today. Who wrote the inexplicable news story—or why they wrote it—remains a mystery.

Ten of the Amazon River's tributaries are as large as the Mississippi River.

SLEEPING MONSTERS

Earth's supervolcanoes have been dormant for thousands of years, but what happens if they wake up?

SOMETHING TO WORRY ABOUT

The term "supervolcano" is something the media came up with and is mostly used to scare peope, but it's also used by some geologists to demonstrate the power of the world's largest volcanoes. The term has no exact scientific definition, but according to the United States Geological Survey (USGS) a supervolcano is capable of ejecting at least 240 cubic miles of scorching lava, ash, gases, and rock into the atmosphere.

When a volcano erupts, the force is measured by the Volcanic Explosivity Index, or VEI. The scale is open-ended, but the highest magnitude ever measured is VEI 8, the size of a supervolcano. To get an idea of how powerful a VEI 8 eruption is, consider this: The eruption of a supervolcano at La Garita (in present-day Colorado) 27.5 million years ago was approximately 105 times more powerful than the Tsar Bomba explosion, a nuclear bomb tested by the Soviets in 1961 and still considered to be the most powerful man-made explosive device ever detonated.

KA-BOOM?

What's it like on earth when this kind of super eruption occurs? No one knows for sure. The last time there was an explosion of VEI 8 was long before written history. So scientists are left to study one of the most "recent" super eruptions—the Toba volcano in Sumatra, Indonesia, which took place about 75,000 years ago—in an effort to gauge the effects it had on the environment and whether those effects pushed humans to the brink of extinction.

Volcanists estimate that Toba ejected an incredible 670 cubic miles of lava, rock, and ash into the atmosphere. By comparison, the worst volcanic catastrophe in U.S. history, the Mount St. Helens eruption that killed 57 people in 1980 released just 0.25 cubic miles of volcanic material. And the famous 79 A.D. eruption of Vesuvius that buried the ancient Roman cities of Pompeii and

Herculaneum did its damage with only 1.2 cubic miles of volcanic debris.

At Toba, an avalanche of lava and rock moving at hundreds of miles an hour killed everything in its path; the damage covered 7,700 square miles—an area about the size of New Jersey. In some places the molten rock and ash was 2,000 feet thick, but destruction wasn't limited to the island of Sumatra. The explosion sent volcanic ash miles into the atmosphere. The ash contained sharp particles of pulverized lava, rock, and volcanic glass shards that killed all the plants and animals in its path. Land more than a thousand miles away was buried in ash, including India and much of Southeast Asia.

But the most widespread effect was on the global climate. Sulfuric gases from the volcano invaded the atmosphere, and the combination of ash, gases, and moisture formed dense clouds that absorbed heat and blocked the sun. The result was what's called a "volcanic winter."

BYE-BYE, NEANDERTHAL MAN

Nobody knows exactly how severe Toba's volcanic winter was, but geological records show that temperatures suddenly dropped in some areas by at least 18°F—and it's possible that the volcanic winter lasted as long as 10 years. Some scientists believe the explosion and climate change killed off 80 to 90 percent of the humans on the planet, leaving only a few thousand in Africa who survived to become our ancestors.

Toba isn't the only volcano associated with species extinction, though. The mystery of why Neanderthals disappeared some 39,000 years ago has long baffled scientists. Now geologists think that their disappearance coincided with the eruption of the Italian supervolcano Campanian Ignimbrite, which caused such severe climate change that it may have wiped out Neanderthal man.

NOT JUST ANOTHER HOLE IN THE GROUND

All of the earth's known supervolcanoes form broad depressions called *calderas*. This means that the largest volcanoes in the world are likely to be broad valleys or lakes that cover hundreds of square miles.

Caterpillars eat constantly and hardly ever sleep.

A caldera's sunken shape is a clue to the way supervolcanoes are created. With all volcanoes, a column of molten rock, or *magma*, rises and comes close to the surface of the Earth. In most volcanoes, the magma comes up through a break in the Earth's crust. But the magma from a supervolcano pools into a chamber underneath the crust that—as it fills up—pushes the crust upward, gradually creating a bulging dome of rock.

When the magma and gases in the chamber develop enough pressure, cracks appear in the dome, and the "roof" of the chamber collapses as thousands of years of collected gases and magma spew out. The eruption empties the magma chambers and the volcano's structure collapses, forming a caldera.

MEET SOME MEGA KILLERS

Most of the supervolcanoes we know about burned out long ago. Others, like Toba, are dormant but could always flare up. Toba's caldera has long filled with water, making it Lake Toba. It doesn't pose much of a threat right now, but there are some other calderas that scientists are keeping an eye on.

Lake Taupo: New Zealand's Lake Taupo caldera is 485 square miles and was a supervolcano. Formed 300,000 years ago, Lake Taupo is responsible for the most violent volcanic eruption in the last 5,000 years. It wasn't a super-eruption, but it's believed to have clouded the air with so much ash that it caused red sunsets thousands of miles away...the ancient Chinese and Romans wrote about them. The caldera is constantly monitored for signs of another eruption, but in the meantime, New Zealand is putting the energy from Lake Taupo's magma chambers to good use: The chambers provide about 8 percent of the country's electricity.

Long Valley: Of the 169 volcanoes in the United States, 18 of the most dangerous are labeled "very high threat" by the USGS. Number 7 on the list is the 200-square-mile Long Valley Caldera in California. It formed 760,000 years ago after an eruption about 3,000 times bigger than Mt. St. Helens. Burning lava covered about 1,500 square miles, and ash spread east to Nebraska, north to Wyoming, and south to northern Mexico.

Will Long Valley erupt again soon? Maybe. One sign that a caldera might erupt is a sudden increase in earthquakes. In 1980 alone, thousands of earthquakes shook Long Valley. In the 1990s, another sign of magma activity showed up in the form of carbon dioxide—a gas present in magma chambers—that began killing trees on Mammoth Mountain, the highest spot on the caldera. Meanwhile on the Long Valley floor, a dome shape of about 100 square miles has slowly risen about three feet, a sign that magma is filling subterranean chambers once again.

Yellowstone: The term "supervolcano" was first coined on a BBC show describing Wyoming's Yellowstone caldera—at about 1,500 square miles, it's more than seven times larger than Long Valley. About 640,000 years ago, the Yellowstone caldera spewed 240 cubic miles of volcanic material into the air. Scientists predict that an eruption of the caldera today would have 1,000 times the force of the atomic bomb at Hiroshima and would cover the entire western half of the United States in three feet of ash, making it uninhabitable for years. Volcanic ash and gases would also cool the global climate, devastate world agriculture, and lead to mass starvation.

Although it's not listed on the USGS's "very high threat" list, the many geysers, hot springs, and boiling mud pots at Yellowstone National Park are proof that it's one of the most active calderas in the world.

DON'T PANIC JUST YET

Most volcanists believe that all the signs we're seeing actually mean that the "imminent eruptions" of these supervolcanoes could be centuries away. So relax—it's still a matter of time…a long, long time.

*   *   *

ANOTHER BEAVER FACT

A small, land-dwelling beaver called *Paleocastor* lived in North America some 20 million years ago. It built complex, spiraling burrows that filled with debris and fossilized, creating twisted stones called "devil's corkscrews."

BELIEVE IT OR NOT!

So you believed the one about the woman who gave birth to a litter of rabbits? Don't worry. Lots of people were fooled by these animal hoaxes.

MER-MONSTROSITY?

Mermaids conjure visions of beautiful singing women with flowing hair and graceful fins. But the "Feejee Mermaid"—displayed by circus mogul extraordinaire P. T. Barnum in the 1840s—did mermaids everywhere injustice. This thing was hideous...a three-foot-long carcass, brown and shriveled, with coarse hair and its mouth open to reveal jagged teeth. For years, the Feejee Mermaid was the star of Barnum's American Museum in New York, bringing in enough tourists to triple profits. The "artifact" had passed through a chain of people, including a sea captain who sold his ship to buy it for $6,000. The mermaid was the only property he owned when he died, and his son sold it to a museum curator and associate of Barnum's.

By then, scientists had dismissed the specimen as a hoax, but Barnum still persuaded people to pay to see it. How? Before the museum began exhibiting the mermaid in 1842, Barnum "conditioned" the public. Using pseudonyms, he wrote to newspapers about an amazing discovery in Fiji (which gave the mermaid its name) and had one of his employees pose as a naturalist named Dr. Griffin to authenticate it. Then, he distributed 10,000 pamphlets to local hotels, stores, and businesses with "facts" about the existence of mermaids. All that press certainly snagged the public's interest.

But modern science eventually proved that this was no mermaid. It was actually a the head of a mummified baby monkey sewed onto a fish body. It probably did come from Asia, though, where fake animal hybrids were often sold to gullible tourists.

BUNNY IN THE OVEN?

In 1726 a bored English housewife named Mary Toft convinced doctors of something ludicrous—that she'd given birth to a litter of stillborn rabbits...in front of a midwife and a doctor, no less. Investigations by the surgeon to King George I and other trusted authorities concluded that she was telling the truth. The surgeon

The seeds of an Indian lotus tree remain viable for up to 400 years.

even went so far as to publish a medical report about her, and people all over the United Kingdom were so sympathetic to her case that they stopped serving rabbit stew. Toft explained the strange occurrence by saying that, while pregnant, she'd been startled by a rabbit and thereafter dreamed of rabbits, was tempted to chase them around, and craved rabbit meat. At the time, people believed that a pregnant woman's thoughts and actions could directly affect her baby's characteristics, so they believed the story.

Obviously, though, Toft was lying, and it eventually came to light that, in a bid for fame and fortune, she had bribed people to bring her dead rabbits, which she hid inside her body and then pretended to deliver. The country was furious, the medical community embarrassed, and authorities eager for punishment—Toft was locked up for four months after a court exposed her as a "cheat."

DINO-BIRD?

In 1999 *National Geographic* made a groundbreaking declaration. A Chinese farmer had discovered a prehistoric fossil that the magazine said was proof of something paleontologists had long suspected: that dinosaurs evolved into birds. The fossil, dug up in the Liaoning Province of China in the 1990s, "revealed" a new species called the Archaeoraptor. It seemed to show a feathered *theropod* (a two-legged, meat-eating dinosaur) that could fly. Nothing like that had ever been found before. The article called the specimen "a true missing link in the complex chain that connects dinosaurs to birds. It seems to capture the paleontological 'moment' when dinosaurs were becoming birds."

A few months later, though, scientists had to admit that they had been fooled. The artifact had actually been put together from at least two real fossils in order to sell on China's booming black market (it fetched $80,000 in the United States). The tail of a small, feathered dinosaur had been attached to the skeleton of an ancient bird, and then filled in with bones from other species. The actual artifacts were almost destroyed by the doctoring, but researchers were able to glean some information from them: Both the dinosaur, now called a Microraptor, and the bird, Yanornis, had been previously unknown to paleontologists. So in the end, it was a real and significant discovery of *two* species…just not the dinosaur-bird as they had initially believed.

YOUR FLIGHT HAS BEEN DELAYED BY...

Sometimes when your airplane doesn't take off on time, it's not just "human" error.

A MOUSE. In August 2011 a flight attendant saw a mouse under the seat of a jumbo jet preparing to depart Sweden for the United States. The flight was delayed because, the airline explained to the 250 passengers, the mouse could chew through wiring on the plane and thereby posed a safety risk. After several hours of trying to catch the mouse, the plane was finally grounded and the unhappy passengers were booked onto different flights. When the mouse still hadn't been found three days later, the airline finally put the plane back to work, saying "all we could do was conclude that it was no longer onboard."

TURTLES. Kennedy International Airport in New York City had to delay several flights one morning in June 2011 when more than 100 diamondback terrapins ambled onto to a runway. The turtles had come from nearby Jamaica Bay, and were headed to a sandy area on the other side of the runway to lay their eggs. Ground crew members were dispatched to hurry the turtles across (they carried them), while flights were delayed for about 30 minutes. A similar incident caused 90-minute delays in 2009.

SNAKES. A Qantas Airlines 737 arrived in Melbourne, Australia, from the town of Alice Springs in April 2009, and then readied to depart for Sydney. But in the midst of offloading cargo, security noticed that a box that was supposed to have 12 snakes in it...had only eight. Four young Stimson's pythons, just seven or so inches long, had somehow escaped from the container. The flight was grounded, and passengers rebooked—although their luggage was not allowed to go with them. When the airline confirmed that Stimson's pythons are not endangered, the plane was fumigated. The dead snakes were later found and disposed of, the plane was put back into business, and the snake-free luggage was sent on to its owners.

JACKALS, LIZARDS, AND RAPTORS. One day in June 2008, all airplane traffic was halted at Indira Gandhi International Airport in Delhi, India, after a swarm of animals, including jackals, monitor lizards, and raptors, swamped the airport's runways. Wildlife officials were called in to clear the animals, and after about an hour, planes were cleared to take off again. The officials said the animals were simply looking for dry land: It was the first day of monsoon season, and sudden rains had caused flooding all over the region. Local newspapers reported that more than 100 flights had been delayed by the animal swarm.

FROGS. A flight scheduled from Wales in the United Kingdom to Florida in 2005 was taxiing toward the runway when the pilot came on the intercom. "Sorry," he said to the 300 or so passengers, "we cannot take off because there are two frogs loose on board." The passengers were hopping mad as they were made to sit in the plane and wait whicle customs officials jumped into the plane's cargo hold and attempted to catch the wayward amphibians. It took more than an hour, after which the plane finally took off. Airline officials defended the decision to delay the flight, saying the frogs might have been endangered—or even poisonous.

A CROCODILE. This is a slightly different kind of animal and plane story, and unfortunately it's tragic, too. In September 2010 a small passenger plane crashed in the Democratic Republic of Congo. The pilot and 18 of 19 passengers were killed. The sole survivor told rescuers that during the flight a crocodile measuring a few feet in length had emerged from a duffel bag in the rear of the cabin. Panicked passengers fled toward the cockpit, and soon after, the plane went down. The survivor said he believed the weight of the passengers collected in the front of the plane caused the crash. According to Tim Atkinson, of Britain's Air Accidents Investigations, "I would say it's extremely unlikely this story holds water. But," he added, "I wouldn't rule it out completely."

Media organizations that reported on the story, including the BBC and NPR, said there were actually two survivors of the crash: the passenger mentioned above…and the crocodile. But, the reports said, the crocodile was killed by rescuers.

FUNNY HEADLINES

Actual headlines—of the animal, plant, and weather variety—ripped from actual newspapers.

Bear Eats Fruit, Takes Stuffed Bear from NH House

Teens Say Cutting Down Trees "Better than Drinking"

Rare Flower Found on Site a Plant, Says Developer

Passing Wind Strands BC Ferry Passengers

MICHIGAN MAN KILLS 3-FOOT GATOR WHILE PICKING CORN

Fish Need Water, Feds Say

PECAN SCAB DISEASE CAUSING NUT TO FALL OFF

Forest Service Employees Donate to Glory Hole

Students Duped by "Tree-Octopus"

Man Learns Lesson in Naked Fight with Javelinas

REASON FOR MORE BEAR SIGHTINGS: MORE BEARS

Man Admits Switchblade Assault in Squirrel Dispute

Town Okays Animal Rule

TERMINAL SMOG NOT LETHAL

CHILD'S STOOL GREAT FOR USE IN GARDEN

CUTS COULD HURT ANIMALS

Lesbian Japanese Monkeys Challenge Darwin's Assumptions

HAVE YOU DRIVEN A FJORD LATELY?

Tips to Avoid Alligator Attacks: Don't Swim in Waters Inhabited by Large Alligators.

TUNA BITING OFF WASHINGTON COAST

Wet, Salty Cat Found in NYC; Did it Swim from N.J.?

DEER AND TURKEY HUNT FOR DISABLED PEOPLE

DRUNK PARROTS ACTING UP AND FALLING OUT OF THE SKY IN AUSTRALIA (AGAIN)

BIG BIRDS

These giant flightless birds are living links to the past—they have more in common with dinosaurs than the little chirpers and tweeters we see every day. We've got a feeling we're not on Sesame Street anymore.

FAST FEET AND FANCY FEATHERS

Title holder for world's largest bird, the ostrich can grow to be nine feet tall and weigh up to 350 pounds. And even though the bird looks gangly, it's an excellent runner, reaching speeds of 40 mph (making it the fastest animal on two feet). Those long, strong legs make the ostrich one tough customer, too. One kick from an ostrich could easily kill a human or any of the bird's natural predators—a list that includes lions, cheetahs, and leopards.

Native to Africa, ostriches are also raised on ranches across North America. Their leather fetches a lot of money, as do their feathers and their meat, which tastes like beef but is leaner. Ostrich farming began in the 19th century, when hats adorned with ostrich feathers became all the rage in women's fashion.

The ostrich bears such a striking physiological resemblance to one particular dinosaur that the ancient creature was named in honor of the giant bird: *Struthiomimus* is from the Greek, meaning "ostrich mimic."

A NATIONAL ICON, MATE

At six feet tall, the emu is the largest bird native to Australia and is second only to the ostrich in height. A brown-feathered nomadic bird, it can run as fast as 30 mph and can leap seven feet straight up into the air. It's also a good swimmer and is capable of paddling across rivers.

Well suited to the sparse, dry Australian terrain, the emu can go weeks without food and days without water. The bird is such a great fit for its homeland that it's become a revered national icon. Besides being a key figure in Aboriginal mythology, emus also appear on the country's coat of arms (along with that other Australian icon, the kangaroo). Also, there are more than 600 places and geographic features across Australia that are named for the bird: Emu Bay, Emu Creek, Emu Heights…you get the idea.

BE WARY OF THE CASSOWARY

Another large bird native to Australia—shorter than the emu, but heavier—is the cassowary. It's also found in the forests of New Guinea and has a striking appearance: fine hairlike feathers cover its body, and its head is a bright sky-blue capped by a sturdy crest made of thick but pliable skin called a *casque*. The purpose of the casque—which looks a little like a shark's dorsal fin—is unknown. Scientists think it might be a kind of helmet that protects the bird's head while it runs through thick forest undergrowth.

The cassowary is shy, but can become extremely aggressive when provoked or threatened, and is considered by many scientists to be the most dangerous bird in the world. It can run as fast as 30 mph and has daggerlike claws to gore opponents. In 1999 a ranger at Queensland Parks and Wildlife in Australia compiled a list of 150 recorded cases of cassowaries attacking humans since the mid-1800s, one of which proved fatal—in 1926 a 16-year-old boy who had attacked the bird with a club was thrown to the ground and kicked in the neck.

WING OR DRUMSTICK, CHARLIE?

The largest bird in South America is the rhea, which roams the woodlands of Brazil and Argentina. At approximately four feet tall, the bird looks like a small, gray ostrich.

In 1834, during the second exploratory voyage of the HMS *Beagle*, Charles Darwin searched the Patagonia region of Argentina for the elusive *lesser* rhea (a relative of the—obviously—slightly larger *greater* rhea, which was generally referred to as simply the rhea). One night while dining on what he had at first assumed was a greater rhea—a delicacy he had enjoyed throughout his Patagonian adventure—Darwin discovered that he was in fact eating a lesser rhea. He promptly sent back to England the parts of the meal he didn't eat. The bird was later classified as *Rhea darwinii*.

GONE BUT NOT FORGOTTEN

Special mention should be made here of two extinct big birds,

Before an earthquake, ponds and canals may give off a strange smell.

because they were, respectively, the tallest and heaviest birds to ever walk the earth.

• **At just over 10 feet tall,** the long-necked moa roamed free in New Zealand until 700 years ago, when the Maoris colonized the area and hunted the bird to extinction. Recent research by the Zoological Society of London suggests that moas took up to 10 years to grow to full size (as opposed to most other birds, which gain full size within a year of hatching). This difference may have led to their extinction: For most birds, it's essential for survival against predators that they grow to full size as fast as they can. For moas, who had no natural predators prior to contact with humans, slow physical development was not a problem...until the Maoris came along and started eating them, turning their bones into tools and jewelry, and using their emptied eggshells as water containers.

• **Slightly shorter than the moa,** the elephant bird is estimated to be the heaviest bird that ever lived. Native to Madagascar, the colossal bird stood at about 10 feet tall and could weigh as much as half a ton. It's unlikely that a bird this big, equipped with a spearlike beak, super-sharp claws, and massive, powerful legs became extinct through hunting. The elephant bird would have simply been too formidable an opponent for the French colonists who landed on Madagascar in the 17th century. It's more likely that the elephant bird's tasty eggs caused their demise. The eggs were roughly the size of a football—bigger even than grapefruit-sized dinosaur eggs—and could feed a family of humans for several days. Scientists believe that the colonizing French turned enough of these eggs into meals that they drove the once powerful elephant bird to extinction.

* * *

IT'S SNOW JOKE

Theoretically, two snowflakes *could* be identical, despite the old adage, but the conditions under which they were created, solidified, and fell to earth would have to be identical, too. And that's probably not possible, given all the variables of any two different spots in the atmosphere at any given time.

WHEN BOYS WERE GIRLS

A thought-provoking story about you—when you were little. (Very little.)

DEEEEP BACKGROUND

Here's a curious thing to ponder: There was a time when each and every *male* human being was female. (Some biologists prefer to describe it as "neutral"—but that's not as much fun, so we're going with "female.") The science behind this state of affairs has to do with how humans (and all mammals) come to be the gender they are in the first place—and it's just plain fascinating.

• Each of us started our lives when a microscopic egg cell from our mother was fertilized by a sperm cell from our father. You probably knew this. But what you may not have known is just how—and when—we became the gender we are today.

• All egg cells are by their nature female: They each contain one X chromosome, the genetic instructions on how to become female. You'd think that sperm cells would naturally be the opposite, but they're not. All sperm cells contain one chromosome, but it can be an X chromosome or a Y chromosome—the genetic instructions for becoming male.

• When an egg is fertilized by a sperm cell carrying an X chromosome, the resulting embryo ends up with an XX chromosome pair. It has, therefore, only instructions on how to become female and will therefore develop into a female human being.

• When an egg is fertilized by a sperm cell carrying a Y chromosome, it ends up with an XY chromosome pair. That means it has the instructions for becoming both male and female. And what happens? Well, nothing…for a while.

MAN-O-PAUSE

All egg cells that are fertilized by Y chromosome–carrying sperm cells end up with an XY chromosome pair and always become male. This is because the Y chromosome is, essentially, an "extra" set of instructions on how to build a human being, and those instructions override the X chromosome instructions.

• During the first six weeks or so after fertilization the female embryo divides, grows, attaches to the uterine wall, and develops an umbilical cord and rudimentary female sex organs.

• During the first six weeks or so after fertilization the *male* embryo divides, grows, attaches to the uterine wall, and develops an umbilical cord and...rudimentary female sex organs.

• Read that last item again.

DADDY'S HOME

Then, about six weeks after fertilization, when the fertilized egg has grown from a microscopic dot many times smaller than the period at the end of this sentence to about ⅛ inch in diameter, the genes on the male Y chromosome wake up, throw out the blueprints, and start bossing everybody around.

• What were once happily developing into female sex organs are now given new plans: What were becoming the clitoris and labia, for example, are now instructed to become the penis and scrotum. And so on.

• Because of this, biologists sometimes refer to female development as the "default" development of mammals, because it's the development that naturally occurs in all embryos after fertilization. Male development is an "augmentation" of the default female plan.

• And that's why it's accurate to say that all of us—even guys—were once female.

ONE FINAL THOUGHT

Why is it that egg cells have only X chromosomes, but sperm cells can have either an X or a Y chromosome? Well, think about it: Female gender is determined by having an XX pair of chromosomes. Females don't have any Y chromosomes. So they can't put any in their eggs. Males, on the other hand, are made of X and Y chromosomes—and can, therefore, put either one of them into sperm cells when those cells are produced.

Air can be expelled from a dolphin's blowhole at speeds of 100 mph.

TO PEE, OR NOT TO PEE?

Strictly speaking, it's liquid in, liquid out—every animal that takes in sustenance must excrete it somehow. But not every animal "goes" in the same way.

• Pill bugs never pee. They have a high tolerance for the ammonia produced by waste and secrete it out through their exoskeleton. (Also, the pill bug drinks through its anus via *uropods*, a pair of appendages that take in water when needed.)

• Technically speaking, most birds don't urinate because they don't have urinary bladders—which is a good thing, since storing urine in a bladder would make them too heavy to fly. (The only bird that does have a bladder is the ostrich, and it can't fly.) When birds poop, they excrete both forms of waste at the same time; the white stuff you see on your windshield is made mostly of uric acid, which is the bird version of pee.

• For the most part, insects that live on land also excrete uric acid instead of liquid urine, which helps them conserve water. Insects that live mostly in water don't have to worry about that, though, so they release waste with more water content. In either case, bugs don't have bladders—they have what are called *Malpighian tubes*, which perform the same function as a bladder.

• Desert rodents such as the kangaroo rat have highly efficient systems. They can recycle the moisture in their breath, and they have specialized tubes on their kidneys that extract water from urine and release it back into their bloodstreams. Like most creatures of the desert, the kangaroo rat excretes uric acid when its body needs to expel something.

• Most snakes don't pee as we know it because they don't have urinary bladders. They secrete their waste along with feces, just like birds do.

• Fish do pee—sort of. They expel liquid waste through a *cloaca*, which serves as a reproductive, digestive, and urinary tract opening. Fish also rid themselves of waste through their gills.

A single rye plant can spread up to 400 miles of roots underground.

FISH FACTS

There's something really fishy about this story.

SO WHAT IS A FISH, ANYWAY?

Deciding what a fish is or isn't can get confusing. Three-quarters of the world is covered with water that is home to more than 30,000 different species of fish. A whale shark, for instance, weighs more than 47,000 pounds, and a clownfish weighs less than an ounce—but they're both fish. Some have excellent eyesight, some are blind, but they can survive in all types of habitats: Pupfish live in desert pools where water temperatures reach more than 100ºF. Icefish, on the other hand, thrive in the freezing ocean around Antarctica. But whatever they look like and wherever they live, most fish (except shellfish) share five characteristics:

- They live in water (although some can leave it for a time).
- They're cold-blooded and take on the temperature of the water they're in.
- They're vertebrates, meaning they have a backbone, or spine.
- They have gills to help them absorb oxygen in water to breathe.
- They have fins.

THE HISTORY OF OUR FISHY RELATIVES

About 500 million years ago, the first animals with vertebrae appeared in freshwater pools and in shallow seas. Called ostracoderms, they had small, flat bodies protected with bony armor. They had no jaws to bite with, and instead slurped up microscopic bits of food from the water and mud. By 360 million years ago, the ostracoderms were extinct, and the planet's waters were filled with the three types of fish that populate them today:

- **Jawless fish** like the lamprey eel and hagfish are descended from ostracoderms.
- **Cartilaginous fish** are jawed fish with skeletons made of cartilage—like sharks, rays, and skates.
- **Bony fish** are jawed fish with skeletons of bone. These make up

the most familiar types of fish: goldfish, guppies, trout, tuna, and the like.

The history of fish is crucial to all life on earth—about 360 million years ago, an unknown species of bony fish developed a way to breathe and navigate on land. That ancient fish-out-of-water then moved to solid ground and is the ancestor of all land vertebrates: amphibians, reptiles, birds, and mammals—including humans.

FISH BEHAVIOR

• A day (or night, if a fish is nocturnal) in the life of a fish might involve hunting, mating, or escaping predators—but it nearly always involves swimming. Most fish swim in a side-to-side movement by contracting muscles on one side, and they're streamlined in a torpedo shape to keep resistance low as they speed through the water.

• All fish with cartilaginous skeletons (like sharks) are meat eaters. Bony fish can be meat or plant eaters, or both.

• Freshwater fish don't drink much because water already permeates their membranes through their gills. Saltwater fish, on the other hand, drink lots of seawater—special cells on their gills pump out the excess salt.

• As fish go about their day, some of them communicate with pops, growls, or other sounds that they make by vibrating organs called swim bladders, which also keep them buoyant. Scientists use underwater microphones to catch sounds that they believe are used to attract mates, scare off predators, warn of danger, and even give directions to help keep other fish from getting lost. Fish have ears inside their heads that can pick up sounds and vibrations in the water.

• Here's the big question: Do fish sleep? They don't have eyelids, so they can't close their eyes, but most of them do go into a motionless, resting state. Perch and catfish rest under logs at night. Coral reef fish rest in crevices of the coral. Sharks keep moving because they have to in order to push water through their mouths to breathe—but scientists believe that they go into a sleeplike state while moving.

The leaves of the Amazonian water lily are so large and strong that they can support a person.

ANIMALS GONE... HUMAN?

They smoke. They laugh. They save people. (These are animals we're talking about.)

HIGH-TECH TONGUES

Orangutans at the Milwaukee County Zoo are proving that people aren't the only ones who go ape over technology toys. Apps for Apes helps bored orangutans in captivity (an increasingly common state for them because their habitat is being destroyed all over the world) by giving them iPads. Just like people, orangutans have their favorite time-wasting apps, including Doodle Buddy, finger painting, and music apps with drums. They also enjoy watching wildlife documentaries (especially the ones that star orangutans). Although these apes do well with touch screens, they're strong animals and can easily break their expensive gizmos, so staff members hold the iPads outside the cages while the orangutans poke their long fingers through the bars to interact with the screen. In the future, Apps for Apes hopes to set up programs to allow orangutans to see and even communicate with each other through Skype.

• Meanwhile in Brisbane, Australia, a female bearded dragon named Crunch puts human gamers to shame. Humans play Ant Smasher by using a touch screen to "squash" flies and ants, while trying to avoid bees. But few humans can play Ant Smasher as fast as Crunch, who licks the screen with her tongue. Her owner, Philip Gith, uploaded a video of her gaming ability to YouTube and turned Crunch into a sensation—the video got 225,000 hits in just a few weeks. Peter Harlow, manager of reptiles at the Taronga Zoo in Sydney believes bearded dragons may be especially adept at Ant Smasher because they're visually oriented: "They look for little insects, and then they go out and grab them" (just like in the game). But even though other bearded dragons might have the skills, so far their owners haven't been able to get the reptiles to emulate Crunch's winning moves.

KLEPTO KITTY

Dusty spends many nights burgling his San Mateo, California, neighborhood and has stolen hundreds of items over the years. Instead of being investigated by the police, though, he was investigated by *Animal Planet* because this burglar is a Siamese cat. Adopted from the Humane Society when he was a kitten, Dusty turned criminal after about a year. His startled owners began discovering strange loot around their house: stuffed animals, Nerf balls, flip-flops, Crocs, bras, underwear, and swimsuits. Dusty's record caper: nabbing 11 items in 24 hours. A cat-behavior consultant interviewed by the *San Francisco Chronicle* admitted that human-style burgling is puzzling in felines. Asked about Dusty, she replied, "I can't say exactly why he's doing it, except it has to do with mixed-up neurotransmitters. I think it's a form of OCD."

LAUGHING APES

Scientists once thought that only people laughed. Now research shows that laughter is fun for other species, too. Researchers carried out "tickling sessions" on apes and human babies. They recorded the sounds that the animals made and, after analyzing them, found a link between baby's laughter and that of apes. Chimps and bonobos—humans' closest relatives—sound the most like us. In fact, the panting laugh chimps make when they play is very similar to the human "ha-ha" sound.

LIGHTING UP

• Chimpanzees share nearly 99 percent of their DNA with humans…and they share bad habits, too. Charlie the chimp began smoking while working as a circus performer and kept it up when he was sent to the Mangaung Zoo in South Africa. The chimp took advantage of lit butts that were tossed into his enclosure by nicotine-addled visitors. (He became internationally notorious after videos showed him puffing away.) Zookeepers did their best to keep Charlie away from tobacco, even as he always did his best to hide his smokes. Surprisingly, Charlie managed to beat the odds despite his addiction—in 2010 he died at age 52. (Chimps rarely make it past 40.)

• Other chimps seem to use cigarettes to get through tough times.

The mountain lion has more than 40 other names, the most of any animal.

At China's Qinling Zoo, a female chimpanzee named Ai Ai took up smoking after her mate died. Then she lost a second mate, and her daughter was moved to another zoo. At that point, Ai Ai smoked heavily and often squealed for cigarettes. To help her kick the habit, keepers gave Ai Ai a new daily regimen that included a walk after breakfast, exercises at night, special treats of "fried dishes and dumplings," and the use of a Walkman. With this "more colorful life," as her keepers put it, Ai Ai stopped squealing and, in 2005, after 16 years of smoking, quit cold turkey.

THE RESCUERS

• One of the first wild animals to become an international hero was Binti Jua, a female western lowland gorilla. In 1996, at the Brookfield Zoo in Illinois, a three-year-old human boy got away from his parents, climbed the wall of the gorilla enclosure, and fell 20 feet to the concrete floor below. Binti Jua immediately went to the unconscious boy...as spectators screamed in fear. But instead of harming the boy, Binta Jua growled to keep approaching gorillas away, and with her own baby clinging to her back, she gently lifted the child and carried him some 60 feet to the access gate where the zoo staff could get him. After a few days in the hospital, the boy recovered. Binti Jua became a hero and was featured as an "intriguing person" in *People* magazine. She even got a medal from the American Legion.

• By far, though, the "animal lifesaver" award goes to dolphins. In 2007, near Monterey, California, a surfer was attacked by a great white shark. He was badly mauled and would have died if a pod of bottlenose dolphins hadn't arrived. They formed a protective ring around the injured man, keeping other sharks away until he made it to the shore. Dolphins in New Zealand used a similar move to protect lifeguards from a prowling great white. Dolphins have also saved whales that get lost in bays or coves, showing them the way to open sea. And an elderly Doberman, stranded in a Florida canal, owes his life to a pod of dolphins that splashed, vocalized, and made a ruckus until a woman saw the exhausted dog and saved him. Skeptics claim animals don't have the heroic altruism of humans, but dolphins keep proving them wrong.

Chalk is made from the fossilized skeletons of ancient sea creatures.

COME SAIL AWAY

Let's take a moment to ponder the ocean.

"Panting and snorting like a mad battle steed that has lost its rider, the masterless ocean overruns the globe."

—**Herman Melville**

"The human animal began as a mere wriggling thing in the ancient seas, struggling out onto land with many regrets. That is what brings us so full of longing to the sea."

—**Sebastian Barry**

"The sea, once it casts its spell, holds one in its net of wonder forever."

—**Jacques Cousteau**

"I pray to be like the ocean, with soft currents, maybe waves at times."

—**Drew Barrymore**

"The sea has never been friendly to man. At most, it has been the accomplice of human restlessness."

—**Joseph Conrad**

"How inappropriate to call this planet Earth when it is quite clearly Ocean."

—**Arthur C. Clarke**

"Blue, green, grey, white, or black; smooth, ruffled, or mountainous; that ocean is not silent."

—**H. P. Lovecraft**

"The cure for anything is salt water—sweat, tears, or the sea."

—**Isak Dinesen**

"Can ye fathom the ocean, dark and deep, where the mighty waves and the grandeur sweep?"

—**Fanny Crosby**

"For whatever we lose (like a you or a me)/ It's always our self we find in the sea."

—**E. E. Cummings**

"For all at last returns to the sea—to Oceanus, the ocean river, like the everflowing stream of time, the beginning and the end."

—**Rachel Carson**

"The sea pronounces something, over and over, in a hoarse whisper; I cannot quite make it out."

—**Annie Dillard**

Most lava flows move slowly, but Africa's Mount Nyiragongo is...

GOING OVER THE FALLS

Next time you're out hiking with friends and you come across a waterfall, amaze them by telling them what kind of waterfall it is. (When they start rolling their eyes and sighing, just keep talking. That's what Uncle John does.)

BACKGROUND

Most of us just think of waterfalls as, well, waterfalls, but geologists, hydrologists (people who study the movement of water), and just plain old waterfall lovers know that they actually come in many different types. Some are broad categories, while others are more specialized, and some waterfalls can be a mixture of more than one variety. Here are the different classifications, followed by a few examples of waterfalls you might have heard of—or even seen for yourself.

• **Cataract:** A general term used to describe large waterfalls that involve the flow of very large amounts of water, a cataract is usually accompanied by rapids both above and below the falls itself.

• **Plunge:** If you see water rushing over the top of a steep cliff and free-falling—not touching the cliff face—for all or a part of its height, you've got a plunge waterfall.

• **Cascade:** Unlike a plunge waterfall, a cascade's water flows down a slope, *cascading* over rocks or ledges on its way down.

• **Block:** A block waterfall is formed when a river or large stream flows over a wide and relatively even ledge, giving the falling water a wide "block" shape. It's also called a *sheet* waterfall, because the falling water resembles a sheet. Both terms are normally used for waterfalls wider than they are tall. If they're taller than they are wide, they're called *curtain* falls.

• **Fan:** A type of cascade waterfall, a fan starts out narrow and gets wider as the water flows downward, spreading out and giving the falls the look of an open fan.

• **Horsetail:** Unlike a fan, a horsetail is a cascade that remains narrow as it flows downward, resembling a long horse's tail.

...known for lava flowing at speeds of up to 60 mph.

• **Punchbowl:** This is a plunge waterfall that forms when a strongly flowing stream or river surges through a small opening and straight down into a round pool—the pool itself is the creation of the falling water over a very long period of time.

• **Segmented:** When a stream or river is separated at or near the top of its height and falls as two or more falls, they're known as *segmented* waterfalls.

• **Tiered:** A tiered waterfall is a single waterfall made up of several smaller steep falls that drop down a series of rock steps.

• **Slide:** This waterfall flows down a smooth, even surface.

• **Chute:** A chute is a cascade waterfall that flows—usually very fast and with lots of white water—between the walls of a narrow canyon.

WATERFALLS YOU MIGHT RECOGNIZE

• **Yosemite Falls** in California is 2,425 feet high, making it the tallest waterfall in North America. It has three sections: The Upper Falls is a 1,430-foot plunge, making it alone one of the tallest falls in the world; the Middle Cascades drops a further 675 feet; and the Lower Falls plunges another 320 feet.

• **Angel Falls** in Venezuela is the highest waterfall in the world, at a staggering 3,212 feet. More staggering: 2,648 feet of that is the initial plunge, before the water even hits the cliff face.

• **Victoria Falls**, on the Zambezi River in Zambia and Zimbabwe, is a classic block waterfall, and stands about 360 feet high. It's about 5,604 feet—that's well over a mile—wide.

• **Niagara Falls** is actually three waterfalls: Horseshoe Falls, American Falls, and Bridal Veil Falls. The first two are block waterfalls; Bridal Veil is a curtain waterfall.

• In 1935 architect Frank Lloyd Wright designed what remains one of his most famous works, **Fallingwater**, a home in southwestern Pennsylvania that incorporates a waterfall into its design. The cascade waterfall, which is part of a five-mile-long creek called Bear Run, is probably the smallest world-famous waterfall. The house itself was declared a National Historic Landmark in 1966.

Snow joke: Ice worms, which live in glaciers, melt if they get too warm.

NATURE'S ANCIENT TREASURE TROVES

Every once in a while nature says, "Okay, I'll quit being so mysterious. Let me open up a great big window to the past for you." And then our knowledge of the ancient world grows by leaps and bounds.

FOSSIL GROVE

Location: Victoria Park, Glasgow, Scotland

Discovery: In 1887 workers excavating the floor of an old quarry while making a road in the city's Victoria Park noticed some strange formations in the rock. The formations looked like stone tree stumps, and each was about four feet high and two feet in diameter.

Treasure: They *were* stone tree stumps. Fortunately, park officials realized they had found something pretty special, and the road was rerouted and the stumps carefully excavated. There were 11 of them, and they even had fossilized root systems. They were the remains of a forest that grew in the region 330 million years ago. That's 100 million years *before* dinosaurs appeared. The trees had been engulfed in several feet of mud, experts say, probably caused by flooding, and over the eons had fossilized. (The upper parts of the trees simply rotted away.) The stumps are still right where they were found—except now they're housed in a special building to protect them. Scientists of several fields continue to study them, looking for and finding clues about the earth of that ancient era. You can even visit the Fossil Grove yourself—it's open to the public from April to September.

MESSEL PIT

Location: Village of Messel, state of Hesse, Germany

Discovery: The Messel Pit is a quarry that had been mined for oil shale since the mid-1800s. The first animal fossil—of a crocodile—was found there in 1875, but nobody seemed to care. By 1900 it was known that there were a lot of fossils there, but mining continued until the 1970s, when that era's oil crisis finally made the mining of oil shale unprofitable. After that, the pit was finally seriously approached by scientists.

Treasure: The sediments in the Messel Pit were laid roughly 47 million years ago, on the bottom of what was then a large, deep lake surrounded by lush, subtropical forests. It was clearly home to an enormous variety of wildlife that was killed off in droves on a regular basis by gaseous eruptions from the lake, which had been formed by an ancient volcano. Creeks and rains carried the animal corpses into the lake, the scientists believe, and they drifted to the bottom, where unique conditions—low oxygen content in the water on the lakebed, for one thing—preserved them incredibly well. Just some of the fossils found in the Messel Pit: the nearly complete skeleton (23 inches long) of a long-tailed lemurlike primate; thousands of fossilized aquatic and terrestrial insects, including beetles with their colors still intact; birds with fossilized feathers; snake, crocodile, turtle, frog, lizard, and salamander fossils; more than 10,000 fossilized fish; and 70 fossilized skeletons of *Propalaeotheriums*—small prehistoric horses—some with tiny, fossilized skeletons of horse embryos still in their wombs.

NULLARBOR CAVES

Location: The Nullarbor Plain, southern Australia

Discovery: In 2002 Father Ken Boland, a priest from Melbourne who also happens to be an avid caver, headed up a team that discovered three new caves in the Nullarbor Plain, a 77,000-square-mile tract of treeless and truly desolate desert. Each of the caves had an opening just a few feet wide at what was the very top of the cave; this meant that any human being who entered the caves had to rappel into them. In the first cave the team immediately found the complete skeleton of a *Thylacoleo carnifex*—or "marsupial lion." The beasts, which grew to nine feet in length, roamed Australia for millions of years, and went extinct just 50,000 years ago. In the second cave, the team found a *Thylacine*—a doglike marsupial better known as the Tasmanian Tiger, which went extinct as recently as the 1930s. The fossil turned out to be more than 500,000 years old.

Treasure: Scientists have since determined that the three caves had stood open for nearly a million years. They also believe that rapidly changing air pressure in and outside the caves may have caused powerful drafts that sucked animals into the caves when they walked too close to the openings. The fall into the caves probably didn't kill the creatures, but once they were sucked in, they were trapped, so they would have just wandered around in there until they died. Their complete skeletons were left to be preserved in the very dry and dark conditions. Thousands of animals died this way. They include many now-extinct marsupials, including several of the mentioned lions; a previously unknown wallaby (similar to a kangaroo), with a sharp, hooked claw on its hind foot reminiscent of a velociraptor's claw; wombats the size of small cars; and a *Procoptodon goliath*—a kangaroo that grew to be nearly 10 feet tall. More than 100,000 bones have been taken from the caves so far—and there are many more left.

THE CRADLE OF HUMANKIND

Location: Gauteng Province, South Africa

Discovery: In 1896 an Italian prospector named Guglielmo Martinaglia blasted away part of a rocky hillside in a gold-mining region about 30 miles northwest of Johannesburg, South Africa. He was actually looking for limestone, which was used to extract gold at the time. He found it—but he also found a huge limestone cave. Soon more caves were found, since known as the Sterkfontein Caves. Fossils were discovered in the caves, but they were seen as little more than objects of curiosity for decades. Then, on April 18, 1947, Dr. Robert Broom, a South African paleontologist, found a skull.

Treasure: The skull was from a member of the species *Australopithecus africanus*, which lived two to three million years ago—and is believed to be an early hominid. Since then, the caves have produced an enormous amount of hugely important finds, including more than a third of the fossils of early hominids ever found anywhere. Some of the other discoveries include the nearly complete fossilized skeleton of an early hominid between 2.2 and 3.3 million years old; evidence of the oldest known controlled use of fire by humans, dating to about 1 million years ago; and the oldest samples of human hair ever found, dating to between 195,000 and 257,000 years old. (The latter was found in a well-preserved pile

The pitohui, a bird from New Guinea, has poisonous skin and feathers.

of hyena dung.) Today a 180-square-mile region around the caves is a designated and protected World Heritage Site, and the finds uncovered there indicate to scientists that the region may indeed be the "cradle of humankind"—the very place where the first humans appeared on earth.

RANCHO LA BREA TAR PITS

Location: Los Angeles, California

Discovery: Native Americans used tar from the pits for centuries, maybe millennia, as waterproofing in things like baskets and canoes. After Europeans started settling the area, bones were often found in the tar—but everyone thought they were from cattle. It wasn't until 1901, when William Warren Orcutt, a geologist with the Union Oil Company, examined the site, that people finally got an idea of what the pits held. Subsequent studies showed that the "tar" was thick asphalt (a kind of petroleum) that naturally seeped up from the ground starting about 40,000 years ago. When the seepage rate was high, substantial "pits" of the stuff formed and quickly became perfect traps for unfortunate animals: Leaves and dust would stick to the tar, and animals would walk or run over the camouflaged surface and become stuck.

Treasure: The site is considered one of the richest fossil deposits from this relatively recent geological period. And asphalt, it turns out, is a really good preservative. More than *one million* fossils have been taken from the pits so far...of more than 650 different species of plants and animals. They include skeletons of about 60 mammal species, many of them extinct, including more than 2,000 saber-toothed cats alone. With them are mastodons, giant ground sloths, short-faced bears, camels, and direwolves (the largest canines known to have existed). Added to that are numerous fossilized reptiles, amphibians, birds, insects, fish, mollusks, and one human: Seventeen bones of a young woman, including a skull, were found in 1914. (The fossilized remains of what scientists believe are a domesticated dog were found beside her.) The La Brea Tar Pits is still an actively studied site—a new trove of fossils from a buried pit were found during construction of a parking lot near the pits in 2009. So expect more fossil news to keep coming our way…well into the future.

La Brea means "the tar" in Spanish.

TEEEEEEEEEEEEEEETH!

Now we grill you with some biting facts to chew on.

• *Megalodon*, Greek for "big tooth," is the name of a huge, extinct shark whose wedge-shaped teeth measured more than seven inches from base to tip. That means the shark was nearly as long as two school buses, and its massive jaws could easily crush one.

• Male snowshoe hares are vicious fighters. Their weapon of choice: sharp teeth. When not fighting each other, the hares use their teeth to strip bark from trees and tear the flesh off carrion. They're one of the few bunny species that eats meat.

• The red-bellied piranha—the most dangerous of the 25 Amazon piranha species—doesn't have very strong jaws. It makes up for that with razor-sharp teeth. How sharp? One bite can take off a human toe.

• The mammal with the most chompers is the long-snouted spinner dolphin; its long jaws hold up to 252 teeth.

• Some slug species have up to 25,000 teeth, called *radula*, on their ribbonlike tongues.

• Mammals are *heterodonts*, meaning they have various types of teeth: canines for tearing, incisors for cutting, molars for chewing, and premolars for grinding.

• Hamsters are born with a full set of teeth that don't stop growing for their entire lives. They must grind them continuously or else the teeth will grow too long.

• The main purpose of teeth is to break down food so it's easy to digest. But anteaters have no teeth, so how do they grind up bugs? When they suck them up through their snouts, they also suck up small pebbles that help to grind the dead ants into mush (and then the anteater passes the stones).

• Elephants grow six sets of molars in a lifetime, which they use to chew tough vegetation. When the last set wears down (at about 65 years old), the elderly elephant looks for softer foliage to eat.

• Sharks are fierce predators, but they're lousy at keeping

their teeth. They're almost constantly shedding them. Some sharks will go through 35,000 teeth in a lifetime.

• Like sharks, crocodiles are also continually losing teeth. They can grow 3,000 in a lifetime.

• In the Middle Ages, sailors in the Arctic harvested spiral-shaped narwhal teeth and sold them as "magical" unicorn horns. Protruding through the left side of the narwhal's upper lip, this bizarre incisor can reach nine feet long. Scientists disagree about what the tooth is used for: either for defense, for mating rituals, or as a sensor that detects temperature and pressure changes in the water. (But they do agree that the horns aren't magical.)

• Two inches doesn't seem that long, does it? Now picture a pair of two-inch-long poisonous snake fangs. That's what the African Gaboon viper uses to strike its prey. They are the longest snake fangs in the world.

• What do giraffes and humans have in common? We both have 32 teeth in our mouths.

• Cone snails have nature's deadliest teeth. Hiding under the seafloor in shallow waters, the cone snail waits until a fish swims by. Then it shoots a tooth like a barbed harpoon connected to a slimy proboscis. Inside the tooth is a toxin so lethal there is no known antidote. The poisoned tooth immediately kills the fish, which the cone snail then reels in and swallows whole.

• Birds with teeth? Sort of. Geese have toothy serrations on their bills. They're not made of the same materials as mammal teeth, but they do perform the same function, and it really hurts when a goose bites you.

• Plants with teeth? No, but the Venus flytrap has leaf extensions, called *trigger hairs*, at the end of its "mouth" that resemble teeth. It doesn't use these hairs for chewing, but, as its name suggests, for trapping. The flytrap doesn't close the hairs all the way. That way, tiny insects can escape and not waste the plant's digestive juices. For larger insects, the teeth act like prison bars...and offer no chance of parole.

ALLERGIES EXPLAINED

You deserve to know exactly what is going on with the sneezing, coughing, stuffy nose, restricted airways, and hives that, in some instances, could actually kill you.

ATTACK!

Allergies are what happen when a person's immune system gets its wires crossed and treats something that is ordinarily harmless like a dire health threat. The human immune system does an amazing job of defending the body against intrusions by disease-causing bacteria, viruses, and toxins. When it detects a threat, it sends an army of germ-killing chemicals to eliminate it. An allergy develops when, for reasons that scientists don't yet understand, a person's immune system mislabels an otherwise-safe substance (called an *allergen*) as dangerous.

One of the most common examples is "seasonal grass pollen allergy" (better known as hay fever). During the spring and summer, pollen is in the air and everyone inhales it—that can't be avoided. For most people, though, it's no big deal because pollen isn't harmful. The immune systems of people with hay fever, however, have a glitch in their programming. They have labeled pollen in the respiratory tract as a direct threat to the body's overall health. So the body's defense chemicals spring into action. The symptoms of hay fever—coughing, sneezing, congestion, itchy throat—are really just collateral damage from the microscopic chemical war being waged inside the throat and lungs. Other allergies, like pet dander or dust allergies, work the same way.

NUTS!

Food allergies are similar, but they're based on the immune system viewing specific food proteins as threats. Common food allergens include the proteins in peanuts, soy, eggs, shellfish, tree nuts, and wheat. Allergies to drugs (like penicillin) and insect stings are also common.

While allergic reactions to pollen and similar substances are often just irritating, reactions to food, medication, and insect stings can be much more severe, even life-threatening, resulting in

...Slowest reptile: The Galápagos giant tortoise moves only about 4 miles per day.

a reaction called *anaphylaxis*,which is essentially the entire immune system freaking out. When this happens, the victim can break out in an itchy rash and hives all over his whole body (although the back is the most common area hit), the throat can swell up and restrict breathing, and blood pressure can plummet, sometimes causing a heart attack. Without quick medical treatment, victims of anaphylaxis can die.

KIDS TODAY ARE JUST TOO DARNED CLEAN!

Doctors aren't sure what causes allergies—or why some people have more severe reactions than others. What they do know is that allergies are on the rise. Surveys done by the National Institutes of Health indicate that the number of Americans affected by allergies has more than doubled over the past 40 years. And oddly, allergy rates appear to be higher in wealthier, more industrialized countries than in poorer ones. These sorts of observations have given rise to the "hygiene hypothesis."

It goes like this: Modern medicine and sanitation practices have created societies in which most children aren't exposed to enough of the right kinds of germs and parasites. Basically, their immune systems don't get enough exercise. Without actual germs to attack, these underdeveloped immune systems attack pollen, peanuts, or wheat proteins instead. Scientists who subscribe to this theory offer as proof studies that have shown lower allergy rates among children who attend daycare than children who stay at home. Kids who grow up around farm animals also tend to have lower allergy rates.

A POUND OF PREVENTION

The bad news for allergy sufferers is that there is no cure. The only way to prevent reactions is to completely avoid contact with the things you are allergic to. The good news, however, is that modern medicine is actually pretty good at treating the symptoms of allergic reactions. Even anaphylaxis is easily treated as long as the victim receives care quickly. (Doctors give the victim a shot of the synthetic adrenaline epinephrine, which stabilizes blood pressure and reduces the swelling that could otherwise close off airways. People with severe allergies often carry an emergency dose of epinephrine with them in a self-injecting device called an EpiPen.)

The scales on a butterfly's wing overlap like roof tiles.

Doctors have also developed medicines that target very specific parts of the body affected by allergic reactions. If you have hay fever, for example, you have probably taken an antihistamine. *Histamine* is one of the chemicals that the immune system releases when it thinks it's under attack. Histamine attaches itself to cells and nerve endings in the affected area, causing swelling and irritation. Antihistamines reverse symptoms by blocking histamines from attaching to those cells and nerve endings.

Some allergies can also be treated with a type of immunotherapy designed to reduce the severity of future reactions. This basically involves injecting small amounts of the specific allergen into the patient over a period of several years in an effort to build up a tolerance. This technique is mostly used for people with severe pollen allergies who have no good way to avoid exposure.

*   *   *

WHEN SNAKES ATTACK!

On page 261, we taught you how to handle attacks from mountain lions, bears, sharks, and bees. Here's one more.

Prevention: Generally, snakes bite only when they feel threatened or surprised, so you can warn them away by making noise while walking in the wilderness. Wear thick boots if you're hiking through snake territory, and don't pick up rocks or pieces of wood, because snakes like to hide under them. If you see a snake or hear a rattle, back up slowly. Give a snake about six feet of distance. And be cautious in the water, too—snakes can swim!

If that doesn't work: Luckily, snakebites are over with one quick jab, and some victims don't even realize they were bitten until they see two puncture wounds on their skin. If a snake bites you, try to note its markings, shape, and size so that you can tell medical responders. Unless you know positively that the species is harmless, assume that it's poisonous. Remain calm and still to keep any venom from spreading. Keep the wound lower than your heart, and call for medical help. If soap and water are available, wash the wound and affix a clean, dry bandage to it. Contrary to popular belief, you should not tie on a tourniquet, apply ice, or suck out the poison. That can make things worse.

Snakes swallow their prey headfirst so the legs won't get stuck in their throats.

WHAT DOES "HYENA" MEAN?

We've all heard these animal names hundreds of times—but where the heck did they come from? Ask no more...

CROCODILE: This word was derived from the Greek *krokodilos*: *kroke*, meaning "pebbles," and *drilos*, meaning "worm." There is some confusion as to whether the first part referred to the crocodile habit of basking on pebbly riverbanks, or to a croc's rough and "pebbly" skin.

GNU: Another name for Africa's wildebeest, the animal got this name from German naturalist and explorer Georg Forster, who in the late 1700s created it from an African word for the 'beest, *i-ngu*. That name came from the Southern Bushman name, which is written in English as *!nu:*, the "!" and ":" designate click sounds in the Bushman language.

ALLIGATOR: This word first made it to English in the 1500s from the Spanish *lagarto*, meaning "lizard." In fact, *legarto* was the original English word for alligator, and it wasn't until the 1620s that the commonly heard *el lagarto*, meaning in Spanish "the lizard," morphed to "alligator" in English.

LEMUR: These Madagascan primates were named by Carl Linnaeus in the 1750s. He took the name from the Latin *lemures*, ghosts meant to be exorcised during the Roman Lemuria festival, in reference to the lemur's seemingly ghostly nocturnal activity.

HYENA: This African doglike animal (which is actually more closely related to cats) was named after a pig. Its name goes back to the Greek *hyaina*, which was derived from the Greek *hys*—meaning "hog" or "swine." This is because of the hyena's bristly fur, similar to a pig's.

EMU: The scientific name of this large, flightless, native Australian bird is *Dromaius novaehollandiae*, Latin for "swift-footed one," and "New Holland," the name given to Australia by the

In 2007 a dog named Rocco sniffed out and dug up a truffle in Tuscany worth $333,000.

Dutch in the 17th century. Their popular name, "emu," goes back to the same century, and is from one of two sources: Some etymologists believe it was derived from the Portuguese *ema*, meaning "ostrich" or "crane"; others think it came from one of the male emu's many vocalizations, this one a long *eeee moooooo*.

JAGUAR: These large cats native to Mexico and Central and South America got their English name from Brazil's Tupi people, who called them *jaguara*, which was actually their name for any large predator.

OCELOT: Another—but smaller—wildcat found in the same region as the jaguar, this name came from the Nahuatl language group spoken by native peoples in Mexico. Except it didn't originally refer to the ocelot—it was the Nahuatls' name for the jaguar.

ORCA: The proper name of the "killer whale" traces its way back to an older English word, *orc*, meaning "large whale," which came from an older French word, *orque*—the name for a variety of mythical sea monsters.

PORPOISE: Derived from the Old French *porpais*—meaning "pork fish." It's believed this was a reference to the porpoise's short snout, which could be said to be piglike.

DOLPHIN: This comes from the Greek *delphys*, meaning "womb." Etymologists say this most likely comes from the fact that the dolphin, being a mammal, has a uterus, or womb, unlike fish. (This is true of all cetaceans, the marine mammal family that consists of all dolphin, whale, and porpoise species.)

OSTRICH. The name for this large, flightless African bird goes back to the ancient Greek word for the bird, *strouthos*, which, oddly enough, meant "sparrow." Their full name for them was actually *strouthos melage*, meaning "big sparrow." They also called them *strouthokamelos*, or "camel-sparrow," because of the ostrich's long neck, which was seen as similar to the camel's long neck.

CATERPILLAR. This one goes all the way back to the Old French name for the familiar rust-brown and black, and seemingly "furry," woolly bear caterpillar, *caterpilose*. What did that mean? "Hairy cat." That, it seems, is what the furry caterpillars looked like to early French observers.

Hawaii is the only place that *Eupithecia* carnivorous caterpillars are found.

UNCLE JOHN'S TRAVEL CLUB

Here at the BRI, we love to travel, and these are three of our favorite lesser-known nature spots.

KEALAKEKUA BAY

Where: The Big Island of Hawaii

Important because... Kealakekua Bay ("Pathway of the Gods") was the site of British explorer Captain James Cook's second landing in Hawaii, in 1779. Cook stayed on the Big Island with his men for a month, keeping journals in which he documented the culture of the native Hawaiians. When Cook left the bay in early February 1779, he was on good terms with the Hawaiians, but after having some trouble with one of his ship's masts, he returned to the island to make repairs. During that stay, a "misunderstanding" caused a deep rift between Cook and the Hawaiians—some historians believe the Hawaiians thought he was a false god; others dispute that. Either way, the Hawaiians weren't happy with Cook the second time around, and after a lot of bad behavior on both sides (the Hawaiians stole Cook's rowboats; he tried to kidnap one of their kings), the locals killed him on February 14. Today a monument commemorating Cook stands on the bay's shores.

What's cool: One of the best snorkeling spots in all of Hawaii, Kealakekua is known for the pods of spinner dolphins that come to feed in the protected waters, as well as hammerhead sharks, turtles, and all kinds of tropical fish.

KUMARAKOM (OR VEMBANAD) BIRD SANCTUARY

Where: Kerala, India

Important because... A former colonial rubber plantation, this 14-acre site is now a safe spot for numerous migratory birds, including Siberian cranes, egrets, herons, and kingfishers. It's been called the best place for birdwatching in all of India.

What's cool: Besides the birds, there are mangrove forests, blooming lilies, and coconut groves for visitors to explore.

Note: If you visit, keep these three things in mind:

• Bring binoculars; the birds live in a natural habitat and won't come up to you like they might in a zoo.

• The birds are most active in the morning; try to get there by 6:30 a.m.

• Be sure to wear long pants and long sleeves. From what we hear, the only creatures at Kumarakom that are more abundant than birds are mosquitoes. They're everywhere...and they're always hungry.

GOLDEN BAY

Where: South Island, New Zealand

Important because... In 1642 Dutch explorer Abel Tasman became the first European to see New Zealand. During a storm, his ship was blown off course and ended up at the north end of the country's South Island. Unsure of where he was (maybe Argentina?), Tasman sent out a few sailors in rowboats to look for fresh water. Before they could get to land, though, the sailors met up with members of the local Maori tribe, who paddled out to them in canoes. After some misunderstandings, a cannon fired in warning, and a Maori war challenge being issued, four of Tasman's men were killed, and the sailors fled the area. Tasman wrote in his journal that sailors should "consider the inhabitants of this country as enemies." He called the area Murderers Bay, a moniker that stood until the 1850s, when gold was discovered and the place got a name change.

What's cool: Golden Bay is known for sandy beaches, calm clear water, and gorgeous scenery. It's also right next door to Abel Tasman National Park, New Zealand's smallest national park (at about 87 square miles), but also one of its most spectacular. The park's most popular activity: hiking the 32-mile-long Coast Track, which takes visitors past sweeping coastal views, near a fur seal breeding ground, and over a 154-foot-long mesh and rope "swing bridge" that straddles the Water Falls River.

NEW KIDS ON THE BLOCK

In 1758, a botanist named Carolus Linnaeus started the modern system of naming and classifying plants and animals. By 2010 biologists had classified 1.7 million species. But those are believed to be just a small percentage of the life existing on earth. Many scientists estimate that another 10 million species remain to be discovered.

GOTHAM BEES AND 'PEDES

In 2009 a bee about the size of a grain of rice, which makes a nest by burrowing in the ground, was discovered in the Brooklyn Botanic Garden. The discovery came during a bee biology survey in New York City. These tiny bees, given the scientific name *Lasioglossum gothamare*, are "sweat bees" because they lap sweat off the skin of humans and animals as one source of food. They also eat regular bee food: pollen and flower nectar. Researchers say the Gotham bee has been buzzing around the city for years pollinating local gardens, but it was so small and looked so much like other small bees that it was confused with other species.

The bee isn't the only new species in town. In 2002 a yellow centipede with 82 legs was discovered in Central Park living off leaf litter. The creature is just 0.4 inches long and was the first new species found in Central Park in more than a century.

THE TASTY *TITANIC*

In 2010 scientists announced the discovery of a new species of bacteria living on the wreck of the *Titanic*. The famous "unsinkable" ship has been sitting at the bottom of the North Atlantic Ocean for more than 100 years, but thanks to *Halomonas titanicae*, it may only be there for another 10 or 20 years. The *Titanic*'s thick hull was made of 50,000 tons of iron, and it now sports many "rusticles," icicle-shaped structures that form underwater on rusting iron. Scientists found the bacteria inside the rusticles. After analyzing the bacteria's DNA, they realized that they'd found a new species. Since then, *H. titanicae* has been tested on steel, which it also likes. The metal-munching microbes concern scientists because they could, theoretically, eat through all kinds of under-

The ratio of bugs to humans on earth: about 200 million to 1.

water structures, including gas and oil pipes. On the plus side, *H. titanicae* could also safely dispose of old, submerged metal ships and tankers.

MONKEY BUSINESS

Although there are millions of undiscovered species in the world, scientists believe that undiscovered larger animals, especially primates, are rare. In 2010, however, the world was startled by photos showing a hunter in Myanmar with a dead monkey never before seen by Westerners. The large monkey is black with white fur on its ear tufts and chin, and its goblinlike face has an upturned nose. In fact, when it rains, the animal must keep its head down so that water won't get into its exposed nostrils.

Scientists named the monkey *Rhinopithecus strykeri*, or the Myanmar snub-nosed monkey, and they launched expeditions to locate the elusive animal, which lives in very rugged, forested country. Finally, in 2012, the first photos of live Myanmar snub-nosed monkeys—including a mother and baby—were released. Unfortunately, researchers also found that there were few of these monkeys left: they are often hunted for food and their habitat is rapidly being destroyed. So wildlife experts continue to work to save the monkeys in the hopes that they won't be lost forever.

DON'T STEP ON THAT!

In 2012 researchers announced the discovery of the world's smallest frog. It's so tiny (about ¼ inch long) that it has been photographed sitting comfortably on a dime. Called *Paedophryne amauensis*, for the Amau village in Papua New Guinea where it was found, this frog almost eluded researchers who tracked a group of them to piles of leaf litter. In the dark, the scientists couldn't find any frogs, so they gathered leaf litter into clear plastic bags to take back with them…and saw tiny frogs jumping in the bags.

The frog has two things in common with most new species discovered these days: It's small enough to be easily overlooked, and it lives in a remote area. What makes this little frog especially important is that it's also the world's smallest vertebrate, an honor that previously went to an Indonesian fish. Scientists hope to study these small creatures to learn how their miniature bodies function, and how they manage to survive.

Neither rats nor horses can vomit.

WHY ARE ANIMALS ANIMAL-SHAPED?

Kids ask the darndest...hold on, why are *animals shaped the way they are?*

ANIMAL ARCHITECTURE

You may have noticed that a whole lot of critters here on earth have a lot of peculiar similarities regarding their bodies. Even in the case of animals that are very different from us, like, say, a frog: We both have a fore section (with a head) and a hind section. The bulk of our sensory organs are located on our heads. We both have an abdomen, located in roughly the same place on our bodies, and it houses the bulk of our vital organs. We have a right side and left side of our bodies, each made up in basically the exact same way as the other. And so on. All in all, for how remarkably different we are, humans and frogs are very similar organisms. More than that, almost *all* animals are designed like this. Amphibians, mammals, fish, birds, reptiles, even insects have this basic body design. The question is why.

The answer lies deep in our history as living organisms. And in digging up the answer, we discovered some extraordinary things about the origins of life itself...and some creatures that don't follow the rules.

A BLOB IS STILL A BLOB

Go back about 800 million years ago and the only living things on earth were single-celled bacteria and primitive multicellular organisms like algae and sponges—and they were nothing but the most primitive blobs of blobbified blobbiness. They had no right side or left side, no front or back, no top or bottom. They didn't even have heads—they were just blobs.

An important thing to note about this, and something that will play into our story in a very important way, is that those bacteria and algae and sponges still exist on earth. And all of them are still blobs. Why? Because they are all descendants of those first bacteria and algae and sponges, and they inherited from them—and still carry—their primitive DNA. That DNA still has the same old instructions about how to build a body, and those instructions say, "Make it blobby!" Luckily for humans, DNA is constantly evolving and changing, and a whole new way of putting bodies together was on the horizon.

WHAT IT CAME DOWN TO

Primitive single-celled organisms such as bacteria aren't in need of a lot of organization. They have no internal organs, and no eyes or arm, or legs. All their equipment, including their DNA, just sloshes around inside them, so they do just fine as blobs.

When the first multicellular organisms came along, things weren't that different. The first groups of cells started working together as parts of one single organism. They were still all the same kinds of cells, so it didn't really matter where any of them were situated in that organism. But after a few million more years of evolution, things changed again, and groups of cells became specialized, each with its own specific functions. These new specialized cells tended to stick together and eventually came to form specific body parts in these new and ever-evolving multicellular organisms. (Look at your own body: Your brain cells are in your brain; your liver cells in your liver; and so on.)

At the same time that all this was happening, nature was also tinkering with how to arrange the new body parts. A lot of different arrangements were tried out, and, through the process of natural selection, some did better than others. And what did nature really seem to favor? Symmetry.

JELLYFISH PIE

Symmetry in biology simply refers to an organism's having roughly identical body parts distributed in the organism in a balanced fashion. A simple example would be your arms and legs: you have two of each, they're basically the exact same in design, and you have one each on each side of your body in about the same place. That's biological symmetry.

Somewhere in the neighborhood of 600 million years ago, scientists believe, the first animals with symmetrical body plans appeared on earth. They were *radially* symmetrical, meaning they had multiple similar body parts that extended outward from a central axis point, like spokes on a wheel. One of the earliest was a primitive jellyfish. You may not have known this about jellyfish, but their bodies are made up multiple (most have four) copies of wedge-shaped body parts that radiate out from their center, like pieces of a pie.

One of the advantages the new creatures had over the blobs was that while the blobs absorbed food and expelled waste through their cell membranes, the creatures had a rudimentary digestive system (with one opening that served as both a mouth and an anus). This allowed for better absorption of nutrients and, therefore, more energy for things like capturing prey. Over the following millions of years, a great diversity of radially symmetrical animals spread throughout the world's oceans. Many still exist today, among them the many varieties of jellyfish, starfish, and sea anemones.

CHOOSING SIDES

By about 550 million years ago, nature had done a lot more tinkering. Fossils tell us that by this time some of those radially symmetrical animals had made a split with their round-bodied cousins. Most importantly, they had developed a rudimentary central nervous system—or the very early forerunner to our brain and spinal cord—and their bodies were arranged around that system. These were the first animals with *bilateral* (meaning "two sides") symmetry. The bodies of these animals have some important characteristics:

• They're organized along a longitudinal axis, that axis being defined by the central nervous system.

• Slice that body along that central axis and you have left and right sides that are mirror images of one another.

• With just a few exceptions, they have a complete digestive tract, with a mouth at one end and an anus at the other.

• They have a head end and a tail end (even if they don't all have tails), and a top and a bottom (or a back and a belly, to put it another way).

• Most of the sensory organs are located on the head.

SUCCESS!

There were a lot of advantages to this new design. For one thing, the more centralized nervous system allowed for more centralized control of the entire organism. That, along with the more streamlined design, allowed animals to become much more mobile creatures. Indeed, most radially symmetrical animals are either very slow, such as the starfish, or they hardly move at all, like sea anemones. Being more mobile provided great advantages to the new animals. Most importantly, they could flee from predators and move toward prey much more easily.

Nature made it abundantly clear that it approved of this new design. Of the millions of different species of animals around today, almost all of them are descendants of those first bilaterally symmetrical animals that appeared some 550 million years ago. That includes all mammals, birds, reptiles, amphibians, fish, insects, worms, cephalopods (octopuses, squid, and such), and even mollusks. No matter how different we all may be, we still carry that ancient DNA and its bilaterally symmetrical body-building instructions. And that's why animals are shaped the way we are.

EXTRAS

• These body plan rules apply to the plant world, too. Picture a buttercup flower. Its has a ring of five nearly identical petals (these are the buttercup "body parts") evenly distributed around a central point. This is an example of radial symmetry in plants.

• Some flowers are bilaterally symmetrical, including those of orchids and peas.

• Most plants' leaves exhibit bilateral symmetry: They're aligned along a longitudinal access—the central vein, known as a *midrib.* The left and right sides on either side of that midrib are mirror images of each other.

• An echinoderm is a marine animal that starts its life as a free-swimming, bilaterally symmetric larva. As it grows, its right side is absorbed into its left side, and it changes form…and grows five legs around a central axis point—meaning it changes from bilateral to radial symmetry in its lifetime. (The brittle star, a relative of the starfish, is an example of an echinoderm.)

Hot air: Herring communicate by farting.

HODGEPODGE

Quick! More animal facts.

• Some Goliath bird-eating spiders have leg spans as wide as 11 inches.

• Ostriches have been known to eat some strange things. One ostrich at the London Zoo ate a pencil, a rope, a handkerchief, an alarm clock, a collar stud, a roll of film, a Belgian franc, three gloves, two old English quarter-pennies, and four halfpennies.

• Seals don't have external ears, just two little ear openings behind their eyes, but they can hear quite well.

• Cobras can't hear anything. It's believed that cobras do the "snake dance" and follow the rhythm of a snake charmer's music simply by swaying to the movements of the musician—not the music itself.

• World's stinkiest animal: According to *Guinness World Records*, it's the striped polecat, which looks a little like a skunk and is native to Africa. One of them kept nine lions at bay with just its smell.

• African elephants have the largest ears in the world, measuring up to six and a half feet tall. Their ears aren't intended to improve their sense of hearing, though. Elephants flap those enormous ears to cool off their bodies.

• Slowest fish: the sea horse, which swims at just 0.01 mph.

• First bird on a U.S. postage stamp: the bald eagle.

• Bears have an exceptional sense of smell. Their brains are only a third the size of the human brain, but the section designated for smelling is five times larger. Their big noses and large folds inside their nostrils house thousands of smell receptors, making their sense of smell even better than a bloodhound's.

• North American opossums have 50 teeth, the most of any land mammal.

• A pigeon's bones are lighter than its feathers.

WHEN WORLDS COLLIDE

Our favorite news story that went viral while we were writing this book was about a baby seal that wandered into a New Zealand home and took a nap on the couch. Aww! Here are some other stories of humans and animals meeting on each other's turf—although the results aren't nearly as cute.

THING 1: Michael Williams, a 36-year-old Australian man
THING 2: Fatso, the largest reptilian resident at the Broome Crocodile Park in Broome, Western Australia

THEY MEET: Williams got very drunk one night in 2010. How drunk? He ended up at the croc park and thought it would be a good idea take a ride on the back of Fatso. The 16-foot-long reptile had other ideas. After Williams jumped on, Fatso rolled over, and over...and over. The croc could have easily killed the drunk man, but only took a chunk out of his leg before letting him crawl away. Said arresting officer Roger Haynes, "Saltwater crocs...once they get hold of you, they are not renowned for letting you go. He's lucky to have escaped with his life."

THING 1: Todd Griffith, an engineer from Fort Meyers, Florida
THING 2: A Muscovy duck
THEY MEET: Muscovys grow pretty large for ducks (10 to 15 pounds), and they have long claws. Males have a dark back, white neck, and a bumpy red face. Griffith got to see a male up close because he was sitting in the chair next to him in a conference room. How did the duck get there? He smashed through a window and landed in the chair. At the time, Griffith was alone and preparing for a meeting. The duck was the first to show up. "He looked at me, like, 'What are *you* doing here?'" A little ruffled but otherwise okay, the duck waddled around the room as Griffith and a few coworkers tried to shoo him out. They finally did, and the duck went back to the drainage ditch behind the building.

THING 1: The Sessions family of Rexburg, Idaho
THING 2: A colony of garter snakes
THEY MEET: Remember the snake-filled dungeon from *Raiders of*

the Lost Ark? That's what Ben and Amber Sessions and their two young kids had to deal with…every day. When the couple bought their five-bedroom house in 2009, they thought they'd gotten a great deal. Their broker had reassured them that all the "snake talk" was overblown; the previous owner exaggerated the serpent story to get out of the mortgage. When the Sessions closed, Ben and Amber signed an agreement stating they knew the house had a snake problem. They could deal with a few harmless garter snakes, right? Wrong. As the weeks and months passed, more and more snakes showed up. "It felt like we were living in Satan's lair," said Amber. Ben called it a "horror movie." At night, the family could hear all the snakes slithering through the walls. They awoke each morning to find snakes all over the floors and even in the garbage. The house, it turns out, was built over a *hibernaculum*, an underground lair where the snakes meet to hibernate. In the end, the serpents won and the Sessions were forced to move out. At last report, the house was abandoned (except for the snakes).

THING 1: JoAnn Lorek, a woman from East Naples, Florida
THING 2: A bottlenose dolphin
THEY MEET: Lorek and some friends were riding in a boat down the Marco River when they spotted some dolphins swimming nearby. The driver slowed down while the passengers all peered over the edge to get a better look. Lorek said, "I just saw this wall of dolphin." The fully grown adult—all 600 pounds of it—leaped out of the water and landed on top of Lorek. Fortunately, it wasn't a direct hit; a fin slapped her in the face and the rest of the dolphin landed on her leg. The bottlenose started thrashing about as the humans scrambled to the other side of the 22-foot-long boat. Luckily, Dorek crawled away before any serious damage was done, although she did have a sprained ankle. It took 10 men—including cops, firefighters, and wildlife officials—to get the animal back in the water. After covering the dolphin's eyes with a towel to calm her down, they tied a rope around her tail and pulled her off. The dolphin seemed okay as she swam away. As for Dorek, she now has a great story to tell. (And she still loves dolphins.)

THING 1: Evan van der Spuy, a competitive mountain biker from South Africa

THING 2: A male red hartebeest

THEY MEET: Did you see the viral video of the cyclist who got waylaid by the gazelle? It wasn't a gazelle—it was a red hartebeest, which is bigger and has pointier horns. Here's the story behind it: Van der Spuy was racing for Team Jeep South Africa in KwaZulu Natal in 2011. As he was zooming down a trail through a pasture, his teammate, Travis Walker, was behind him…with video camera in hand. Walker saw the animal running across the field directly toward van der Spuy. He yelled out, "Buck!" But it was too late—both rider and beast were going too fast for either to alter course, and the buck slammed headfirst into van der Spuy's side. The rider hit the ground in a heap while the hartebeest stumbled a bit and then ran away. When Walker reached his friend, he was moaning in pain. Luckily, the only injury van der Spuy received was a stiff neck, but his bike and helmet were both quite damaged.

THING 1: Makayla McEvoy, a seven-year-old Australian girl

THING 2: An adult eastern gray kangaroo

THEY MEET: Sure, kangaroos look cute and cuddly…until one brutally attacks a little girl. The incident took place on New Years Day 2012 at a campsite in New South Wales. Makayla was playing by herself, not too far from her parents. There were a few kangaroos nearby, but they were a common sight at the camp and usually stayed well clear of people. Not this kangaroo. For some reason, it saw the little girl as a threat, hopped over, and started pummeling her. "All I could see was grey, grey, grey," said Makayla from the hospital. She was beaten up pretty badly, but thankfully her stepdad ran over and chased the 'roo off before any serious damage was done. Makayla said she still loves kangaroos and wants to be a veterinarian when she grows up.

*   *   *

AN ACTUAL POLICE REPORT

Buffalo, New York: A caller reported a large black and tan Doberman was in the area of Garden Court. Police reported it was only a giant porcelain deer.

ANIMAL ORGIES

At certain times every year, huge masses of creatures congregate at their favorite breeding grounds. Consider yourself invited to observe swarms of critters as they go about the business of propagating their species. (They don't mind if you watch.)

RED CRABS

When and where: During the last quarter of the moon in November or December on Australia's Christmas Island

The dirty details: Every winter, Christmas Island is overtaken by more than 50 million (some say as many as *75 trillion*) red crabs. When the weather's just right, the males venture out of their inland burrows, start marching to shore, and are joined by crabs of both sexes on the way. They're dependent on moisture to survive, so the migration halts if the weather gets too dry. Moving at just 3 mph for up to 12 hours a day, the crustaceans sometimes so impede the island's streets and walkways that park rangers have to close roads and construct temporary walls and bridges to help the animals cross the island safely.

When the crabs arrive at the coast, the males dig burrows and mate with a partner. Two weeks later, before the new moon, the females lay their eggs onshore at the turn of high tide. (Scientists think that's when mother crabs are least likely to get swept away by waves.) The eggs hatch on contact with the water, and the babies stay in the ocean for the next month. Meanwhile, their parents trek back inland, where they remain until the next year's festivities.

PALOLO WORMS

When and where: One week after the full moon in October or November in the South Pacific, especially Samoa

The dirty details: Palolo worms spend almost their entire lives deep in coral rock under the ocean. Every year, the worms emerge for just a day or two. In preparation for spawning, the rear half of their bodies becomes engorged with either sperm or eggs. Then, just before dawn, the foot-long worm splits, and the rear reproductive end rises to the surface while the front half sticks around and regenerates. Tens of thousands of the tail segments spiral up and simultaneously dissolve, releasing their eggs or sperm and turning the water a milky white. The sperm fertilize the eggs, which eventually sink and find homes in the coral. Many of the tails don't make it to the spawning stage, though, because of one main predator: the local Polynesians who crowd the beaches to collect the worm tails—a delicacy that's eaten raw.

RED-SIDED GARTER SNAKES

When and where: April and May in the Interlake area of southern Manitoba, Canada, especially in the Narcisse Snake Dens

The dirty details: Male red-sided garter snakes are not what you'd call sensitive to the needs of their female counterparts. When a female snake emerges from her winter den, sluggish and unsuspecting, up to 100 males swarm over her. Attracted by her pheromones, the males join with her to form what's called a "mating ball." In a frenzy, the group slides across the ground together, onto rocks and even climbing up trees, fighting for a chance to mate. This can go on for up to two hours. When a male gets close enough, he extends one of his two *hemipenes* (penises) and does the deed. Adding to the mating ball confusion, some males release a female hormone that lures the other male snakes away, and then sneak back to the female so they can have her all to themselves, at least for a while.

Eventually, the female escapes and gives birth to about 30 live snakes. Garter snake mating has become a spectator sport: Visitors to the Narcisse Snake Dens in May 2011 were treated to the sight of around 15,000 snakes going at it at once.

MEXICAN FREE-TAILED BATS

When and where: In the winter, in caves in Mexico—including one in Nuevo León where more than 140,000 bats congregate to mate

The dirty details: Researchers are only now discovering the specific caves in Mexico where millions of Mexican (also called Brazilian) free-tailed bats go when they migrate south every year. Because bats are nocturnal and elusive, not a lot is known about their lives deep in caves or even high up on buildings. However, scientists believe that both male and female Mexican free-tailed bats are promiscuous. The females gather together, and males swoop in and make mating calls. In a flurry, the males aggressively grab hold of any partner that's not taken and mate with her. Then the males move on to another. After conception, all of them return north to roosts where the mothers deliver one baby each.

GREEN SEA TURTLES

When and where: In the spring, on Raine Island in the Great Barrier Reef and in the Costa Rican village of Tortuguero (which means "land of the turtle")

The dirty details: Named for the color of the body fat under their shells, green sea turtles are wise old parents—they don't begin spawning until they're at least 30 years old. And even then, only the males can breed every year—for females, it's every two to four years—which is part of the reason they're endangered. But they do have ways of ensuring the survival of their species. At nesting time, two or more males court each female underwater, swimming around her, bumping her, and knocking other males away from her. While one pair is mating, another male will grab onto them (creating what's called "a mating ball") and attempt to join the party. Sometimes as many as four males join in.

This group mating is a good thing: it helps achieve genetic diversity and a higher likelihood of survival for the young. The female even stores sperm inside her body to fertilize batches of eggs months later. Females stick around their breeding colonies until the summer and fall. Then tens of thousands of them crawl onto the sand and dig pits in which they lay 100 to 200 eggs each. That sounds like a lot, but given the number of predators that prey on green sea turtles and their eggs and hatchlings, only 1 in 1,000 eggs will survive to adulthood.

* * *

WATCH YOUR HEAD

Though most are dust by the time they reach the atmosphere, thousands of tons of rock have fallen to earth from outer space. In 1920 an African farmer plowing his field unearthed a nine-foot meteorite made of iron. It has been named "Hoba" (for the farm where it was found), weighs more than 66 tons, and is the largest known meteorite on earth.

FEAR FACTOR

Man. Beast. Fear. Quotes.

"We humans fear the beast within the wolf because we do not understand the beast within ourselves."

—**Gerald Hausman**

"Suspicion, the offspring of fear, is eminently characteristic of most wild animals. Courage and timidity are extremely variable qualities in the individuals of the same species, as is plainly seen in our dogs."

—**Charles Darwin**

"Perhaps the wilderness we fear is the pause within our own heartbeats, the silent space that says we live only by grace. Wilderness lives by this same grace."

—**Terry Tempest Williams**

"There are very few monsters who warrant the fear we have of them."

—**Andre Gide**

"The wolf that one hears is worse than the orc that one fears."

—**J. R. R. Tolkien,**
The Fellowship of the Ring

"Fear helps me from making mistakes, but I [still] make lot of mistakes."

—**Steve Irwin**

"If you talk to the animals they will talk with you and you will know each other. If you do not talk to them, you will not know them, and what you do not know, you will fear. What one fears one destroys."

—**Chief Dan George**

"A cat bitten once by a snake dreads even rope."

—**Arab proverb**

"There is no living thing that is not afraid when it faces danger. True courage is facing danger when you are afraid."

—**L. Frank Baum,**
The Wonderful Wizard of Oz

"I had a linguistics professor who said that it's man's ability to use language that makes him the dominant species on the planet. That may be. But there's another thing that separates us from animals. We're not afraid of vacuum cleaners."

—**Jeff Stilson**

A FEW OF OUR FAVORITE PARASITES

How many parasites can exist in a human or animal's body? Better not to think about it. Let's just leave it at scads.

MEET THE PARASITES

We generally think of parasites as nasty little creatures that attach themselves to us and suck our vital juices. Well, that's what they are, and that's why they're called parasites. But there's more to them than that.

Here's the official definition of a parasite: An organism that benefits from its relationship with another organism, its *host*, at the expense of said host. The word has its root in the ancient Greek *parasitos*, meaning "one who eats at the table of another." The parasitic organisms that affect a huge variety of hosts range from fairly benign to downright horrifying. Consider, for example, the parasite that eats and then takes over the role of its host's tongue. Really. (More on that soon.)

To give you a peek (at a safe distance) into the wonderful world of parasites, we've picked out a few of our favorites. Some you'll recognize, some you won't, and some might just give you nightmares. So, welcome to another beautiful day in parasites!

GYPSY MOTH CATERPILLAR BACULOVIRUS

This is a viral parasite, which is redundant, since all viruses are parasites. And viruses do one thing—they infect the cells of living things and trick them into replicating, thereby getting *themselves* replicated, something they can't do on their own. In this case, the baculovirus infects a gypsy moth caterpillar and, creepier than that, somehow manages to affect its behavior. An infected caterpillar will climb to the top of whatever tree or plant it's on. Then the virus liquefies the caterpillar…and the liquefied caterpillar drips down onto other caterpillars below it. Because the liquid is teeming with baculovirus—the dripped-on caterpillars become infected, too, and the parasite's life cycle begins again. In 2011 scientists actually isolated the gene in the baculovirus that makes the caterpillars act this way.

MISTLETOE

And you thought it was just a Christmas decoration. Mistletoe is actually a parasitic plant that uses trees, shrubs, and birds as hosts. It comes in hundreds of species and, whether you knew it or not, you've probably seen their distinctive leafy clumps in infected trees. The plant's life begins with poop: a bird defecates; the poop sticks to a branch of a tree; a mistletoe seed in the poop sprouts; and modified roots, known as *haustoria*, grow out of it. (Think about that the next time you're waiting for a kiss under a sprig at Christmastime.) Anyway, the haustoria secrete enzymes that eat through the tree's bark and hard outer surface, and into its living tissue. Once it gets in there, the young mistletoe steals water and nutrients from the tree. When it matures, the mistletoe produces seeds inside berries, birds eat the berries—and thus begins the poop part again. Severe mistletoe infestations can do serious damage to trees, and can even kill them.

Bonus: Mistletoe is a *hemiparasite*, or "half parasite," meaning it is not completely dependent on its host because it can produce its own food. Mistletoe grows leaves and, like other green plants, relies on photosynthesis to provide it with food.

THE AFRICAN EYE WORM

Perhaps during your travels through a tropical rain forest in West Africa, you were bitten by a deer fly. It hurt, but you didn't notice that, while it was biting you, tiny worms crawled out of its proboscis and into your skin. They were African eye worms, or "loa loa" worms, short for their species name, *Loa loa filariasis*. Once under your skin, the worms began traveling around your body, feeding on your blood. Over the next few years, the worms grew—some of them by now three inches long—and you developed red, itchy bumps on your skin, caused by the worms. Some of the worms died, and your body reacted by forming itchy, pus-filled bumps around the dead worms' remains. Other worms made their way to your eyes…where they wriggled across the surface of your eyeballs. (You'd need surgery to remove them.) Some may have made their way to your brain, causing brain swelling and possible death (although that's very rare these days). In the meantime, female worms laid thousands of eggs that took up residence in your blood, spinal fluid, and lungs. If you're bitten by another deer fly, it ingests some of the eggs, which grow into worms. If the fly bites another human, the worms will travel down its proboscis, and start the life cycle of the African eye worm all over again. Have a great trip!

TONGUE-EATING LOUSE

The tongue-eating louse is a parasitic marine crustacean that lives in the Pacific Ocean, where it uses the spotted red snapper fish as its host. A young tongue-eater initiates the relationship by crawling into a snapper's mouth via its gills. It makes its way to the base of the fish's tongue and proceeds to suck all the fluid out of the tongue, which eventually withers away completely. The louse then attaches itself to the remaining nub of the tongue with its hind legs. From this point, it takes over the role of the fish's tongue, eventually growing to almost two inches in length. The fish can even maneuver the louse-tongue with muscles remaining in its tongue nub, using it to hold prey, and whatever else fish do with their tongues. Fish infected with the creatures—amazingly—do not seem overly affected and continue to live normal lives, complete with their creepy new tongues.

THE GREEN-BANDED BROODSAC

A relative of the more famous tapeworm, which infects human digestive tracts, this parasitic flatworm infects snails and birds. Like mistletoe, the green-banded broodsac begins life in a pile of bird poop, in this case as eggs. A snail comes along and eats the bird poop, the eggs hatch, go through a couple of life stages, and end up in the host snail's tentacles. The normally dull-looking tentacles become bright, pulsating, swollen, green, yellow, and red appendages on the snail's head. Worse: The snail normally uses those tentacles to detect light—which it avoids to evade predators—but the virus causes the tentacles to lose their light-sensing ability. The snail eventually wanders into open daylight, a bird sees its bright, pulsating, colorful tentacles, which look a lot like tasty caterpillars, and eats them, ingesting a new batch of broodsac eggs. And, just like mistletoe…only a lot creepier…it all starts again.

PROVERBS, NATURALLY

The beauty and wonders of nature transcend nationality.

Every animal knows far more than you do.

—Nez Perce

The heart is but the beach beside the sea that is the world.

—Chinese

When a man moves away from nature, his heart becomes hard.

—Lakota

No matter how long the winter, spring is sure to follow.

—Guinean

The earth is mankind's only friend.

—East African

The best time to plant a tree was 20 years ago. The second-best time is today.

—Chinese

When elephants fight, the grass gets hurt.

—East African

Man is preceded by forest and followed by desert.

—French

All riches come from the earth.

—Armenian

Everyone must pay his debt to nature.

—German

Nature without effort surpasses art.

—Latin

The tiger depends on the forest; the forest depends on the tiger.

—Cambodian

Nature does nothing in vain.

—Romanian

Listen to the voice of nature, for it holds treasures for you.

—Huron

Just let there be a forest, and there is sure to be a forest spirit.

—Russian

In nature, there is no such thing as a lawn.

—Albanian

In a moment the ashes are made, but the forest is a long time growing.

—Senecan

When the last tree has been cut down, the last river has been polluted, and the last fish has been caught, only then do you realize that money can't buy everything.

—Native Amer.

More than half of America's wetlands have been drained in the last 100 years.

THE HIGHEST ANIMALS

And we don't mean up a tree...

DO THEY OR DON'T THEY?
A lot of what's been written about "animals that get high" is nonsense. Biologists point out that just because an animal eats something containing a chemical compound that can cause intoxication in humans doesn't mean the chemical affects the animal in the same way. And even if it did, that doesn't mean the animal set out to become intoxicated—maybe it was just hungry. On the other hand, anyone who's ever watched a cat with catnip knows there's *something* to the stories. That's a good place to start.

CATS

Drug of choice: Catnip

Background: Catnip is native to Europe and Asia, where it's been used for a variety of medicinal purposes (most commonly as a relaxing tea) for thousands of years. Brought to the New World by early European colonists, it now grows wild all over the United States and southern Canada. Its active ingredient is *nepetalactone*, an organic compound found in an oil produced in the plant's leaves.

Animal stoners? Sure looks like it. Here's what happens: Nepetalactone binds with olfactory receptors in cats' noses. What it does after that, nobody knows, but there's no question that nepetalactone makes cats experience some kind of high. On smelling it for just a few moments, cats will rub themselves on the plant, bite the leaves to release more oil, sniff it, and then act completely whacked out for a few minutes. They writhe around, yowl, run in circles, play with things that aren't there...or just go gaga and drool until the effects wear off. (Pretty much like Uncle John and his friends used to do in the 1960s.)

Extra: It's actually *sniffing* the plant that gives cats that stimulative effect. If they eat it, it acts as a sedative. About 70 percent of cats are affected by catnip. It's genetic—they get high off of catnip only if Mom and Dad did.

BIGHORN SHEEP

Drug of choice: Lichen

Background: Bighorns live in the high (as in northern) mountainous regions of western Canada and the U.S. Because much of their time is spent in snowy, rocky terrain, where there is often not a lot of plant life, they've learned to eat what's available, which includes the extremely hardy plantlike life that is lichen.

Animal stoners? Probably not. Though stories abound of bighorn sheep climbing sheer rock faces to get to tiny clumps of lichen because they really want to get wasted, there's little evidence to back up those stories. Plus, no one ever seems to say exactly how the bighorns are affected by the lichen or what might be in the lichen that would cause intoxication. There *are* stories of lichens that contain toxic and possibly psychedelic compounds, but we couldn't find even a single story that gave the species name of the lichen doing the intoxicating—which would have to be included to make such a story credible.

WALLABIES

Drug of choice: Poppies

Background: Poppy flowers contain potent psychoactive substances called *opioids*. They work by interacting with opioid receptors, which are found in the brain, spinal cord, and digestive tract of humans and other animals. Once attached to those receptors, opioids block transmissions of pain messages to the brain. They also act on the brain's pleasure centers, causing feelings of euphoria. Drugs like morphine and heroin are made from opioids.

Animal stoners? Oh, yeah. The island state of Tasmania in Australia has enormous poppy farms, and is the largest producer of opioids for pharmaceutical use in the world. It's also home to a lot of wallabies. And wallabies apparently have opioid receptors—and like to use them. "They would just come and eat some poppies and they would go away," poppy farmer Lyndley Chopping told ABC in 2009. "They'd come back again, and they would do their circle work in the paddock." By "circle work," Chopping meant that the wallabies would eat poppies, and then, seemingly stoned out of their gourds, hop around in circles, making "crop circles" in the poppy fields. Then they'd fall asleep. The Tasmanian govern-

...winter, spring, summer monsoon, and winter monsoon.

ment said it was looking into ways to stop the wallaby drug parties, both for the sake of the farmers and the wallabies.

REINDEER

Drug of choice: Fly agaric mushrooms

Background: This mushroom species (*Amanita muscaria*), found on every continent except Antarctica, contains several psychoactive compounds, the most active being *muscimol*, which causes heightened senses, a variety of emotions, and visual and auditory hallucinations. This is why the plants are also known as "magic mushrooms."

Animal stoners? What was the question again? Oh, right, like we said, these mushrooms grow all over the world, and that includes the Arctic regions of Europe and Asia, where native reindeer eat them as a regular part of their diet, even digging deep into the snow to find them. This has led to stories in newspapers and on the Internet under headings like "Flying reindeer flying high on magic mushrooms!" But little evidence is ever given that the mushrooms actually affect the reindeer, and no scientific studies have been undertaken to prove or disprove it. The reindeer might just be eating them because there's not a lot else to eat on the tundra. The stories are very likely linked to evidence that reindeer-herding peoples, including the Chuchki and Koryak people of Arctic Russia, use fly agaric mushrooms in religious ceremonies. So maybe the stories originated with people, who, while high on 'shrooms...thought the reindeer were high, too.

MALAYSIAN PEN-TAILED SHREWS

Drug of choice: Alcohol

Background: A species of tree shrew found only in Malaysia, this little mammal grows to four to six inches in length, and is so named for its long tail, which ends in a feathery tip (like a pen made from a bird's feather). Pen-tailed shrews spend much of their lives in the branches of the bertram palm tree, which produces blooming flowers year-round...which in turn produce a nectar that ferments into a booze with about 3.8 percent alcohol (about the same as the average beer).

Animal stoners? Probably not. Pen-tailed shrews consume one thing and one thing only: the booze-laden nectar of the flowers of the bertram tree. They're the only animal in the world known to have developed such a diet. And they drink a lot of it: the equivalent of about nine glasses of wine per day. (Did we mention that they're just six inches long?) But although they are regularly included on lists of animals that get high, no matter how much alcohol they drink, pen-tailed shrews don't appear to get drunk. Scientific studies show them suffering no impairment whatsoever even after huge nectar-booze binges. Scientists have no idea why this is, but hope to study the alcohol-swilling tree shrews further in hopes of learning something about human alcohol poisoning.

EXTRAS

• Black lemurs on the island of Madagascar regularly capture giant millipedes and bite them gently so that the millipede will shoot out a defensive chemical cocktail that the lemurs then rub on their skin, which kills mites and repels insects. Video evidence of millipede-nibbling, twitching, goggle-eyed lemurs suggests the chemical concoction also gets the lemurs pretty wasted.

• Cane toads were introduced into Australia to eat bugs that were decimating sugarcane crops. Well, they didn't do what they were supposed to do and instead have become a major nuisance. One unexpected downside (among many) of the cane toad invasion is the toxin they secrete from glands on their backs—a defensive measure that keeps predators from wanting to eat them. It turns out that dogs seem to get high on the toxin. Over the last few years, there have been a number of reports of dogs licking cane toads' backs, becoming wobbly and glassy-eyed, and then, after recovering…going back for more toad-licking goodness.

• One more thing to consider: We know that many plants rely on animals for their survival—from honeybees that pollinate flowers to birds that spread seeds via their poop. More than a few scientists have suggested that plants, via natural selection, may have developed their intoxicating substances as a way to give animals a "prize" in exchange for helping them out, in order to gain an advantage over other plants.

Colored feathers are stronger and more resistant to wear than white feathers.

NATURAL SELECTION FOR NATURAL DUMMIES

If you're already well versed in the biological process known as natural selection...well, this is for the rest of us.

ONCE UPON A TIME...

...long, long ago, there was a land known as the Kingdom of the White Moths. It got that name from a species of moth that lived in great numbers in the kingdom. The moths spent their nights in flight, eating and looking for mates, and their days resting on tree trunks. Resting on trees was a potentially dangerous thing for the moths to do, however—because they were a favorite food of birds. Fortunately for the moths, a kind of lichen grew on the surface of the tree trunks, and that lichen, like the moths, was white. So the moths were camouflaged and very difficult for the birds to see.

Sometimes when baby moths were born, they weren't white—they were black. (There was nothing unnatural about this, it just happened, just as two blond-haired parents might have a child with dark hair.) Such an unlucky baby moth would stand out on white lichen like, well, a black moth on white lichen—and a bird would spot it and gobble it up in no time. So it goes without saying that there weren't a lot of black moths around. And this is the way it went, for ages and ages, in the Kingdom of the White Moths. Then...something happened.

LICHEN DISLIKE

After many, many centuries, humans living in the kingdom discovered ways to take coal from the ground in enormous amounts, and to use it to power great new factories. Soon there were coal factories everywhere, and they spewed thick black smoke from their smokestacks. This, it turned out, was a disaster for the white moths. The white lichen that had for so long been their safe resting spot happened to be extremely sensitive to the black smoke, and in no time at all, the white lichen died out and disappeared.

Now there was nothing for the white moths to rest on but the dark bark of the trees. The moths stood out like, well, white moths on dark trees, and they began to be gobbled up by hungry birds, who now had no trouble seeing them.

And what of the formerly *unlucky* black moths? They were no longer unlucky at all—because now they were the ones that were safely camouflaged on the dark-colored trunks of the trees. And because they passed their dark coloring on to their offspring, their descendants flourished, too. Soon there were no white moths at all—except for a few odd *unlucky* ones, who were quickly eaten by hungry birds. The Kingdom of the White Moths was now the Kingdom of the Black Moths.

That, readers, is a simple but accurate enough description of the evolutionary process known as natural selection.

THE KINGDOM

The scenario you just read was obviously dressed up to read like a fairy tale—but it really happened. The "kingdom" was central England, and the "long, long ago" was the 1800s. The moth was the peppered moth (*Biston betularia*), well known and studied by British naturalists for centuries. In the early 1800s, peppered moths—which were light colored with dark specks, hence their "peppered" name—were common in central England and were usually found resting on light-colored lichen growing on the surface of trees. Then, in the mid-1800s, the Industrial Revolution surged into full gear, and coal-powered factories sprang up all over Britain. The emissions from the factories resulted in a noticeable change to the English countryside. One of those changes was the disappearance of the light-colored lichens that grew on trees.

In the early part of the century, roughly 98 percent of the moths in the region were white, and just about 2 percent were dark. By the mid-1800s, it was about 50–50, and by the end of the century, 98 percent of all peppered moths were black; only 2 percent were white. Nature had indeed "selected" the black moths for survival.

FIRST BUT NOT QUITE FOREMOST

The concept of natural selection is commonly associated with 19th-century naturalist Charles Darwin, and he indeed coined the

The world's smallest rodent, the pygmy jerboa, can run as fast as a horse.

term in his groundbreaking 1859 publication, *On the Origin of Species*. But as Darwin himself noted, he wasn't the originator of the idea. Since the time of the ancient Greeks, scholars had been proposing similar theories to explain all the different kinds of life on earth. And especially since the beginning of the Scientific Revolution in the 16th century, scientists had been proposing a *how* for those theories and were inching ever closer to Darwin's ideas. A few standouts:

• **In 1790 German philosopher Immanuel Kant**, noting the similarities among different animals—number of limbs, bone structure, etc.—proposed that different animal species may have had common ancestors and had developed into different types of animals by undergoing a slow progression of changes over millions of years. He did not, however, propose *how* this might happen.

• **In 1801 French naturalist Jean-Baptiste Lamarck** said that all life was constantly undergoing minor changes. As for how that happened, Lamarck thought that animals could pass on to their offspring characteristics they had acquired during their lifetime. A classic example of this was Lamarck's belief that giraffes had long necks because they stretched to eat leaves high in trees, and over many generations, this stretching led to longer and longer necks. Known as *Lamarckism*, the theory was wrong, but it was still widely believed well into the 20th century.

• **In 1798 English scholar Thomas Malthus** published a study on population that said organisms such as plants and animals naturally produce too many offspring and the resulting overpopulation resulted in things like disease and famine, which in turn resulted in the death of many members of the overpopulating species. (Malthus published this as a warning: He proposed limiting the number of children people could have—to save the human race from the dangers of overpopulation.)

THEN CAME DARWIN

In 1838 Charles Darwin read Malthus's study on population. He had by this time already spent more than a year studying evolution and, more precisely, how species changed over time. Malthus's work proved to be the catalyst that set Darwin's theory in motion. From Darwin's autobiography, written in 1876:

There are viruses, fungi, and insects that "zombify" other creatures by infecting their brains.

> In October 1838, that is, fifteen months after I had begun my systematic inquiry, I happened to read for amusement Malthus on Population, and being well prepared to appreciate the struggle for existence which everywhere goes on from long-continued observation of the habits of animals and plants, it at once struck me that under these circumstances favourable variations would tend to be preserved, and unfavourable ones to be destroyed. The results of this would be the formation of a new species. Here, then I had at last got a theory by which to work.

This was in 1838. Darwin spent the next 21 years developing his theory, studying a wide variety of plant and animal species, and sharing his ideas with just a few people, before he finally published *On the Origin of Species* in 1859.

THE DETAILS

So what exactly was Darwin's theory? In a nutshell:

• All species of life produce far more offspring than can actually survive.

• This results in a "struggle for survival" between members of a species.

• Every species experiences *random variation*, meaning that each member of any given species is born a little different from every other member, whether in size, shape, color, or other traits. (Just look at you and your family if you doubt this is true.) Most importantly—many of these new traits, although not inherited from parents, can be passed on to offspring.

• Some of those traits provide an advantage to those who have them over those who don't, and make it more likely that they, and their offspring—and, most importantly, their particular traits—will survive and flourish, while others will not.

• This process, repeated countless times over very long periods of time, can lead to enough physical changes in a given species that entirely new and different species can emerge from older ones.

SINCE DARWIN

By the time of the publication of *On the Origin of Species*, Darwin had already been a respected scientist for several decades. The book was an immediate international success, and even though it had its detractors, over the course of the next decade Darwin's theory of natural selection became almost universally accepted science. The progress of science in the time since its publication has only reinforced its foundations.

Probably the most significant support to Darwin's theory of natural selection came with the modern science of genetics. We now know, for example, that what causes the variations Darwin said were the primary engine behind natural selection and evolution itself are genetic mutations, or mutations to tiny bits of DNA. We tend to think of those as something out of science fiction, but genetic mutations happen all the time.

MUTATION STATION

Here's a quick explanation of how genetic mutations happen, and how they drive natural selection:

• DNA reproduces by replicating itself—and it is very common for little errors to happen during that process. Sometimes a piece of a gene ends up in the wrong spot. Or pieces are missing altogether. These are mutations, and they happen to the DNA in your own cells all the time.

• When this happens in reproductive cells—sperm or egg cells in animals—the mutations can be passed to offspring. The mutation or mutations will then be a part of that offspring's DNA, and can in turn be passed on to future offspring.

• Most mutations have no effect whatsoever on the offspring. But some do, whether it's a change in hair or eye color, bone length or strength or susceptibility to heat or cold—they might even make an offspring immune to a disease that its parents weren't immune to.

• Some of these new traits might give the offspring a better chance of survival, and then those new traits—caused by the lucky genetic mutations—become more common within the species.

• Picture tiny changes happening in this way a hundred thousand times over millions of years, and you begin to understand how, for example, a small, furry, bearlike animal became what we know today as a seal. It's all got to do with natural selection.

EXTRAS

• The phrase "survival of the fittest" was coined by British scholar Herbert Spencer in 1864, after reading *On the Origin of Species*. Darwin added it to the book for the fifth edition, in 1869.

• Although he came up with it himself, Darwin was not a fan of the term "natural selection," because he felt it implied that something was "selecting" something, when in fact the very randomness of the variations was a fundamental ingredient in the process.

• *Sexual selection* is a specific kind of natural selection described by Darwin as evolutionary changes to an organism that specifically have to do with its ability to mate—even if it harms that organism's ability to survive. As an example, Darwin pointed to the male peacock, and how the one with the most extravagant tail feathers is more likely to be chosen by a female, thereby passing down his genes, and subsequently his tail feathers, to descendants. But those huge feathers are hard to carry around, and make the male peacock an easier target for predators.

• Darwin also coined the term "artificial selection," and you can probably guess what it is: People who breed dogs, cats, flowers, cattle—they're all taking part in an artificial form of natural selection. Instead of nature favoring random genetic traits, the humans are choosing individuals with desired traits and breeding them with different individuals that have different desired traits—to create very different kinds of organisms.

• An example of how drastically artifical selection can change an organism: Cauliflower, cabbage, broccoli, and kale are all bred descendants of the same plant—wild mustard.

• In 1956 Great Britain passed the Clean Air Act, and pollution levels from coal-powered plants and other, newer sources quickly declined. The light-colored lichen returned to trees, and in some areas of central Britain, as many as 90 percent of the peppered moths are now light-colored again.

A single baobab tree can store over 30,000 gallons of water in its trunk.

THE POOP-EATERS

If you collected all the poop that all the animals in the world pooped in just one day, we bet you could build a pile that stretched all the way to Uranus and back.

TEST RUN

Animals make a lot of poop, that's a fact. Luckily, nature has at least one way of putting it to use that is not only extraordinarily beneficial to the very existence of life on earth, but extraordinarily grotesque as well.

The scientific name for the practice of eating feces is *coprophagy*, and it comes in a variety of categories. A few: *autocoprophagy* (eating one's own feces), *allocoprophagy* (eating the feces of other members of your species), and *heterospecific coprophagy* (eating the feces of other species).

Okay, that was a test run: If you're not completely grossed out and still with us, let's move on to some specific examples.

EARTHWORMS. The more than 3,000 different species of earthworms play an important part in maintaining the earth's terrestrial ecosystems by being nature's recyclers of decaying organic material, which includes animal feces. They gobble it up and poop it out as nutrient-rich *castings* that are essential for good soil, which is in turn essential for the creation of more plants, more plant-eaters, more plant-eater-eaters, and more poop-producers. Worms are therefore *very* important in the great poop-circle of life. You can even make (or buy) a feces-eating worm composter (worm composting is called *vermicomposting*) for your house pet's poop; the worms eat the poop and convert it into fertilizer. Some people even have vermicomposting outhouses for human poop.

DUNG BEETLES. There are about 4,500 species of dung beetles, and they feed almost exclusively on dung. Most are found in Africa, where they evolved along with large herbivores like buffaloes and elephants, who seemingly dropped the dung beetles' favorite foods several times a day. Most species are *rollers*: they get a clump of dung, often several times bigger than they are, and push it with their powerful back legs, roll it along the ground, and eventually bury it to use as a food source. Sometimes, when romance is in the air, a male and female will roll a dung ball together, find a suitable spot to bury it, and mate underground. Later the female lays her eggs in the dung ball, and when the dung beetle babies hatch, they eat the dung. Other dung beetles are *tunnelers* that bury dung where they find it; others still are *dwellers* that live right inside piles of dung.

ELEPHANTS. Baby elephants start off life with sterile intestines, meaning their intestines contain none of the necessary microbes animals use to digest food. So they eat their mom's poop to "colonize" their guts with the microbes, making them good to go with digestion for the rest of their lives. (Human babies get their *gut flora*, as it's called, primarily during contact with their mother and her microbes during birth, and then by being around microbey humans, putting their fingers in their mouth, and so on.)

SLOTH MOTHS. Sloth moths evolved alongside sloths in Central and South America. Adult moths spend their entire lives in the fur of sloths, feeding off secretions from the sloths' skin, and from algae that naturally accumulates in sloth fur. One large sloth can be home to more than a hundred moths at any given time. Sloths are arboreal, meaning they live in trees, where they spend most of their time sleeping—they also spend about six hours a day looking for food. But they don't poop where they eat: About once a week, a sloth climbs down to the ground, digs a hole...and takes a dump. (They do so in the same spot every time, and cover the dump afterward.) When the female moths smell the poop, they fly out of the sloth's fur, find said dump, and lay a bunch of eggs in it. When the eggs hatch, the sloth moth caterpillars eat nothing but sloth poop. When they become moths they fly away—and find another sloth to call home.

Bonus: In 2001 biologists at a research site in the Amazon rain forest in Peru found a sloth inside a latrine. It was eating human feces. Since then, sloths have been found in the site's latrines at

...A. One reason: They eat food rather than producing their own.

least 25 times. The biologists are at a loss to explain the strange behavior, but said the sloths must have learned that there was some nutrition to be had from the poop.

KOALAS. The young koala drinks only its mother's milk for the first six to seven months of its life and remains in the pouch all that time, slowly growing and developing eyes, ears, fur, etc. At about 22 weeks, its eyes open and it begins to peep out of the pouch. From then to about 30 weeks, it feeds on a substance called *pap*, a specialized form of feces that forms an important part of the young koala's diet. The pap allows a baby koala to make the transition from mother's milk to eucalyptus leaves, rather like a human baby is fed mushy food when it starts to eat solids. Pap is soft and runny and thought to come from the koala's cecum. Besides being a rich source of protein, pap allows the mother koala to give her baby the gift of the microorganisms from her own digestive system that are essential to the digestion of the eucalyptus leaves that will make up most of its diet for life.

* * *

MORE BEHOLD...THE TURTLE

"In the beginning, there was a great tortoise who supported the world. Upon him, all ultimately rests. He is all wise and can outrun the hare. In the night his eyes carry him to unknown places."

—William Carlos Williams, "The Turtle"

"I picked the tortoise up and she blinked at me with her upside-down eyelids. I felt instantly calm. Her eyes were soft brown. Her skin felt like an old elbow."

—Jessica Grant, *Come, Thou Tortoise*

"Anytime you see a turtle up on top of a fence post, you know he had some help."

—Alex Haley

LAKE-STREMES

The largest, oldest, hottest, and otherwise strangest lakes on this here planet Earth.

• **Largest lake:** The Caspian Sea covers 750 miles from north to south, and on average it's 200 miles wide. (The Romans called several large lakes "seas" because they were salty, and the names stuck.) This immense lake borders five countries: Azerbaijan, Iran, Kazakhstan, Russia, and Turkmenistan. The Caspian Sea is an *endorheic lake* (a body of water that doesn't flow into the ocean) and contains some salt, but it's still three times less salty than the ocean.

• **Largest lake system:** The Great Lakes of the United States and Canada include Superior, Michigan, Huron, Erie, and Ontario. Together they form the world's largest lake surface area—more than 95,000 square miles. The Great Lakes also contain about 20 percent of the world's surface freshwater.

• **Oldest and deepest lake:** About 30 million years ago, Lake Baikal in Siberia formed when the earth's crust pulled apart to create a rift valley that is 5,369 feet (more than a mile) deep. Lake Baikal has more freshwater than any other lake in the world—including the Great Lakes, even though it has only about an eighth of their surface area.

• **Highest lake:** In the Andes Mountains, at 20,965 feet above sea level, is a lake in a crater on Ojos del Salado, the world's highest volcano.

• **Lowest lake:** Located between Israel and Jordan, the Dead Sea sinks more than 2,300 feet below sea level. (Its surface alone lies at 1,320 feet below sea level.) Nothing but bacteria and algae live in this "dead" lake, which is almost six times saltier than the ocean.

• **Clearest lake:** Blue Lake in New Zealand has a horizontal visibility (how far you can see in front of you) of about 230 to 260 feet. Some scientists say it's the clearest lake in the world. Why?

Minerals and other particles that could cloud the water are filtered out when they pass through landslide debris to enter the lake.

• **Hottest lake:** Boiling Lake on the Caribbean island of Dominica has its basin in a fumarole that's almost 200 feet in diameter. A fumarole is a hole in the planet's crust that emits heat from underground, and this particular fumarole heats Boiling Lake to 197°F.

• **Weirdest lake:** Jellyfish Lake on the island of Palau is a saltwater lake that was cut off from the Pacific Ocean millions of years ago...with golden jellyfish trapped inside. The jellyfish survived by feeding on algae, and over time, with no predators, they lost their ability to sting.

• **Most-buried lake:** The Lost Sea in Tennessee was discovered in 1905 by a 13-year-old boy who was playing in a cave and found an opening that lead to a lake 140 feet underground. Now known to cover more than 13 acres, it's America's largest underground lake.

• **Iciest lake:** Vostok Lake in Antarctica lies more than two miles under the ice and has been buried for about 25 million years. Believed to be as large as Lake Ontario, Vostok is one of the world's biggest freshwater lakes.

For some lake FAQs, grab a Jet Ski and head over to page 85.

* * *

THE STONE-EATERS

Many animals with gizzards—digestive organs used to grind up food—swallow small stones, ranging in size from sand grains to hefty pebble. Gizzards take the place of teeth, grinding up food in order to aid digestion. Some stone-eaters: chickens, nutcrackers, ostriches, some trout species, crocodiles, alligators, seals, and earthworms.

World's longest bug: Chan's megastick, a stick insect discovered in 2008, can be 22" long.

HE DID WHAAAT?

They say love is blind, but for some of nature's amorous couples, love is just plain bizarre.

SEXY SPARROWS

If your parents ever lectured you about the birds and the bees, they probably didn't mention the promiscuity of these feathered friends. Take female saltmarsh sparrows, for instance. Ninety-five percent of them regularly cheat on their mates. And the dunnock, or hedge sparrow, is even more notorious. She gives her mate a loving peck, then goes off to find a handsome guy with shiny breast feathers, a sign of good genes. Not only does she begin an affair, she invites her lover to share the family nest. Soon she's got two males helping raise the little ones, though neither male knows exactly which, if any, chicks are his. Zoologists say the female does it to guarantee more offspring and as a kind of insurance policy in case one male is infertile.

PEEING PORCUPINES

The old joke goes, "How do porcupines make love? Very carefully." Kind of true, but there's more to it than that...and it isn't pleasant. When love strikes, the male begins whining—basically, the porcupine version of bursting into song—and then he rises up on his hind legs. If the female is attracted to him, she'll do the same, and as they're facing each other, the male will spray his beloved with a stream of urine and soak her from head to foot. Then the actual mating begins.

HORNY GUPPIES

In the rivers of Trinidad, female guppies are usually a drab brown gray, but when they're fertile, they have their choice of brightly colored males. While the female mulls over her prospects, the guys get impatient and chase or nip at her to encourage her to hurry up. The males get so excited that they'll even pester females that aren't fertile, and may try to sneak a quick sexual interlude if that uninterested female gets distracted. So the girl guppies have developed their own defense to ward off the pesky males: A desperate female will swim to predator-filled parts of the river. Because they're so drab, it's possible for females to keep out of sight and out of danger, but the males are much too colorful to risk following them.

HE-SHE OYSTERS

Pacific oysters never move from their spot in a tide pool, but they still manage to have an extremely productive love life. Mating, or "spawning," season begins as the springtime weather warms. A few male oysters spawn, encouraging the rest in a kind of chain reaction. As the sperm-filled water bathes the females, they release hundreds of millions of eggs. To prevent more than one sperm from fertilizing the same egg—which would result in the death of the embryo—the oysters produce thousands of different varieties of each, which include several different proteins. Only a sperm with the same protein as an egg can fertilize it. The most interesting part? All oysters start out as males, regularly releasing sperm, but after a few years, some of them switch and become females.

BAWDY BONOBOS

Bonobos are apes native to Africa, and are related to chimpanzees. They live communally with very little infighting, but with plenty of sexual activity. For bonobos, sex is as common as a handshake—and not limited to male-female copulation. Nearly anything goes with bonobos: They use sex to ease tensions, make up after fights, encourage close relationships, and keep the group cooperative rather than competitive. Besides being the only known animals to French kiss, they're also the only primate besides humans to engage in mating for purposes other than procreation.

LONELY LADY LIZARDS

New Mexico whiptail lizards have no opposite sex: They're all female. They reproduce by *parthenogenesis*, meaning that their eggs require no fertilization and their offspring are all female with no male chromosomes. Yet—and here's the really strange part—whiptails still perform a mating ritual with one lizard acting like the male and the other acting like the female. The ritual stimulates whichever lizard is playing the female role to ovulate and lay eggs. Why do they act out copulation? Some scientists believe this pseudo mating encourages fertility, but they aren't sure why.

Bad news, Santa: One reindeer subspecies, the arctic reindeer, is already extinct.

RESEARCH SHOWS...

...that we live in a very interesting—
and often really weird—world.

GO AHEAD—SMELL MY GENES

"Smelly monkeys have left scientists wondering if one way to find the partner of your dreams is to follow your nose. They have found evidence that a female mandrill monkey sniffs out a mate with different genes—and they think that we might be wired the same way. 'Mandrills are quite closely related to humans,' says Dr. Jo Setchell from Durham University's Anthropology Department.' Our results support the idea that humans might choose genetically compatible mates'...The team suggests females are using body odor to work out which males have a different genetic makeup to produce strong and healthy offspring. The scientists say the monkeys are relying on a group of genes which helps build proteins involved in the body's immune system and affects body odor by interacting with bacteria on the skin."

—SkyNews, November 2009

DOMO ARIGATO, HERR RAT-O

"Rats can tell the difference between Dutch and Japanese, suggests a new study. But it is not because some spy agency has bioengineered them to eavesdrop on conversations in Tokyo or Amsterdam. They are simply recognizing the difference in rhythmic properties of the languages, says Juan Toro, a neuroscientist at the University of Barcelona in Spain...Toro's team trained rats to recognize either Dutch or Japanese—by pressing a lever in response to a short sentence—and then exposed them to sentences they had not heard before, in both languages. They found that the rats responded significantly more often to the language they had been trained in. However, the rats could not tell the difference if the sentences were played backwards or were spoken by different people."

—*New Scientist*, January 2005

An animal epidemic is called an "epizootic."

NOT SO BIRD-BRAINED AFTER ALL

"Magpies can recognize themselves in a mirror, highlighting the mental skills of some birds and confounding the notion that self-awareness is the exclusive preserve of humans and a few higher mammals. It had been thought only chimpanzees, dolphins, and elephants shared the human ability to recognize their own bodies in a mirror. Helmut Prior, of the Institute of Psychology at Goethe University in Frankfurt, and his colleagues tested their magpies by marking the birds' bodies with a red or yellow dot that could only be seen in a mirror. They found the birds regularly scratched the mark on their body, proving they recognized the image in the mirror as themselves and not another animal. The result throws into question some basic ideas about how our brains work."

—**Reuters, August 2008**

IT POOPS, THEREFORE I AM

"Tiny snails can survive being eaten by birds—and the gastropods come out the other end perfectly healthy, a recent study says. Researchers studying feces of Japanese white-eye birds had noticed a surprising number of intact snail shells, especially of *Tornatellides boeningi*. So Shinichiro Wada, a graduate student at Tohoku University in Japan, and colleagues fed more than a hundred snails to captive white-eyes, and 55 to captive brown-eared bulbuls, another bird known to eat *T. boeningi*. The team found that roughly 15 percent of the snails passed through both bird species' guts alive. One snail even gave birth shortly after emerging—apparently unfazed by its incredible journey."

—***National Geographic Daily News*, July 2011**

* * *

NOT QUITE THE CUDDLY CHARACTER

Not one bit like his cute cartoon namesake, the Tasmanian devil lives up to his moniker. Not only do his screams strike fear in the hearts of anybody who hears him, the fierce, elusive creature smells like the carcasses of dead animals...his favorite food.

THE WORLD'S GREENEST BURGS

Dorothy had to travel to Oz to find a green city, but today, she'd be able to find one in spots all across the globe—even back home in Kansas.

GREEN POWER TO THE PEOPLE

Cities put an enormous strain on the environment: They use more than 75 percent of the world's energy and release more than 75 percent of the world's carbon dioxide and other pollutants into the environment. More than half the people on earth (over 3.5 billion) live in cities, and by 2050, that number is expected to reach 70 percent. The future could be bleak: more lung disease from more pollution, increased global warming, mountains of waste, and concrete everywhere. But the people who live in the world's greenest cities are pioneering a future that's very different.

VANCOUVER, CANADA

Population: 603,000

How green is it? Often called the greenest city in Canada, Vancouver has more than 200 parks in a region that's surrounded by spectacular beaches, forests, and mountains. The city leads the world in the production of hydropower, which supplies 90 percent of its electricity. And one of Vancouver's most famous innovations is the use of solar-powered trash-compactor bins on public sidewalks: The bins can hold five times the amount of conventional trash cans, so they need to be emptied only once a week instead of every night, which saves on the need to use the city's gas-powered fleet of garbage trucks.

Vancouver has also been adding new streetcar lines and bike lanes, and it has constructed nearly 250 miles of "greenways," special corridors for pedestrians and cyclists that connect parks, nature reserves, historic sites, neighborhoods, and shopping areas. And 40 percent of commuter and tourist day trips in Vancouver involve walking, biking, or using public transportation.

REYKJAVIK, ICELAND

Population: 120,000

How green is it? In the 1970s Iceland relied on imported coal for 75 percent of its energy. Today all of its electricity is produced from hydroelectric and geothermal power. The hydropower source is flowing water from melting ice that turns turbines to make electricity. The geothermal power uses the heat and steam of Iceland's volcanoes to do the same. The only fossil fuel the city uses is for its cars and fishing fleets.

But Icelanders even consider that to be too much: To get down to zero use of fossil fuels, Reykjavik is working on a changeover to cars and ships fueled mainly by electricity and hydrogen. In 2003 Shell opened its first hydrogen filling station in Reykjavik to service hydrogen-powered public buses. By the mid-21st century, Iceland plans to have most of its fishing fleet running on hydrogen and all of its cars and buses powered by alternative fuels.

COPENHAGEN, DENMARK

Population: 1.2 million

How green is it? Like Reykjavik, Copenhagen has been addressing environmental issues for decades. The result is that the water in its harbors and canals is so clean people actually swim in them. There are also more than 186 miles of bike paths in the metro area, and there are places where residents and tourists can borrow bikes for free. (Really.) Some major streets even have a "green wave" system so bike riders can speed through intersections without stopping—they hit timed green lights the entire way. The result is that nearly 55 percent of Copenhageners bike to work or school.

The city is already filled with parks, but plans are in the works to guarantee that by 2015 at least 90 percent of Copenhagen's population will be within walking distance of a park or beach. About 20 percent of the city's electric power comes from wind turbines, hydroelectric power, and biomass (energy from organic matter like wood, straw, and organic waste), but the goal is to stop using coal altogether. The city is encouraging residents to buy electric and hydrogen-powered cars and is investing more than $900 billion so that, by 2025, Copenhagen will have reduced its coal and oil pollution to zero.

SAN FRANCISCO, CALIFORNIA

Population: 805,000

How green is it? San Francisco was the first city in the United States to pass a mandatory recycling law, and the first to ban the use of plastic bags. Meant to lessen the amount of garbage that goes into landfills, those 2009 edicts have worked so well that San Franciscans now recycle 77 percent of their waste. (All that recycled garbage weighs about twice as much as the Golden Gate Bridge!) New laws also mean cleaner air: Public transportation runs on 20 percent biodiesel fuel (made from used cooking oil), and a green taxi law has resulted in 92 percent of the city's cabs running on alternative fuels.

Even though it's famous for its fog, San Francisco has proved that solar can work in overcast locales: The 60,000-square-foot solar system on the city's convention center generates enough electricity to power the entire center during events, and 24,000 solar panels atop a reservoir provide electricity for city buildings, including a hospital, the airport, and police and fire stations.

CURITIBA, BRAZIL

Population: 3.5 million

How green is it? Curitiba is the capital of the Paraná state in Brazil, and despite facing severe poverty and overcrowding, it consistently wins recognition as one of the most beautiful, livable, and green cities in the world. In 1968 the city had less than 10 square feet of greenery per person, but careful urban planning—minimizing urban sprawl, planting trees, and protecting local forests—has turned that into 500 square feet for each inhabitant. Curitiba now boasts 16 parks, 14 forests, and more than 1,000 green public spaces.

Curitiba is also internationally famous for its Bus Rapid Transport (BRT) system. Reliable and cheap, the BRT vehicles run as often as every 90 seconds in dedicated bus lanes. Eighty percent of the residents use the buses—that's more than two million riders a day. Also famous for its garbage disposal system, the city provides an alternative for low-income families who don't have garbage pickup: They can bring in bags of trash or recycling, and exchange them for bus tickets, food, school supplies, or toys. The result: A clean city where the poor live better and more than 70 percent of the waste is recycled.

GREENSBURG, KANSAS

Population: 900

How green is it? It's not a big city, but the small town of Greensburg still embodies the spirit of environmentalism. In May 2007 a tornado demolished 95 percent of the town. When the residents rebuilt, they decided that their new buildings would meet internationally recognized standards that would make their town as energy-efficient and environmentally friendly as possible. The winds that once almost destroyed the town now power a wind farm that provides electricity to all of Greenburg's homes and businesses. This incredible comeback has made the town a center for environmental businesses and ecotourism, and young residents who once vowed to go away to college and never come back now say there's no place like home. In 2011 *Budget Travel* magazine put Greensburg on its top 10 list of the "Coolest Small Towns in America." And we think that's pretty cool.

* * *

WHAT A COINCIDENCE

Glen Kerley was fishing off the coast of West Sussex in southern England in February 2009 when he caught a 25-pound cod. He gutted it...and found a cell phone in its belly. He took the phone's SIM card out, put it in his phone, and was able to read some of the dialed numbers. He soon got ahold of the girlfriend of Andrew Cheatle. The couple was out shopping—for a new cell phone for Andrew—because he'd lost his on the beach in West Sussex a week earlier. "I know it sounds a fishy tale," Cheatle said, "but it is 100 percent true."

MA NATURE'S HIT SQUAD

We all know that lions and wolves are fierce and deadly predators, but what about falcons...and doodlebugs?

SPEED DEMONS

Peregrine falcons are such talented killers that for centuries people have used the females (they're larger) to hunt. Falcons can spot their prey—usually a medium-sized bird—from five miles away and bear down on it faster than any other animal. They dive at speeds of more than 200 mph, striking their victims in midair with closed talons. At that speed, the blow usually means instant death...but not always. If the prey is only unconscious, the falcon quickly breaks its neck. If it's not too heavy (like one of those mid-sized birds), the falcon will carry it away. Otherwise, the peregrine will drop it to the ground and eat it where it lies.

DEADLY GANGS

Orcas (killer whales) aren't whales at all—they're the largest members of the dolphin family, and they live and hunt in family groups called pods. Nicknamed "sea wolves" (because they behave like wolves when they hunt whales), orcas separate out the weakest for killing, and different pods have developed ingenious techniques depending on their location and prey: In the Antarctic, where seals rest on ice floes, an orca pod will swim together to create huge waves that knock the seals into the water. Orcas have also been known to attack and kill great white sharks by holding them upside down until the shark loses consciousness and suffocates. And back in the 1800s, an orca pod formed a killing partnership with humans: The orcas would herd and trap baleen whales so the whalers could harpoon them. In return, the humans gave the pod the right to take the first spoils from the dead whales' carcasses.

BABY KILLERS

Doodlebugs are only half an inch long and are the larvae of adult winged antlions, which resemble dragonflies. When it comes to being killing machines, doodlebugs are brilliant engineers. The tiny insect gets its name from the winding, doodlelike trails it leaves as it looks for the best place to dig a killing pit. In sand or sandy soil, doodlebugs dig a two-inch-deep cone-shaped pit, making sure that the sides of the pit are steep so that they'll collapse if disturbed by an ant or other crawling insect. When the sides of the pit collapse, the prey falls to the bottom, where the doodle bug is waiting to eat it.

SHOCKING DEATHS

Electric eels are actually a type of knifefish. They live in the muddy rivers of South America where they can barely see, and they have to come to the surface every 10 minutes to breathe. They don't have any teeth. Instead, they stun or kill their prey with about 600 volts of electricity, about five times the shock you'd get if you were silly enough to stick your finger into a wall socket. Electric eels have been known to produce enough current to power a microwave, knock out a horse, and even kill a human. They attack their prey by discharging an electrical signal into the water or touching their prey. Just one touch from their tails can disable a human or large animal, but they mostly use this superpower to knock out fish, frogs, and small mammals before swallowing them whole.

ZOMBIE INVADERS

This may be the scariest story of all. Parasitic hairworms live and mate in freshwater, but they spend the beginnings of their little larvae lives inside of grasshoppers. Scientists aren't exactly sure how the worms get on land to infect the grasshoppers, but they suspect that when the hairworms first hatch, mosquitoes eat the microscopic larvae and carry them around until the hairworms reach adulthood. Grasshoppers eat dead mosquitoes, and that's probably how they get infected with hairworm larvae. Inside a grasshopper, a hairworm quickly grows to several times the length of its host's body as it eats everything it can of the grasshopper's insides while keeping the poor skeletal insect alive. The hairworm is also busy making proteins that take over the grasshopper's brain and nervous system to create an enslaved, zombified insect. The grasshopper, which can't swim at all, suddenly develops a suicidal compulsion to find water and dive in. As the grasshopper drowns, the worm emerges to swim away and find a mate.

Eighty-five percent of all life on earth lives in the oceans.

A WEB OF TRICKERY

"The wisdom of the spider is greater than that of all the world together."
—West African proverb

WATCH OUT FOR TRICKSTERS
Animal myths and fables appear in many cultures and have been passed down orally for thousands of years to teach life lessons and explain why nature works the way it does. One of the most common characters to appear in these stories is "the trickster," usually an animal con artist that's always trying to get something for nothing. Sometimes, these animals are tripped up by their own greed and then used as an example of how not to behave. Other times, they are considered to be brave folk heroes because they'll take on anyone—stronger animals, kings, even gods. They have a special appeal to those who are oppressed by the powerful in society and are fighting for freedom against unjust rules. Here are a few of our favorites.

ANIMAL TRICKSTER: Anansi the spider

FROM: West Africa

BACKGROUND: Some of the most universal trickster fables began in Africa with Anansi the spider, who often gets into trouble because his greed trips him up. Other times, though, he wins because he's so ruthless and clever.

ONE STORY: Long ago, all tales were about the god Nyankupon, but the spider Anansi wanted all stories to be about him. When he broached the subject with Nyankupon, the god agreed…on one condition: Anansi had to bring him a jar full of live bees, a boa constrictor, and a tiger.

The next day, Anansi set off on his quest. He took a clay pot to the bees and told them he was arguing with Nyankupon, who didn't believe that bees were capable of flying into the pot. The angry bees showed Anansi that, of course, they could fly into his pot…and then the spider sealed it up and sent it to Nyankupon.

Next, Anansi went to visit Boa Constrictor and showed the snake a long stick. He said that no one believed Boa Constrictor was as long as the stick, so the snake laid himself alongside it to prove just how long he was. Anansi quickly tied him to the stick and sent the snake to Nyankupon.

On the third day, the spider sewed up his own eye and began shouting near Tiger's house that he could now see wonderful things. When Tiger begged Anansi to help him see the wonderful things, the spider quickly sewed up Tiger's eyes and took the helpless animal to Nyankupon. Amazed at Anansi's cleverness, the god revised the world's stories so they'd all feature the spider as the main character.

ANIMAL TRICKSTER: Mouse Deer

FROM: Indonesia

BACKGROUND: A mouse-deer is a small, hoofed mammal found in Sumatra, Borneo, Malaysia, and Indonesia. In Indonesian fables, the character of Mouse Deer is humble and small, but also very cunning. Despite his size, he's never eaten by larger and more powerful enemies.

ONE STORY: One evening, Mouse Deer stole a farmer's cucumbers, so the farmer set out a trap that caught Mouse Deer. The farmer put him in a cage, and the farmer's wife began preparing a feast that would feature Mouse Deer meat. As Mouse Deer sat worried in his cage, he saw Dog and asked if he were coming to the party. Mouse Deer explained that he was the farmer's new pet and they were having a party to honor him. At first, Dog didn't believe it, because the farmer wasn't the partying type. But when Dog saw the farmer's wife busy in the kitchen, he changed his mind and wanted to be invited to share the food. Mouse Deer said Dog could come if he waited in the cage, so Dog removed the stick that kept the cage closed. As soon as Dog stepped inside, Mouse Deer bolted out of the cage and locked Dog in. When the farmer arrived, he was furious to find Dog instead of Mouse Deer and began hitting Dog, who ran off immediately.

ANIMAL TRICKSTER: Coyote

FROM: The American Southwest

BACKGROUND: The coyote appears as the chief trickster in the folklore of several Native American tribes. He possesses supernatural abilities like transformation and magic, and is considered to be responsible for bringing humans fire, daylight, and even the buffalo, which were hunted by the Native Americans for centuries.

ONE STORY: When the earth was new, a monster named Humpback imprisoned all the world's buffalo in a corral in the mountains. Humpback kept a close eye on the buffalo and hoarded their meat for himself and his son. Coyote and a group of humans sneaked up on Humpback's home on the mountain and scouted out the situation—the humans ultimately decided they were afraid of Humpback and his power. But Coyote noticed that Humpback's son had no pet. So when the group returned home, Coyote announced that he would change himself into a bird called Killdeer and go back to the mountain. Coyote flew right to Humpback's son, who took him home for a pet.

Coyote hoped to be able to get into the corral, but Humpback threw him out. So Coyote changed himself into a dog, hoping that animal would be allowed to stay. At first, Humpback yelled that he would have no mangy dog in the house, but the son held loved his new pet and refused to let Humpback harm him. Eventually, Humpback let Coyote stay…but not in the house. He put Coyote put into the corral with the buffalo. So Coyote started barking and yipping and caused a stampede. The buffalo then broke free from their corral and ran off to wander the earth… and provide meat for humans.

ANIMAL TRICKSTER: Br'er Rabbit

FROM: The American South

BACKGROUND: Africa's trickster tales traveled the New World on slave ships, where the cunning, crafty Br'er Rabbit, a hare usually dressed in oversized trousers and a work shirt, was born. He survived by his wits, not any physical power, and got the better of nearly every animal he came across.

ONE STORY: One day, Br'er Rabbit was suffering from thirst and met up with Miss Cow in a field. She'd never given him any milk, not even when he'd needed it for his sick wife, so he was pretty sure she wouldn't just give it to him now either. Thinking quickly, Br'er Rabbit chatted with Miss Cow and, after pointing out the persimmons in a nearby tree, asked her to help him knock them down. Miss Cow ran at the tree several times, but the persimmons weren't ripe and so wouldn't fall. Finally Miss Cow took such a big run that her horns got stuck in the trunk.

Br'er Rabbit promised to get help, but instead returned with his family and milk pails...and they milked Miss Cow dry. After the rabbits left to drink their milk, Miss Cow managed to free her horns from the tree, but she was so angry that in the morning she placed them back in the trunk's holes and waited. Pretty soon, Br'er Rabbit came back for more milk, and Miss Cow raced after him. Br'er Rabbit dove into the Briar Patch (where he lived), and with only his head sticking out, Miss Cow didn't recognize him. She asked if he'd seen a rabbit, and he directed her down a far-away road. She galloped off, and Br'er Rabbit laughed himself to sleep.

* * *

TWO RANDOM NATURE FACTS

• The mounds created by Australian compass termites rise out of the grass like thick tombstones that become much thinner as they reach the top. The thin tops of the mounds help the termite homes avoid blazing midday heat, while the flat fronts and backs always face north and south so that they can be warmed by a bit of the more tolerable early morning and late afternoon sunshine. The way these termites build—to take advantage of the movement of the sun—is being copied by some architects.

• The oldest known whole rocks on earth were found in northern Quebec, Canada, in 2008. Unlike regular *amphibolites*—types of metamorphic rocks—that are dark green or black, these are beige or brown and have been dubbed "faux-amphibolites." Their age has been calculated at 4.28 billion years old, and since the earth is believed to be 4.5 billion years old, these rocks may have been part of the very first crust ever formed on the planet's surface.

MORE TINY BUBBLES

On page 265, we introduced four animals that rely on bubbles for survival. We couldn't believe it, but we found four more.

BEWARE MY BUBBLES

Eastern lubber grasshoppers get their name from the fact that "lubber" means a clumsy person—and these are some of the clumsiest insects in the animal kingdom. About three inches long with red or yellow stripes, they can't fly, they're terrible jumpers, and they can't even walk fast. They do, however, have great defenses, one of the best being bubbles. The grasshoppers' bright colors tell predators that the animals are toxic to eat, and if a predator ignores that warning, there are other things the grasshoppers can do…like lift a wing, emit a loud warning hiss, and force a bubbly liquid out of their breathing holes. When the bubbles in the toxic foam pop, they release a terrible smell, and most predators, realizing they're dealing with a nasty-tasting insect, will give up before the lubber uses its other trick…and throws up on them.

THE BUBBLE BOATERS

The violet sea snail can't swim, but it still manages to spend its entire life floating in the tropical and subtropical oceans. Inside its beautiful purple shell, this happy-go-lucky drifter is pushed along by the currents and the wind…while clinging to a raft of bubbles. As soon as violet sea snails are born, they build their rafts by stirring up the water to create bubbles that they glue together and protect with mucus secretions. Then they attach themselves to the bottom of the bubble raft and float along, just beneath the water's surface, eating any tiny sea creatures that swim by. Because they're only an inch across and their shells are paper-thin, violet sea snails are light, and so their relatively sturdy rafts support them throughout their drifting lives.

BUBBLY REAL ESTATE

Spittlebugs, or "cuckoo spit," are *nymphs* (immature insects) that do their growing on the stems of plants. They pierce the stems, suck out the sap, and then excrete a liquid—through their back ends and openings in their abdomen—that they pump into bubbles. The bubble froth is a perfect home. It hides spittlebugs from predators, insulates them against heat and cold, and protects them from drying out in the sun. Plus, the slimy, bubbly froth has an acrid taste that works as extra insurance to keep predators away. Inside their foam homes, the bugs feed on their plant and molt five times, growing larger each time. When spittlebugs reach adulthood, they're a dull tan or brown and about ⅛ to ¼ inch long, with wings. They also become some of the best jumpers in the insect world—at that point, most people know them as froghoppers.

HOW TO WALK ON WATER

Water shrews live in long systems of burrows along the foliage-sheltered banks of streams and lakes. Their homes have an entrance above the water because these small (about six inches long) mammals hunt in the water for fly larvae, shrimp, and small fish. They're also excellent swimmers, assisted by the air bubbles that get trapped in their thick fur and help to buoy them up. Their feet and tails are fringed with long, stiff, bristly hairs that have two functions: They help the shrews to swim by pushing the water aside, and—on the animal's feet—trap bubbles between the hairs. These bubbles are so buoyant that they keep the water shrew's feet at the surface so the animal can actually run across the surface of the water.

* * *

ANOTHER REAL POLICE REPORT

Rock Hill, Missouri: Police were informed by a resident on Raritan Drive that an area family was taking over the minds of local dogs and turning them against their owners. Police were advised that the only way to protect the pooches was to install a force-field on their heads when going outside. Police responded.

MORE FEATHER FACTS

On page 32, we started talking about some of the amazing properties of bird feathers. Here's the rest of the story.

WHAT THE WELL-DRESSED BIRD IS WEARING

Birds are among the most colorful animals on earth—due to their feathers, of course. Most feathers are colored by pigment in their keratin. Black, gray, and brown feathers are tinted with melanin that birds naturally produce in their bodies. Yellow, red, and orange pigments in feathers are produced by carotenoids in the foods birds eat. The color blue in feathers is different because it's created by the structure of the feathers: Blue feathers have microscopic pockets of air that reflect and scatter light so that our eyes see the blue end of the spectrum. Green feathers can be a mix of the structurally created blue and pigment-created yellow. The colors worn by the bird kingdom's best-dressed bird—the peacock—are produced by thin layers of keratin that reflect light to create iridescence like the colors in a soap bubble.

THE HEIGHT OF FASHION

These intricate, colorful feathers help a bird do what no machine has ever been able to duplicate—they can take off, soar, dive, and land with instantaneous, lightning-fast speed.

• Birds have specialized contour feathers, called *flight feathers*, the longest, stiffest, strongest feathers on a bird. Flight feathers on birds' wings are different from other feathers because they have one vane that's more narrow than the other. The shape allows wing feathers to cut through the air with less resistance, or drag. And the long, stiff flight feathers on the tail provide stability.

• A bird's wings are covered with contour feathers, which—along with a number of flight feathers—create a slick, smooth surface and an airfoil shape (like the wing of an airplane). As a bird flaps its wings, air flows quickly and evenly over the top of the wing as the air underneath moves slowly. This creates lower air pressure above the wing and higher air pressure beneath it, a combination that lifts the bird upward when it takes off and helps thrust it forward in flight.

• The strength of its stiff, strong flight feathers supports the airborne bird. A bird can also move each of its feathers independently using tiny muscles in the skin, and the feathers on the wing can bend into aerodynamic shapes that reduce drag or deflect air to propel the bird in flight. Flight feathers on the tail move in various directions like a rudder to help steer birds through the air.

PRACTICAL FASHION

Feathers have many other functions besides flight:

• Down feathers do such a good job providing insulation that birds can keep their body temperature at about 104°F in all kinds of climates. Even penguins manage to maintain their body temperature in Antarctica's subzero climate.

• Feathers also help in the quest for food. An owl's wings have fluffy feathers on their undersides, and the edges of their flight feathers are fringed so that they don't disturb the air, both of which help the owl fly silently and swoop down on unsuspecting prey.

• There's a reason that most female birds have feathers in dull shades of tan and brown—it's a version of camouflage that makes them hard to see when they're sitting on their nests (which, by the way, are often lined with feathers). Males, on the other hand, sport brightly colored feathers so they can show off during mating season and impress the ladies.

• Finally, our kudos go to the Namaqua sandgrouse for one of nature's most creative uses of feathers. This super dad lives in Africa's Kalahari Desert. To get water to his baby chicks, he flies to a water hole—as far as 50 miles away—and each belly feather soaks up eight times its weight in water. Then he flies back to the nest so the chicks can drink the water from his feathers.

* * *

The whistling swan, found all over North America, can have as many as 25,000 feathers during winter, more than any other bird.

MORE Q & A

Thinking about domesticating a zebra for your next horse show? This might make you think again.

WHY ARE THERE 24 HOURS IN A DAY?

A. Thank the ancient Egyptians, the first people known to divide up day and night. According to them, days generally lasted 10 hours (longer in summer), and nights were 12 hours (shorter in summer). There were also two "twilight hours," one at dawn and another at dusk.

Q. WHY CAN'T SOME ANIMALS BE DOMESTICATED?

A. First we should probably explain what "domesticated" means. A domesticated animal is one that has been bred over time to be used to having humans around and to possess the traits humans like best. All dogs are descendants of wild wolves, for example, but your Morkipoo or black Lab was selectively bred over thousands of years to preserve its human-friendly qualities (like being house-trained) and get rid of the undesirable ones (like attacking people as prey). This is not the same as a tame animal, which is one that has become so acclimated to humans that it isn't threatened and can even be taught to do tricks or act in movies. Bart, a Kodiak brown bear that appeared in films like *White Fang* (1991) and *Legends of the Fall* (1994), was tame but not domesticated.

Of all the animal species on the planet, humans have managed to domesticate only a few of them. Why? Author and scientist Jared Diamond suggests that it's because an animal can be successfully domesticated only if it meets the following criteria:

1. Has a flexible diet: The animals can't be too picky, and they have to be able to survive on cheap, accessible food (so it's easy for humans to feed them).

2. Has a fast growth rate: The animals must grow quickly enough that their human herders will see a return on their investment.

3. Is easy to breed: The animals have to procreate easily under the conditions where humans keep them.

4. Is easy to get along with: Horses are naturally more gentle than zebras, which have a reputation for being vicious. That's why domestication succeeded with horses but failed with zebras.

5. Doesn't panic: Lots of animals will freak out when they're corralled or restrained. Cows, however, are pretty easygoing, so they were not difficult to domesticate.

6. Adheres to a social hierarchy: Domestication works only if the humans are in charge. Solitary animals like grizzly bears don't go for that.

Q. WHY DO STARS TWINKLE?

A. Stars are huge, like our sun, which is also a star. But because they're so far away, they look small to our eyes. (Okay, maybe that part's obvious.) But when the light from those distant suns reaches us, it bumps into the gases, dust, salt, water vapor, and other things that make up the earth's atmosphere. Those things, plus distortions caused by the light traveling millions of light years through open space, are always briefly getting in the way of the light's path from the stars to our eyes. So it looks like they twinkle. In space, though, where there's no atmosphere, the stars appear as steady streams of light that don't twinkle at all.

Q. WHY DON'T THE OCEANS FREEZE IN WINTER?

A. One reason is that they're always moving. The oceans contain huge amounts of water that are in constant motion—they rarely ever sit still long enough to freeze. Plus, water from warmer oceans is always flowing into the colder ones and changing the temperatures. Another reason is that the oceans are full of salt, which has a lower freezing point than water.

There are two exceptions, however. At the North and South Poles, the ocean does freeze. The surface of the Arctic Ocean at the North Pole, for instance, freezes 10 to 15 feet down, insulating the water beneath it and keeping it from freezing completely.

* * *

Earliest known reptile: Hylonomus, which looked like a modern lizard, lived about 312 million years ago.

THE STORY OF BATS

No, not Joey "Bats" Scigliani, Uncle John's best friend growing up in New Jersey, but bats, you know, those flying things.

Evolutionary biologists believe that bats first appeared on earth between 70 and 100 million years ago, having evolved from gliding, shrewlike insectivores.

• Around 50 million years ago, the earth went through a warming period, creating conditions in which insects thrived...along with their most voracious predators—bats. It was around this time, scientists believe, that bats acquired *echolocation*: the ability to navigate—and hunt and capture flying insects—in complete darkness using their unique sonar system. This is believed to have first occurred in what is now North America.

• The ability to fly gave bats a distinct advantage over other mammals. It made it easier for them to move to new territories, and because of this, bats began to spread farther and farther around the planet, diversifying into many different species as they did.

• Roughly 35 million years ago, bats in tropical regions began eating fruit, rather than insects. You don't need sonar to find fruit—so these bats lost their echolocation abilities. They also started foraging during the day and sleeping at night. Many also became much larger than their insect-eating cousins.

• All bat species that exist today are descended from either these small, echolocating insect-eaters, or the large, non-echolocating fruit-eaters. These are the two great bat suborders: Microchiroptera, or microbats; and Megachiroptera, or megabats. The names are somewhat deceiving—some megabats are smaller than some microbats, but generally, megabats are the larger of the two.

• Bats of both orders continued to diversify. Today there are 1,240 species total—that's about a fifth of all known mammal species. Just 186 of them are the fruit-eating megabats.

• Exceptions to the no-sonar fruit bat rule: The Egyptian fruit bat (*Rousettus aegyptiacus*), along with just a few other species in the same genus, use echolocation, but they don't use it to hunt. They're fruit-eaters that use it only for navigation.

• Today bats live everywhere on earth except for the Arctic, on Antarctica, and on some remote oceanic islands.

• As bats diversified into more species, their behavior changed drastically—especially regarding diet. About 70 percent of all bats eat insects, and most of those catch them in flight.

• Several fruit bat species also eat flower nectar, which they lap up with long tongues, like hummingbirds. There are also several carnivorous bat species, all of them echolocating microbats. These capture and eat frogs, lizards, other bats—some even eat birds, catching them in flight.

• One species, *Myotis vivesi*, found around the Gulf of California, catches and eats fish and crabs right out of the water, grabbing them with the very long, sharp-clawed toes of their feet.

• Three bat species have adapted to survive on nothing but blood. These are, of course, the vampire bats, and they're found from Mexico to South America. The common vampire bat feeds on the blood of mammals such as tapirs and domesticated livestock, whereas the other two species—the white-winged vampire bat and the hairy-legged vampire bat—drink the blood of birds.

• The world's smallest bat is the Kitti's hog-nosed bat, also called the bumblebee bat, native to Thailand and Burma. It measures just 1⅓ inches in length, with a wingspan of about 6 inches. The largest bat is the Giant golden-crowned flying fox, native to the Philippines. It's about 13 inches long, with a wingspan of more than 4 feet.

• Bracken Cave located near San Antonio, Texas, is home to a colony of approximately 20 million (some estimates say 40 million) Mexican free-tailed bats. It is not only the largest bat colony in the world—it is the largest natural collection of any mammal in existence (aside from human cities).

DISASTER PREP 101

Do you know what to do when the weather gets wild? Uncle John to the rescue!

TORNADO!

How to prepare: If you live in a tornado-prone area, make sure you know where to go if one might be coming your way. If you've got a basement, that's the best place to be. Have a radio, batteries, medical supplies, and food stocked there. The second-best place is a ground-floor windowless room, closet, or hallway far from heavy objects. If a tornado warning is issued, watch for signs of a funnel cloud. Just beforehand, the sky may turn green, you may see an approaching cloud of debris, or the storm could suddenly become eerily still and quiet. If you hear what sounds like an approaching freight train or airplane, that means a tornado is close.

What to do during: If you're in a building, move away from windows. Go to your safe zone and hunker down under some sturdy furniture, or climb into the bathtub and pull a mattress over you. If you're driving and see a twister far away, you might dodge it by making right-angle turns away from it—tornadoes are less likely to move in that direction. But if a funnel cloud comes near your car or mobile home—get out! Both can be easily blown around by tornado winds, some of which have topped 300 miles per hour. If you're stuck outdoors, it's safest to lie facedown in a low area or a ditch, away from trees. Protect your head and neck with your hands.

EARTHQUAKE!

How to prepare: Though earthquakes are more common in California than in other places in the U.S., nearly all 50 states are at risk for them. All households should have an emergency survival kit in a heavy-duty airtight container by the front or back door. Pack a pair of shoes and toiletries (the most commonly forgotten items) and at least three days' worth of food, water, and supplies. It's also important to scope out the safest place in your house or office, as well as a safe zone in every room. Experts no longer recommend standing in a doorway during an earthquake. The best place will be far from windows, glass, and heavy objects that might fall. That might mean standing against an interior wall.

What to do during: If there's time before the shaking gets serious, go to your closest safe spot, drop to the ground (preferably under a heavy desk), and protect your head. If you're in bed, stay there and hold a pillow over your head. Most injuries occur when people try to run outside or to another room, so stay put! If an earthquake hits while you're driving, stop the car away from power lines, trees, and overpasses, and stay there. Tremors last only a minute or so, but beware of aftershocks over the next few hours and days.

HABOOB!

How to prepare: If you've never heard of one of these, you probably don't live in the American Southwest. The word may sound a little funny, but there's nothing amusing about a *haboob* (Arabic for "strong wind"). Dangerously strong windstorms that can generate a wall of dust up to two miles high and 50 miles wide, they don't happen only in the Arabian desert; they also hit the arid and semiarid regions of Australia, Arizona, New Mexico, and Texas. When weather reports say a haboob is coming, be prepared for winds over 60 miles an hour, falling trees, power outages, and flight delays. And as always in the desert, have extra water at home and in your car at all times.

What to do during: The best defense in a haboob is to stay inside a building, with the windows and doors shut tight. If you get caught on the road, turn your car's air conditioner to "recirculate" to avoid breathing dust. There might be lots of tumbleweeds in the road, but don't go out of your way to swerve around them; they look mean but they crumble easily when hit. Visibility will likely be reduced—sometimes to near-zero—from the dust and heavy rain that may accompany a haboob. At that point, pull over and turn off the lights. Set the emergency brake and take your foot off the brake pedal (these storms can be disorienting, and you don't want your lights to serve as beacons for other vehicles that might follow you onto the shoulder and hit you). It's safest to stay in a car or building until the storm passes. If you're caught outside, cover your face as best you can, try not to breathe in too much dust, and seek shelter.

TSUNAMI!

How to prepare: Unlike many other natural disasters, this one comes fast—and with very little warning. A tsunami (from Japanese for "harbor wave") is a giant wave that comes as part of a series of waves triggered by an earthquake on the ocean floor. Often, the quake happens too far off the coast to be detected. But if you're near the beach when you feel tremors, follow the advice for earthquakes above, then immediately head for higher ground. There might not be time for the authorities to issue a warning, so you're on your own here. One surefire sign of an impending tsunami is when the ocean suddenly recedes dramatically from its usual level, exposing ground that's usually underwater even during low tide. But that doesn't always happen—sometimes there's no sign at all.

What to do during: It is imperative to evacuate the coast before a tsunami arrives, or at least take shelter on the topmost floor of a reinforced concrete building. The wall of water can reach 100 feet high and speed along at hundreds of miles an hour. Big tsunami waves travel far inland. The deadliest tsunami on record crossed the Indian Ocean in 2004 and drowned more than 230,000. There isn't much you can do if you get caught in one, except hang on to something stationary and keep your head above water. Be prepared for several waves, with subsequent waves often larger and stronger than the first.

* * *

KISS KISS!

Chagas disease is transmitted to humans by insects known as "kissing bugs," commonly found in the American Southwest. The bugs are nighttime bloodsuckers that commonly bite the faces of sleeping humans. How do kissing bugs spread the disease? By dropping their feces right in the bites they make on your face (which are often near the eyes or mouth). Tiny parasites in the droppings make their way into your bloodstream and infect you. Sweet dreams!

NATURAL NAMES

Everyone wants their child's name to be special. How about something that honors the natural world?

Aidzig: young deer (Armenian)

Aihe: dolphin (Maori)

Flora: flower (Latin)

Aeniera: snow (Welsh)

Hokulele: shooting star (Hawaiian)

Ren: water lily (Japanese)

Ashley: ash wood (English)

Gimli: fire (Norse)

Balarka: rising sun (Sanskrit)

Conall: wolf (Irish/Scottish)

Betoto: owl (Swahili)

Deniz: sea or ocean (Turkish)

Bustan: orchard (Aramaic)

Cerise: cherry (French)

Chaga: goat (Sanskrit)

Chandran: shining moon (Indian)

Citali: star (Aztec)

Aurora: dawn (Latin)

Colombina: little dove (Italian)

Dorcia: deer, gazelle (Greek)

Mesi: water (African)

Fiala: violets (Czech)

Alon: oak (Hebrew)

Gajaraja: king of the elephants (Sanskrit)

Genesee: beautiful valley (Native American)

Guido: forest (German)

Haupuehuehu: snowflake (Hawaiian)

Jacintha: hyacinth (Dutch)

Jessamyn: jasmine (Persian)

Chi: twigs or branches (Vietnamese)

Drake: dragon (Middle English)

Ria: river (Spanish)

YOU'LL NEVER SEE A TASMANIAN TIGER

These animals roamed the earth for millions of years but, in fairly recent times, disappeared forever. Your parents or grandparents might have seen some of them but—sorry!—you never will.

ANIMAL: Dodo
LIFE STORY: Most people have heard of the dodo bird, but most of them haven't heard the *whole* story. The dodo lived only on Mauritius, a remote island in the Indian Ocean. Geological evidence shows that Mauritius was formed by volcanic activity about 8 million years ago, and eventually became lushly vegetated. When a species of Asian pigeon started migrating there, some of them decided to stay. Over millions of years, the pigeons evolved into the dodo: a grayish bird about three feet tall and weighing as much as 50 pounds, with short yellow legs, a long and stout beak, and tiny wings no longer suitable for flying. With no predators and abundant food, the dodos felt free to roam the island and build unprotected nests right on the ground.
GONE: In 1598 Dutch explorers started using Mauritius as a stopover on their way to points farther east and south, becoming some of the first humans in history to ever see the dodo. Over the next decades dodos were hunted to some degree, but were, fortunately for them, considered not particularly tasty. Unfortunately for them, the Dutch introduced animals like rats and pigs to the island, so the unprotected dodo eggs and chicks didn't stand a chance. Exactly when they went extinct is unknown, but by the 1680s the dodo was gone forever.

ANIMAL: Rodrigues solitaire
LIFE STORY: A large flightless bird like the dodo, the Rodrigues solitaire was found only on the island of Rodrigues, about 350 miles east of Mauritius. In fact, recent DNA studies of the bird's bones show it descended from dodos that left Mauritius before

Some species of moray eels have such large mouths that they cannot close them.

they lost the ability to fly. Written descriptions—and the one surviving drawing done by someone who actually saw the birds—show it looked something like the dodo, but was tan in color, had a much shorter beak, and had bony growths on each of its wings, which the males used as weapons during breeding battles.

GONE: The island of Rodrigues was colonized by the French in the 1690s. Like the dodo, the solitaire was easy to capture, but even worse, the French thought of it as a delicacy. In less than a century the solitaires were hunted to extinction.

ANIMAL: Quagga

LIFE STORY: A relative of the zebra, the quagga lived on the grasslands of what is now South Africa, unlike its black-and-white cousin, whose territory extends much father north. It differed from the zebra by being brown instead of white (except for its legs and tail) and had black stripes only on the front of its body—primarily on the neck and head. The quagga (the name comes from a native name for all zebralike animals) survived for 200,000 years or so. Once classified as its own species, recent DNA tests have proven that the quagga was a subspecies of the common zebra.

GONE: Dutch colonists began hunting the quagga for food in the 1830s, but not for themselves. They didn't like quagga meat; they killed them to feed to their servants. And kill them they did. By the 1870s, the quagga was extinct in the wild. The last living specimen died on August 12, 1883, in a zoo in Amsterdam.

ANIMAL: Thylacine, or Tasmanian tiger

LIFE STORY: First, the name: Known scientifically as the thylacine, meaning "dog-headed," and called "tiger" because it had vivid stripes on its back from about its shoulders to its tail, it was also known as the Tasmanian wolf because it looked so much like a dog. But it wasn't related to dogs (or tigers) at all; it was actually more closely related to the kangaroo, which means it was a marsupial, and like the kangaroo, it had a pouch. But unlike the kangaroo, the Tasmanian tiger was a carnivore, living off smaller marsupials and birds. It once roamed all of Australia, including the island of Tasmania, which was attached to the Australian mainland for millions of years until sea levels rose about 12,000 years ago. Fossil evidence shows that the thylacine thrived in Australia for at least 4 million years.

GONE: The thylacine disappeared from the Australian mainland more than 2,000 years ago, probably because of competition with a real dog, the dingo, which was introduced to Australia about 4,000 years ago. The dingo never made it to Tasmania, however, so the thylacine still survived in large numbers there when the British began settling the island in the 19th century. Before long the thylacine was branded a sheep killer, and ruthlessly hunted down. There were so few left by the 1920s that efforts were finally made to save them, but it was too late. The last thylacine died in a zoo in Hobart, Tasmania, on September 7, 1936.

Sad final note: Studies performed in 2011 found that the thylacine's jaws, which were very long and narrow, weren't strong enough to kill sheep. They had been killed off for no reason at all.

ANIMAL: Pyrenean ibex

LIFE STORY: The Pyrenean ibex was a mountain goat native to the Pyrenees in France and Spain, known especially for the long, thick horns that curved gently back and away from its head. It existed in large numbers until the 1400s, with some decline in the following two centuries due to loss of habitat.

GONE: As the use of firearms for hunting grew in the 18th and 19th centuries, the number of Pyrenean ibex dwindled. By 1900 there were only about 100 of them left, and far fewer by the end of the 20th century. The last of them, a 13-year-old female that scientists had named Celia and who had been captured and released with a tracking device, was found dead in the mountains in January 2000. She had been killed by a falling tree.

Extra: In 2009 a team of Spanish and French scientists announced that they had successfully cloned a Pyrenean ibex, using tissue that had been taken from Celia before her death. The resulting birth of a living clone made the Pyrenean ibex the first animal in history to be brought back from extinction through cloning. Unfortunately, it is also the only animal known to have gone extinct twice: the young animal died just seven minutes after its birth due to malformations in its lungs. No others have been successfully cloned since.

France's Oak Chapel church is built inside a living 800-year-old oak tree.

LOOK WHAT I FOUND!

From a thighbone that's thousands of years old to brand-new ways to recycle plastic, the 21st century has brought us some amazing (and weird) discoveries.

NOT TONIGHT, DEAR

The discovery: In 2009 Dr. Rachel Grant was monitoring the breeding patterns of common toads spawning at San Ruffino Lake, Italy. Suddenly, in the midst of the breeding period, 96 percent of the male toads gave up on love and hopped away. Two days later, all the toads had completely split the scene. Grant puzzled over this sudden exodus. Toads don't suddenly quit spawning, and there was no unusual weather to account for their flight. Three days later, a 6.3 magnitude earthquake struck. Its epicenter was in L'Aquila, a city about 46 miles from the lake. The toads didn't return to the lake until after the last aftershock. Then they got back to business as usual.

A real find: The L'Aquila earthquake killed 297 people—a tragedy that could have been prevented if scientists had been able to predict the coming disaster. NASA scientists began working with Grant to find out if there were some kind of signal before and during the earthquake that made the toads leave the area.

The team discovered that underground rocks subjected to pressure (like that of a coming earthquake) release charged particles that reach the air and ionize it with massive amounts of positive airborne ions. (Ions are atoms or molecules that have an unequal number of protons and electrons, making them volatile.) These positive airborne ions react with groundwater, turning it into chemicals like hydrogen peroxide. Hydrogen peroxide would be toxic, or at least irritating, to the toads and would explain why they left the lake. The ions also cause stress in animals, another reason the toads might abandon their mating ritual. If further research supports the theory of ionized air as an earthquake signal, toads fleeing groundwater combined with other signs of nature reacting to positive ions could help predict earthquakes in the future.

THE MAMMOTH PROJECT

The Discovery: Woolly mammoths were elephant-like animals of the Ice Age that stood 9 to 15 feet tall and had long, black shaggy fur. They appeared more than two million years ago and went extinct about 10,000 years ago.

In 2011 Russians discovered a woolly mammoth thighbone so well preserved that it contained bone marrow with apparently undamaged genetic material. In a project with scientists from Japan, the Russians want to use the bone to try to clone the extinct animal. They'll be replacing the nucleus of an egg cell from an African elephant with the nucleus of a mammoth cell that was extracted from the marrow. Then they will insert the egg into a surrogate mother, probably an elephant.

A real find: Scientists have been trying to find viable DNA from a woolly mammoth since the 1990s in the hopes of bringing the big animals back. Will it work? No one is sure, but a 2009 attempt to bring back the Pyrenean ibex (extinct for 10 years) with DNA from the animal's skin led to the cloned ibex dying from breathing difficulties within minutes of being born. Some scientists question whether cloning—a tricky process even with living species—can actually reproduce an animal that's been extinct for thousands of years. Even if the experiment is successful, they point out, the animal will have some DNA from the elephant egg and wouldn't be pure woolly mammoth. However, an excited public would still flock to see it, and a live (mostly) woolly mammoth could create interest in protecting other animals that are in danger of becoming extinct.

GATOR AID

The discovery: Scientists at McNeese State University in Louisiana have found that the state's alligators have an enviable immune system. Male alligators have vicious territorial battles that can lead to severe injuries. They live in swampy water filled with all kinds of infectious microbes, yet they usually recuperate from injuries, even the loss of a limb, and regain their health instead of succumbing to infections.

McNeese State professor Mark Merchant was curious about the gators' great healing powers. After drawing blood from alligators and exposing it to 16 strains of bacteria and viruses, including a strain of HIV, Merchant and his team found that the alligator blood killed all 16 bacteria. Human blood serum (or blood plasma, the part of the blood that doesn't include red or white blood cells or clotting agents) could take down only six. Others, including the HIV, were immune to the alligator blood. Further research showed that an alligator's immune system could also kill many types of fungi.

A real find: A growing number of diseases are developing resistance to antibiotics, and although alligator blood can't be injected into a patient to cure strep throat or AIDS, it may hold the key to new, more powerful antibiotics to fight these diseases. In particular, scientists are studying proteins called *peptides* that appear in the alligator blood. These peptides attack invading germs, and drugs are already being developed from the peptides, though they've yet to be tested in humans. In the meantime, scientists propose that the National Institute of Health in Washington, D.C., sequence the genome (basically, map the order of the long chains of nucleic acids that make up the DNA) of the alligator because a better understanding of this reptile and its mighty immune system could help us in the war against disease.

PLASTIC MUNCHIES

The discovery: In 2008 students from Yale University's Rainforest Expedition and Laboratory discovered an interesting fungus in the rain forests of Ecuador. It's called *Pestalotiopsis microspora*, and back at the Yale lab, the students discovered that the fungus has the ability to eat a type of plastic called polyurethane. The fungus can live and prosper on a steady diet of polyurethane, and it can do so in anaerobic conditions (where there's no oxygen). That means this fungus can break down polyurethane that's buried or lying under tons of garbage at the bottom of a landfill.

A real find: Polyurethane has long been a problem for landfills and because it used in millions of products and can last for generations without breaking down. But the *Pestalotiopsis microspora* discovery means that nature could finally degrade the tons of polyurethane foam and other polyurethane plastics in landfills. Conservationists also point out that this important new fungus is another reason to preserve the amazing biodiversity in Amazon rain forests.

TOE YOU SO

An anatomical discovery: In 1706 an elephant fell over and died in Dundee, Scotland, and surgeon Patrick Blair dissected it, reporting that it had six toes. Blair's dissection notes were soon corrected by later scientists who countered that elephants had only five toes along with an extra shaft of cartilage, though why that cartilage was there remained a mystery. Finally, in December 2011, researchers at the Royal Veterinary College in London announced that they'd used CT scans, dissection, and electron microscopy to solve the toe secret. It turned out that Blair was right…sort of. He'd found an elongated sesamoid bone that acts as sixth toe in elephants. In most animals and humans, a sesamoid bones give leverage to tendons (like the patella bone in the knee), but in an elephant, this digit is attached to the big toe in the middle of the fatty pad of an elephant's foot. The bone faces in the opposite direction from the other five toes, and it transfers weight from the elephant's foot into bone and ankle joints, helping the big animals balance their massive bulk.

A real find: The discovery of the sixth toe hardly matters to the elephants that use it to stand no matter what it's called. But it solved a 300-year-old mystery for scientists and helped veterinarians better understand elephant anatomy. It also gave a clue to the evolution of elephants. Their ancestors were small and lived near water. As they became land-based about 40 million years ago and were growing ever larger, they developed the toe to help them carry their weight.

*　*　*

GROOVY

Scientists believe that the first venomous organisms were *conodonts*, tiny marine creatures that looked like eels. They made their appearance hundreds of millions of years ago and became extinct during the late Triassic period, about 200 million years ago. What makes them the likeliest candidates for being the first of their kind? Most predators with toxic bites carry venom in grooves of their teeth that run from the root to the tip. The conodont is the oldest known creature to have such grooves.

THE NEED FOR SPEED

It's a hurry-up world for most humans, but animals move at their own pace.

• When it's diving, the peregrine falcon flies at speeds of up to 200 mph. When it's not diving, the bird still comes close to 65 mph.

• The cosmopolitan sailfish is the fastest creature in water, speeding along at about 70 mph.

• Cheetahs are the fastest animals on land, hitting a maximum speed of more than 65 mph in short bursts. Coming in a close second: the pronghorn deer, at just under 53 mph.

• A lion can run short distances at about 50 mph.

• Sauropods, an order of dinosaurs that includes the Brachiosaurus, could weigh up to 100 tons and lumbered along at about nine feet per second—that's a little more than 6 mph.

• Coyotes and dogs can run 40 to 45 mph at their fastest.

• On land, the giant tortoise moves at just 0.13 mph, but it can swim a lot faster: about 22 mph.

• That symbol of slowness, the sloth, usually moves at just 0.08 mph. It can take a sloth an entire day to climb down from a tree.

• An elephant would probably lose a race to a rhino—elephants can generally run 25 mph, but rhinos are capable of speeds of up to 40 mph.

• The black mamba slithers along at 12 mph, which makes it the fastest snake around.

• The common vampire bat runs at speeds of about three feet...per second.

• Camel spiders can move at a speed of up to 12 mph.

• Some New World vultures beat their wings in flight once per second; that's the slowest wing beat of any bird.

• The slowest creature in the world is the slug, which cruises (sluggishly) along at 0.03 mph.

• Gibbons are capable of *brachiating* (swinging from tree limb to tree limb) at speeds up to 35 mph.

Chickens run at about 9 mph.

MORE BEAR FACTS

On page 101, we gave you "Da Bears," the story of bears all the way back to when they first split from their canine cousins around 20 million years ago. Here are a few more unbearably mind-blowing tidbits...about bears.

• Bears deep in the wild are active any time of the day or night. But near civilization, they've adapted and are considered *crepuscular*—mostly active at dawn or dusk.

• A female bear is called a *sow*. A male bear is a *boar*. And a group of bears is a *sleuth* (or *sloth*).

• Common bear myth: "Bears have an incredibly powerful sense of smell, but they can't see very well." This is hogwash. Bears can see at least as well as humans during the day, and much better at night. Like many animals, the back of bears' eyes are coated with a membrane called the *tapetum lucidum*, which reflects light and greatly enhances night vision.

• If you spot a bear too close to town in Churchill, on the shores of Hudson Bay in the far north of Manitoba, Canada, you're advised to call a special number. The bear will be tranquilized and put in the "Polar Bear Jail," an old airplane hangar outside town—until it can be flown away and dropped off far from civilization.

• The Hindi word for bear is *bhalu*—and that was the inspiration for Rudyard Kipling's bear character Baloo in *The Jungle Book*.

• When sloth bear cubs are ready to leave their birth cave at about seven weeks old, they (there are usually two of them) ride on their mother's back to and from feeding grounds—and even up into trees. They do this for the first six months of their lives. Sloth bears are the only bears that carry cubs this way.

•"Bile bears" are Asiatic black bears that are kept in captivity in Asia, often in horrible conditions, so that bile can be extracted from their bodies. Bile is a digestive enzyme produced in the liver and stored in the gallbladder of mammals, and bears happen to produce a whole lot of it. It's been used in traditional Chinese medicine for ages, as a cure for a number of ailments, from rheumatism to erectile dysfunction. It contains a chemical compound called *ursodeoxycholic acid* (UDCA), which has been shown to reduce cholesterol levels, and is even effective against some liver ailments. UDCA is also made artificially by pharmaceutical companies today, but the caging of bile bears is still a big problem for the extremely endangered species.

• Most bears are really bad hunters. That's because they have short backs and short, very thickly muscled back legs—meaning they're built for strength, not speed (although they can reach 30 mph per hour in bursts). That's one reason bears eat so much vegetation and fruit. The only exception to this rule is the polar bear, which evolved into a ruthless and very capable predator.

• A bit larger than a house cat, the red panda is a mammal that lives in trees in a region overlapping the giant panda's. It's neither a panda nor a bear—red pandas are closely related to raccoons. It does eat bamboo, though (and small mammals, eggs, and berries).

• Countries where brown bears can be found in the wild: Norway, Sweden, Finland, Estonia, Belarus, Latvia, Russia, Romania, Ukraine, Slovakia, Poland, Czech Republic, Bosnia and Herzegovina, Croatia, Slovenia, Greece, Macedonia, Albania, Austria, Italy, Bulgaria, Spain, France, Turkey, Georgia, Azerbaijan, Syria, Iraq, Iran, Turkmenistan, Kazakhstan, Uzbekistan, Tajikistan, Kyrgyzstan, Afghanistan, Pakistan, India, China, Mongolia, North Korea, South Korea, Japan, United States, and Canada.

• In 1975 a cave was discovered in Romania's Apuseni Mountains. In it were the fossilized remains of cave bears, a species related to brown bears (and a bit larger) that went extinct about 27,000 years ago. They're so named because most of their fossils have been found in caves. The Romanian cave was nearly a mile long and included 140 fossilized cave bear skeletons. Evidence suggests all the bears were in the cave alive at the same time—when a landslide closed the cave opening. They starved to death...but not before they'd done their best to eat each other. Most of the bones show signs of damage from teeth and claws.

• During the Middle Ages, fossilized bones of cave bears were believed to be the bones of dragons.

Male and female cobras work together to guard their eggs.

MISCENATURALLANEOUS

You can read more random, totally not-related-in-any-way stories—except that they all concern something very weird from the wild world of nature—in another article with this exact same made-up title on page 275.

HE LICKED A TURTLE'S EYEBALLS

In 2008 Calvin "Clicker" Embry was at a Fourth of July celebration in of his hometown of Wayne City, Illinois, when he grabbed a snapping turtle from the back of his truck and prepared to show a crowd of people his unique talent: turtle hypnosis. Embry was a turtle hunter and had performed the trick many times over the years. He rubbed the reptile's belly, which, he explained to the crowd, puts turtles to sleep. "I can usually kiss him on the snout, then lick their eyeballs before they wake up," he said later, "but something went really wrong." What was it? The turtle woke up...and latched its jaws onto Embry's tongue just as he was going to lick its eyeballs. A friend finally got the turtle off by working a knife around in its jaws, and Embry went to the hospital. He's still missing a piece of his tongue today.

TOAD GO "BOOM"

In 2005 more than 1,000 toads exploded over the course of a few days around a pond in Hamburg, Germany. According to witnesses, the toads would swell up as if a gas were being injected into their bodies, eventually reaching three times their normal size, before exploding in a sticky mess more then six feet in diameter. Scientists were baffled. Some said it must be a virus; others that the toads were committing suicide by explosion. (Although those last ones might not have been *real* scientists.) A vet examined the exploded toad corpses—and was surprised to find their livers missing. That led to the conclusion that a recent influx of crows to the area was behind the bizarre phenomenon: crows are known to peck their way through the skin of living toads to pluck out their livers—the only parts of toads, apparently, that crows find tasty. After enduring this unwelcome procedure, experts explained, the toads must have employed their normal defensive move of making themselves look larger than they actually are by inflating their lungs and puffing themselves up. But without their livers, which normally help hold their lungs in place, the toads simply kept expanding until they exploded.

TOAD TESTS

In the 1930s British zoologist and weird experimenter Lancelot Thomas Hogben introduced to the world his latest achievement: A surefire pregnancy test for women. How did it work? You injected a woman's urine into a female African clawed toad. If the toad laid eggs within the next 12 hours—the woman was pregnant. If not—she wasn't. The test worked, he explained, because hormones present in the urine of pregnant women are similar to hormones found in female African clawed toads. It was such a surefire test (with the added bonus that it didn't kill the frogs—they could be used for the test again and again) that the African clawed toad pregnancy test was the most popular pregnancy test in the world for decades—and was even in use up until the 1960s, when more modern, less *toady* tests were finally invented.

OH DEER

Tom Satre, 60, was skippering his 62-foot *Alaska Quest* charter boat near Juneau, Alaska, in October 2010 when his sister, Sharon Kelly, spotted something odd: Four deer swimming straight for the boat. Weirder: When the deer arrived, they started circling the boat. Figuring the deer had been chased into the water by wolves, Satre opened up the boat's back gate—and he and Kelly helped the animals scamper onboard. The four, all young bucks, collapsed, and spent the trip back to harbor lying in the back of the boat, shivering. When they arrived at shore, three of the deer quickly jumped onto the dock and disappeared into the nearby forest. The fourth, which Kelly said seemed to be suffering from hypothermia, needed a bit of massaging and coaxing. But it was soon up and gone, too. Satre told reporters later, "My daughter, Anna, and son, Tim, helped the last buck to its feet. Anna later told me that the experience was something that she would never forget—and I suspect the deer felt the same way."

MASTERS OF DISGUISE

Some animals are masterful at using their appearance, movements, sounds, and even smells to pretend to be something they're not...all to get a meal, a place to live, find love—and, of course, not be somebody's dinner.

WANNA BEES

In 1861 Henry Bates became one of the first naturalists to investigate a particular type of mimicry. He discovered that, among the butterflies he'd collected in the Amazon, the normal butterflies imitated the bright colors and patterns of the unpalatable and poisonous butterflies that the birds refused to eat. Today, it's called "Batesian mimicry" when a tasty, harmless animal tries to avoid being eaten by imitating a dangerous or unpalatable one. Take the bee fly, for instance. Birds love to eat flies, but for obvious reasons, they don't eat bees because they might get stung. The bee fly is just a stingless fly, but it's tough to tell that at a glance: It's hairy like a bee and has a similar coloring. It imitates the bee's hovering movements, too, using its long, thin tongue, or proboscis, to feed on flower nectar like a bee. It even buzzes like a bee.

THE SNEAKY GUY GETS THE GIRL

The side-blotched lizard of the Pacific coast has a complicated and competitive love life that scientists have described as a "rock-paper-scissors" mating competition. The mating game involves three varieties of male side-blotched lizards—orange-throated, blue-throated, and yellow-throated—each of which has a different mating strategy. Orange lizards are aggressors that defend large territories and a large harem of females; they fight the blue lizards to take their females. Blue lizards have fewer females, but after mating they stay around and form lasting bonds; they guard their females even at the expense of conquering more territory. The yellow lizards are sneaky types that don't collect either females or territory, but when they're in the mating game they mimic female lizards. By pretending to be females, they avoid the blues (who are busy guarding their females anyway) and sneak into the orange lizard's harem. While the orange lizard is busy watching out for invaders, the little yellow-throated intruders mate with his neglected females. Once the deed is done, the yellows sneak away, and the orange-throated lizard is none the wiser.

EYES IN THE BACKS OF THEIR HEADS

Predators that try to sneak up behind the tiny (6¾ inches tall) pygmy owl are startled to see two wide-open eyes staring back at them. The "eyes" are really black feathers on the back of the pygmy owl's head, but they look so real that most predators give up and go elsewhere. African scops owls are about the same size as pygmy owls, but they rely on a different sort of camouflage: Their grayish coloring helps them blend in with tree bark. Not only that—they can also stretch their bodies to look thinner and then sway, which makes them look like a tree branch waving in the wind. But maybe the best of the small owl mimics are the burrowing owl chicks that mimic the sound of rattlesnakes to scare off predators.

ROYAL IMPOSTORS

Imagine being able to move into a palace, pretend to be the real ruler, and trick everyone into giving you the royal treatment. Curious? Meet the mountain alcon blue caterpillar, whose body is covered with a waxy coating of chemicals that mimic those of ant larvae. Soon after it hatches, the caterpillar drops to the ground and waits for a parade of ants to pass by. The ants pick up on the caterpillar's mimicking chemicals with their antennae and carry the trickster home thinking it's one of their own. Once the mountain alcon blue is inside the ant nest, it gets the same treatment a queen would: great food and the best TLC the ant world has to offer. In fact, if the colony is short of food, the ants will actually feed their own larvae to the intruder. Why? Because the mountain alcon blue also mimics the raspy sounds that an ant queen makes. It's not until the caterpillar becomes a butterfly that the ants finally realize they've been duped and go on the attack. That's when the con artist makes a quick getaway.

NOW YOU SEA IT, NOW YOU DON'T

How good is the mimic octopus of Indonesia? Possibly the best on the planet. A second or so is all it takes for this small brown-and-white octopus to change its color, shape, and skin texture. As it propels itself through the water looking for its own dinner—small fish, crabs, or worms—it mimics various venomous or dangerous sea creatures to protect itself.

When it needs to look like a lionfish, it hovers and spreads its arms wide while letting them trail in the water like a lionfish's venom-tipped rays. Or it might let its arms droop delicately down to resemble a poisonous jellyfish. To imitate a poisonous flatfish, the octopus pulls its arms together, flattens out, and undulates though the water like a flatfish does. And it's smart enough to mimic the creature that would best get it out of trouble. When it wants to scare away an aggressive damselfish, it will bury all but two of its long arms in the sand and change color so that its arms, suddenly banded with gold and black, look like two swimming sea snakes—the damselfish's worst enemy. Not surprisingly, this brainiac octopus also knows how to mimic a crab, and when another crab shows up looking for a mate, the mimic octopus eats it.

* * *

WHO NEEDS WEATHERMEN?

Before satellite photos and Doppler radar, people relied on nature to predict the weather. One instrument they used was the weather stick. Invented by North America's Abenaki Indians, it's just a slender, 16-inch-long, barkless branch from a balsam fir tree. It works like this: You nail the weather stick to a protected outside wall (like on a porch) so that it protrudes horizontally and parallel to the ground. When the weather is dry, the stick curls up. When rain is on the way, the stick bends toward the ground. It's what meteorologists call a *hygrometer*—an instrument that predicts storms by measuring moisture in the air.

What makes a weather stick react this way? Due to the way that balsam trees grow, some branches' cells are more compressed than others. Compressed cells react more to moisture and dryness than regular cells. Weather sticks have compressed cells on their top side, and when these absorb a lot of moisture (right before a rain), they make the top of the stick longer than the bottom. That forces the stick to curl down. When the weather is dry, the top cells dry out and shrink faster than the bottom, making the bottom of the stick longer and pushing it up.

The right whale got its name because it was considered the "right" whale to hunt.

THE FELINE-AVIAN WAR

One of the most epic conflicts of our time is taking place right now. It pits cats against birds...and cat lovers against bird lovers.

BYE-BYE, BIRDIE

The setting: A suburban backyard. A small flock of starlings vie for a spot on a suet block that hangs from a limb. On the ground below, opportunistic dark-eyed juncos hop around, quickly eating the seeds that have fallen in the garden.

But there is a predator lurking.

Slinking low beneath a nearby shrub, a tabby cat inches closer, her tail twitching with excitement. Then—as a distracted junco pauses to ponder a seed that it has dropped—the tabby strikes! With lightning speed, her front paws pin the fluttering junco to the ground. The other birds scatter. With one well-placed bite, the tabby fatally wounds the junco. Biting again, she tears off the little bird's head...and then triumphantly carries the "trophy" to her owner's back door.

DRAWING UP THE BATTLE LINES

That gruesome scene is playing out in yards everywhere—as well as in fields, parks, alleys, and even on the balconies of high-rise apartment buildings. The domesticated cat has had a profound impact on the world's sparrows, warblers, swallows, and other small songbirds. But what exactly is that impact? The numbers are hotly contested, and emotions run high. Making it really confusing: It's nearly impossible to count all the songbirds and cats in the world, especially because many of the cats are strays. And determining exactly how many bird deaths are due to cat predation is even more difficult. That being said, here's a rundown of what each side says, and what part you may play in the Feline-Avian War.

MEET THE FLOCKERS

The leading avian advocate is the American Bird Conservancy (ABC), a nonprofit organization formed in 1994. They report that domestic cats kill roughly 100 million songbirds annually in the United States alone. Worldwide, that number is estimated to be

Approximately 40,000 people are bitten by cats in the U.S. each year.

between 500 million and 1 billion per year. ABC senior policy adviser Steve Homer states that cats are having "population-level effects" on birds: "About a third of the birds in the U.S. are in decline, and cats have been identified as one of the more significant factors in this decline." ABC says that house cats are primarily responsible for at least 33 avian extinctions since the 1600s. The National Audubon Society adds, "Cats kill not only birds that visit our backyards, such as the eastern towhee, American goldfinch, and song sparrow, but also WatchList species such as the snowy plover, wood thrush, and black-throated blue warbler, and endangered species such as the least tern and piping plover."

As such, scientists have classified house cats as an invasive species, meaning that their mere presence throws the natural ecosystem out of balance. Songbirds are crucial to the survival of countless plant species as well as other wildlife because they spread seeds and keep pesky insect populations at bay. Also, they're an important food staple for natural predators. ABC and Audubon even claim that cats are adding to the negative effects of climate change. How? As the world warms, insects' numbers will grow. With fewer birds to eat them, the bug problem could get out of control.

MAN-MADE MONSTERS

But is little Fluffy really destroying the planet? And even if she is, whose fault is it? Bird advocates place the blame squarely on humans. Domestic cats did not exist in large numbers until our ancestors in Egypt tamed wild cats several thousand years ago (which is actually a very brief time biologically). Since then, humans have been breeding house cats to become lean, mean hunting machines. Historically, the cats' primary targets were mice and rats (whose numbers are doing just fine, in case you were wondering). But the birds have proven to be the collateral damage. Wild songbirds, for the most part, have not adapted to outwit clever kitties. Before house cats came along, the songbirds' fiercest predators were snakes and larger birds of prey. Today, house cats pose a much larger threat than anything wild.

As you might expect, classifying house cats as ruthless killers has made cat lovers' fur stand on end. Their rebuttal: Cats aren't even as big of a threat to wild songbirds as buildings are. Each

Mudpuppies are the only salamanders that make sound—a doglike barking.

year, hundreds of millions of songbirds meet their end by flying into plate-glass windows. Add to that the bird deaths attributed to cars, airplanes, power lines, and wind turbines, and that number climbs to more than a billion—every year. But even those menaces aren't the greatest threat to birds. What is? Habitat loss due to human encroachment. That, say cat advocates, is more to blame than cats for the 33 recent avian extinctions.

THE CLAWS COME OUT

The posturing and accusations flung about from both sides can get downright nasty. Cat lovers accuse bird lovers of skewing data to make cats look worse than they are. Case in point: In 2010 scientists at the Smithsonian Conservation Biology Institute tagged 69 catbird fledglings and observed them at three suburban parks over a few months. Their findings: "Predation caused 79 percent of the deaths of juvenile gray catbirds." Forty-seven percent of those were attributed to domestic cats. After the report was released in March 2011, cat advocates came out in full force to repudiate it. Cat activist and columnist Peter J. Wolf wrote, "The people responsible are far more interested in making scapegoats out of the cats than they are in any rigorous scientific inquiry." Basically, say Wolf and other critics, the researchers' numbers are way off. They point out that only six cat attacks were actually witnessed by the scientists, and that the rest of the dead birds were more likely killed by raccoons or owls.

According to a 2011 *Mother Jones* article by Kiera Butler titled "Are Cats Bad for the Environment?" scientists have actually been threatened for presenting findings that put cats in a bad light. Butler wrote, "In 2005 research by Stan Temple, an emeritus professor of wildlife biology at the University of Wisconsin–Madison, was cited by a panel that proposed studying cats' impact on birds in that state. In response, he received several death threats. 'You cat-murdering bastard,' one activist wrote...'I declare open season on Stan Temple!'"

STRAY CAT STRUT

What makes this such a fiery topic is that if the bird people get their way, a lot of cats will have to die. And if the cat people get *their* way, a lot more birds will die. But is it really that simple?

Of 350 species of eucalyptus, koalas can digest only 20, and prefer just five.

Before we go any further, it's important to understand that the war on cats is being fought on two fronts—against outdoor cats that have warm homes to sleep in at night, and against cats that don't.

The numbers vary, but stray and feral cats have been deemed even more harmful to bird populations than pet cats. What's the difference between stray and feral? A stray cat once had a home from which it was ejected or ran away. A feral cat was born free, but its feline ancestors had homes.

There are hundreds of millions of these houseless house cats roaming the world, and it's more than the birds' welfare that is at stake. Feral and stray cats threaten natural predators by stealing their food sources. They can also spread germs and disease…and not just to wildlife. Health officials at the Center for Disease Control are concerned that feral cats can pose a health hazard to humans due to the spread of rabies and a parasitic disease called *toxoplasmosis*.

QUALITY OF LIFE

The debate heats up even more when it comes to how to deal with all these strays. Most bird advocates say euthanize them. That notion is justified by the claim that, according to the American Bird Conservancy, strays "lead short, miserable lives." By that notion, killing them is doing them a favor. Strays certainly do have it tougher than their cared-for kitty counterparts—facing daily dangers from speeding cars, malicious humans, dogs, coyotes, foxes, wild cats, birds of prey, and the aforementioned diseases.

But even with these shorter lives—which some research posits is less than half the life span of pet cats (about 12 to 15 years)—each feral cat will take down hundreds, if not thousands, of little creatures in its five or six years. What these free-roaming cats eat varies greatly by region, but on average, about 70 percent of their wild diet consists of small mammals, about 20 percent is birds, and the remaining 10 percent is reptiles, amphibians, and insects. On some islands, birds make up nearly 100 percent of the feral cats' diet.

THE BIG FIX

The cat lovers dispute this "short, miserable" notion about ferals' lives, but they do concede that these cats need our help. There are three alternatives to killing feral cats: Leave them alone so nature can take its course, adopt them, or spay and neuter them to keep the population in check. Because the cats are not a natural part of the ecosystem, it's unwise and almost impossible to just ignore them. It's also impossible to adopt them all (as a walk through just about any animal shelter will prove).

The third solution—fixing them—is more realistic. There are about 250 feral cat advocacy groups in the United States pushing for this solution. The biggest player is Alley Cat Allies (ACA), founded in 1990 by Louise Holton (who prior to that had studied cheetahs in Africa). "It is not ethical to protect one innocent animal by doing something cruel and inhumane to another," says Holton. "Lethal control of cats cannot be ethically justified. Birth control and altering human behavior are both proven methods of humane control that work. Alien, exotic, feral, or invasive species of animals—whatever you choose to call them—are just as much the victims of human greed, neglect, and ignorance."

CANNED CONSPIRACY

To make this matter even murkier, there's another big player in the Feline-Avian War: pet food companies. In Kiera Butler's *Mother Jones* article, she reports that feral cat groups have "enjoyed generous grants from cat food vendors like PetSmart and Petco." Business-wise, it makes sense: More people feeding stray cats means more pet food sales. And this is a multibillion-dollar industry that isn't about to give up on a major slice of its market. Does that mean feral cat protection groups are in the pockets of the pet food companies? The accusations are certainly out there, and money does flow. But Holton and her contemporaries maintain that they have one goal in mind, and it isn't to sell pet food.

HERE KITTY, KITTY...

One cat-saving method you may have heard about is called Trap-Neuter-Return, or TNR. It's been put into place in several U.S. cities, including San Francisco, Miami, and Chicago, and many more cities are considering it. Here's how TNR works:

- Humane traps are placed among feral cat colonies.

• Captured kitties are taken to a vet to be spayed or neutered. Most are given rabies shots; some are given other vaccinations.

• The cat is then returned to the wild. (Its ear is also tagged so trappers won't capture it again.)

The effectiveness of TNR depends largely on who is presenting the findings. The cat people say it is working great. Alley-Cat-Allies points to many success stories, including an 11-year study on a Florida college campus: "At the end of the study, the [feral cat] population had decreased by 66 percent."

The American Bird Conservancy doesn't agree: For the practice to actually start to reduce the feral cat population, they claim that 71 percent of the world's free-roaming cats would have to be captured and fixed. That adds up to tens of millions of cats at cost of about $100 per cat, all paid for by the cities where the animals live. That's a pretty tough sell in harsh economic times, especially in lieu of a recent conclusion by the American Veterinary Medical Association that fixing feral and stray cats will have virtually no impact on their overall numbers.

There is one other possible solution: a drug that will sterilize feral cats through ingestion. One big problem: No such drug exists, and researchers aren't even close to discovering it. But the Oregon-based Alliance for Contraception in Cats and Dogs has teamed up with orthopedic surgeon Gary Michelson, who made a fortune inventing medical devices. Michelson founded a nonprofit group in 2005 to help end America's feral cat (and dog) overpopulation and has offered a $25 million award called the Michelson Prize to anyone who does manage to synthesize an edible pet prophylactic. So far, no takers.

TIME TO COME IN

So how do bird-admiring cat owners go about living with the fact they may be subsidizing a killer? The solution for outdoor pet cats, obviously, is to bring them inside and keep them there. (Too bad cats don't really do leashes.) That's the main goal of ABC's Cats Indoors! campaign. The group contends that indoor cats are much healthier, safer, and do not pose a threat to wildlife.

However, if you take a walk through just about any neighborhood, you'll see that the human custom of owning outdoor cats

Only black-and-white North American mammals: porcupines and skunks.

isn't likely to go away anytime soon. It's one thing to raise an indoor cat from kittenhood to stay inside, but to adopt a stray and then try to keep it inside is much more difficult, if not impossible. That being said, there are a few things you can do to help reduce the effects of this very serious and complicated problem:

• Spay and neuter your pets, whether they're indoor or outdoor.

• Don't feed stray cats. This may seem illogical: If you feed a stray, doesn't that mean it will kill fewer birds? Not necessarily. Studies show that the hunting instinct is independent of hunger. Stray cats should be dealt with just like other wild animals. Game officials are pretty clear on this one: Keep your food inside. (Besides, cats won't be the only animals coming to your yard for the free meal.)

• If there is a TNR program where you live, you can report stray cat sightings, and someone will come and take the animals and fix them.

• Put a bell on your cat's collar. That might give its potential prey an extra second of warning. However, ABC argues that this trick doesn't work that well. Why? Birds have thus far not adapted to perceive a ringing bell as a threat.

• If you want to let your cat go outside, but don't want it to kill birds (and you have a lot of money), construct an enclosure that keeps your cat in the yard, but doesn't allow birds to fly in.

• Conversely, if you want to create a cat-free bird zone, build a fence that keeps the cats out but lets the birds in.

• There are a few cat repellents that you can buy, including oil of mustard (*allyl isothiocyanate*), citronella, citrus oil, eucalyptus oil, geranium oil, lavender oil, lemongrass oil, menthol, and even nicotine. These work to varying degrees.

• Other ways to keep cats out of your yard: Get a dog, or install motion-activated sprinklers to get the feline hunter all wet.

• Can you train a cat *not* to kill? No. Cats are biological predators. If they are outside, they will hunt…and then present to you the carcass as if you were a Mafia kingpin they hoped to impress. No wonder birds are so afraid of us.

The skin of a newborn naked mole rat is transparent—you can see its organs.

CREEPY-CRAWLY QUOTES

Bugs instill thoughts in us that—like them—are both profound and silly.

"If you think you're too small to be effective, you've never been in bed with a mosquito."

—**Betty Reese**

"When I was five years old, I saw an insect that had been eaten by ants and of which nothing remained except the shell. Through the holes in its anatomy one could see the sky. Every time I wish to attain purity I look at the sky through the flesh."

—**Salvador Dalí**

"The ant is knowing and wise, but he doesn't know enough to take a vacation."

—**Clarence Day**

"If you step on people in this life, you're going to come back as a cockroach."

—**Willie Davis**

"I always felt that insects are the general rule, and everything else is a special case."

—**Paul Bystrak**

"The butterfly counts not months but moments, and has time enough."

—**Rabindranath Tagore**

"In nature there is no evil, only an abundance of horror: the plagues and the blights and the ants and the maggots."

—**Isak Dinesen**

"I ate a bug once. It was flying around me. I was trying to get it away. It went right in my mouth. It was so gross!"

—**Hilary Duff**

"Human knowledge will be erased from the archives of the world before we possess the last word that a gnat has to say to us."

—**Henri Fabre**

"We hope that, when the insects take over the world, they will remember with gratitude how we took them on all our picnics."

—**Bill Vaughan**

"So, naturalists observe,
a flea has smaller fleas that
on him prey; and these have
smaller still to bite 'em;
and so proceed ad infinitum."

—**Jonathan Swift**

A single acre of the Amazon rain forest may house 3.5 million ants.

WORDS GENETICISTS USE

It's amazing how much you can find out about a subject just by learning its terminology. (Like Uncle John says: "If you know what 'gas pedal' means, you've pretty much mastered the art of driving!") So here are some important terms from the study of DNA, heredity, evolution, and other things "geney"...to help get you up to speed.

Adaptation: Term used to describe the process by which an organism changes—structurally, functionally, or otherwise—via natural selection, with the result of making the organism better suited to its environment. The process by which we acquired our opposable thumbs is an example. Also used to describe the result, i.e., our thumbs are adaptations.

Allele: One of two or more different versions of a gene found in the same place on a chromosome and having the same function. For example, the gene for hair color in humans is located at a specific spot on a specific chromosome, but different alleles of that gene result in many different hair colors.

Amino acid: Chemical compound found in cells. Of the many different amino acids, 20 are especially important as the building blocks of proteins. Those 20 can be linked together in long chains—in a variety of sequences—to form the millions of different proteins important to all cell functions. Our cells naturally construct 11 of the 20—the rest we get from food.

Base sequence: There are just four different chemical "pieces" that link together end to end to form the chainlike molecule known as DNA. Known as *nucleotide bases*, they are: adenine (A), guanine (G), cytosine (C), and thymine (T). The base sequence is the order in which they link up. One section of DNA might start "TTCTAAAGTC," another might start "AAAGCATTGG," and so on. Determining the exact sequence is essential in identifying different genes and learning their functions.

Cell: Fundamental structural unit of all living things, most basically defined by being encased in a membrane that allows for a regulated inner environment suitable for proper cell functions, along with the presence of DNA to govern those functions.

Chromosome: A molecule of DNA, in the form found in the nuclei of eukaryotic cells. In humans there are 23 pairs of chromosomes—one of each pair comes from each of our parents.

DNA (deoxyribonucleic acid): The chainlike molecule found in all living cells that is the source of the chemical instructions by which cells and organisms reproduce, pass on inheritable information to offspring, and function throughout their lives.

Eukaryotes: The more advanced of the two types of cells found in all living things. Meaning essentially "good nucleus," eukaryotic cells are defined by having DNA in the form of chromosomes contained inside a well-defined nucleus. These cells are found in all organisms in the four kingdoms of life, a classification system that breaks things down into animals, plants, fungi, and protists, which are any organisms (like protozoa or algae) that aren't plants, animals, or fungi. (*See* prokaryotes.)

Evolution: The process by which populations of living organisms change over successive generations through inheritance of continually changing traits, those changes being caused by genetic mutation, hence their inheritability.

Gene: A segment of DNA found in a specific location on a chromosome and having specific genetic functions.

Gene expression: The process by which a gene performs its function, most commonly via the production of proteins that then act as messengers of sorts inside cells. Also, in all cells, some genes are "turned on" and others "turned off." This is controlled chemically. The "on" cells are expressed; the "off" cells are repressed.

Genome: The entire genetic makeup of a given organism. The human genome, for example, is different from the mouse genome, and both are different from the banana genome.

Junk DNA: Portions of DNA for which no function has yet been determined. Roughly 98.5 percent of human DNA is junk DNA.

Marker: A tiny section of DNA with a unique and known base sequence with a known location on a specific chromosome. Markers are used in a variety of ways. If one is located in or near a gene known to cause a genetic disease, for example, it can be used to determine if that disease has been passed on to children.

...A. They can only breathe through their noses.

Phylogenetics: The study of the relationship between different organisms through evolution.

Prokaryotes: The more primitive of the two cell types. Meaning basically "before nucleus," prokaryotic cells are defined by their lack of a nucleus: Their DNA is in the form of one ring-shaped molecule that simply floats around inside the cells. Prokaryotic cells are found in just two kingdoms of life: Bacteria and Archaea. (*See* eukaryotes.)

Proteins: Molecules made up of chains of amino acids that are the means by which DNA transmits its instructions regarding cell function. Proteins are actually copies of the molecular makeup of genes or sections of genes, and are distributed throughout cells in order to carry out those instructions via chemical interactions.

RNA (ribonucleic acid): Molecular compound very similar to DNA that DNA uses to create (or *synthesize*) proteins.

Speciation: The process by which new species arise through natural selection.

Trait: An observable characteristic of an organism as determined by that organism's genotype.

Transformation: The process by which sections of DNA are incorporated into the DNA of another. (Transformation occurs naturally in some species of bacteria. It can also be done artificially in laboratories.)

Variation: The physical differences among individuals within a given population of the same species as a result of the presence of different alleles. (For example, the difference in size and fur color in a given population of wolves.)

Zebrafish: A small, tropical freshwater fish popular with geneticists. Zebrafish develop quickly—from embryo to larvae in just three days—and they're transparent, meaning their development can be easily observed. Geneticists can alter an embryo genetically (chemically inducing specific genes to turn on or off, or removing or adding genes from other organisms) and see the effect in days. (You can buy zebrafish in different fluorescent hues; this has been accomplished by inserting genes responsible for fluorescence extracted from luminescent jellyfish into zebrafish embryos.)

Lead was one of the first metals used by humans, dating back to about 6500 BC.

THE TENREC'S TALKING QUILLS

And a few other stories about some remarkable animal sounds, how they're made, and, in one case, what they do to the genes of the little ladies that hear them.

TENREC QUILLS

In 2011 a BBC film crew ventured far into a rain forest on the island nation of Madagascar and got close-up video of the back of a tenrec—a pointy-nosed little mammal covered in long quills that looks like a cross between a shrew and a hedgehog. The shot they got was of a group of very short, specialized quills on the tenrec's back, which the tenrec obligingly rubbed together, producing high-pitched noises—so high that they can't be heard by the human ear. (The crew recorded the sounds with the kind of devices used to record the ultrasonic echolocation noise produced by bats.) More than that: It was clear that the tenrecs were using the sounds to communicate with one another. The production of sound in this way, by rubbing body parts together, is known as *stridulation*, and it's most famously done by insects like crickets and cicadas. The BBC filming of the tenrecs was the first time mammals have been filmed producing sound via stridulation. And tenrecs are the only mammal known to use the technique.

MANAKIN FEATHERS

The club-winged manakin is a small redheaded bird of the order Passeriformes, also known as the "perching birds" (the sparrow is in this same group), native to the northern Andes Mountains in South America. If you're ever lucky enough to observe one, you might see the little bird thrust its head down while simultaneously thrusting its wings straight up behind its head and vibrating them. And you'll probably be shocked to hear a loud, very clear, and high tone like a violin note. The club-wing's ability to do this has been known for ages, but it's been just in the last few years that ornithol-

Kiwis are the only birds that hunt using their sense of smell.

ogists have determined how the birds are able to produce the sounds. They do it through use of very specialized wing feathers. Each of the birds' wings has one feather with several ridges on its shaft. Next to each of these feathers is another feather, each with a stiff tip section. When the manakin lifts its wings up, it rubs those feathers over the ridges of its neighbors incredibly quickly—more than 100 times a second. The result is that, through acoustic properties too complicated to go into here, the frequencies of the sound produced pile up and multiply, resulting in the very pure musical tone the manakin is known for. The unique call is used by male club-wings to attract mates, and females appear to prefer the males that can make the loudest of these sounds.

Bonus: The club-wing and a few other manakin species are the only birds in the world known to produce sound via stridulation, although the club-wing's is by far the most musical. One of its cousins, the white-bearded manakin, produces a sound like a firecracker, or a whole string of firecrackers, going off, all through the use of its specially adapted feathers.

SNAKE CLOACAL POPPING

"Cloacal popping" is a polite, scientific way of saying "farting." And two species of snakes, the Sonoran coral snake and the western hook-nosed snake, both natives of the American Southwest and Mexican northwest, can use their cloacas—their all-purpose anal openings—to produce popping sounds. (They actually sound like high, squeaky human farts.) Luckily for us, and humanity in general, herpetologists have studied the farting snakes extensively, and determined that they produce the sounds manually, by contracting muscles to force air out of their cloacas. The only theory herpetologists have been able to come up with for why the snakes do this is that, since both snakes live in the same region, and do it only when threatened, it must be used as a defense mechanism against a similar predator. (How this might work is unknown—maybe the farting sounds just frighten a predator for long enough for the farting snake to escape.)

Bonus: Studies have shown that the western hook-nosed snake produces louder snake farts than the Sonoran coral snake. The hook-nosed's fart can exceed 70 decibels...about as loud as the average TV show.

Myth-information: A fish's growth is in no way affected by the size of its tank.

FRUIT FLY GENES

In October 2011 scientists at the University of St. Andrews in Scotland made an unexpected discovery: The mating song of a male fruit fly activates the genes in female fruit flies. They were able to make the discovery because not only has the DNA sequence of the fruit fly been completely mapped, geneticists even know what each specific gene within that sequence does. Armed with this new knowledge, the researchers were able to play recordings of male fruit fly mating songs—a deep, throaty song produced by the males' wings—to females, then study their genes. Which genes did they find activated by the males' love songs? The ones that boost the females' immune systems. This makes sense, since fruit fly mating is not always a nice business for females: Males often stab the females right through their abdomens to deliver their sperm, and females can be infected with disease or even killed during sex. So the immune system boost—turned on by a love song—is a plus.

EXTRA

• In June 2011 a team of European scientists announced they had determined that the water boatman was the loudest aquatic insect in the world. The tiny bugs, just two millimeters long, can produce a sound measuring 99 decibels—as loud as an orchestra heard from the front row. The aquatic boatman produces the sound, the team said, through stridulation…in this case by rubbing its penis against its abdomen.

• The male oyster toadfish makes a call like a foghorn to attract mates. It produces the sound by vibrating special muscles attached to its swim bladder, a gas-filled organ that lets fish control their bouyancy. The muscles vibrate at more than 200 times a second, making them the most rapidly contracting muscles known to science. One oyster toadfish call can last as long as an hour.

• Tiger moths are known to produce ultrasonic clicking sounds through the use of special *tymbal organs* on their bodies. In 2009 scientists in North Carolina put the tiger moths and one of their chief predators, brown bats, together in a special chamber fitted with ultrasonic detectors. The scientists found that the tiger moths produced their ultrasonic clicks when a bat approached—and in doing so "jammed" the bat's sonar, thereby thwarting an attack.

HOW TO "GO" OUTDOORS

Because sometimes Uncle John is "Wild" John—and Wild John knows how to treat the outdoors right.

BACKGROUND

You're probably aware that when you're out camping, backpacking, riding a wild river, or on some other kind of outdoor adventure, it's not a good idea to do your "business" in the same spot where you're going to be cooking dinner or pitching your tent...for obvious reasons. And there are other reasons, such as keeping a likely spot for future campers clean, and more importantly, not contaminating water sources. And if you think just your little old poop won't hurt anything? Well, what if the other millions of people who go camping every year thought the same thing? Could make for a lot of *crappy* adventures in the future.

For those reasons, there are recommended ways of properly disposing of your feces and urine. It's pretty simple, and it makes a big difference.

1. Choose a spot. Find a location at least 200 feet from your camp (or anybody else's); from any roads or trails—human or animal—that you can locate; and from any water, including lakes, ponds, swamps, rivers, or creeks—no matter how small they are. (The average adult step is about 2½ feet—so take about 80 steps to measure 200 feet.) You also want to ensure that you have not chosen an area that will drain into any water the next time it rains. And if you're staying in the area more than one night—remember where you went. You don't want to use the same area twice, and you want to keep all the spots you use as far away from each other as possible.

2. Dig a hole. Use a shovel, garden spade, stick, or whatever works, and dig what is called a *cathole*—because it's similar to the hole a cat digs when it does its business. But don't just dig any old hole. You want your feces to end up in the topsoil, the rich, loose soil at the surface, and not in the subsoil, the harder, denser soil deeper down. That's because topsoil is teeming with creatures such as worms and grubs that feed on decaying organic matter—including animal poop. (Subsoil is made up primarily of minerals, and is not home to large amounts of poop-eating critters.) Almost as soon as you make your "deposit," a multitude of creatures will begin devouring it and, in the process, begin turning it into more nutrient-rich topsoil. To ensure that you stay in the topsoil layer, dig down just 6 to 8 inches. And make the cathole just big enough—or about 4 inches in diameter.

2. Save the soil. Don't throw the soil everywhere as you dig. Place it right next to the hole, and keep the top section—the part with plants and roots attached—separate from the loose soil.

3. Do that thing you do... We're pretty sure you can handle this part, but there's an extra: Several environmental organizations say that after you're done, you should take a stick and mix your poop up with soil in the hole, to get the decomposing process started even faster. (This, it turns out, is not for everyone—but do what you can.)

4. Cover up. Cover the feces with loose soil, then put the pieces with plants and roots attached on top, to disguise the hole as best you can. You can also put leaves on the top to hide it even better.

5. Do not bury toilet paper! TP must be carried out, and flushed down a toilet when you get home or to suitable facilities. (Plan ahead and bring plastic zipper bags just for this purpose.) It doesn't decompose quickly enough to be buried as shallow as poop, and the danger of it being dug up by an animal or left to surprise another hiker—maybe you!—is too great, not to mention that it could be a disease spreader. Note: Technically, you can burn used toilet paper, but that could be a fire hazard and carrying it out is the best method for dealing with it environmentally in any case. And remember—you can always use leaves or sticks instead of paper. If you do, just make sure and bury them too. (And be sure the leaves and sticks don't come from poison oak or ivy.)

6. Wash your hands! What, were you born in a barn?! Wash your hands, for goodness' sake!

EXTRAS

• Urine is actually pretty harmless stuff, so you don't need to dig a hole for it or carry it out. It is recommended, however, to pee at least 150 feet away from camps, trails, and water.

• Got a large group of people who are going to be staying at a backcountry site for a while? Some places allow you to dig a latrine, rather than a cathole, for convenience's sake. This means digging a trench about 6 feet long, and, again, 6 to 8 inches deep. Use it starting at one end, and cover deposits as they occur, topping with the top section of the topsoil just as you do with a cathole.

• Don't poop in the snow! If you're camping or hiking in snow-covered territory—plan on carrying all your poop out. It's the only way to do it in an environmentally sound way.

• In the desert? Again: plan on taking your poop home. There is generally not enough topsoil in deserts to allow for quick decomposition of feces. Tip: Poop on a flat rock, bag it, and smear what remains with a stick. This will alow the sun to kill pathogens in the feces quickly, and the wind will later scatter the harmless remains.

• Adding a little kitty litter to your poop baggie makes dealing with it—both smell-wise and texturally—a less unpleasant experience.

• Feminie hygiene products have to be bagged and carried out. They take a very long time to decompose, and burning them does not work, as they require a very hot fire to incinerate completely.

• Trouble squatting? Plant a cheek on a log. Or grab a thin but strong tree trunk with two hands for support.

• If you're in a river canyon and you can't get 200 feet way from the river, it is advised to take all feces out in bags—and to pee right in the river, as this will disperse your urine better than it would be if you peed in the dirt on shore.

* * *

Q. WHY DO BATS HANG UPSIDE DOWN?

A. Their legs are too weak to support them standing up.

A BLOOMIN' PAGE

Q. What does Uncle John have in common with a goat?
A. They both love flowers.

"It is at the edge of a petal that love waits."

—**William Carlos Williams**

"The flower is the poetry of reproduction. It is an example of the eternal seductiveness of life."

—**Jean Giraudoux**

"We inhale a flower's ardent aroma and, no matter what our ages, we feel young and nubile in a world aflame with desire."

—**Diane Ackerman**

"We can complain because rose bushes have thorns, or rejoice because thorn bushes have roses."

—**Abraham Lincoln**

"A rhododendron bud lavender-tipped. Soon a glory of blooms to clash with the cardinals and gladden the hummingbirds!"

—**Dave Beard**

"Flowers are like human beings. They thrive on a little kindness."

—**Fred Streeter**

"If you pass by the color purple in a field and don't notice it, God gets real pissed off."

—**Alice Walker**

"I perhaps owe having become a painter to flowers."

—**Claude Monet**

"To create a little flower is the labor of ages."

—**William Blake**

"Where flowers bloom so does hope."

—**Lady Bird Johnson**

"I am not a lover of lawns. Rather would I see daisies in their thousands."

—**W. H. Hudson**

"I'd rather have roses on my table than diamonds on my neck."

—**Emma Goldman**

"I've made an odd discovery. Every time I talk to a savant I feel sure that happiness is no longer a possibility. Yet when I talk with my gardener, I'm convinced of the opposite."

—**Bertrand Russell**

KILLER PROTEINS

You can't see them without a microscope, and the body's immune system can't see them at all. But they caused a panic in the 1990s. Does the phrase "mad cow disease" ring a bell?

MAD COWS AND ENGLISHMEN

In the 1990s and early 2000s, mad cow disease was front-page news in the United Kingdom. Cows infected with it lost control of their ability to do normal things—like standing up and walking. Eventually, they died. Even more scary, humans could catch a similar disease by eating contaminated beef. Mad cow was stealthy, lethal, and had a long incubation period (sometimes months or years). So even though the risk of transmission to humans was incredibly low—the organism that causes mad cow disease was found only in bovine brains and spinal tissue, so most cuts of beef, even from infected cows, were safe—it was terrifying. And it got even more scary as scientists learned more about it.

Researchers believe that mad cow disease, officially known as *bovine spongiform encephalopathy* (BSE) is caused by malformed proteins called *prions*. Cow and human bodies use hundreds of different proteins—long molecules that are precisely folded to fit certain functions, like puzzle pieces. The trouble begins when one or more prions—basically, "misfolded" proteins—enter the body and begin to turn all the normal proteins into copies of themselves. Unrecognized by the immune system, the disease eventually spreads throughout the body, including to the spine and the brain, where it does the most damage.

MAD PERSON DISEASE

In humans, the disease isn't called "mad cow" or BSE. It's known as variant Creutzfeld-Jakob disease (vCJD) because its symptoms mimic another prion disease: Creutzfeld-Jakob disease (CJD), which is 100 percent fatal and for which there are no known treatments. CJD was named for the two German neurologists who first recognized its symptoms in the 1920s. Sufferers exhibited memory loss, personality changes, and dementia, followed by muscle twitches. Once the symptoms began, the patient had about 12 months to live. Because so many other diseases have similar symptoms, CJD was difficult to diagnose and couldn't be confirmed until the victim died and an autopsy was performed. Before the 1990s, CJD mostly affected people in their late 60s, and in about 85 percent of cases, the cause of the disease was unknown.

In 1990s Britain, though, people in their 20s started presenting with CJD symptoms. After study and investigation, scientists discovered that many of the patients had eaten beef infected with the dreaded mad cow disease.

FOR WHOM THE BELL TOLLS

BSE first spread to cattle because of the practice of using animal remains in cattle feed—the theory goes that BSE jumped from sheep, where it is known as "scrapie," to cattle in this way. Once the link to vCJD was made in Britain, the government put strict regulations in place to try to stop the epidemic: 179,000 cattle died of BSE there, and an additional 4.4 million were destroyed as a precaution. About 200,000 cattle were also diagnosed worldwide, but that number wasn't nearly as high as it could have been. Measures to prevent the export of British cows in the 1990s are likely responsible for the disease mostly staying in Britain.

The human toll has been far smaller: More than 200 people have died of vCJD since the 1990s, 171 of them in the UK. Only one American was diagnosed, and she likely contracted the disease while living in England. There is still no cure for BSE or vCJD—prions can't be destroyed in meat by cooking or radiation—and since the disease can take decades to manifest, scientists believe that we likely haven't seen the end of it.

UP ALL NIGHT

The human version of mad cow disease isn't the only human prion disease, however. There are several, all of which are incredibly rare. Of these, the most bizarre is *fatal familial insomnia* (FFI), which affects fewer than 40 families worldwide. FFI is genetic—and it's dominant, which means that if one of your parents has it, you have a 50/50 chance of developing it yourself.

Like other prion diseases, it's the result of misfolded proteins that slowly and progressively kill brain cells. But unlike the others,

Fish scales are separate; reptile scales are connected in a single sheet.

the cells most affected are in the thalamus, which controls sleep. Over a period of about a year and a half, a patient's brain slowly forgets how to sleep. The symptoms vary from patient to patient, but follow a general pattern of sleeping less and less each night, which results in panic attacks, hallucinations, and loss of short-term memory and cognitive and motor skills. Sleep medications don't help. And, in the end, everyone with this disease dies of it. It is unclear whether the insomnia itself causes death, but the symptoms indicate that it might.

UNCLE PETE IS BAD TO EAT

Kuru is another prion disease that was passed from generation to generation—but not by heredity. Sometimes called "cannibal's disease," it mostly infected members of the Fore tribe on the island of Papua New Guinea, just north of Australia. Between 1957 and 1968, kuru killed 1,100 people in a tribe of 8,000. The symptoms are similar to Creutzfeld-Jakob disease: muscle twitches and an unsteady gait progressing to the complete inability to move. The illness was named "kuru" after the tribe's word for "shake." But unlike other prion diseases, there was no associated dementia. Once the symptoms appeared, death followed in six months to a year.

Eight times more women died of kuru than men, which proved to be a clue as to the cause. The Fore practiced mortuary cannibalism—in other words, they ate their dead family members. The men took the choice cuts and the women ate what was left over, including the brain, where the prions were concentrated.

Once doctors realized that cannibalism caused kuru, the Australian government and local missionaries made sure that the practice ended. By 1968 the disease was all but wiped out. Sixteen years later, a team of medical researchers at the University of California–San Francisco isolated the kuru prion...just in time to help stem the outbreak of mad cow disease in the UK.

* * *

A GROANER

Q: What do you call a snake that becomes a Canadian law officer?

A: Mountie python.

ODD ANIMAL PREGNANCIES

It's not all "Boil some water! Get some towels!" Some animals handle making babies (or not making babies) in their own unique way.

BACKGROUND

We humans tend to project our way of doing things onto other animals, and that even includes our way of reproducing: "Oh, look at the cute mommy mouse getting ready to have her little babies." And then we get upset when mommy mouse meets a new man, aborts the pregnancy, eats the fetuses, and mates with the new guy. Well, nature's a tough neighborhood. And wild animals have had to devise a complete package of strategies for dealing with the innumerable dangers they confront on a regular basis—a package so complete that it's even meant devising different and sometimes just plain bizarre pregnancy strategies. Here are a few you might find interesting.

DELAYED IMPLANTATION

This occurs in several carnivorous mammals, and is the reason these animals have surprisingly small babies. Bears, for example, have relatively long gestation periods—about eight months for the larger bear species—but give birth to remarkably tiny newborns: Polar bear and grizzly bear newborns weigh less than a pound at birth, and panda newborns weigh just three to four ounces (about the size of a stick of butter). The reason for this is that female bears have a biological safety mechanism called *delayed implantation*. In most mammals, including humans, a fertilized egg implants—attaches to the wall of the uterus—within days of fertilization. Implantation triggers the appearance and growth of a placenta and umbilical cord, through which the new embryo will be nourished. This quick implantation means the embryo will be nourished for almost the entire duration of the pregnancy. But bears don't do this. After mating, normally in midsummer, a female's fertilized egg just floats around in the uterus. When it comes time for her to hibernate, months later, the egg will finally implant—but only if the bear has eaten enough in the ensuing months. If food is scarce and the mother hasn't built up enough fat reserves for hibernation, hormonal signals cause the egg to be aborted. This ensures that cubs won't be born into an environment that can't sustain them. If there *is* enough food, and Mom's good and fat, the egg implants in November or December, and the mother gives birth during hibernation, about two months later. This relatively short development time, regardless of the long total gestation time, is why newborn bears are so tiny. Other species that employ delayed implantation include badgers, weasels, river otters, and wolverines.

DELAYED FERTILIZATION

Several bat species in colder regions of the world actually hibernate, some for up to six months each year. This creates a dilemma for reproduction: Bat young develop inside the womb for about two months—and the young must be born shortly after hibernation ends if they're going to develop and fatten up enough to make it through the following year's hibernation. Work out the timing, and that means parents would have to mate during hibernation. But they can't, because their bodies shut down almost completely during this time. So what do they do? They mate just before hibernation, but no eggs are actually fertilized. Under *delayed fertilization*, a mated female stores the sperm she receives from a male in her uterus, then, months later in the early spring, finally uses it to fertilize an egg. This means the young are born in late spring or early summer—and the youngsters have time to fatten up before the cold weather arrives again.

MARSUPIAL DELAYED IMPLANTATION

One of the chief characteristics that define marsupials is their remarkably short pregnancies. In even the largest, the red kangaroo, the period between mating and birth is only 29 to 38 days, after which a surprisingly underdeveloped fetus is born. (It's just an inch or so long—and it doesn't even have back legs yet!) The real development happens in what is a sort of "outside womb"—the famous marsupial pouch, in which the newborns attach them-

The Khasis people of India "grow" living bridges from rubber-tree roots.

selves to teats and go through their primary development period, which can last for several months. A problem arises here because a female can become pregnant almost immediately after giving birth, but she can't keep having babies every 35 days when she's already got one in her pouch! To deal with this, when a marsupial mother with a joey (that is, a baby) in her pouch mates, the fertilized egg or eggs will simply float in the uterus (pretty much like the bears) until the mother is done suckling the baby in her pouch. Then the egg will finally implant. This enables females to become pregnant again very quickly should a suckling joey die, and it's why marsupials can reproduce almost continuously. (And that's why there are roughly 25 million kangaroos in Australia...more than the country's 22 million humans.)

PREGNANCY BLOCK

This occurs in a few rodent species, including mice and some lemmings. Using the mouse as an example: If an already pregnant female comes across an unfamiliar male mouse (or even comes across just the *scent* of a strange male), she is likely to have a hormonal reaction that causes her to spontaneously abort her fetuses. The system is believed to have developed because male mice often kill and eat the young of other males as a natural part of male mouse rivalry. It's therefore more efficient energy-wise—and survival in the wild is all about using energy efficiently—for the pregnant mouse to abort her fetuses and mate with the new male, rather than waste the energy on completing the pregnancy just to watch the new guy eat the kids. Often the mother will also eat the aborted fetuses—because why would she let good food go to waste?

Bonus: The pregnancy block is also known as the "Bruce effect," after British zoologist Hilda M. Bruce, who first noted the phenomenon in 1959.

* * *

Houseflies and butterflies can taste the plants and objects on which they land using special taste sensors on their feet.

GREAT BALL OF FIRE

The earth's core is about 4,000 miles belowground. As of 2011, humans had managed to drill down a whopping...7.5 miles. Only 3992.5 to go!

CAN YOU DIG IT?

In 1864, Jules Verne wrote a science-fiction novel called *A Journey to the Center of the Earth*, in which a trio of explorers make their way to the earth's core and find prehistoric animals, poisonous gases, subterranean waterways, and other natural hazards and phenomena. Although some ideas from science fiction eventually became realities (airplanes, scuba diving, space stations, and robots, to mention a few), mankind hasn't made much progress getting to the center of the earth.

In 1970, a year after Neil Armstrong walked on the moon, the Soviet Union decided to launch a scientific voyage in the other direction. The Soviets organized the Kola Superdeep Borehole project on the Kola Peninsula in northwest Russia. Their plan was to dig deeper toward the center of the earth than anyone had ever gone before. With the core of the earth an incredible 4,000 miles belowground, Soviet scientists seemed to set their sights pretty low—they were hoping to make it at least nine miles down.

Using specially designed drills and drilling techniques, the Soviets began drilling SG-3, a borehole nine inches wide, into the ground. Progress was incredibly slow, however, and by 1989, SG-3 had reached a depth of only 7.5 miles. Then, the drillers began meeting some unexpected and overwhelming obstacles. For one, temperatures soared to 356°F. Plus, some of the rocks took on the characteristics of flowing asphalt—whenever the drill was pulled out to replace a worn drillbit, the asphaltlike rock would fill in the hole again and gum up the works.

These difficulties and a shortage of funds ended the SG-3 project. As of 2012, the project's 7.5 miles remain the deepest that humans have gone into the center of the earth.

BECOMING AN INSIDER

Since the temperatures are so high beneath the Earth—and since it's tough to dig with a melted shovel—geologists use other methods to discover what it's like in the red-hot center. One way is by measuring seismic waves, the energy waves given off during earthquakes. Seismic waves pulsate through the planet, and go faster or slower depending on the kind of rock they encounter. From the speed of seismic waves, scientists get clues about the types of rocks that make up the earth's interior.

More clues come from the magnetic fields emanating from the center of the earth, and geologists also use computer simulations and laboratory experiments to more get information. After they put all the clues together, geologists came to the conclusion that the inside of the earth is made up of three layers: the surface, the mantle, and the core.

BREAKING THE CRUST

The earth's thin surface layer is called the crust, the outermost rocky shell. The crust is mainly made up of light granite rock and it varies from about 12 miles thick under the plains to 43 miles thick under mountain ranges. On the ocean floor, the crust is made up mainly of basalt rock. Heavier than granite, the basalt crust is also much thinner, ranging from 4 to 7 miles thick.

Even though the ground beneath our feet seems solid and strong, the crust is actually pretty thin, comparatively, just a few miles of rock wrapped around a planet that's about 8,000 miles in diameter. At the very bottom of the crust is the *Mohorovicic discontinuity*, named for the Croatian seismologist Andrija Mohorovicic, who proposed it in 1909. Fortunately for us, that mouthful of a term is commonly shortened and just called the "Moho."

Discontinuities are boundaries between the earth's different levels, and the Moho is the boundary between the top two. The Soviets never reached the Moho, so it remains unseen and mysterious, but thanks to seismic waves, we do know that its temperatures can reach 1,300°F with pressure (the weight of rock against the push of gravity) of more than 4 million pounds per square foot. Those astounding numbers for heat and pressure only get greater as you move deeper into the earth.

Healthy diet: Coyotes eat fruits and vegetables, especially in the fall and winter.

MEETING THE MANTLE

Beneath the crust and Moho lies the mantle, a 1,770-mile-thick layer of rock that makes up more than three-quarters of the earth's volume. The mantle's rock is denser and heavier than the crust's. It can reach temperatures of 1,600°F in the upper mantle, and it gets more than twice as hot near the bottom. In the deepest regions, mantle rocks get so hot and soft that they can flow like warm wax.

Most people think of the earth's insides as solid and stable, but the mantle's heat currents keeps things stirred up. In a process called *convection*, the hottest rocks at the lower section of the mantle become lighter and are always rising to the surface. When they cool they get heavier, begin to sink, and the process keeps repeating itself.

There are places where red-hot, molten rocks from the mantle rise all the way to the earth's crust, break through weak spots, and come pouring out of volcanoes as lava. This gives geologists a peek at bits of rock that were once inside the earth. Lava also reveals that the hot mantle has the power to create new landmasses...like the Hawaiian Islands, whose volcano, Kiluea, is still active and spewing lava into the ocean.

ARE WE THERE YET?

Beyond the mantle is the earth's core, the least-known part of our world. It wasn't until the turn of the 19th century that geologists even began hypothesizing that the earth had a core. From seismic studies, however, scientists discovered that there was a core made up of at least two parts:

• The outer core is about 1,370 miles thick and made up mostly of iron and nickel alloy that has turned into swirling, molten metal at temperatures of about 8,000°F. Heat currents and convection keep the metal moving, and because the core is mainly iron, it generates a powerful magnetic field. From deep inside the earth, that magnetic field keeps the needle of a compass pointing north. But it's changeable—130,000 years ago a modern compass would have pointed south. That magnetic field is also crucial to life on the crust because it shields the planet from deadly cosmic rays and damaging radiation from outer space.

Many Arabian horses have one less rib and one less lumbar bone than other horse breeds.

• Finally, the center of the earth is a solid ball made up mainly of iron and is roughly the size of the moon. This is the planet's inner core, and it contains radioactive materials that are responsible for the intense heat inside the earth. The inner core burns at an estimated 10,000°F, comparable to the heat of the sun. Despite that intense heat, however, there are so many millions of pounds of pressure on the center of the earth that its atoms stay crowded together and it remains solid.

GETTING DOWN

The more scientists learn about the inside of the planet, the more obvious it becomes that actually seeing it would be incredibly difficult. A tale of traveling to the center of the earth might always remain science fiction. But scientists are determined to keep looking. In the 21st century, an international scientific partnership called the Integrated Ocean Drilling Program picked up the challenge. They're taking a Japanese drill ship equipped with six miles of drilling pipe and new drilling technology, and going out to the middle of the Pacific Ocean where the crust is thinnest "to obtain for the first time a section of the lower oceanic crust—the material lying just above the mantle." After investigating sites off Hawaii, Baja California, and Costa Rica, they hope to start heading toward that elusive Moho by 2020.

* * *

THE CRUELEST MONTH

The United States has more tornadoes than anywhere else in the world. The National Weather Service ranked April 2011 as the country's most active tornado month on record, with 753 tornadoes (592 more than the previous decade's April average of 161). The largest tornado outbreak ever recorded in the United States also occurred that month, from April 25 to 28, a four-day span that's now known as the 2011 Super Outbreak. That's when 353 tornadoes touched down in 21 states, from Texas to New York. April 27, 2011, was the worst day in history for U.S. tornado fatalities: 320 people were killed, and by the time the month was over, 364 people had been killed.

Q. What is *Microbacterium hatanonis*? A. Bacteria that live in hairspray.

OUR BACTERIAL ORIGINS

Deep inside every single cell in each of our bodies is a mysterious little pack of cellular stuff called mitochondria, which provides a service so essential that biologists describe it as central to the very existence of higher life on earth. And it just may have come to us as a bacteria.

LITTLE ORGANS

Most people remember—with various amounts of horror—those middle school science teachers who were so skilled in Boredom 101 that they could almost put you in a trance. And remember when they tried to teach you the basics of cell biology? Well, welcome back to middle school! (We're kidding...sort of.)

The most important thing you need to know first involves *organelles*. These are the subunits of cells, each with its own functions. Basically, they're the tiny "organs" of cells—hence their name. The most well known is the *nucleus*. It's the largest organelle; each cell has just one and it holds the cell's DNA. Here's another: the *ribosomes*. These are very tiny; there can be many thousands in a single cell and they basically help the DNA do its various jobs. But the organelles we're here to talk about are the *mitochondria*. These are much larger than ribosomes, but still smaller than the nucleus. There can be from one to thousands in a cell, and they're most often described as the "power plants" of cells, because it's their job to convert food into the fuel that allows cells to function.

That's all basic cell science. What's not so basic is how mitochondria ended up inside our cells in the first place.

CELL ME A STORY

Somewhere around 3.8 billion years ago, by best estimates, in the primordial sea of mishmashing elements interacting with one another in the fetid, gaseous, lightning-plagued laboratory that was the early earth, the very first life as we know it came into being. It came in the form of the very first cells. Cells are life. All life—from amoebas to mushrooms to trees to animals like us—is made up of cells.

There was already a lot of complex chemical stuff going on by this time—molecules were even doing things like replicating themselves (this was primitive, pre-cell genetic material!)—but it wasn't until molecules evolved membranes, and thereby became actual cells, that things really took off. That's because inside a cell, a tiny, sealike environment full of replicating molecules was created. More importantly, those molecules were all stuck together in one tiny spot. This meant that a chemical team of sorts was assembled inside these early cells. That led to increased complexity of chemical interactions, which led to more complex cell functions, which finally resulted in the characteristics that made those cells alive. Most significantly, they developed the ability to absorb through their membranes the nutrients they needed to survive, and to expel waste through them too. The cells also developed the ability to go through cell division, thereby creating new copies of themselves.

TALKING ABOUT AN EVOLUTION...

Those first living cells, as amazing as they were, were extremely primitive compared to later, more evolved cells. The early cells were called *prokaryotes*: primitive, single-celled organisms with very disorganized inner structures. They didn't even have organelles or a nucleus yet. Their necessary equipment—including their primitive, single, ring-shaped molecule of DNA—just kind of floated around inside the cells' liquid interior.

For the next hundreds of millions of years, the chemical teams inside those cells were very busy, and about 2 billion years ago, a new type of cell appeared: *eukaryotic* cells. They were much larger than prokaryotes—up to 100 times larger. They had well-formed organelles, and their DNA was contained within a nucleus. Plus, that DNA was no longer in a ring shape—it was now configured into several separate pieces (which we today call *chromosomes*).

These were monumental changes. Just as the presence of a membrane allowed cells themselves to become more complex and thereby develop higher functions, the presence of membranes on organelles allowed this to happen once again—only now on a much grander scale.

SPACE INVADER

Now you've got to picture this messy, wet world, with a bunch of big, complex eukaryotes, and a bunch of much smaller, primitive prokaryotes doing their business in the water, absorbing nutrients and secreting out waste.

The prokaryotes, they were primitive, yes—but they were fine. They're still around today, in fact: They're bacteria. That's right, the first living things on earth were bacteria. (They've evolved a lot themselves since then, but they're all still primitive single-celled organisms with highly disorganized inner structures.)

Now here's the weird bit: According to the best available science, about 1.5 billion years ago, one of those eukaryotic cells swallowed up some of those little bacteria...and didn't digest them. The bacteria survived inside the sealike environment of the eukaryote, and even kept dividing and making copies of themselves in there. When the big eukaryote itself divided and made copies of itself, the copies had the bacteria inside them, too. Over time, a relationship developed between the eukaryotes and the bacteria. The bacteria got all the nutrients they needed inside the cells, while being protected from the outside world. In return, the eukaryotes got their own nourishment—because the bacteria produced what turned out to be a "superfuel" for cells. So, in time, those bacteria became the permanent "power plants" of eukaryotic cells. In other words, those bacteria became mitochondria.

THE EVIDENCE

This theory of a bacterial origin of mitochondria is known as *endosymbiotic theory*. The origins of the idea go back to the 1920s, but it wasn't thoroughly addressed or widely known until 1981, when Dr. Lynn Margulis of the University of Massachusetts–Amherst wrote about it. The theory was widely ridiculed at the time—but not anymore. In the years since Margulis's paper was published, scientific progress, especially in the area of genetics, has repeatedly bolstered her theory. Some key points:

• Mitochondria have what is described as a "double-walled" outer membrane, unlike other organelles, which have single-walled membranes. That double-walled outer membrane is very similar to the outer membranes of bacteria.

• Mitochondria have their own DNA separate from the DNA found in a cell's nucleus. It is in the form of one ring-shaped molecule—the same form as that of bacterial DNA.

• Bacteria divide via a process called *binary fission*. It is a very different, more primitive process than the one used by eukaryotic cells, which is known as *mitosis*. When mitochondria undergo cell division inside cells…they do it via binary fission, like bacteria do.

CONCLUSION

The appearance of mitochondria in cells some 1.5 billion years ago led to one of the most profound transitional events in the history of life on earth. The extra energy provided by the mitochondria's "superfuel" (an enzyme known as *adenosine triphosphate*, or ATP) allowed eukaryotic cells to evolve explosively from there on out. In the next million years or so—a blink of an eye in terms of evolution—life went from primitive single-celled organisms to multicellular plants and animals. Another 500 million years after that, human beings appeared.

There is, of course, a lot more complicated science involved in all this, much more complicated than most of us nonscientists can grasp. And endosymbiotic theory is just that—a theory—so it has its detractors, but it also has very broad support among scientists today. If it's true, all this wonderful life around us—on land, in the sea, in the air—might be here because a primitive little bacteria got eaten by a cell...and decided to stay.

EXTRAS

• *Prokaryotic* means "before kernel" in Greek. The "kernel" refers to the nucleus, or, in this case, the absence of one. *Eukaryotic* means "good" or "true" kernel.

• The "symbiotic" in *endosymbiotic* means "living together," and refers to a common occurrence in nature where two or more organisms intermingle in some way, with one or both organisms getting some benefit. (A classic example is the relationship between bees and flowers, in which bees get food and flowers get pollinated.) *Endo* simply means "inside," and refers to the fact that in this case one of the participants is inside the other.

• The oldest known fossils were the remains of bacteria found in Western Australia, estimated to be about 3.4 billion years old.

Enteropneusta means "gut breathing."

• Plant cells have mitochondria, but they also have organelles called *chloroplasts* that are responsible for the process of photosynthesis, which uses energy from the sun to provide plants with food. Chloroplasts have their own DNA in the form of one ring-shaped molecule. They also divide by the process of binary fission, like mitochondria and bacteria. In fact, it's believed that chloroplasts, like mitochondria, are the descendants of bacteria that were swallowed up by early eukaryotic cells. (There are, in fact, still bacteria species that use photosynthesis).

• A parasitic bacteria called *Rickettsia prowazekii* causes typhus, a disease that has killed millions of people over the last 2,000 years. Recently, geneticists have discovered many similarities in the genes of both *Rickettsia prowazekii* and mitochondria, and believe they are closely related. (We'll leave you to ponder that irony in more depth by yourself.)

* * *

WHAT A COINCIDENCE

The day after Thanksgiving 2008, Randall Koch, on leave from the army for the holidays, was fishing with his brother and a friend on Sam Rayburn Lake in southeast Texas. Koch had just caught an eight-pound bass that had flopped around the boat, when his friend found an old high school class ring on the boat's floor. There was a name engraved inside the ring: Joe Richardson. Koch used his brother's iPhone, and searched for Joe Richardsons in the area. "We found him on the fourth or fifth call," Koch said. That night, Koch drove to Buna, Texas, in the state's northeast, and handed Joe Richardson his high school ring. He'd lost it while fishing on Sam Rayburn Lake…in 1987…21 years earlier. "We didn't actually see the ring come out of the bass's mouth," Koch stressed to reporters, "but how else could it have gotten into the boat?" That remains a fishy mystery. Woo-OOO-ooo…

A single African aardwolf can eat 105 million termites per year.

ALL THINGS GREAT AND SMALL

When "itsy-bitsy" and "humongous" aren't descriptive enough.

• The **Hercules moth** is the largest of its species, with a wingspan of 10 to 13 inches.

• The largest living creature in any category is the **blue whale** at about 100 feet long. That's more than the length of two school buses.

• The teensy **goby fish** found in the waters surrounding the Marshall Islands in Micronesia measures just a half inch as an adult.

• A **giant sequoia** that's big enough to have a name—General Sherman—is the largest living single-stem tree at 275 feet tall. The tallest tree overall is Hyperion, a **coast redwood** that measures almost 380 feet tall.

• At 18 feet long, the **king cobra** is the largest venomous snake species in the world. The longest nonvenomous snake: an **anaconda** that measured almost 30 feet long.

• The largest rodent in the world is South America's **capybara**, which grows to more than four feet long. The largest rat is from Papua New Guinea and grows to just under three feet in length.

• **Huntsman spiders** have been known to grow to the size of dinner plates (nearly 12 inches).

• The fungus ***Armillaria bulbosa*** is a single organism that extends through 37 acres of forest in the state of Michigan. Another kind of *Armillaria*, this one in eastern Oregon, has spread across some 2,000 acres of forest soil.

• The fairy fly is about 0.001 inch long.

• The **cardón cactus**, found in Mexico, is the world's largest—the tallest one measures 63 feet high.

Young hedgehogs shed their "baby" spines and grow new, permanent, "adult" spines.

WHY SO BLUE, CRATER LAKE?

Here's the story of an enormous volcano that blew its top, leaving behind one of the most beautiful, otherworldly places on earth: Crater Lake National Park—home of the planet's bluest water.

WHAT GOES UP...

Rising roughly 12,000 feet above sea level, Mount Mazama wasn't the highest of the Cascades volcanoes. Its peak fell slightly short of Mount Shasta (to the south in California) and Mount Ranier (to the north in Washington). But in terms of pure mountainous girth, Mazama was the undisputed heavyweight champion of the Pacific Northwest. For more than 400,000 years, the composite volcano grew layer by layer in spits and spurts over top of a giant subterranean magma chamber in what is today southern Oregon. Mild eruptions, lava flows, gassy vents, and glaciation created a rugged landscape marked by frequent change.

The biggest change occurred just 7,700 years ago (a mere blip on the geologic time scale). Mount Mazama erupted in spectacular fashion. Ten cubic miles of ash and lava shot 30 miles into the sky. Pyroclastic flows laid waste to entire pine forests. One lava flow carved out 40 miles of what later became the Rogue River. Ash covered the ground as far away as Nebraska. The eruption ranks as a VEI 7, or "super-colossal," on the USGS's Volcanic Explosivity Index. (The scale only goes up to 8.) Put into perspective, Mazama's eruption was 42 times stronger than Mount St. Helens' blowup in 1980. Geologists believe it to be the most violent Cascades eruption of the past million years.

...MUST COME DOWN

Because Mount Mazama was so wide, after all the lava emptied from the chamber, there was nothing left to hold up the mountain. Result: Several million tons of earth, rock, and ash collapsed into the chamber. When the dust cleared, what had been a mountain was now a mountain-sized hole. The volcanic *caldera* formed a nearly perfect circle six miles wide and 4,000 feet deep.

Over the next few centuries, the volcanic activity slowly subsided while the caldera steadily filled up with snow and rain. Crater Lake was born.

CLASH OF THE TITANS

Because the eruption occurred so recently (in terms of the earth's history), there were witnesses. The Klamath and Modoc Indians both lived nearby, and the mountain blast shook them to the core. The Klamaths' name for Mazama was *Moy-Yaina* ("Big Mountain"). According to their creation myths, living deep inside the mountain was Llao, the spirit chief of the underworld. One day, he emerged and saw a beautiful maiden named Loha wandering in the forest. Llao fell in love with Loha, but she was the chief's daughter, and rejected the hideous god. Angry, Llao sent fire and thunder from the mountain over nearby Klamath Lake. The people would have perished if not for Skell, the spirit chief of the sky. He fought on their behalf and defeated Llao. To ensure that he could never return, Skell covered Llao's lair with earth and then filled the hole with water. The Indians renamed it *Tum-sum-ne* ("Mountain with the Top Cut Off"). And Crater Lake was born.

That story was passed down for thousands of years, and for the most part, the Indians stayed away from Crater Lake (although there are stories of at least one brave explorer who ventured into the fuming caldera before it filled with water). The Indians, believing the lake to be sacred ground, also kept its existence a secret from white settlers. A group of gold prospectors finally discovered the lake by accident in 1853. Struck by its beauty, they spread the word to others. Before long, curious adventurers made the difficult journey through thick forests, across hardened lava fields, and up the steep terrain to see it for themselves.

THE FATHER OF CRATER LAKE

One such adventurer was William Gladstone Steel, who had been hearing stories of the lake's splendor ever since he was a teenager in the 1870s. Steel finally made it to the southwestern part of the rim (a spot called Discovery Point) in 1885. He was amazed: "All the ingenuity of nature seems to have been exerted to the fullest capacity to build one grand awe-inspiring temple the likes of which the world has never seen before."

The Asiatic gliding frog can glide up to 50 feet.

Rising from 1,000 to 2,000 feet above the shore, the rim of Crater Lake offers incredible views. The first sight that struck Steel (and most visitors) was the crystal-clear blue water. It was bluer than the sky. Across the lake, the vertical cliffs of the rim were also colorful, marked by towering castles of orange lava deposits, bright yellow lichen, white speckles of snow, and forests of evergreen trees. On a calm day the view is extra special: Glassy reflections on the water create abstract patterns of the shore six miles away.

Steel was also taken by Crater Lake's other prominent feature, a conical island that rises more than 700 feet out of the southwestern portion of the lake. It's also covered with volcanic rock and forests of pines, fir, and hemlock. Reminding Steel of a sorcerer's cap, he named it Wizard Island. Over time, Steel named several more of Crater Lake's features, including Llao Rock and Skell Head. And he was the one who called the ex-mountain Mazama, the name of a mountaineering club he belonged to.

A PARK IS BORN

Steel became Crater Lake's biggest advocate. He brought in tourists, scientists, surveyors, and developers. In 1886 he hired Clarence Dutton of the United States Geological Survey to measure the lake's depth. "As the visitor reaches the brink of the cliff," wrote Dutton, "he suddenly sees below him an expanse of ultramarine blue of a richness and intensity which he has probably never seen before, and will not be likely to see again." Steel and Dutton knew the lake was deep, but it wasn't until they lowered a piano wire at various points along the surface that they grasped just how deep: nearly 2,000 feet.

Steel was instrumental in convincing President Theodore Roosevelt to designate the area as the sixth U.S. national park in 1902. However, if Steel had gotten his way, there would have been a lot of development there: He wanted to build an elevator to take visitors from the top of the rim to the shore, and a bridge to Wizard Island. His colleagues at the National Park Service wanted to keep the area pristine, though, and Steel lasted only three years as Crater Lake's superintendent before he was ousted.

Today, there is minimal evidence of man's impact at the park. There's a lodge and a gift shop on the south rim, and the 33-mile-long Rim Drive blends into the landscape as it circles the lake. It

Gorillas use at least 22 vocalizations to communicate.

offers dozens of amazing viewpoints, but most of the road is closed during the long winter. Even so, the national park is open year-round, and gets about 500,000 visitors annually.

A LAKE LIKE NO OTHER

Crater Lake wears its geologic past on its sleeves. You can actually look at the inside of a sleeping volcano. Here's some of the science and superlatives of the "Gem of the Cascades."

• **That's seep.** Modern sonar readings show that Dutton was pretty close to the mark. The lowest part of the lake bed is 1,949 feet beneath the surface. That ranks Crater Lake as the deepest lake in the U.S., and the ninth deepest on earth. If the Empire State Building were lowered into the lake (not counting for water displacement), by the time the ground floor reached the bottom, the top of the spire would be 500 feet *below* the surface.

• **A perfect balance.** Most of the world's lakes are fed by streams and rivers, and drain into streams and rivers. Crater Lake does neither. It is filled solely by precipitation. (Average rainfall per year: 66 inches. Average snowfall: 44 feet.) The lake loses its water through evaporation (and to a lesser extent, by seepage into the porous rock). These processes—precipitation and evaporation—balance each other out so well at Crater Lake that the surface rises and falls only by a few feet every century. (A single drop of water's "residence time" in the lake is about 150 years.) Plus, because of Crater Lake's great depth, the surface rarely freezes.

• **I can see clearly now.** Crater Lake contains what may be the clearest, purest water known to exist. In most lakes that boast clear water, you can see about 16 feet below the surface in broad daylight. But in Crater Lake, it's possible to see to depths of more than 100 feet. The deepest scientific measurement has been 142 feet, a world record. Several factors contribute to the lake's clarity: Because no rivers run into it, no silt gets deposited. There's little pollution because of Crater Lake's remoteness (the nearest big cities—Portland, San Francisco, and Reno—are each hundreds of miles away). There are also very few organic materials or dissolved minerals in the water, and the human impact around and on the lake is minimal.

• **The blues.** How can the water be so clear—and so blue—at the same time? Actually, it's so blue *because* it's so clear…and so deep. Here's how it works: As sunlight penetrates the lake, it absorbs all the colors of visible light except for blue, which it reflects back. The deeper and clearer the water, the more blue gets reflected.

• **New growth.** Wizard Island is one of two new volcanoes that have risen out of Mazama's caldera (the other is still underwater). At barely 6,000 years old, the island is very young, yet many of the trees that grow on it are very old, some more than 800 years. There's a trail that winds through forests and large lava rocks to the top of Wizard Island's cone, which contains its own small caldera.

• **Phantom ship.** Mazama's demise unearthed some very old rock formations, including Crater Lake's other island, Phantom Ship. This spire of 400,000-year-old andesite lava was left behind by an ancient eruption. When viewed from the rim, the island looks like an old sailing ship, hence the name. The rocky spires rise 163 feet above the surface; the island itself is about 300 feet long. Clinging to the rocks are an astounding seven species of trees.

• **The old man of the lake.** More than a century ago, a large hemlock tree fell from somewhere on the rim and landed in the lake. Since then, the 30-foot-long tree has been traveling along the surface, carried by the wind, with only a few feet of its exposed, bleached trunk bobbing above the water. It's somewhat of a mystery as to why this tree—and no other—has become a floating island. Just another curiosity of Crater Lake.

• **Life will find a way.** Crater Lake might seem inhospitable—the rim is more than 7,000 feet above sea level, and most of the year it's blanketed in snow. But like all volcanic regions, it has a thriving ecosystem. The most abundant life are the mangled, windswept trees. There are also several species of colorful wildflowers that enjoy their "spring" in September due to the area's high elevation—among them Indian paintbrush, penstemon, lupine, monkey flower, and shooting star. Black bears, elk, mule deer, and bald eagles share the park with foxes, pikas, squirrels, snowshoe hares, several species of songbirds, and big, furry moths. Most surprisingly, there are rare black garter snakes that live on Wizard Island. They've adapted to blend in with the dark rocks.

• **Into Llao's domain.** There have been a few scientific expeditions—manned and unmanned—to see what lies at the bottom of Crater Lake. Scientists have learned that the area is still active—steam vents enter the water at great depths. That allows primitive life-forms to exist more than 1,000 feet below the surface, which actually receives faint bits of sunlight on clear days. But perhaps the biggest surprise came at depths of 100 to 460 feet along the lake walls—forests of moss several stories thick.

• **Gone fishin'.** Can you fish in Crater Lake? Yes, but there is just one access point to the lake itself at the bottom of a steep, mile-long trail from the rim down to Cleetwood Cove. Docked there are the only two boats allowed on the lake. Operated by the National Park Service, they take visitors to and from Wizard Island. The lake itself has no native fish, but William Gladstone Steel introduced some fish and shrimp in late 19th century. A few more stockings occurred over the next few decades, but the practice was stopped in 1941 to preserve the water's natural purity. However, some kokanee salmon and rainbow trout still live in Crater Lake. Fishing from the rocky shore of Wizard Island offers anglers one of the most exotic places on earth to cast a line. (You can also swim in Crater Lake, but the water is quite cold, rarely topping 60 degrees in the summer.)

• **Beyond the rim.** There's a lot more to the park than just the lake. One attraction is the Pumice Desert. This five-square-mile area lies just north of the rim. Small, light lava rocks—which cooled after Mazama erupted—form a layer several feet thick. Although it looks from a distance to be lifeless, there are 14 species of plants that thrive in this desert. Another incredible geological feature of Crater Lake is known as the Pinnacles—a steep river canyon full of hardened steam vents that stick up like spikes out of the sloping walls. And what would a Pacific Northwest park be without a waterfall? Vidae Falls cascades down the south side of the old mountain. Get there in late summer for the wildflower displays.

THE FUTURE OF CRATER LAKE

Will the volcano erupt again? Most likely. The constant change that shaped the region is stull in flux. What scientists don't know is how much magma—if any—still remains in the chamber, and just how much pressure is building up. Future activity is likely to happen just east of the lake, where the geologic "hot spot" now lies. What's more worrisome is the chance of a large earthquake causing landslides and huge waves on the surface. A really cataclysmic seismic event could rupture the rim wall and cause the lake to drain, creating a flood of 4.6 trillion gallons of water. But for now, Mazama remains at rest.

* * *

KNOW YOUR CASCADES

• Extending for 700 miles from northern California to British Columbia, the Cascades range makes up the North American portion of the Pacific Ring of Fire. The highest point is the peak of Mt. Rainier, at 14,411 feet above sea level.

• There are 20 major volcanoes in the Cascades. In California, Lassen Peak and Mount Shasta; in Oregon, Mount McLoughlin, Crater Lake, Mount Thielsen, Diamond Peak, Mount Bachelor, Newberry Caldera, Broken Top, Three Sisters, Belknap Shield Volcano, Mount Washington, Three-Fingered Jack, Mount Jefferson, and Mount Hood; in Washington, Mount Adams, Mount St. Helens, Mount Rainier, Glacier Peak, and Mount Baker.

• Two Cascades volcanoes have erupted in the past century—Lassen Peak in 1915, and Mount St. Helens in 1980. A few others have burped a bit. And who knows which one of the mountains will be sending forth more thunder and fire in the not-too-distant future…and what will be left behind.

• Here's a great Cascades volcanic hike: the Mount St. Helens Ape Cave Lava Tube in southern Washington. Bring a strong flashlight and a coat—it's a constant 42°F. At more than two miles, Ape Cave is the longest lava tube in the continental U.S. It formed during an eruption of Mount St. Helens...2,000 years ago.

THE LAST LIST

And now, we bid a belated good-bye to some things that you'll probably never again see in the natural world.

• **The last western black rhino** disappeared from the wild sometime in 2011. They now exist only in zoos.

• **The last breath you took** was 4 to 5 seconds ago.

• **The last major earthquake on the New Madrid fault** was a 5.5 magnitude quake that struck southern Illinois in 1968. Lying under Missouri, southern Illinois, western Tennessee, and western Kentucky, the New Madrid fault is said to be much more dangerous and unstable than any fault on North America's West Coast.

• **The last time the Mississippi River ran backward** was during a series of earthquakes along the New Madrid fault on February 7, 1812.

• **The last major eruption of Mount Vesuvius** took place from March 18 to 29, 1944. Vesuvius, you might remember, was responsible for killing thousands in the city of Pompeii in AD 79.

• **The last Caspian tiger** was spotted in the wild in 1957. Once plentiful in central and southern Asia and the Middle East, the cat was largely killed to protect livestock.

• **The last year without any rain in Death Valley** was 1953.

• **The last time that Africa's Lake Victoria ran dry** was around 12,000 BC. The second-largest lake on earth, Victoria is naturally shallow and, therefore, sensitive to climate changes. So it might run dry again.

• **The last natural (not originating in a laboratory) case of smallpox** occurred in Somalia in 1977. The World Health Assembly declared smallpox to be eradicated in 1980.

• **The last opportunity you had to hear a Bachman's warbler** was more than 20 years ago. The bird, once inhabiting an area as far south as Louisiana, as far north as Kentucky, and all over the Carolinas and Georgia, hasn't been seen since 1988.

Russian scientists use crab enzymes to treat burn victims.

ANSWERS

THE LIMONOLOGY QUIZ, PAGE 100

1. **y)** Structure of internal organs
2. **l)** Chemistry of living things
3. **q)** Distribution of life on earth
4. **v)** Plants
5. **i)** Crustaceans
6. **m)** Cells
7. **t)** Growth of organisms
8. **e)** Ecosystems
9. **a)** Insects
10. **w)** Animal behavior
11. **d)** DNA
12. **u)** Plant distribution on earth
13. **p)** Amphibians and reptiles
14. **n)** Tissues of living things
15. **z)** Fish
16. **g)** Inland waters
17. **j)** Mammals
18. **f)** Sea life
19. **b)** Microorganisms
20. **x)** Structure of organisms
21. **s)** Fungi
22. **r)** Nervous system disorders
23. **k)** Birds
24. **o)** Extinct life
25. **c)** Disease
26. **h)** Drugs and their effects

THE ANIMAL TOE QUIZ, PAGE 155

1) Four. The two middle toes are the largest, and sit at the front of the foot. These take much of a pig's weight on dry ground, whereas the outer two, which are smaller and situated behind the two main toes, come into use more so in mud.

2) 10. Unlike the three-toed sloth, whose name corresponds to the number of toes it has on *each* of its feet, the two-toed sloth has two toes on its *fore* feet only, and three toes on each of its rear feet. Bonus: Carolus Linnaeus gave these sloths their genus name, *Choloepus*, in 1758. It means "lame foot" in Latin, presumably because Linnaeus saw the presence of just two toes on the creature's front feet as a disability.

3) Two face forward and two face back. The two that face forward are the equivalent of your second and third toes. The two that face back are equivalent to your big toe and fourth toe.

Parrotfish teeth never stop growing.

4) Cormorants and boobies have *totipalmate* feet, meaning all four of the birds' toes are webbed. Ducks and geese have *palmate* feet, where only the three of the toes are webbed, and one unwebbed toe faces toward the rear.

5) The ostrich. It has one fairly enormous toe—about seven inches long, with a broad, stout nail/claw on it—and one smaller toe (on the outside of each foot), about four inches long and thinner than the big toe, with no nail whatsoever.

6) Equidae, the family that includes horses, zebras, and donkeys. Like the pigs, they are ungulates—hoofed animals—but in this case they have one large, single-toed hoof.

7) The toes are fused from the base to just before the claw—but they still have their own claws. That gives this order of marsupials one of their defining features: the appearance of having a single second toe on their hind feet…with two claws sticking out of it.

8) 26. The Milwaukee Animal Rescue Center in Greendale, Wisconsin, rescued an orange-and-white tabby named Daniel in October 2011. Daniel has a fairly common feline genetic condition called *polydactylism*, which causes the cats to grow extra toes. Daniel has two extra toes on each foot, though, which is rare. (The world record for the number of toes on a cat, according to *Guinness World Records*, is 28.) Shortly after the shelter got Daniel, owner Amy Rowell found out that her rent was about to be doubled. She decided to buy the building, and used the many-toed Daniel to help: She put out a call for donations, asking people to donate $26—$1 for each of Daniel's toes. By December, they had raised $110,000 and were on their way to a new home.

9) Eight. That means that Acanthostega was one of evolution's early attempts, you could say, at giving tetrapods digits—but it didn't work. Acanthostega's evolutionary line died out after just a few million years. When five-fingered tetrapods appeared—about 340 million years ago—it *did* work, and all surviving tetrapods today are the descendants of those early and successful five-fingered beasts.

10) Dan Aykroyd, Ashton Kutcher, and Joseph Stalin

11) One of his toes. (You didn't really expect us to say "his

Until 1997, killing a panda in China was a crime with an automatic death penalty.

spleen," did you?) Fisherman Donald Gunn lost his right thumb in an accident at sea. Surgeons at Aberdeen Royal Infirmary replaced it with the second toe from his left foot.

12) Dogs, alligators, and crocodiles

13) Two-toed sloth, three-toed sloth, three-toed skink, three-toed box turtle, Santa Cruz long-toed salamander, long-toed stint (a wading bird), short-toed snake eagle, pink-toed tarantula, Helena's stump-toed frog (it's got really short toes), and the stump-toed gecko (it's also got really short toes).

MEET THE BURROWERS, PAGE 163

1. c. Since the Middle Ages, there have been weather predictions on February 2. In Germany, a badger was used to predict the weather (if he cast a shadow, it was six more weeks of winter). As Germans immigrated to Pennsylvania in the 1800s, they substituted the groundhog. America's first official Groundhog Day was in 1886 in the town of Punxsutawney, when a cloudy day and no shadow predicted an early spring.

2. b. *Alice's Adventures in Wonderland* (1865), in which Alice falls down the rabbit hole, is set in England, where rabbits were introduced by the Romans about 2,000 years ago. The species became one of England's worst pests, and they cost the British economy about $400 million a year in damage to crops, businesses, and infrastructure.

3. a. River otters build a comfortable burrow with an entrance from the water, and a tunnel that goes to their sleeping nest. But when they're not resting, these active animals spend little time underground. They hunt fish and romp near the river, where they enjoy sliding down hills into the water, wrestling, and playing water tag.

4. d. Shakespeare used the term "shrew" to describe his fierce, ill-tempered heroine, Kate, in the comedy *The Taming of the Shrew.* (It wasn't a compliment because all species of shrews are little terrors.) Generally the size of a mouse and sometimes only as big as a thumbnail, these tiny mammals will hunt and kill insects and animals that are bigger than they are, including other shrews.

Rattlesnakes give birth to live young.

5. d. Dung beetles are a burrowing owl's favorite food. In the spring, during mating and nesting season, the male owl lines his burrow with mammal dung, usually from cattle. The dung helps insulate the burrow, and it also lures the dung beetle and other insects that will help feed the owls and their young.

6. c. The three-inch long naked mole rats are mammals, but they live in underground colonies like ants or termites. Their colonies have workers that dig the tunnels, search for food, and tend to the queen, who gives birth to a colony of as many as 300 individuals. Naked mole rats can run backward and forward equally as fast, because they use their face or tail whiskers to navigate rather than their eyes.

7. a. Meerkats live in southern Africa in *mobs* (groups) of up to 25 animals. The award-winning TV series *Meerkat Manor* followed the lives of a mob called the Whiskers, which was led by a very successful matriarch named Flower. For five years, Flower helped the Whiskers survive famine and territorial challenges from neighboring meerkats, until she died of a snakebite and was succeeded by her daughter, Rocket Dog.

8. b. In special sections of their burrows, moles store live worms to eat during the winter. To preserve a live worm, they bite off its head segments, which paralyzes but doesn't kill the worm. Moles have been known to store up to 470 paralyzed worms in just one underground chamber.

9. a. Sand dollars, those white circular disks found on beaches along the Atlantic and Pacific coasts, are actually dead and are the skeletons of a marine animal that's an echinoid, or "spiny skinned creature," like sea urchins. By the time a sand dollar washes up on the beach, it's been bleached by the sun and no longer has the purplish covering of tiny spines it had when it was alive. Those tiny moving spines help the creature crawl along the ocean floor and burrow into sandy and muddy ocean bottoms where it eats tiny particles of plankton and animals. (Note: Not all sand dollars are dead...only the white ones. Live sand dollars are dark purple, and they live just under the sand, making them harder to spot.)

10. c. Fennec foxes live in the Sahara Desert, where they burrow into the sand to escape the heat. People can become very attached to these animals with their funny ears, big eyes, beautiful sandy fur, and affectionate, lively dispositions. When aviator/author Antoine de Saint-Exupery crashed in the Sahara in 1935, he worried about being rescued and was comforted by an encounter with a wild fennec fox. Years later, when he wrote *The Little Prince*, Saint-Exupery's admiration for the fennec fox led to the character of a wise desert fox that gives the young prince some famous advice: "One sees clearly only with the heart. What is essential is invisible to the eye."

GENUS & SPECIES, PAGE 264

1. v
2. s
3. a
4. d
5. r
6. e
7. k
8. g
9. l
10. p
11. b
12. o
13. w
14. i
15. j
16. u
17. q
18. h
19. t
20. c
21. n
22. m
23. f

* * *

THE FISH KNOWS

In 1989 a fish named Oscar made it into *People* magazine. Oscar, who lived in the aquarium in the biology lab at Southern California's Corona del Mar High School, became famous for predicting earthquakes. He was a one-eyed South American red oscar fish that normally swam upright. But biology teachers noticed that the fish always swam on his side several hours before a nearby earthquake. After keeping track of Oscar's swimming habits, his keepers found that he'd predicted at least 15 earthquakes over a period of three years. Oscar was even observed resting on his side (normally he rested in an upright position) the night before the big 1989 San Francisco Bay earthquake that measured 6.9 on the Richter scale and caused widespread damage.

A starving ribbon worm can eat 95 percent of its own body...and survive.

THE LAST PAGE

FELLOW BATHROOM READERS:

The fight for good bathroom reading should never be taken loosely—we must do our duty and sit firmly for what we believe in, even while the rest of the world is taking potshots at us.

We'll be brief. Now that we've proven we're not simply a flush-in-the-pan, we invite you to take the plunge: Sit Down and Be Counted! Log on to *www.bathroomreader.com* and earn a permanent spot on the BRI honor roll!

If you like reading our books...
VISIT THE BRI'S WEB SITE!
www.bathroomreader.com

- Visit "The Throne Room"—a great place to read!
- Receive our irregular newsletters via e-mail.
- Order additional *Bathroom Readers*.
- Read our blog.

Go with the Flow...

Well, we're out of space, and when you've gotta go, you've gotta go. Tanks for all your support. Hope to hear from you soon. Meanwhile, remember...

Keep on flushin'!